Marja E. Meinl   Electronic Complaints

Kulturen – Kommunikation – Kontakte

Hartwig Kalverkämper (Hg.)

Band 18

Marja E. Meinl

Electronic Complaints

An Empirical Study on British English and German Complaints on eBay

Frank & Timme
Verlag für wissenschaftliche Literatur

Cover: The subject matter of the present book is COMPLAINTS, the logical structure of which is represented by the model <“Something has happened” and “There has been a controversial reaction to the event”>. It addresses two ways of acting which constitute a whole, but which nevertheless oppose each other.
The chosen labyrinth effectively portrays this dialectic model of action with its dualistic forms and structures: the two shifted offset squares with their unique labyrinthine structures form a holistic single unit. Autonomy (accomplishment, complaint), controversy (complaint, criticism, refusal) as well as the holistic communicative act (sequence of action and complaint, linking of texts, intertextuality, interconnected text types) are represented with this artistic labyrinth, which therefore serves as an adequate visual metaphor for the pragmatic subject of this book.

Source of the labyrinth: Ulrich Koch: Labyrinthe. Irrwege, Wirrgärten und Suchbilder und ein Ariadnefaden zum Herausfinden. Mit einem Vorwort von Hans-Peter Niebuhr. München: Deutscher Taschenbuch Verlag 1987, Nr. 31: „Vier Ecken“.

ISBN 978-3-7329-0030-5
ISSN 1868-8306

Herstellung durch das atelier eilenberger, Taucha bei Leipzig.
Printed in Germany.
Gedruckt auf säurefreiem, alterungsbeständigem Papier.

Zugl. Dissertation an der Philosophischen Fakultät
der Rheinischen Friedrich-Wilhelms-Universität Bonn, 2010

www.frank-timme.de

To my Father

Table of Contents

Acknowledgements

This project would not have been possible without the support of many people who deserve my deep gratitude.

First, I would like to thank my supervisor Prof. Dr. Klaus P. Schneider (University Bonn, Germany) for his support, advice, and encouragement during these years. My further heartful thanks go to Ejo Zimmermann, who not only patiently taught me the statistics I needed, but also most skilfully introduced me to SPSS. Furthermore, I want to express my gratitude to Christoph Henn, editor of the *eBay Magazin*, who was always eager to help me with questions concerning eBay. Also many thanks go to my proof-readers Fanny Bates and Ryan Dux for their invaluable feedback and suggestions for linguistic improvements.

My sincere appreciation goes to my parents, who emotionally and financially supported me throughout my studies, making my academic career possible.

Last, but by no means least, I would like to express my deep gratefulness to my husband Michael Meinl who has always supported me by his boundless patience and good humour, but most importantly by his infinite love.

List of abbreviations

?	The reason for complaining could not be identified.
#	Absolute frequencies
%	Relative frequencies
BrE	British English
Capitalisation (words)	Capitalisation of words
Capitalisation (message)	Capitalisation of the whole message
CMC	Computer-mediated communication
CMD	Computer-mediated discourse
CofP	Community of Practice
CP	Cooperative Principle
D	"Double complaint", i.e. a user complains for two reasons at the same time.
D_Statis	The German Federal Statistics Office and the Statistical Offices of the Länder
Demonstrative pronouns	Demonstrative pronouns followed by nouns denoting the complainee
Ex.m. (single)	Single exclamation marks
Ex.m. (repeated)	Repetition of exclamation marks
(Item) DIFF	Data set: 'Item different than expected', i.e. a user complains about the fact that the item s/he received was somehow different than s/he expected it to be.
(Item) DIFF-D	Data set: 'Item different, double-complaint', i.e. a user complains about the fact that the item s/he received was somehow different than s/he expected it to be, in addition to another reason for complaining.
FVF	Final value fee
G	German

Intensifier (downgrading)	Intensifier used to aggravate the mitigating effect of downgrading modifiers
Intensifying features CMC (downgrading)	Intensifying features of CMC used to aggravate the softening effect of downgrading modifiers.
(Item) NR	Data set: 'Item has never been received', i.e. a user complains about the fact that s/he has never received the item.
(Item) NR-D	Data set: 'Item never received, double complaint', i.e. a user complains about the fact that s/he has never received the item in addition to another reason for complaining.
NPBA	Non-paying bidder alert
p	Probability level
PP	Politeness Principle
Pronouns (complainee)	Pronouns referring to the complainee
Pronouns (eBay community)	Pronouns addressing the eBay community
Repet. other punct. m.	Repetition of punctuation marks other than exclamation marks
T	"Triple complaint", i.e. a user complains for three reasons at the same time.

List of tables

List of figures

Chapter 1: Introduction

"The Internet? We are not interested in it" - Bill Gates, 1993
(http://www.quotesandsayings.com/gbillgates.htm)

Despite Bill Gates' lack of interest in the Internet, illustrating his pessimistic prognosis of its acceptance, the World Wide Web nowadays enjoys great popularity as a new means of communication. It has opened up a wide range of possibilities for its users. At the same time though, its usage demands new communicative skills, not only due to the different mode of communication, but also since the Internet connects speakers from a wide range of cultural and linguistic backgrounds.

As studies on cross-cultural, intercultural, and interlanguage communication have shown, different cultural norms can result in misunderstandings, communication breakdown, and/or the formation of stereotypes (cf. Clyne et al. 1991; House 1993, 1996a, 1996b, 2000; House and Kasper 1981; Miller 2000; Murphy and Neu 1996; Trosborg 1995; Tyler 1995). However, almost all of these studies have focused on spoken communication only, thus leaving a large research gap as to whether these findings also apply to other language modalities such as writing or "computer-mediated communication (CMC)" (Herring 1996: 1), also known as electronic discourse (cf. Davis and Brewer 1997). The latter is especially worth investigating due to the immense increase in computer usage as well as the large number of culturally different speakers "meeting" every day on the Internet.

Research on CMC started in the 1980s. Since then many studies have focused on describing the diversity of electronic text-types, the particularities of the communicative situations involved, and the specific linguistic features of this rather new language modality (cf. Abbott 2002; Bader 2002; Bays 1998; Bergs 1999; Claridge 2007; Herring 1996; Maynor 1994; Raettig 1999; Siever et al. 2005; Wenz 1998; Werry 1996; Yates 1996). Another branch of CMC research has investigated gender differences and gender asymmetries in online communication (cf. Brail 1996; O'Brian 1999; Brown 2000; Cherny 1994; Cohen 2001; Ess 1996; Gilboa 1996; Hall 1996; Harcourt 2000; Herring 2003, 2004b; Kiesler et al. 1984; Sutton 1994). Additionally, "broader metapragmatic issues" (Herring et al. 2013: 23), such as code alternation and genre in CMC, have attracted scholarly attention (cf. Androutsopoulos 2013; Androutsopoulos and Hinnekamp 2001; Giltrow 2013; Giltrow and Stein 2009; Goldbarg 2009; Heyd 2008; Paolillo 2011; Siebenhaar 2006). However, the areas of cross-cultural pragmatics or speech act analysis have still mainly been neglected. With regard to the latter, it is especially worth looking at complaints in CMC, since the vast spread of the Internet has been accompanied by an ever-growing interest in e-commerce (cf. Albrecht et al. 2007: 708) where this type of speech act is very common, so that the complaining behaviour between sellers and buyers from all over the world has definitely increased. Due to the fact that not only the interlocutor's face, but also financial losses are at stake in business transactions, misunderstanding your trading partner's complaints can be particularly detrimental. It is hence of crucial importance to avoid these misunderstandings, but this can only be achieved if more cross-cultural research provides insight into speakers' cultural norms when complaining.

Faced with the lack of attention to cross-cultural differences in CMC, which is especially important regarding complaining behaviour, the present study wants to contribute to this still undiscovered research area by comparing British English and German complaints in CMC, precisely on eBay.

This study is thus anchored in the field of cross-cultural pragmatics, and the main approach taken is speech-act based. However, as complaints are always embedded in discourse and thereby occur as post-event, the present investigation certainly also takes the contextual factors of the data into account, thus additionally drawing on research from discourse analysis.

The overall aim of this project is a comparison of the British English and German production of computer-mediated complaints and, consequently, a description of similarities and differences, of which the latter may lead to misunderstandings in cross-cultural electronic communicative situations.[1] Specifically, the collected complaints were analysed according to five categories: the use of complaint strategies, the chosen level of directness, the employment of modification, the use of pronouns, and the handling of features

[1] For differences between British English and German speakers that led to misunderstandings in spoken interactions see, for instance, House and Kasper (1981), Möhl (1996), and Trosborg (1995).

of CMC. In light of these categories, the following research questions guided the investigation.

1. Do British and German traders' computer-mediated complaints differ with regard to the five categories of analysis?
2. Does the reason for complaining influence their linguistic choices?
3. Does it make a difference whether they have one or two reasons for their online complaint?

To find answers to these research questions, British and German complaints were taken from the British and German feedback forum of the online auction house eBay and analysed according to the five categories. The results were then statistically compared. Apart from contributing to research on cross-cultural pragmatics and thereby being relevant for the improvement of cross-cultural communication, this study is significant for research on complaining behaviour as well as for research on CMC. What is more, its findings are also fundamental for the areas of interlanguage research and second language teaching, since knowledge of British and German speakers' communicative norms when complaining in CMC is essential for further in-depth analyses of learners' interlanguage, which will aid the production of effective teaching materials.

The present report is divided into eight chapters, structured as follows. The theoretical background information of the present study is given in Chapter 2 and 3. More precisely, in Chapter 2 important theories regarding complaints within cross-cultural pragmatics are explained. Hence, a brief overview of pragmatics and the key concepts of speech act analyses with focus on complaints is given. This is followed by descriptions of relevant (im)politeness theories and a clarification of important terms related to pragmatics across cultures, i.e. contrastive, cross-cultural, and intercultural pragmatics. Chapter 3, on the other hand, gives a theoretical summary of the chosen modality of communication, namely CMC. Here, CMC is defined, its history briefly presented, and approaches to classifying computer-mediated discourse (CMD) are outlined.

Chapter 4 turns to the methodology of the present study, focusing on its data. Consequently, the chosen database and its contextual features are described. Additionally, the data collection procedures are outlined, the advantages and disadvantages of the present data are discussed, and its statistical analyses are briefly explained. In Chapter 5 the different categories of analysis are presented. Each category is described and the procedures of data analysis are explained. In Chapter 6 the results of this study are illustrated following the order of the research questions and in Chapter 7 discussed in light of previous research on complaints as well as (im)politeness theories. Last but not least, Chapter 8 concludes this report by pointing at implications of the present results for the improvement of cross-cultural communication and language pedagogy, as well as making suggestions for future research.

Chapter 2: Complaining within cross-cultural pragmatics

As mentioned in the introduction, the present study is anchored in the field of pragmatics, a rather "'young' science" (Mey 1998: 716) which, since its beginnings in the late sixties and early seventies, has not only expanded its scope very rapidly but also become an extremely popular research area.
This chapter begins with a brief description of pragmatics and presents the definition used in this study (2.1.), followed by a characterisation of important pragmatic theories, which are relevant for the present study. These include theories in the field of speech act analysis, which are crucial when dealing with complaints (2.2.). Furthermore, important theories of (im)politeness are explained (2.3.) and relevant terms within the field of pragmatics across cultures are defined (2.4.), which helps to clarify the chosen methodological approach.

2.1. Pragmatics

Since the pragmatic turn in linguistics, many different definitions of pragmatics have been put forward (cf. Crystal 1985: 240; Gass 1997: 20ff.; Reynolds 1995: 5). Although many researchers have referred to Charles Morris's (1938) famous concept of pragmatics as "the study of the relation of signs to interpreters" (Morris 1938: 6), no agreement has been reached so far as to what pragamtics actually is or what it is not.
Regarding the present study, Mey's (1993) definition has been chosen as a working definition. He says, "*Pragmatics studies the use of language in human communication as determined by the conditions of society*" (Mey 1993: 6). His definition illustrates the shift of researchers away from analysing purely linguistic means to also dealing with extralinguistic factors, hence the user's context in society.
These two sides are also represented in Leech's (1983) distinction between the areas of pragmalinguistics and sociopragmatics. Pragmalinguistics is, on the one hand, "the study of the more linguistic end of pragmatics", which means that researchers "consider the particular resources which a given language provides for conveying particular illocutions" (Leech 1983: 11). Examples of such resources are the use of realisation strategies or means of modification.

Sociopragmatics, on the other hand, "is the sociological interface of pragmatics" (Leech 1983: 10). Hence it focuses on the influence of extralinguistic factors on a particular illocution, such as social distance, power relations or the cultural background of the interlocutors. As the present study is concerned with participants of different cultural backgrounds, yet at the same time compares the linguistic means the subjects use in complaining in CMC, this study incorporates both areas of Leech's (1983) concept of pragmatics.

Apart from this, pragmaticians divide their field of research into micro- and macropragmatics (cf. Mey 1993, 1998). As the prefixes indicate, the former is "the study of language in smaller contexts", which has traditionally been understood "as comprising the sentence (and its immediate surroundings)" (Mey 1998: 728). Researchers in this field consequently deal with topics such as speech acts, reference or anaphora. When focusing on macropragmatics, the interest is on "user interaction, in various ways, and in a number of settings" (Mey 1998: 728). Thus conversational analysis, pragmatics across cultures, social aspects of pragmatics, or metapragmatics are research issues here. Although the present study addresses a cultural aspect in a computational environment, the centre of attention is on the speech act of complaining and hence on micropragmatics.

2.2. Speech act analysis

Because this study focuses on complaints, this subchapter turns to relevant theories of speech act analysis. Thus, the basic assumptions of speech act theory are presented (2.2.1.) and a brief description of discourse analysis (2.2.2.), specifically of the integrated model developed by Edmondson (1981) (2.2.2.1.), is given. These concepts are relevant when the focus shifts to the speech act under investigation, complaints (2.2.3.). Reasons for choosing complaints are given (2.2.3.1.) and the nature of complaints are explained (2.2.3.2.).

2.2.1. Speech act theory

Since the beginnings of pragmatics, speech act theory has been one of the most influential theories in this field. Due to its suitability for studies focussing on language in use, speech act theory has been used as a theoretical approach in many studies (cf. Barron 2003; Blum-Kulka et al. 1989; House and Kasper 1981; Möhl 1996; Trosborg 1995) including the present one. Therefore, this subchapter provides a brief overview of its fundamental claims.

The foundations of speech act theory were laid by J. L. Austin, a British professor of philosophy, whose William James Lectures, which he delivered at Harvard University in 1955 and were published posthumously as "How to Do Things with Words" (1962), led to an enormous interest in speech acts. In the following years, speech act theory was highly influenced by his student follower, John Searle, and resulted in linguists turning away from "truth-conditional semantics" (Barron 2003: 11), which was prevalent at that time. The fundamental claim of speech act theory is that speech is action, and hence each sentence a speech act[2] which is created when "speaker/writer S makes an utterance U to hearer/reader H in context C" (Allan 1998: 927).

Austin (1962) was the first to isolate a hierarchy of acts that are performed simultaneously when speaking (adapted here):

> (1) locutionary act: the uttering of a certain sentence with a certain sense and reference.
> (2) illocutionary act: the performing of utterances which have a certain (conventional) force, such as informing, ordering, warning, undertaking, etc.
> (3) perlocutionary act: the bringing about of effect upon the feelings, thoughts or action of the hearer, audience or other people.
>
> (Austin 1962: 108)

In other words, when producing an utterance, a speaker does not only express something about the world (locution), but at the same time has an intention uttering his words (illocution), which he hopes to have the desired effect on the hearer (perlocution).

Perlocutionary effects have often been neglected by speech act theorists, as it has been argued that they fall outside of linguistics, because they are not part of language per se but instead responses to the illocutions in utterances (cf. Allan 1998: 928). What linguists, however, have looked at closely are the intentions of speakers, namely the illocutionary act. These reveal the way a speaker wants his utterance to be interpreted by a hearer, regardless of the way it is phrased. This is of great importance, since one proposition may occur in different illocutionary

[2] The notions of 'spoken' and 'speaking' also properly include writing for simplicity of exposition.

acts, as in the utterances "Jack, take out the garbage", "Jack, will you take out the garbage?" and "Jack will take out the garbage". Although they all have the same proposition, namely that Jack will take out the garbage, these utterances differ in their illocutions: the first being an order, the second a question and the last a prediction. Yet, to make the inference of the intended illocutionary force of an utterance easier, a speaker can use illocutionary indicating devices such as performative verbs, word order or intonation. In addition to that, Searle (1969: 55ff.) declared that certain "felicity conditions" have to be met for an act to be performed. In a second step, he extracted the following set of rules which help to recognise a given speech act: the *propositional content rule, the preparatory rule, the sincerity rule,* and *the essential rule*. However, despite the mentioned illocutionary force indicating devices and given rules for speech acts, a speaker's intention need not always be recognised by a hearer, in which case the illocution is not felicitous and the perlocution consequently unsuccessful.[3] In contrast to Austin (1962), Searle (1969) only regards recognition of the intention as essential to the accomplishment of a speech act and not the subsequent behaviour:

> In the case of illocutionary acts we succeed in doing what we are trying to do by getting our audience to recognize what we are trying to do. But the 'effect' on the hearer is not a belief or response, it consists simply in the hearer understanding the utterance of the speaker.
>
> (Searle 1969: 47)

Furthermore, Austin (1962) was the first who developed a speech act classification to achieve some order in the large amount of different speech acts, which is in principal a lexical classification of so-called illocutionary verbs. Lexical groupings make reference to the syntactic environment of the verb, leaving Austin with five classes: *expositives, verdictives, commissives, exercitives,* and *behabitives*. Since Austin's approach (1962) there have been many further proposals of how to classify speech acts (cf. Ballmer 1979; Ballmer and Brennenstuhl 1981; Searle 1975; Wierzbicka 1987). The most widely accepted among them is still Searle's (1975) taxonomy (cf. Schneider 1988: 61), which has been adopted in many studies (cf. House and Kasper 1981;

---

[3] The distinction between illocutions that may be felicitous (*geglückt*) and perlocutions that may be successful (*erfolgreich*) can also be found in Roth (2002: 33) and Linke et al. (2001: 188f.).

Möhl 1996; Trosborg 1995) including the present one. Similar to Austin's model, Searle's (1975) classification comprises five categories for which he used four criteria: illocutionary point, direction of fit, psychological state of speaker, and prepositional content. He thus distinguishes the following five classes of speech acts:

1. *Representatives* (later renamed *Assertives*) have a truth value, show words-to-world fit, and express S's belief that *p*.
2. *Directives* are attempts to get H to do something, therefore they show world-to words fit, and express S's wish or desire that H do A.
3. *Commissives* commit S to some future course of action, so they show world-to-words fit, and S expresses the intention that S do A.
4. *Expressives* express S's attitude to a certain state of affairs, specified (if at all) in the prepositional content. There is no direction of fit; a variety of different psychological states; and "the propositional content must [...] be related to S or H" (Searle 1975: 357f.).
5. *Declarations* bring about correspondence between prepositional content and the world, thus direction of fit is both words-to-world and world-to-words. Searle does not mention any psychological state for declarations.

Apart from that, speech acts are often further divided into direct and indirect speech acts depending on the relationship between their form and function. Precisely, while in a direct speech act "the speaker says what he means", he "means something more than what he says" (Searle 1980: viii) when using an indirect one. An example of the latter is for instance the utterance "Isn't it cold in here" (Sadock 2006: 69), whereby a speaker does not actually seek a hearer's agreement, but rather requests for some improvement of the uncomfortable situation. Due to the fact that some indirect speech acts have already been used very frequently in particular situations and the addressee is no longer burdened with an actual calculation of the intended illocution, they have been denoted conventionally indirect speech acts. They are distinguished from non-conventionally indirect speech acts, which are less obvious and hence still require the effort of inference.

Nevertheless, despite all the praise speech act theory has received since its origin, there have also been some aspects of criticism which are important to keep in mind. One of the main critical points is that speech act theory only focuses on the single utterance itself by establishing the illocutionary force of an utterance by its form. The broader context of the conversation and its interactional aspects are thereby deliberately neglected. However, since conversations do not simply consist of one speech act following another but are more complex in that there is an interplay and dependency between different utterances, the focus on isolated utterances alone cannot suffice for a real understanding of the whole conversation. Yet, this criticism can be levelled in the present study, as the chosen data consists of electronic complaints which are at the very most followed only by a reply and a follow-up comment. Consequently, it is due to this specific communicative situation that interlocutors simply cannot engage in larger conversations, so a wider discourse context is not neglected but naturally not present. What is more, the interactional aspect of turn taking cannot be considered in the present analysis, as the data of this study consists of asynchronous CMC in which interruptions or overlaps are simply impossible.

Another criticism of speech act theory mentioned in the literature is that a speaker may have several intentions at the same time when voicing his speech act, so more than just one illocution is involved. Kasper (1989: 41) and Wiezbicka (1991: 199), however, point out that a hearer can unambiguously infer the illocutionary force of an utterance in most cases. This is made possible "to a large extent, due to unmistakable linguistic cues" (Wierzbicka 1991: 199). As far as the present database is concerned, there are even visual signs preceding each feedback comment, clearly signalling whether a praise, neutral comment or complaint follows, thereby making any uncertainty about the interpretation impossible.

Furthermore, research in the field of speech act theory has also been censured for leaving out the analysis of any paralinguistic or non-verbal aspects of language (cf. Geis 1995: 13ff.). This aspect is yet again irrelevant concerning the chosen data, since this absence of paralinguistic and non-verbal cues is a defining characteristic of text-based CMC.

So all in all, the discussion above reveals that, although criticised, speech act theory is generally a very suitable concept for studies in pragmatics, especially with regard to the particular communicative situation of the present data.

2.2.2. Discourse analysis

The criticism that speech act theory focuses on the speech act in isolation and hence neglects the utterance's context, led to the development of discourse analysis. Researchers in this field have undertaken a variety of analyses of language above the sentence level, embracing research areas such as linguistics and literary and film theory (cf. Mc Houl 1994: 940; Potter and Wetherell 1987: 6f.).

With regard to the present study, the linguistically-based approach of discourse analysis is relevant. Edmondson's (1981) discourse model is followed when analysing the interactional position of the collected complaints, since it does not only look at the interactional structure, but also concentrates on the speech act. A brief description of this model is given below.

2.2.2.1. An integrative model of discourse

Edmondson's (1981) model, which has been adapted in Edmondson and House (1981), is based on role-play data collected in the research project "Communicative Competence as a Learning Objective in Foreign Language Teaching", conducted at the University of Bochum in Germany. Similar to the approach taken by Sinclair and Coulthard (1975) it adopts a rank system, i.e. functional units of discourse are presented in a hierarchical order.

According to this model, the act is the smallest unit of interactional structure, followed by the move, the exchange, the phase, and finally the complete interaction. The move and exchange constitute the primary focus in this model, whereby the move is defined as "the smallest element by means of which a conversation is developed" (Edmondson 1981: 6f.). It is to be distinguished from a turn, which in the simplest way consists of one interactional move, but usually of more. In his model, Edmondson (1981) identifies a number of different moves that may occur in different sequences in order to build an exchange. Most important in this respect are the Initiate, Satisfy, Contra, and Counter. While an Initiate starts the exchange, a Satisfy is a move which leads to an outcome, either positive or negative, thereby bringing the exchange to an end. A Contra, on the other hand, is "an attempt on the part of the producer of the Contra to cause his conversational partner to withdraw the preceding Proffer" (Edmondson 1981: 88). Additionally, addressees may choose a Counter to response to an Initiate in case they want "to cause the content of the preceding move [...] to be amended, qualified, or withdrawn in light of the content of the Counter" (Edmondson 1981: 89). Counters and Contras are hence very similar. These moves, however, differ in that a Counter calls for a specific response while a Contra does not. The different types of moves make up an exchange which is defined as:

> a conversational unit in which both partners together reach a conversational *outcome*, i.e. they reach a point of agreement, and the conversation may then proceed to further business, or indeed to a closing ritual.
>
> (Edmondson and House 1981: 38, original emphasis)

An exchange consists of at least two interactional moves: an Initiate and Satisfy which are produced by two different speakers. Exchanges may, however, also have complex structures, for instance, when an Initiate is followed by several Contras until a Satisfy occurs. Exchanges also link with one another to form a conversational phase, which makes up the last level in Edmondson's (1981) model, namely the full interaction.

In contrast to Sinclair and Coulthard (1975), Edmondson (1981) does not only focus on the interactional structure but combines speech act theory and the study of interaction in his model. Utterances which speakers produce, and thereby contribute to a conversational event, have a dual function: an illocutionary as well as an interactional function. Accordingly, speech acts in conversation do not only have an illocutionary force but are also elements of the interactional structure, which are significant for the progression of the conversation. In Edmondson's model (1981), discourse is thus always analysed in two ways: for the illocutionary and the interactional value. The utterance "Hey, you've not washed up yet." (Edmondson and House 1981: 36) would thus be classified as a complaint (illocutionary act) and similarly as an Initiate (interactional move).

2.2.3. The focus of the present study: complaints

Having outlined theories relevant to speech act analysis, the focus now turns to the chosen speech act itself, i.e. complaints. Specifically, the reasons for choosing this type of speech act are given (2.2.3.1.), then the nature of complaints is described from a speech act as well as from a discourse perspective (2.2.3.2.).

2.2.3.1. Reasons for choosing complaints

When planning a research project in the area of speech act theory, it is certainly important to first decide which particular speech act one wants to investigate. Regarding the present study, the decision was made to investigate the speech act of complaining for the following reasons.

Because complaints are very common and essential speech acts in everyday life, their analysis is, of course, highly significant. Hence, researchers in the areas of cross-cultural, intercultural, and interlanguage pragmatics (cf. Cohen and Olshtain 1993; Geluykens and Kraft 2003; House and Kasper 1981; Katz 1987; Kraft and Geluykens 2002, 2004; Möhl 1996; Murphy and Neu 1996; Nakabachi 1996; Olshtain and Weinbach 1987, 1993; Trenchs 1994; Trosborg 1995; Weinbach 1988) have already focused on this type of speech act. However, almost all of these studies have only examined spoken communication, leaving a large research gap as far as other language modalities, such as writing or CMC, are concerned. This research gap needs to be filled, especially in the area of CMC, given the vast spread of communication via the Internet, which has been accompanied by an ever-growing interest in e-commerce (cf. Albrecht et al. 2007: 707), where complaining behaviour is very common. Consequently, the amount of complaints between sellers and buyers from all over the world has definitely increased. Gaining insight into how these traders use this particular speech act is therefore a compelling need.

With regard to the field of cross-cultural pragmatics, there have been very few studies comparing British English and German native speakers (cf. Geluykens and Kraft 2003; House and Kasper 1981; Möhl 1995), which are the focus of the present study. More research in this field is thus definitely needed.

What is more, the studies on cross-cultural, intercultural, and interlanguage communication have revealed that different cultural norms can result in misunderstanding, communication breakdown and/or the formation of stereotypes (cf. Clyne et al. 1991; House 1993, 1996a, 1996b, 2000; House and Kasper 1981; Miller 2000; Murphy and Neu 1996; Trosborg 1995; Tyler 1995).

These negative consequences are especially important in the case of intrinsically face-threatening acts like complaints, as they themselves represent a source of conflict (cf. Boxer 1993a, 1993c; Brown and Levinson 1987 [1978]; Murphy and Neu 1996; Olshtain and Weinbach 1993; Trosborg 1995). Given the fact that complaints are frequently used in business transactions, in which not only the traders' faces but also financial consequences are at stake, the occurrence of misunderstandings in complaints is more devastating than in any other type of face-threatening act. Their avoidance is hence of crucial importance and can only be achieved if more cross-cultural research is conducted giving insight into native speakers' cultural norms when complaining.

Moreover, culturally specific complaining behaviour causes problems for learners of all cultural backgrounds. These difficulties are even more severe given the non-ritualistic nature of complaints. Cross-cultural studies like the present one are therefore needed as a starting point, since a knowledge base about native speakers' cultural norms is an essential prerequisite for further in-depth analyses of learners' interlanguage and thus for the production of effective teaching materials.

In addition to that, the face-threatening nature of complaints (cf. Brown and Levinson 1987 [1978]) allows an analysis of the use of mitigating devices such as indirectness and modification, which are also key issues of potential difficulty for foreign language learners.

Last but not least, the non-hearer-supportive nature of complaints (cf. Edmondson and House 1981) also makes it very likely that the data analysis can be extended to the notion of impoliteness, an area which is often neglected in politeness research. Impoliteness research could especially benefit from the specific CMC situation dealt with by this study, namely highly emotional situations involving the speaker's intensified anger and the addressee's absence when the speaker formulates his/her complaint.

2.2.3.2. Characteristics of complaints

When focussing on complaints, one must distinguish between direct and indirect complaints[4] (cf. D'Amico-Reisner 1983; Boxer 1993a, 1993b, 1993c; Edwards 2005; Wolfe and Powell 2006). While indirect complaints, which are also referred to as 'griping' and 'grumbling' (cf. Boxer 1993b: 2), have the function of establishing rapport and solidarity between a speaker and hearer, a speaker making a direct complaint expresses his/her disapproval of a past or ongoing action which does not conform with the speaker's expectations and interests. The consequences of this action are at cost to the speaker, who holds the hearer at least partly responsible for or capable of remedying the perceived offence (cf. D'Amico-Reisner 1983; Boxer 1993a, 1993b, 1993c; Edmondson and House 1981; Olshtain and Weinbach 1987, 1993; Möhl 1996; Trosborg 1995). Direct complaints are the focus of this project and will for the sake of simplicity henceforth be called "complaints".

According to Searle's (1976) taxonomy, complaints are expressives, since speakers express their feelings and attitudes to a certain state of affairs. Their psychological state is that of annoyance and anger, which they may or may not mention in the propositional content. The propositional content is thereby the complainable, thus related to the speaker and hearer of the interaction. Despite being a rather common speech act, Searle never explicitly illustrated his rules for the occurrence of the speech acts of complaining. Fritz and Hundsnurscher (1975) have hence made an attempt to apply Searle's rules to this type of speech act (Fritz and Hundsnurscher 1975: 84; translated from German). A is thereby the speaker, B the addressee, p the utterance expressed, and the x the committed offence:

1. *propositional content rule*: by expressing p, A predicates a performed (or unperformed) action x of B.
2. *preparatory rules*:
    - 2.1. A assumes: B has (or has not) done x.
    - 2.2. A assumes: B (like A) understands x to be of scheme X (and not XY).
    - 2.3. A assumes: B can be held responsible for x (or not-x).
    - 2.4. A assumes: B has (or has not) done x on purpose.
    - 2.5. A assumes: B violated the norm N by doing (or not doing) x.

[4] The notions of *direct* and *indirect* are used differently in this case than in the distinction between direct and indirect speech acts (see 2.2.).

2.6. A assumes: B accepts the norm N.

3. *sincerity rule*: A really wanted B to do (or not to do) x.

(Fritz and Hundsnurscher 1975: 84)

In their application, Fritz and Hundsnurscher (1975), however, left out Searle's essential rule, which can be applied to the speech act of complaining as follows:

4. *essential rule*: the utterance counts as an undertaking to show one's annoyance, disapproval and anger.

When looking at the distinction between a felicitous complaint and a successful complaint (see 2.2.), neither recognition of intent nor a perlocutionary effect is observable if this effect only comprises feelings of sorrow, regret or guilt without the performance of any redressive action. However, regarding the present data it can be argued that the specific symbol preceding each electronic complaint (see 4.1.2.) guarantees a hearer's intention uptake and hence a felicitous complaint. Whether this complaint then also evokes any feelings of regret or guilt cannot be observed, especially not in the case of the chosen asynchronous CMC data, in which complainers, being absent when the addressees receive their comments, cannot even see the addressees' facial expressions when they are reading their comments. A successful performance of complaints can hence only be determined if a reply is given which makes an addressee's sense of responsibility clear.

Given that complainers wish to express their anger about a committed offence, complaints are face-threatening acts (FTA) according to Brown and Levinson's (1987 [1978]) politeness theory. In light of their distinction between positive and negative face, complaints are clearly threats to a hearer's positive face, as they go against a person's wish to be liked, approved of, and respected (cf. Brown and Levinson 1987 [1978]). At the same time though, complaints also threaten the hearer's negative face, since complainers ask the hearer to cease or not to repeat an offensive action and sometimes even ask for some sort of repair (cf. Boxer 1993a; Kraft and Geluykens 2002; Olshtain and Weinbach 1987, 1993; Rader 1977). They hence clearly impede a hearer's freedom of action.

As speakers usually want to avoid threatening their interlocutor's face, they are caught in a conflict between their illocutionary and social goals, and thus face specific "payoffs: *a priori* considerations" (Brown and Levinson 1987: 71). On the one hand, a complaint may result in a breach of a speaker's social goal of maintaining harmony between himself/herself and the hearer, and on the other hand, it helps to get rid of one's frustration and anger and to regain one's own emotional balance, also called catharsis (cf. Wolfe and Powell 2006: 17). Although speakers flout the hearer-supportive maxim when voicing a complaint (cf. Edmondson and House 1981: 47), Edmondson and House (1981) argue that they are justified in committing this speech act, as the social balance between the speaker and hearer has already been disturbed by the hearer's prior or ongoing offence. Seen in this light, complaints can be regarded as the beginning of a struggle to regain social balance between the speaker and hearer which is important for harmony and the smooth flow of communication.

Because face must be saved in a successful communication, complaints are often made more socially appropriate by the use of indirectness or external and internal modification. The former thereby leaves addressees with more freedom in their interpretation, i.e. whether they want to recognise the specific utterance as a complaint. The use of modification, on the other hand, reduces the imposition a complaint is likely to have on the complainees. An example of modification would be the use of an apology for the following face-threatening act, thereby showing one's concern for the hearer's face.

However, whether a complaint is really voiced by a speaker and how it is linguistically realised depends on situational variables, such as the severity of the offence, the social distance and power relations between the participants, as well as on the speaker's personality (cf. D'Amico-Reisner 1983; Möhl 1996; Olshtain and Weinbach 1987; Tatsuki 2000).

Given that complaints are very variable in form, they are more difficult to identify theoretically than more formulaic speech acts such as requests or apologies. In context, it is hence often impossible to distinguish them from closely related speech acts such as disapproval, criticism, accusation, warning, threat and insult, which are likely to appear at the same time and elicit similar reactions (cf. Laforest 2002: 1597). While Brown and Levinson (1987 [1978]) seem to regard acts of disapproval, complaint, criticism, accusation etc. as distinct from one another, various studies dealing with complaints have shown that these acts overlap, so that it is not necessary and may not even be useful to distinguish very clearly between them (cf. House and Kasper 1981; Laforest 2002; Olshtain and Cohen 1983; Olshtain and Weinbach 1993; Trosborg 1995; Wolfe and Powell 2006). Thus, what is called complaint in the present study

includes, as in previous studies devoted to complaints, these closely related and overlapping acts mentioned above.
As far as the interactive structure of discourse is concerned, complaints are often initiating speech acts provoked by the preceding offence (cf. Edmondson and House 1981: 147). Nevertheless, they can also occur as Contras (cf. Edmondson and House 1981: 151). In the clearest case of complaints, the alleged offence was committed by the addressees themselves, while other complaints are made by third parties (cf. Edmondson and House 1981: 144). Regarding the present data, the electronic complaints are initiating moves addressed directly towards the complainee, who is held responsible for the perceived offence. All complaints are typed and sent to an addressee, who is spatially separated from the sender, and thus lacks any further non-verbal or auditory cues. As far as the exchange level of Edmondson's (1981) discourse model is concerned, the collected complaints are either followed by a reply or remain unanswered. If a reply is given, this may be a satisfying move, hence bringing the exchange to an end. On the other hand, replies may also be Contras or Counters leaving the end of the exchange open. In this case, as well as when a complaint is not answered, the interlocutors may conclude their specific exchange outside the feedback forum using email, telephone or personal contact.

2.3. Theories of (im)politeness

Since the late 1970s there has been a great deal of interest in 'politeness', resulting in the development of various politeness theories (cf. Arndt and Janney 1979; Brown and Levinson 1987 [1978]; Fraser and Nolen 1981; Gu 1990; Ide 1982; Lakoff 1977; Leech 1983; Watts 1989). Despite this flourishing research, the confusion about the term politeness itself unfortunately still remains, since different phenomena have been discussed under its heading. There have, for instance, been researchers advocating the "social-norm view" of politeness (Fraser 1990: 220f.) which sees politeness as "[…] proper social conduct and tactful consideration of others" (Kasper 1994: 3206), and is, for instance, described in etiquette books. Other scientists have used the terms 'deference' or 'register' as synonyms for politeness which, though related, signify different things. In contrast to politeness, deference and register are sociolinguistic concepts, i.e. a speaker has no choice as to whether to use the deferent form or more formal language, since "usage is dictated by sociolinguistic norms" (Thomas 1995: 152). On the contrary, politeness is a pragmatic phenomenon and hence concerned with "[...] ways in which the relational function in linguistic action is expressed" (Kasper 1994: 3206). In other words, it affects how language is strategically used to achieve such aims as improving or maintaining interpersonal relationships. It is this pragmatic view of politeness that is meant when using the term in the present study.

This subchapter deals with famous approaches to the study of (im)politeness from a pragmatic perspective. In accordance with Fraser's (1990) categorisation, the first three are labelled the conversational-maxim view (2.3.1.), the face-saving view (2.3.2.), and the conversational-contract view (2.3.3.). These are complemented by two post-modern approaches to politeness, namely the concept of relational work (2.3.4.), and the concept of rapport management (2.3.5.). Finally, a model solely focusing on the counterpart of politeness, i.e. impoliteness is demonstrated (2.3.6.).

2.3.1. The conversational-maxim view

Both the conversational-maxim view and the face-saving view of politeness are concerned with conflict-avoidance and are based on Grice's model of verbal interaction (cf. Grice 1975). These theories therefore fall in line with Grice's opinion that speakers are rational individuals who share common goals in interactions. The goals are governed by Grice's Cooperative Principle (CP) (cf. Grice 1975: 45) which consists of four maxims: the Maxim of Quantity, Quality, Relation, and Manner. According to Grice's theory, in smoothly ongoing interactions speakers adhere to the CP. There are, however, many incidents in everyday communication where interactional partners violate one or more of the maxims but still understand each other perfectly. An example is a conversational partner asking: "Could you pass me the salt, please?" In voicing this polite request instead of an imperative, the speaker flouts the Maxim of Manner which states that one should avoid obscurity and ambiguity but be brief and orderly. In Grice's theory, politeness is thus merely seen as a violation of the CP.

Politeness researchers therefore argue that Grice's model is insufficient for the analysis of real conversation, as it fails to explain the frequent use of politeness. They criticise that Grice only stresses the referential function of language, while, in contrast to that, they also take its relational function into account. Given these two different functions of language, speakers are often caught in a conflict, having to decide whether maximum efficiency or politeness is more important.
Leech, the best known representative of the conversational-maxim view, extended and thereby 'rescued' Grice's formerly insufficient CP. He came up with the Politeness Principle (PP) which refers to the relational function of language and is in par with Grice's CP. The two are thus related in that a breach of the CP can be explained by a reference to the PP. Leech (1983) formulated his PP as:

> 'Minimize (other things being equal) the expression of impolite beliefs.' [...] 'Maximize (other things being equal) the expression of polite beliefs.'
>
> (Leech 1983: 81)

Polite and impolite beliefs are thereby beliefs that are in some way favourable and respectively unfavourable to the hearer or to a third party. Like the CP, the PP consists of a number of maxims which, according to Leech (1983), stand in the same relationship to the PP as Grice's (1975) maxims to the CP.[5] The main maxims are the Maxim of Tact, Generosity, Approbiation, Modesty, Agreement and Sympathy, which all operate along specific pragmatic scales.[6] These maxims are formulated in the imperative mood, which, however, does not mean

---

[5] In Leech's (2007) incarnation of his Principles of Pragmatics approach, to which he still broadly adheres (cf. Leech 2007: 174), he reformulates his maxims of politeness. In doing so, he avoids the term 'maxim', since it is so easily misunderstood (cf. Thomas 1995: 168) and instead prefers the term 'pragmatic constraint' which equals Spencer-Oatey and Jiang's (2003) 'sociopragmatic interaction principles (SIPs)'. In the reformulated version (Leech 2007), the different constraints, as the former maxims, go in pairs and also work on similar lines. In contrast though, the pragmatic constraints do not relate to the PP anymore but to a super constraint, the Grand Strategy of Politeness (GSP) which reads as follows: "In order to be polite, *S* expresses or implies meanings which associate a high value with what pertains to *O* (*O* = other person(s), mainly the addressee) or associates low value with what pertains to *S* (*S* = self, speaker)" (Leech 2007: 181, italics in original). As opposed to the PP, the GSP thus does not only refer to the hearer but involves both the self/speaker and other person(s) which are mainly the addressee.

[6] In the reformulated version of his approach, Leech (2007) extends the number of scales along which politeness operates by "self-territory" and "other-territory" (in-group membership vs. out-group) (cf. Leech 2007: 194) to also account for the more group-oriented Eastern cultures.

that they are intended to be strict rules. They are rather normative and relative in their application. In his approach, Leech (1983) associated all maxims with particular illocutionary forces and related them to Searle's (1969) categorisation of illocutionary acts which has also been used for the present study. Accordingly, the speech act of complaining has been classified as belonging to Searle's (1969) category of expressives (see 4.2.). Therefore the related Maxim of Approbiation is looked at more closely. The Approbiation Maxim is hearer-oriented and states:

> (a) Minimize dispraise of *other* [(b) Maximize praise of *other*]
>
> (Leech 1983:132, original emphasis)

When applying this maxim to the speech act of complaining, the best operation of this maxim is, of course, not to complain at all. There are, however, situations in each society in which complaints, i.e. dispraise of other are in varying degrees are acceptable. In these cases the directness scale, along which the Approbiation Maxim functions, becomes relevant. Accordingly, the more indirect a complaint is phrased in such situations, the more closely a speaker adheres to Leech's (1983) Approbiation Maxim, and hence the more polite s/he is. The following examples of the present data set illustrate this connection.

(BrE, NR 71)[7] too useless for words

(BrE, NR 88) Total idiot & waste of space!!! cheque cancelled forthwith!!!

While a complaint is expressed in both cases, the first complainer minimises the dispraise of the other in being very indirect. According to Leech's model, s/he is more polite than the second complainer who phrases his/her complaint very bluntly. Thus, even if one speaker expresses dispraise of another, in Leech's (1983) view they still have the choice to be polite in varying degrees, by choosing different levels of directness.

Since its first publication, Leech's (1983) theory has not only triggered a lot of research but has also been the reason for much controversy. On the one hand, it has been praised for its usefulness in cross-cultural research (cf. Thomas 1995: 167f.). Cross-cultural differences in politeness are in this approach explained by proposing that speakers of different cultural backgrounds weigh the maxims differently (cf. Leech 1983: 80; Thomas 1995: 168). On the other hand, Leech's model has spawned at lot of criticism. It has mainly been censured for the

[7] For an explanation of the references in brackets, see Chapter 5.

unlimited number of maxims which can be produced to explain every perceived regularity in language use (cf. Barron 2003: 17; Spencer-Oatey 2000b: 39; Thomas 1995: 167). This makes Leech's approach "at best inelegant, at worst virtually unfalsifiable" (Thomas 1995: 167). Furthermore, empirical research has revealed that there is not always a positive correlation between politeness and indirectness (cf. Blum-Kulka 1987: 136ff.; Blum-Kulka 1990: 269ff.; Held 1996: 78), making Leech's equation of indirectness and politeness untenable. Moreover, Kasper (1990) criticises the conversational-maxim view for its lack of any empirical basis (Kasper 1990: 194), and is supported by Watts et al. (1992: 7) and Taylor and Cameron (1987: 97) who judge Leech's theory to be too theoretical to apply to real language. A final critical aspect concerns Leech's narrow focus on the polite side of language and his neglect of all types of uncooperative communication (cf. Trosborg 1995: 25).

2.3.2. The face-saving view

Brown and Levinson's (1987 [1978]) politeness theory has remained the most influential one until today (cf. Eelen 2001: 3; Thomas 1995: 168). Brown and Levinson's approach is also related to the Gricean framework in so far as they regard the violation of Grice's maxims as a consequence of politeness.

Central to this theory is the assumption of individuals' rationality, i.e. their capacity for logic reasoning, as well as their possession of face which has been adopted from Goffman (1967) and is defined as:

> the positive social value a person effectively claims for himself by the line others assume he has taken during a particular contact. Face is an image of self delineated in terms of approved social attributes – albeit an image that others may share, as when a person makes a good showing for his profession or religion by making a good showing for himself.
>
> (Goffman 1967: 5)

In interactions, face "[…] can be lost, maintained, or enhanced, and must be constantly attended to" (Brown and Levinson 1987: 61). In their politeness theory Brown and Levinson have, however, not only adopted Goffman's (1967) concept of face but also expanded it. They consequently differentiate between positive and negative face, which they formulate as two opposing face 'wants'. While positive face refers to a person's wish to be liked, approved of and respected, the latter designates a person's "rights to non-distraction – i.e. to freedom of action, and freedom of imposition" (Brown and Levinson 1987: 61). Being based on Austin's (1962) speech act theory (see 2.2.), Brown and Levinson claim that most speech acts are inherently face-threatening acts (FTAs), i.e. they either threaten the hearer's, the speaker's, or both face wants. Since there is a mutual dependency between one's own and the interactant's face, the aim of each participant is to maintain each other's face in conversation. They hence engage in face management. In doing so, each conversational partner chooses a particular politeness strategy, which s/he believes to be the most appropriate one in order to mitigate the face-threat involved. Each speaker has thereby a selection of five super strategies at his/her disposal (Figure 2.1) which are associated with a number of substrategies. The super strategies are arranged in an order of increasing politeness and indirectness, Super Strategy 1 thereby being the most direct and impolite, Super Strategy 5 the most indirect and polite.

Figure 2.1: Brown and Levinson's (1987) super strategies for doing FTAs (Brown and Levinson 1987: 69).

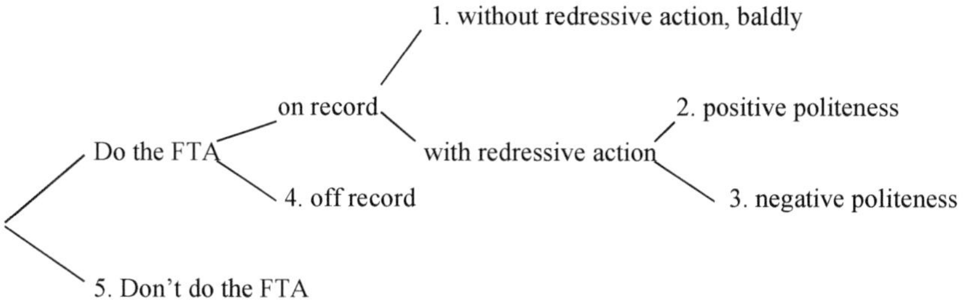

The most direct way of performing an FTA is to do it *bald on record*, in which case Grice's (1975) maxims are followed, making clarity and conciseness prominent. With the choice of Super Strategy 2, *do the act with redress (positive politeness)*, the speaker uses expressions of solidarity, thereby attending to the hearer's positive face-wants. If a speaker, on the other hand, wants to pay attention to the addressee's negative face-wants, s/he employs Super Strategy 3, *do the act with negative redress (negative politeness)*. The speaker hence uses expressions of restraint to provide the hearer at least superficially a way out. When choosing the most indirect way in performing an FTA, a speaker does the act *off record*, i.e. avoids unequivocal impositions and rather tries to disguise his/her face-threat by being ambiguous. Substrategies of this super strategy include hints, metaphors or ellipsis. If the speech act at hand is perceived as too face-threatening, a speaker can also refrain from performing it. In doing so, s/he is most indirect and polite, but, at the same time, misses to express his/her own needs.

Which of the five super strategies is chosen in a given situation, i.e. what kind and amount of politeness is employed, is determined by the 'weightiness' of the face-threat. This is calculated from three social independent variables, namely the perceived social distance between the interactants (D), the perceived power relations between the speaker and the hearer (P), and the absolute rank of imposition (R), i.e. how threatening a speech act is perceived to be in a specific culture. The weightiness of a particular face-threat can be calculated by adding these three variables together. This is illustrated in the following formula, where x denotes a speech act, S the speaker, and H the hearer:

$W_x = D(S, H) + P(H, S) + R_x$

With regard to the relationship between politeness and the weightiness of the face-threat, Brown and Levinsons's model predicts that the greater the face-threat at hand, the more indirect and polite the chosen super strategy will be. The three social variables which constitute the degree of face-threat are thereby seen to be culture-specific (cf. Brown and Levinson 1987: 76), consequently resulting in culture-specific views of the severity of the face-threat, and thus a culture-specific strategy choice. The core theoretical notions of these social variables, each individual's possession of positive and negative face, the principle of face-threat, and the operation of rationality are, on the other hand, claimed to be universally valid.

Being the best known politeness theory, Brown and Levinson's publications (1987 [1978]) have triggered numerable reactions, both positive and negative (cf. Bilbow 1995; Kerbrat-Orecchioni 1997; Lee-Wong 1998; Macauley 1996). Among the former are, for instance, the praise for its social significance (cf. Eelen 2001: 5; Turner 1996: 3) as well as its easy applicability, which has resulted in a large amount of further research.

However, there has also been a lot of criticism which cannot be overlooked. One of the major concerns relates to Brown and Levinson's (1987 [1978]) claim of universality. Specifically, it has been argued that Brown and Levinson's treatments of politeness have a Western bias in that they emphasise an individualist ethos which, however appropriate to the West, does not fit to the Eastern ethos of identifying with the group in which each person has a place defined by obligations and rights in relation to superiors, equals and inferiors (cf. Gu 1990; Ide 1989; Koutlaki 2002; Mao 1994; Matsumoto 1989; Wierzbicka 1991). Accordingly, Mao (1994) claims that Brown and Levinson's concept of face is at variance with the Chinese concepts of *miànzi* and *liǎn* and according to Gu (1990) their concept of politeness does not match the Chinese concept of *lǐmào*. Similarly, Ide (1993) censures Brown and Levinson's neglect of the Japanese concept of *wakimae* or *'discernment'*, despite its necessity to explain the Japanese socially constrained politeness or *teineisa*.

In addition to that, Gu (1990) and Matsumoto (1988) criticise Brown and Levinson's assumption of a universally-valid positive correlation between face and politeness, as they suggest that it is not the avoidance of face-threat that is decisive in an interaction but rather the participants' social standing.

Another significant criticism relates to the importance of context. Brown and Levinson have been blamed for dealing with single utterances only, thereby ignoring the significance of the sequential position of an utterance as well as the situational factors involved (cf. Fraser and Nolen 1981; Kienpointner 1997; Locher and Watts 2005; Meier 1995a). Sentences are, however, not inherently polite or impolite, independent of the context in which they are uttered, so that "one and the same type of speech act can be polite in some contexts, but impolite or even rude in other contexts" (Meier 1995a: 383ff.).

Related to this issue is the criticism of Brown and Levinson's belief of a direct relationship between increasing weight of contextual factors and increasing politeness. In her empirical research on American middle class speakers Wolfson (1988: 32ff.) has, for instance, revealed that intimates, status unequals and strangers use approximately the same level of politeness which is lower than the one used by non-intimates, status equal friends, co-workers and acquaintances. Due to this politeness pattern she proposes a bulge model which explains the given distribution with the fact that the most need for politeness is in situations in which the interlocutors' relationship is negotiable.

A further censure concerns the formula for calculating the weightiness of a face-threat. Apart from the assumed equal weight of the social factors D, P and R, their independence has also been questioned, since P and D may, for instance, have an impact on R, and a high P difference between the interlocutors may influence the participants' perception of D.

Moreover, not only Leech's (1983) politeness theory but also the face-saving view has been criticised for its claim of a positive correlation between politeness and indirectness (see 2.3.1.). It is equally doubtful to assume that positive politeness is more often used in situations of lower face-threat than negative politeness, as it has to be taken into account which of the two face-wants is actually threatened (cf. Turner 1996: 6). Furthermore, a single utterance can be oriented to both the positive and negative face simultaneously (cf. Thomas 1995: 176), thus refuting Brown and Levinson's claim that positive and negative politeness are mutually exclusive.

In addition to that, Brown and Levinson's face-saving view has been criticised for being a rather negative and pessimistic view. Held (1996), Holmes (1995) and Kerbrat-Orecchioni (1997), for instance, point out that politeness should not only be seen as a means of avoiding or mitigating FTAs, but additionally as a means of expressing positive aspects of interlocutors by the use of 'Face-Enhancing-Acts' (cf. Kerbrat-Orecchioni 1997: 14).

Locher and Watts (2005) therein go as far as to censure Brown and Levinson for not having developed a theory of politeness but rather a theory of facework. Accordingly, they claim that much of what is thought to be polite is, according to their model, in fact socially appropriate or, as they call it, "politic behaviour" (cf. Locher and Watts 2005: 17).

Finally, the face-saving view, like other theories of politeness such as Lakoff's (1975) or Leech's (1983) (see 2.3.1.), has been blamed for advocating a rather idealistic assumption about communication in that it ignores the negative counter-part of politeness, i.e. intentional impoliteness or rudeness, which is a well-recognized phenomenon in people's interactions (cf. Culpeper et al. 2003: 1548; Kienpointner 1997: 256; Locher and Watts 2005: 10). Kasper (1990) thus correctly points out that "Future studies will have to address the function of rudeness as complementary behaviour to politeness" (Kasper 1990: 211).

2.3.3. The conversational-contract view

The conversational-contract view was first presented by Fraser and Nolen (cf. Fraser 1975, 1990; Fraser and Nolen 1981). Similar to Brown and Levinson's (1987 [1978]) politeness theory, this view is based on Grice's (1975) CP and recognizes the importance of Goffman's (1967) notion of face. In contrast to the former though, it is discourse- rather than speech-act-based, leading to significant differences between these frameworks.

Central to the conversational-contract view is the assumption that when entering a conversation participants have an understanding of some initial rights and obligations which determine, at least in the beginning, their expectations of the other participant(s). This set of rights and obligations forms the conversational contract (CC) between the interactants which is seen as a changeable rather than stable concept, as it can be renegotiated throughout the course of the interaction. The CC thereby consists of three components which differ in their variability. The first is conventional thus seldom negotiable. Examples include the obligation to speak loud enough, to use a mutually intelligible language, or to abide by turn-taking rules. Similarly, the second component is rather fixed, since it is "imposed by the social institutions applicable to the interaction" (Fraser 1990: 232). The third is, however, "determined by previous encounters or the particulars of the situation" (Fraser 1990: 232) and hence renegotiable in the light of contextual factors such as power, social distance, or each speaker's role.

Politeness, in this view, is not an additional aspect of interaction but a part of it. It can therefore be found in every utterance as long as it is perceived as appropriate by the participants of the conversation, and thus in line with the terms and conditions of the CC. Consequently, being polite does not involve making the hearer 'feel good' as in Leech's (1983) approach, nor avoiding or mitigating a face-threat at hand as in Brown and Levinson's (1987 [1978]) theory. It is rather seen as the norm which is expected and thus not noticed by the participants. Violations of the CC, i.e. utterances that are perceived as impolite, however, are recognised.

The underlying motivation for polite behaviour is thereby seen in the speaker's intention to be cooperative, and consequently to abide by the CP. Indeed, it is not sentences which are "*ipso facto* polite [...]. It is only speakers who are polite, and then only if their utterances reflect an adherence to the obligations they carry in that particular conversation" (Fraser 1990: 233). However, whether or not an utterance is then really perceived as polite remains in the hands of the hearer.

The conversational-contract view can clearly be commended for its attempts to account for the dynamic and changing nature of politeness and conversations. However, it has also been criticised for its abstract and imprecise nature which makes this approach difficult to apply to empirical data (cf. Thomas 1995: 177). In addition to that, Locher and Watts have censured that politeness is regarded as the norm in this framework, and accordingly goes unnoticed (cf. Locher 2004; Locher and Watts 2005). In contrast to that, they claim that not only impolite but also polite behaviour is recognized in interactions, as politeness exceeds interactants' expectations. A more detailed account of their theory is given in the following section (2.3.4.).

2.3.4. The concept of relational work

In their approach, Locher and Watts (2005) criticise that politeness research influenced by Brown and Levinson (1987 [1978]) does not deal with politeness but with mitigation of FTAs in general. As a consequence, much of what has been defined as polite in literature is, according to them, merely appropriate behaviour. They hence argue for a discursive approach to politeness which reduces politeness to a much smaller part of facework than was previously thought. The origins of this strand of thinking can be traced back to Watts' studies (1989, 1992) which have further been developed by Kasper (1990), Watts (2003), Locher (2004, 2006b), and Locher and Watts (2005). Central to this theory is the notion of relational work which they define as "the 'work' individuals invest in negotiating relationships with others" (Locher and Watts 2005: 10). Relational work thereby comprises a continuum of behaviour spanning from impolite to over-polite with appropriate and polite behaviour in between (see Figure 2.2).

Figure 2.2: Relational work and its polite (shaded) version, illustrated with respect to the judgments on (im)politeness, appropriateness and markedness (Locher 2004: 90).

R E L A T I O N A L   W O R K

◁				▷
	negatively marked	unmarked	positively marked	negatively marked
◁				▷
	impolite	non-polite	polite	over-polite
◁				▷
	non-politic/ inappropriate	politic/ appropriate	politic/ appropriate	non-politic/ inappropriate

Locher and Watts thus argue to replace prior dichotomies of polite and impolite behaviour (cf. Brown and Levinson 1987 [1978]; Culpeper 1996, 2005; Culpeper et al. 2003; Escandell-Vidal 1996; Fraser 1990; Lakoff 1973; Leech 1983; Meier 1995b; Mills 2003, 2005) with a continuum in which politeness only represents a small part of relational work (column 3 in Figure 2.2). Additionally, they are in favour of a further distinction within appropriate behaviour (cf. Locher 2004; Locher and Watts 2005; Watts 1989, 1992, 2003), namely non-polite yet appropriate/politic behaviour (column 2 in Figure 2.2) on the one hand, and appropriate/politic but similarly polite behaviour (column 3 in Figure 2.2) on the other. The term politic has thereby been introduced by Watts (1989) who defines it as "that behaviour, linguistic and non-linguistic, which the participants construct as being appropriate to the ongoing social interaction" (Watts 2003: 257). Politic behaviour hence describes behaviour which is seen as appropriate in lay people's perceptions, because it is the kind of behaviour they would expect to happen in this situation.[8] Polite behaviour, in contrast to that, goes beyond what is expected and is hence seen in this approach as *surplus* (cf. Kasper 1990; Locher 2004; Watts 1989, 1992). Given these definitions, Kasper (1990), Watts (1989, 1992), and Locher (2004) clearly differ from Fraser's (1975, 1990) view in that politeness is not only regarded as unmarked appropriate behaviour, but as a marked behaviour, which stands above the norm

[8] In later work the terms 'politic' and 'appropriate' are used as synonyms. Since the term 'politic' is as loaded as the term 'politeness', Culpeper (2008) argues for the use of the more neutral and at the same time more transparent term 'appropriate' (cf. Culpeper 2008: 43).

and is thus recognised in interactions, as it goes beyond interactants' expectations.

As far as the motivation for polite behaviour is concerned, the researchers' opinions diverge. While Watts (1992) claims that polite behaviour is mainly non-altruistic and egocentric, since it aims to make others have a better opinion of oneself (cf. Watts 1992: 51), Kasper (1990) sees its motivation in "ensuring comity, social harmony, and counterbalancing potential conflict" (Kasper 1990: 208). Locher (2004) thereby takes a middle position by combining these assumptions, as she believes that both aspects can be expressed with or understood as polite behaviour (cf. Locher 2004: 90f.).

In order to define relationships among interactants, the entire spectrum of social behaviour is needed. Locher and Watts' framework of relational work is thus equivalent to Halliday's (1978) interpersonal level of communication in which interpersonal rather than ideational meaning is negotiated.

Although the term 'facework' signifies the same breadth of behaviour covered by Locher and Watts' concept of relational work, they prefer the term 'relational work', since 'facework' has mainly been used to describe polite and appropriate behaviour only, thereby excluding the negatively marked types of relational work.[9]

The majority of relational work that participants invest in interactions is of an unmarked nature and thus goes unnoticed (column 2 in Figure 2.2). Yet, with regard to marked behaviour three different kinds can be distinguished: *impolite/non-politic/inappropriate* (column 1 in Figure 2.2) and *over-polite/non-politic/inappropriate behaviour* (column 4 in Figure 2.2) comprise relational work which is perceived in a negative way. In addition to that, marked behaviour can also be positively marked in which case it is *polite/politic/appropriate* (column 3 in Figure 2.2).[10] Accordingly, polite behaviour is always politic, but politic behaviour not always polite. At the same time though, there are no clear-cut boundaries between the different categories

[9] Spencer-Oatey speaks about rapport management in this respect (cf. Spencer-Oatey 2000a, 2000b, 2002, 2005, 2007) (see 2.3.5.).

[10] For the distinction between the marked and unmarked case cf. Fraser and Nolen (1981).

presented in Figure 2.2, since they are a matter of negotiation between the communicative partners involved.[11]

To explain why participants behave in a certain way in specific situations and on which basis they judge their interlocutor's relational work, Locher and Watts (2005) refer to the concept of frame (cf. Escandell-Vidal 1996; Tannen 1993) or habitus (cf. Bourdieu 1990). While frame is defined as "structures of expectation based on past experience" (Tannen 1993: 53) or "an organized set of specific knowledge" (Escandell-Vidal 1996: 629), habitus is central to Bourdieu's Theory of Practice and signifies "the set of predispositions to act in certain ways, which generates cognitive and bodily practices in the individual" (Watts 2003: 149). These terms thus express that on the basis of previous experience with relational work in social practice, individuals develop cognitive structures representing specific social norms. In interaction, these norms do not only direct the individuals' own social behaviour but also serve as guidelines to determine the appropriateness and markedness of the other interlocutors' relational work. Most of the time these processes pass off unconsciously. Furthermore, in every Community of Practice (CofP) (cf. Buchholtz 1999; Eckert and McConnel-Ginet 1999; Holmes and Meyerhoff 1999; Lakoff 1973; Lavé and Wenger 1991; Meyerhoff 2002; Wenger 1998) these norms are always negotiated over time and therefore subject to change.

Central to Locher and Watts' (2005) concept of relational work is Goffman's (1967) notion of face which also constitutes a significant pillar of Brown and Levinson's (1987 [1978]) politeness theory (see 2.3.2.). In contrast to the latter though, Locher and Watts argue in line with Goffman (1967) that face is not inherent in each individual but rather constructed in every individual discourse. Face is thus socially attributed anew in each specific interaction, which implies that every individual can have a large number of faces. Locher and Watts (2005) hence equate them with "masks, on loan to us for the duration of different kinds of performance" (Locher and Watts 2005: 12), which an individual may even want to change within the course of an interaction, as we are not "tied to just one single role" (Locher 2006b). Given this discursive concept of face, relational

[11] Given that the distinction between the different behavioural categories is not absolute but rather fuzzy, Culpeper (2008) argues to see them as scales (cf. Culpeper 2008: 23).

work comprises a more comprehensive notion of face than previously presented by Brown and Levinson (1987 [1978]).

Crucial to Locher and Watts' (2005) discursive approach of politeness is the fact that it is based on the notion of first order politeness (politeness1), i.e. the lay concept of politeness, rather than second order politeness (politeness2) which makes use of the terms "polite" and "politeness" as theoretical constructs (cf. Watts et al. 1992). As they claim that no linguistic expression is inherently polite and, at the same time, individuals' realisations and understanding of utterances may vary due to their different habita, Locher and Watts see no point in maintaining a universal theoretical concept of politeness (cf. Locher 2006a, 2006b; Locher and Watts 2005). Instead of imposing second order principles on linguistic data, whose results often do not coincide with individual's perception of politeness, they want us "to recognize that terms such as 'impolite', 'polite' or 'appropriate' are inherently evaluative and normative" (Locher 2006b: 252). Similar to Fraser and Nolen's model (cf. Fraser and Nolen 1981: 96), it can thus neither be taken for granted that a particular linguistic utterance is similarly evaluated by everyone involved in the interaction, nor that a speaker's intention to be (im)polite is necessarily perceived as such by the addressee.

Given this evaluative and norm-oriented character of politeness, Locher and Watts argue for their discursive approach to politeness in which "there is an ongoing struggle over forms of appropriateness in any given group of people over time" (Locher 2006a: 734). This struggle is thereby less severe among interactants who are familiar with the norms of behaviour established in a specific CofP, and have consequently developed a very similar habitus in this respect. Newcomers to this particular community are, on the other hand, more likely to differ in their evaluations of appropriateness, revealing the importance of experience and acculturation to find the appropriate level of relational work.

All in all, this more recent approach to politeness certainly has to be praised for demonstrating the importance of the specific context of an interaction as well as the necessity to take human beings' individuality into account when making judgements about politeness. In addition to that, their concept of relational work also includes impolite behaviour which has mainly been neglected in preceding politeness theories. What is more, although Locher and Watts criticise prior frameworks on politeness, they still do not miss their worthiness. Regarding

Brown and Levinson's (1987 [1978]) politeness theory, for example, they praise the researchers for the enormous insights they have given us into human behaviour as well as for their astute description of linguistic strategies which are valuable tools when analysing relational work in interaction. Moreover, they demonstrate the applicability of their own model to naturally occurring data (cf. Locher 2006b: 258ff.; Locher and Watts 2005: 17ff.), giving their approach an empirical basis.

However, a consequence of this elusive concept of politeness which underlies Locher and Watts' approach, is that politeness is declared not to be a predictive theory (cf. Watts 2003: 142). Yet this is incompatible with researchers' aim to explain a particular communicative behaviour (cf. Leech 2007: 104). Terkourafi (2005) therefore states: "What we are then left with are minute descriptions of individual encounters, but these do not in any way add up to an explanatory theory of the phenomenon under study" (Terkourafi 2005: 245). Indeed, if participants' evaluation of (im)politeness is not explicitly the topic of their interaction, data analysis remains only on the basis of what the researcher takes as evidence for politeness or impoliteness or, in case of a weaker claim, even only of 'potential' (im)politeness. The procedure of data analysis is thus not that different from the way data is interpreted in studies of politeness2.

In addition to that, Culpeper (2008) criticises that despite these scholars' politeness1 approach, they failed to "offer an authoritative account of the lay person's use of politeness terms" (Culpeper 2008: 20), which can, as he suggests, be made up for by a corpus-based exploration of the terms.

2.3.5. The concept of rapport management

In line with previous researchers (cf. Fraser and Nolen 1981; Holmes 1995; Locher 2004; Watts 2003), Spencer-Oatey (2000a) regards politeness as a social judgement in that no sentence or linguistic construction is inherently polite or impolite, rather (im)politeness is "an evaluative label that people attach to behaviour, as a result of their subjective judgement about social appropriateness" (Spencer-Oatey 2005: 97). People's judgements thereby primarily depend on their expectations which in turn are based on their beliefs about behaviour.

Given Spencer-Oatey's (2002) interest in the social-psychological component of the management of relations, the main focus of her approach is on the motivational concerns underlying the management of relations (cf. Spencer-Oatey 2002: 530). Unlike previous researchers on politeness, she does not take language as her starting point but proposes a model that starts with the management of relations and is hence called 'rapport management' model (cf. Spencer-Oatey 2000b, 2002, 2005, 2007). In her approach she avoids the term 'politeness', not only due to the confusion of this term (see. 2.3.), but also since it only emphasises the harmonious aspect of social relations thereby neglecting incidents in which language is used to keep or even attack social relations (cf. Spencer-Oatey 2000a: 2f., 2005: 95). Her framework of rapport management, like Locher and Watts' (2005) approach, has thus a broader focus aiming to examine "not only the behavior that enhances or maintains smooth relations, but any kind of behavior that has an impact on rapport, whether positive, negative, or neutral" (Spencer-Oatey 2005: 96).

Similar to Brown and Levinson's (1987 [1978]) framework, also in Spencer-Oatey's model of rapport management interactant's face is an important issue, which, following Goffman (1967), she defines as "the positive social *value* a person effectively claims for himself [*sic*] by the line others assume he has taken during a particular contact" (Goffman 1967: 5, cited in Spencer-Oatey 2000b: 13f., Spencer-Oatey's emphasis). Yet, instead of adopting Brown and Levinson's (1987 [1978]) concept of face, she proposes a modified conceptualisation of face and rapport thereby taking into account the criticism which has often been claimed against Brown and Levinson's (1987 [1978]) concept of negative face, namely that they have over-emphasised the notion of individual freedom and autonomy, and that they have ignored the interpersonal or social perspective on face (cf. Ide 1989; Mao 1994; Matsumoto, 1988).[12]

[12] For Spencer-Oatey's discussion about the insights that theories of identity, especially Simon's (2004) Self-Aspect Model of Identity and Brewer and Gardener's (1996) theory of levels of identity, can offer for the conceptualisation and analysis of face, see Spencer-Oatey (2007).

Spencer-Oatey's (2000b) approach thus incorporates both one's individual or personal identity as well as one's identity within a group.[13] To account for the fact that interactants must orient to both their individual face needs and also reconcile these with the norms and expectations of a specific group, the rapport management model involves two main components: the management of face which is associated with *value*, and the management of sociality rights which is oriented to *entitlements*. Face management is thereby divided into two interrelated categories (see Table 2.1): *quality face* which is the desire to be viewed positively and thus is equivalent to Brown and Levinson's (1987 [1978]) notion of positive face, as well as *identity face*, which is group oriented and designates the desire to be respected in our social roles, e.g. as a group leader, valued customer, or close friend (cf. Spencer-Oatey 2000b: 14, 2002: 540). Similarly, *sociality rights* are divided into two interrelated categories (see Table 2.1): *equity rights* which describe the desire to be treated fairly and not be unduly imposed upon by others. They hence help to uphold people's independent construals of self (cf. Markus and Kitayama 1991) and thus equal Brown and Levinson's (1987 [1978]) definition of negative face wants. Spencer-Oatey (2005) thereby distinguishes three aspects which relate to the equity entitlement.[14] Firstly, *cost-benefit* consideration, i.e. the principle that people should not be exploited or disadvantaged. Secondly, *fairness and reciprocity*, namely the belief that costs and benefits should be fair and kept in an approximate balance. And thirdly, *autonomy-control*[15], that is the belief that people should not be controlled or imposed upon.

The second component of the *sociality rights* are the *association rights* which express our fundamental belief that we are entitled to association with others and have positive relationships with them. Again there are three issues related to them,[16] namely *involvement,* i.e. the principle that people should have

[13] The distinction between individual identity and social identity corresponds to a large extent to that between independent and interdependent construals of self (cf. Markus and Kitayama 1991; Morisaki and Gudykunst 1994; Ting-Toomey and Kurogi 1998).
[14] In former publications, Spencer-Oatey distinguishes only two aspects that relate to *equity rights* (cf. Spencer-Oatey 2000b, 2002).
[15] In previous work, the aspect *autonomy-control* is called *autonomy-imposition* (cf. Spencer-Oatey 2000b: 14, 2002: 540).
[16] In former publications, Spencer-Oatey distinguishes only two aspects which are related to association rights (cf. (Spencer-Oatey 2000b, 2002).

appropriate amounts and types of "activity" involvement with others, *empathy*, which designates the belief that people should share appropriate concerns, feelings and interests with others,[17] and finally, *respect*, which is the belief that people should show appropriate amounts of respectfulness for others (cf. Spencer-Oatey 2005: 100). For an overview of the components of rapport management see the following Table 2.1.

Table 2.1: Components of rapport management (Spencer-Oatey 2000b: 15).

	face management (personal/social value)	**sociality rights management (personal/social entitlements)**
personal/independent perspective	quality face (cf. Brown and Levinson's positive face)	equity rights (cf. Brown and Levinson's negative face)
social/interdependent perspective	identity face	association rights

Regarding the definitions of the four components of rapport management, it becomes obvious that both the management of face and the management of sociality rights have a personal component: *quality face* and *equity rights* respectively, and a social component: *identity face* and *association rights* respectively (see Table 2.1).

Accordingly, social relations may be threatened in two ways in Spencer-Oatey's (2000b) model: either through face-threatening behaviour or through rights-threatening behaviour, whereby either of the two components of face or sociality rights may be under attack.

Different cultures may thereby place different emphasis on the four components of rapport management, revealing the culture sensitivity of Spencer-Oatey's (2000b) framework. Specifically, culture may impact the relative sensitivity to the varying components so that rapport management may be needed more for one aspect than for another. Furthermore, people's conceptions of rights and obligations are likely to be culturally influenced. And finally, cultures may differ in the strategies they prefer for mitigating rapport threatening behaviour (cf. Gudykunst 2000; Spencer-Oatey 2002; Ting-Toomey and Kurogi 1998).

[17] In prior publications (cf. Spencer-Oatey 2000b: 14f., 2002: 541), *involvement* and *empathy* are called *interactional association/dissociation* and *affective association/dissociation*, respectively.

Spencer-Oatey's (2000b) model is clearly laudable for its contextual and cultural sensitivity, demonstrating its post-modern view of politeness. Furthermore, this approach has the great advantage that it allows for teasing apart the individual and group influences on participants' behaviour in a given interaction. This is extremely helpful when investigating CMC data as the present study does, since in many CMC modes, group membership plays a significant role, leading to the fact that the virtual presence of other online group members clearly influences members' linguistic behaviour (cf. Graham 2007, 2008).

With regard to the subjects of the present study, two types of group membership in relation to CMC can be distinguished. On the one hand, eBay users belong to the eBay community in which a good reputation is crucial for future transactions. Consequently, the virtual presence of the other members of the eBay community has a strong impact on member's linguistic choices. On the other hand, eBay users also belong to the huge group of Internet users, who all may surf on eBay's websites without being registered, since eBay is a public domain. Yet, given that Internet users who are just 'lurking' on eBay's feedback forum are not allowed to do business on this online marketplace and are hence no potential trading partners, their influence on eBay member's communicative behaviour is presumably only low. However, since 'lurkers' may join the eBay community, the impact of their virtual presence should not be neglected.

2.3.6. A model of impoliteness

As mentioned above (cf. 2.3.1. and 2.3.2.), many famous politeness theories have been criticised for their disregard of the counterpart of polite behaviour. Although there have also been studies extending the scope of these politeness theories to the area of confrontational communication (cf. Bousfield 2006, 2007, 2008; Cashman 2006; Craig et al. 1986; Culpeper 1996, 1998, 2005, 2008; Graham 2007, 2008; Hatipoğlu 2007; Kienpointner 1997; Lakoff 1989; Limberg 2008; Penman 1990; Spencer-Oatey 2002, 2005; Tracy 1990), the number of studies focusing on impoliteness has remained disproportionate compared to the vast amount of studies on politeness. This dearth of research on the apparent 'dark' side of social interaction (Austin 1990) is not only telling since any adequate account of the dynamics of interpersonal communication needs to consider both polite and impolite behaviour (cf. Craig et al. 1986; Culpeper et al. 2003; Spencer-Oatey 2000b; Tracy 1990), but also because researchers have shown that in some contexts conflictive communication is rather common and not just "marginal to human linguistic behaviour" (Leech 1983: 105). These contexts include, for instance, settings such as army training (cf. Culpeper 1996, Bousfield 2008), police-public discourse (cf. Bousfield 2008; Limberg 2008), interactions between traffic wardens and care owners (cf. Culpeper et al. 2003), political discussions (cf. Harris 2001), courtroom trails (cf. Harris, 1984; Lakoff 1989; Penman 1990), family discourse (cf. Vuchinich 1990), doctor-patient discourse (cf. Mehan 1990), adolescent discourse (cf. Goodwin and Goodwin 1990), or fictional texts (cf. Culpeper 1998; Liu 1986; Tannen 1990).

Contextual factors which have been shown to facilitate impolite behaviour are, for instance, an imbalance of power, since "the more powerful participant has more right to be impolite" (Culpeper 1996: 345), or interlocutors' conflictive interests in equal relationships with high social distance, as for example in competitions, where everyone's aim is to win. In relationships with low social distance, on the other hand, the variable affect (liking/disliking) seems to have an impact, since Slugoski and Turnbull's study (1988) has revealed that speakers care less for their interlocutor's face when the relationship is one of dislike. And finally, Infante and Wigley's study (1986) points to genetic factors having an influence in that some people are predisposed towards aggressive behaviour.

Given that scholars of this field come from different theoretical camps, it is not surprising that also with regard to the term 'impoliteness' no common agreement on its definition has been reached. The lowest common denominator can be summarised as follows: "*Impoliteness is behaviour that is face-aggravating in a particular context*" (Bousfield and Locher 2008: 3, italics in original), revealing that researchers at least agree on the importance of context. Yet most scholars would also agree that this definition is insufficient, which has led to many differing elaborations on this term (cf. Bousfield 2008; Culpeper 1996; Culpeper et al. 2003; Mills 2005; Spencer-Oatey 2005; Terkourafi 2008).

Facing the necessity of deeper and more accurate insight into impolite behaviour, Culpeper developed his well-known model of impoliteness in 1996, which he and his colleagues improved in 2003, until he came up with an incarnation in 2005. However, since even the enhanced version retained fundamental deficiencies, most notably its previous dependence on Brown and Levinson's (1987 [1978]) notion of face as well as its retention of the category *bald, in record impoliteness*, Bousfield (2008) modified Culpeper's model even further.[18] The definition of impoliteness which thereby underlies Bousfield's (2008) approach is phrased as follows:

> I take impoliteness as constituting the issuing of intentionally gratuitous and conflictive face-threatening acts (FTAs) that are purposefully performed:
> 1) Unmitigated, in contexts where mitigation (where mitigation equates with politeness) is required and/or,
> 2) With deliberate aggression, that is, with the face threat exacerbated, 'boosted', or maximised in some way to heighten the face damage inflicted.
>
> Furthermore, for impoliteness to be considered successful impoliteness, the intention of the speaker (or 'author') to 'offend' (threaten/damage face) must be understood by those in a receiver role.
>
> (Bousfield 2008: 132)

Accordingly, impoliteness only exists if both the speaker and addressee (in a two party interaction) intend and perceive face-threat respectively.[19]

Further assuming that face is always an issue of interaction and that the 'positive' and 'negative' face strategies often systematically combine in interaction (cf. Culpeper et al. 2003: 1560ff.; Harris 2001), Bousfield (2008) restructures Culpeper's model (2005) along simpler lines. Specifically, he merges the original five super strategies of impoliteness and the "meta-strategy" of *sarcasm* (cf. Culpeper 2005: 42) into two main 'tactics'[20] under which the existing linguistic strategies for performing impoliteness can be subsumed. These two tactics are as follows:

---

[18] For a discussion of the deficiencies of the most recent version of Culpeper's (2005) model, see Bousfield (2008: 134ff.).

[19] Definitions on impoliteness mainly differ in the role they attribute to the recognition of intentions in the understanding of impoliteness. While some researchers, like Bousfield, make the hearer's understanding of the speaker's intention the key for impoliteness (cf. Bousfield 2008: 132; Culpeper 2005: 38, 2008: 36), others claim that the recognition of intentions is the basis of rudeness rather than impoliteness (cf. Terkourafi 2008: 70).

[20] Bousfield (2008) prefers the term 'tactic' to clearly differentiate his approach from the concept of '(super)strategies'. However, he points out that both are "unhappy terms" (Bousfield 2008: 152), since in light of their meaning in military service 'tactics' are in fact what Brown and Levinson (1987 [1978]) misnamed in their approach as 'strategies', and the 'tactics' he identifies should rather be called 'strategies' (Bousfield 2008: 152).

(1) On-record impoliteness

On-record impoliteness constitutes the use of strategies to explicitly attack the interlocutor's face, construct it in a non-harmonious or conflictive way, or to refrain from expected face wants or rights of the recipient, or even a combination thereof. Due to the context in which these strategies are employed, the aggravation of face is clear and unambiguous.

(2) Off-record impoliteness

Off-record impoliteness signifies the use of strategies to indirectly communicate the intended face-threat by way of an implicature (cf. Grice 1975, 1989). The speaker can hence easily deny to have intended the offence. Yet, given the context in which the strategies are used, the speaker's real intention "clearly outweighs any others" (Culpeper 2005: 44).

Culpeper's notions of *sarcasm*[21] and the *withholding of politeness* are classified in Bousfield's model under the heading of off-record impoliteness. They are described as follows:

(a) Sarcasm

Sarcasm designates the use of strategies or combinations of them which on the surface maintain or enhance the recipient's face. In the context in which they occur they are, however, obviously insincere, and thus have the opposite effect, i.e. threaten, attack, or damage the addressee's face.[22]

(b) Withhold of politeness

Withhold politeness denotes the absence of politeness in contexts where it would be expected or even taken as obligatory.

A major advantage of this outlined model is clearly that it is employable alongside traditional (cf. Goffman 1967), culture-specific (cf. Brown and Levinson 1987 [1978]), and more contextually and culturally sensitive (cf. Spencer-Oatey 2002, 2005) concepts of face, making it "an adaptable adjunct to existing models of face" (Bousfield 2008: 139). Furthermore, the different strategies of impoliteness which have been pointed out in previous models (cf.

---

[21] Culpeper's (1996) notion of *sarcasm* is thereby close to Leech's (1983) understanding of *irony*. He nevertheless prefers the term *sarcasm*, since *irony* can refer to enjoyment or comedy, while *sarcasm* is always employed as a means to achieve social disharmony.

[22] Similar to Culpeper (1996, 2005), also Bousfield (2008) defines *sarcasm* as the opposite in *functional* terms to *banter* (cf. Leech 1983). He hence calls *banter* the "*Sarcasm's* polite 'mirror-tactic'" (Bousfield 2008: 152, italics were added).

Culpeper 1996; Culpeper et al. 2003; Cashman 2006) can all be categorised as one of the tactics described above, which shows the wide range of different means of impoliteness that are captured by this approach. And finally, Bousfield (2008) demonstrates the applicability of his model on empirical data taken from television 'docusoaps' or 'fly-on-the-wall' documentary serials. Future research will certainly have to prove its applicability on other types of data, among which the present project may serve as an example (see 7.2.).

2.4. Pragmatics across cultures

Given that the present study is not only located in the area of pragmatics but more specifically focuses on a comparison of pragmatic issues across cultures, it is important to clarify the most important terms with regard to this research area. This subchapter therefore begins with an explanation of the initial approach taken to compare the pragmatics within and between cultures (2.4.1.). This is followed by a clarification of the terms cross-cultural and intercultural pragmatics (2.4.2.) which have often been used interchangeably in literature, although marking different communicative situations. Finally, the concept of culture is outlined (2.4.3.), as it is a basic element for the cross-cultural approach taken in this study.

2.4.1. Contrastive pragmatics

Since the origin of pragmatics there has been a growing number of studies comparing pragmatics within and between different cultures. Initially researchers chose a contrastive approach, thus focusing on pragmalinguistics in their comparison, thereby neglecting the sociopragmatic side of language. This approach takes for granted the assumption that language use is universal, i.e. that all cultures share not only the same speech acts as well as strategies and linguistic means for their realisation but also have the same theoretical framework in common. This assumption of universality has been hotly debated in literature (cf. Blum-Kulka et al. 1989: 8ff.; Wierzbicka 1991: 67ff.). Many investigations confirm this view, showing that a number of language areas seem to be universal, as for instance, the use of pragmatic routines (cf. Coulmas

1981b), a sensitivity for the importance of contextual variables (cf. Brown and Levinson 1987 [1978]), the basic speech act categories (cf. Kasper and Schmidt 1996) or the means of modification (cf. Blum-Kulka 1991).

However, some researchers have also uncovered cultural variation regarding the use of language. For instance, Wiezbicka's study (1985) reveals a difference in pragmalinguistic conventions across cultures, as her study shows that an ability question is a conventionalised request in English but not in Polish (cf. Wierzbicka 1985: 148ff.). Further areas proven to be culture-specific in language use include the weighting of the contextual factors in a situation (cf. Takahashi and Beebe 1993) or some specific speech acts which differ due to differences in institutional structures (cf. Kasper and Schmidt 1996). It is these culturally different interactional styles which result in different preferences for modes of communicative behaviour and hence have often been shown to lead to miscommunication, communicative breakdowns, and/or the formation of stereotypes (cf. Clyne et al. 1991; Günther 2000; House 2000; House and Kasper 1981; Murphy and Neu 1996; Spencer-Oatey and Xing 2000; Thomas 1983; Trosborg 1995; Tyler 1995; Žegarac and Pennington 2000).

Given the increasing amount of studies revealing culture-specificity in language use and the possibly resulting misunderstandings, the initial contrastive approach, based on the assumption of universality, was increasingly replaced by a cross-cultural perspective.

2.4.2. Cross-cultural versus intercultural pragmatics

In contrast to contrastive pragmatics, the field of cross-cultural pragmatics embraces both sides of language: pragmalinguistics and sociopragmatics. House (1986) hence calls it "an important new branch of contrastive linguistic studies because in any two languages different features of the social context may be found to be relevant in deciding what can be expressed and how it is conventionally expressed" (House 1986: 282).

However, there is some confusion regarding the terms cross-cultural and intercultural pragmatics, since they are often used interchangeably although they do not have the same meaning. Cross-cultural communication focuses on comparative studies of interpersonal communication in different cultures, i.e.

data is obtained independently from different cultural groups and compared to one another regarding a particular aspect of interest (cf. Spencer-Oatey 2000a: 4). Intercultural communication, on the other hand, considers interaction among people representing different cultures. Research in intercultural pragmatics is hence interested in "how people understand one another when they do not share a common cultural experience and how culture is constructed by interactants with different national, ethnic, and racial backgrounds" (Kecskes 2004: 2).
The best known project in the area of cross-cultural pragmatics is the Cross-Cultural Speech Act Realisation Project (CCSARP) in which Blum-Kulka et al. (1989) compared the realisation modes of requests and apologies in seven different languages and language varieties. Given that the focus of the present study is on a comparison of the realisation of a particular speech act between two cultures, it is also located in the area of cross-cultural pragmatics. As the concept of culture is of crucial importance for the chosen cross-cultural perspective, an attempt to characterise this concept follows.

2.4.3. Culture

The term *culture* is derived from Latin *cultura* stemming from *colore*, meaning "to cultivate, to worship" (cf. "culture, *n.*" *The Oxford English Dictionary*. 2nd ed. 1989. *OED Online*. Oxford University Press. 4 December. 2008, http://dictionary.oed.com/). But in spite of its importance for many research areas, the notion of culture has remained very vague, lacking a clear definition until today (cf. Hofstede 1993: 18f.; Knapp and Knapp-Potthoff 1987: 4; Koole and Ten Thije 1994: 55; Spencer-Oatey 2000a: 3). Already in 1952, the American anthropologists, Kroeber and Kluckhohn (1952) compiled a list of 164 definitions of "culture" in their publication "Culture: A Critical Review of Concepts and Definitions", a number which has certainly further increased by now. However, despite this vast array of different definitions of culture, most of the anthropological definitions have at least three basic elements in common, precisely that culture is man-made and learnable, it is related to human groups rather than to individuals, and it is found in symbols and action (cf. Koole and Ten Thije 1994: 55ff.).

Of more importance for the present study though, is the close relation between culture and language which was first expressed in the nineteenth century by the German philosophers Johann Herder (1744-1803) and Wilhelm von Humboldt (1762-1835). This idea was later taken over by the American anthropologists Edward Sapir and Benjamin Lee Whorf, resulting in the well-known Sapir-Whorf hypothesis which states that our language predisposes how we experience and interpret our surroundings (cf. Sapir 1962: 68ff.; Whorf [1940] 1956: 221). While the strong version of this language determinism was discarded, a weaker version is still accepted today.

Furthermore, the originally simplistic view of culture in linguistics has given way to a more complex picture over the years. In other words, culture in communication is no longer seen as a homogenous system of knowledge and beliefs which is shared as a functional whole by people of a particular nation. Cultural phenomena in speech are nowadays regarded as dynamic, situational, and context-dependent (cf. Bloommaert 1998; Kecskes 2004; Rampton 1985; Risager 2005). However, this diverse and changing nature of culture does not make cross-cultural studies pointless since, in addition to its dynamic nature, culture is at the same time characterised by a certain regularity. Precisely, prior experience and communicative encounters of an individual result in memorised "relatively standard cultural behavior models and expectations " (Keckskes 2004: 21) which are more similar in one cultural group than another.[23] In a given context, these existing communicative repertoires are then activated and applied, whereby unexpected behaviour of an interactant can lead to misunderstandings, communicative breakdowns, and/or the formation of stereotypes. As a consequence, the concept of culture in cross-cultural pragmatic research has to be regarded as much more complex than once thought, which makes cross-cultural investigations more multi-layered but not less fascinating.

When the term 'culture' is used in the present report, it is operationalised in terms of national or regional political identity, i.e. of British English and German speakers. This is not to deny that members of these groups are a

[23] The term 'cultural group' thereby need not refer to a whole nation. Similarly, the term 'cross-cultural' is nowadays not only used to imply speaking different languages. Accordingly, Terkourafi (2008) states: "Speaking the same language but not adhering to the same, recognisable conventions is enough to cause the impression that different 'cultures' are at play" (Terkourafi 2008: 64).

heterogenous set of people. However, it is clearly an impossible aim to adequately deal with the different factors that are associated with each interactant so that the present report remains deliberately limited in this respect.

Chapter 3: Computer-mediated communication (CMC)

Having chosen the World Wide Web as the data source for the present study, a short introduction into CMC is given in this chapter. This includes a brief description of CMC (3.1.) and its history (3.2.), as well as an illustration of the attempts that have been made to classify the vast variety of CMC forms (3.3.). These include a short presentation of former approaches (3.3.1.) as well as a more detailed description of the recent faceted classification scheme (3.3.2.) which has also been applied to the data of the present study (see 4.3.2.).

3.1. Definition of CMC

Following Herring's (1996) definition of CMC, it is defined in this study as "communication that takes place between human beings via the instrumentality of computers" (Herring 1996: 1). As the present study examines electronic complaints from the feedback forum of eBay, using analytical tools of speech act theory for its data analysis, it is located in the area of CMC. However, since the position of the collected complaints in discourse and their situational context are also investigated in the present analysis and taken into account when discussing the received results, this study is similarly situated in the area of computer-mediated discourse (CMD), a sub branch of CMC, distinguished by its use of methods of discourse analysis (cf. Herring 2001: 612).

In light of the ever continuing progress in computer technologies, such as the invention of web cams, the area of CMC research is always extending. Nonetheless, most CMC currently in use is still text-based, i.e. messages are typed on a computer keyboard and read as texts on the computer screen, either immediately after their production (synchronous CMC), or at a later point in time (asynchronous CMC). These texts are sent either to one person or to many people simultaneously who usually do not share the location of the message sender. There are many different forms electronic texts can take, such as email, real-time chat, discussion groups, or, as in the present study, the form of a feedback comment. Despite their different forms which are partly influenced by the different technical and situational features connected with their use, all these different "forms have in common that the activity that takes place through them is constituted primarily – in many cases, exclusively, by visually presented language" (Herring 2001: 612). Hence, given the absence of other communicative channels, CMC stresses the importance of language itself, through which interactants present themselves, establish contact, and build relationships, thus making it a fascinating area for linguistic research.

3.2. A brief history of CMC

CMC is a rather recent phenomenon which has experienced a vast upswing in a very short period of time. Its beginnings can be traced back to the 1960s when communication via computer networks was first designed in the United States for the purpose of national defence (cf. Levy 1984; Rheingold 1993; Wiest 1997). Since then CMC has quickly attracted the interest of a wide range of users. First used by computer scientists in the 1970s (cf. Hafner and Lyon 1996), it became famous among business and academic professionals in the 1980s (cf. Herring 2001) and is used today by thousands of people throughout the world. Although in the 1990s male users had greatly outnumbered females in this medium (cf. Balka 1993; Smith et al. 1997; Truong 1993), female participation has increased along with the overall growth in CMC usage, so that today gender differences in the use of this medium have been balanced out. The enormous increase in CMC users from 15,000 modems in operation in 1970 (cf. Collot 1991: 14) to 250,000 modems in 1980 (cf. Collot 1991: 14), to an approximate number of 1.020 billion Internet users in 2006 (cf. Albrecht et al. 2007: 707) was not only supported by the rise of commercial Internet service providers but also by the decrease in prices of the equipment needed and for the Internet connection itself (cf. Federal Statistical Office and the Statistical Offices of the Länder (D_Statis) 2007a). This development enabled a much wider range of people to afford communication via computer networks, leading to an 'electronic revolution' (cf. Benson 1993) and opening up new possibilities for everyday communication. Regarding the continuing rapid progress in computer technologies which have greatly simplified and innovated computer use, the importance of CMC in our everyday lives will definitely further increase and affect our communication.

As soon as scholars came in touch with this new medium, research on CMC began to develop. Early works from the mid-1980s include Naomi Baron's (1984) study on the effects of "computer-mediated communication as a force in language change" which was soon followed by Denise Murray's (1985) work on real-time messaging systems at IBM. In the early 1990s, researchers also began to apply analytic tools of discourse analysis to CMC, hence founding the new subdiscipline of computer-mediated discourse (CMD) (cf. Baym 1993, 1996; Ferrara et al. 1991; Reid 1994). Nevertheless the term "computer-mediated discourse" was not introduced until March 1995 at a pre-session of the Georgetown University Round Table on Languages and Linguistics organized by Susan Herring (Herring 2001: 623). Since then, research in the fields of CMC and CMD has rapidly expanded and led to an ever growing group of researchers fascinated by these research fields.

On the other hand, it should not be overlooked that in the early stages of this active interest in CMC, misunderstandings about this medium arose. Properties such as "egalitarian", "anonymous", "impersonal", "fragmented", and "spoken-like" were subscribed to it, failing to take the different types of CMC into account (cf. Herring 2001: 613). Later research, however, has by now revealed that language transferred via computer networks is in fact sensitive to a variety of technical and situational factors, making it more complex and variable than implied by earlier descriptions.

3.3. Classification of computer-mediated discourse (CMD)

Attempts to classify discourse are not new but can be traced back to traditional discourse analytic concerns. Precisely, discourse analysts have traditionally classified their spoken and written data into types according to criteria comprising modality, number of participants, text or discourse type, and genre or register (cf. Biber 1988; Chafe and Danielewicz 1987; Longacre 1996; Swales 1990). Since classification helps to get a precise overview of the important properties of the data under investigation, thereby making explicit which features are shared by data of the same discourse type and setting it apart from other types, it clearly facilitates data analysis.

With the rise of the Internet and the development of a vast and ever growing variety of forms of CMD, researchers of computer-mediated communication clearly face the same demands to classify their data, thereby challenged by the new properties of the medium. Thus, since the 1980s researchers have continuously tried to organise CMD into categories that would facilitate its analysis and use. Among these various attempts, three earlier approaches can be distinguished which are described first (3.3.1.), before Herring's (2007) more recent classification scheme is illustrated (3.3.2.).

3.3.1. Earlier approaches to classifying CMD

In the beginning, researchers tended to characterise CMD as a single, homogeneous genre or communication type. Due to these linguists' experience in dealing with the two language modalities of speech and writing, they tried to classify CMD in relation to them (cf. Ferrara et al. 1991; Maynor 1994; Murray 1988; Werry 1996; Yates 1996). In doing so, they asked whether CMD is a type of writing, as it has to be typed and read as text on the computer screen, or whether it should be regarded as "written speech" (cf. Maynor 1994), given its rapid transmission, informality, and features of orality. Others thought of it as an intermediate modality between speech and writing, sharing features of both, being unique though in its communicative process (cf. Ferrara et al. 1991; Murray 1990).

By regarding CMD as one consistent type of communication which somehow has to be posited next to speaking and writing, followers of this early approach clearly overgeneralised about computer-mediated language. Despite this obvious drawback of this "globalizing approach" (cf. Herring 2007: 7), there are still researchers advocating this view in recent years (cf. Crystal 2001; Hiltrop 2003). Crystal (2001), for instance, regards "Netspeak" as a global variety of online language, sharing specific features regardless of the Internet situation (cf. Crystal 2001: 81ff.). Examples of these features include the use of specific abbreviations and word formations, emoticons, new spelling conventions, and a minimal use of punctuation.

However, with the vast spread of the Internet and the simultaneous increase in its users, people became aware of the fact that CMD is much more diverse and complex (cf. Baym 1995; Herring 1996). Researchers' focus hence shifted from a global to a more specific approach, describing the communicative and linguistic feaures of different genres of CMD, such as email (cf. Baron 2000), multi-user dimension (MUD) (cf. Cherny 1999), Internet Relay Chat (IRC) (cf. Werry 1996), or other Chat systems (cf. Raettig 1999). Herring (2002) refers to these as "socio-technical modes", different CMC subtypes with unique technical characteristics. She also stresses that labels, such as email or IRC, do not only describe the different underlying CMC systems but also refer to social and cultural conventions which have been developed among their users.

Although the genre and mode approaches present a more complex picture of CMD, they can still be criticised for their inaccuracy (cf. Herring 2007). While the concept of genre may "be applied to communication at different levels of specificity" (Herring 2007: 3), the mode approach primarily refers to technologically-defined CMD types, thereby neglecting the importance of social variables which potentially impact participants' language use. Another drawback of these genre and mode approaches is that they rely on already existing and well-known CMC systems (cf. Swales 1990), so it remains questionable whether they are flexible enough to also account for new emerging forms of CMD (cf. Herring 2007).

Regarding the third approach to structuring the different forms of data, researchers classified their CMD data according to pre-defined sets of categories. Murray (1988), for instance, used Hymes' (1974) "ethic grid" to characterise her data consisting of CMD among workers of a U.S. technology organisation, while Collot (1991) and Collot and Belmore (1996) applied Biber's (1988) model to describe the communicative components of their data taken from Bulletin Board Systems (BBS). It is also worth noting Baym's study (1995: 141). Like Biber (1988: 28ff.) she applied factors such as the purpose of the communication, the temporal structure of the group, and the characteristics of the group and its members, to her data of television soap opera fan newsgroups. However, in contrast to Biber's (1988) approach which comprises eight categories, Baym's classification is limited to only five, thereby missing important variables such as participants' social evaluation (cf. Biber 1988: 31), the language participants use, or the fonts they have at their disposal (cf. Danet and Herring 2007).

Given that researchers did not aim primarily at classifying CMD in all these approaches mentioned but rather pursued goals such as separating their CMD data from other data types or finding variables which were likely to explain the specific linguistic characteristics of their database, their attempts to classify CMD remained unsystematic and imprecise. In addition to that, they were not flexible enough to also account for new forms of CMD which are emerging every day. Facing the lack of a systematic, objective, and widely applicable classification system, Herring (2007) developed a faceted classification scheme for CMD which systematises and also extends previous efforts to classify CMD data. In doing so, she highlights those features which have been shown to most directly impact users' linguistic choices, and allows for the identification of a much more accurate picture of different CMD types than previous approaches. Her classification scheme is hence an important prerequisite for CMD data analysis. Furthermore, as it is not based on pre-existing modes, it can be applied to all different forms of CMD, including already existing but also newly emerging and more experimental ones. Given these advantages over the former approaches, Herring's (2007) classification scheme has been chosen to be applied to the data of the present study (see 4.1.2.) and is hence described in more detail below.

3.3.2. The faceted classification scheme of CMD

Underlying Herring's (2007) scheme is the assumption that CMD is subject to two types of influence, namely medium (technological) and situation (social), which are in an unordered and non-hierarchical relationship. Each type of influence consists of a number of categories or "facets" derived from empirical evidence gained through CMD research. Accordingly, the first set of categories relates to technological features of CMC systems and the second to social or situational factors describing the communicative context. The categories of each list are listed in no specific order but may (or may not) interact, just as medium and social factors may (or may not) influence one another. Furthermore, each list of categories has to be thought of as being flexible and open ended. In other words, when applying this faceted classification scheme to a CMD sample, unimportant factors with regard to the data in question can be left out, while others which condition users' online discourse should be added.

An overview of the medium and social factors which have been observed to condition CMD and are thus part of Herring's (2007) classification scheme is given in Table 3.1 and Table 3.2. An application of this scheme to CMD data demonstrates the specific realisation of each category, thereby revealing a nuanced account of the CMD sample under consideration.

Table 3.1: The medium factors of Herring's classification scheme (Herring 2007:13).

M1	Synchronicity
M2	Message transmission (1-way vs. 2-way)
M3	Persistence of transcript
M4	Size of message buffer
M5	Channels of communication
M6	Anonymous messaging
M7	Private messaging
M8	Filtering
M9	Quoting
M10	Message format

As Table 3.1 illustrates, Herring's (2007) classification scheme comprises ten medium factors. The first refers to synchronicity of participation which, with regard to online discourse, may either be synchronous or asynchronous. While participants have to be online simultaneously in synchronous CMC systems such as chat systems, messages in asynchronous systems are stored at the addressee's site and can be read at any later point in time. A typical example of an asynchronous type is the email system. Given that synchronicity clearly differs with regard to traditional forms of written and spoken communication, it has been shown to be a useful category for comparing different CMD forms with regard to these language modalities (cf. Condon and Cech 1996; Yates 1996). Moreover, Herring (2004a) and Ko (1996) have revealed that synchronicity has an effect on the structured complexity of messages as well as on users' pragmatic and interactional behaviour.

The second medium factor describes how messages are transmitted. This may either be message-by-message, character-by-character or line-by-line.[24] The differing speed of message transmission thereby influences users' turn-taking

[24] Cherny (1999) speaks of one-way and two-way transmission in this respect, referring to message-by-message and character-by-character transmission respectively.

procedures and decides whether simultaneous feedback or interruptions within a participant's turn are possible (cf. Herring 2002).

"Persistence of transcript" relates to the period of time messages are stored on the system. While, for instance, email messages remain accessible until the user deliberately deletes them, participants' turns in chat systems only remain readable until the viewing window becomes filled with messages. The oldest message is then always deleted when a new one emerges on the screen. As studies have shown, a longer persistence of CMD does not only result in an increase in users' metalinguistic awareness but also makes it easier for them to follow online discourse and take part in more than just one conversational thread (cf. Herring 1999).

"Size of message buffer" is associated with the maximum length messages can have. Regarding emails, the message buffer is usually unlimited. Yet in some chat systems as well as text messaging systems of mobile phones, message size is limited to a specific number of characters, thereby influencing participants' choice of discourse organisation strategies (cf. Condon and Cech 2001) or the likelihood that language will be structurally abbreviated (cf. Anis 2007).

In light of the recent developments of computer technology, the number of different "channels of communication" available in CMC systems has definitely increased. Nowadays, systems providing a visual channel not only make use of texts but also of static and animated graphics. Furthermore, technical developments of audiochats, videos or videoconferencing systems additionally supply an audio channel (cf. Chou 1999; Herring et al. 2002). The presence and content of video images has thereby been shown to influence gender distribution in discourse on educational websites (cf. Herring 2002).

The factor "anonymous messaging" is associated with CMD situations in which participants use nicknames instead of their real names. In this respect it is important to differentiate between CMC systems in which participants' name and email address are verified and those in which this is not the case. Research on this issue has shown that anonymity has an effect on the degree of self-closure (cf. Kiesler et al. 1984), antisocial behaviour (cf. Donath 1999), and play with identity (cf. Danet 1998).

Another important medium factor relates to the issue whether CMD takes place in a private or public manner. In private messaging, senders deliberately choose the recipient(s) of their message, as for example in email systems. In contrast to that, messages in many chat systems or feedback forums remain public and can hence be read by anyone online. A third option is enabling users to have both private and public messaging at their disposal, offered to users in some CMC systems such as IRC or MUDs.

Furthermore, CMC systems differ with regard to filtering mechanisms. While recipients can always ignore messages, some systems enable that specific messages are automatically filtered. Similarly, quoting is handled differently by each CMC system. In emails, for example, the received message is always mechanically repeated in the reply, allowing the responder to type between the lines of the quoted message and directly refer to specific contents. In other systems, quoting requires more effort in that users have to copy and paste passages they want to refer to, which affects the likelihood and manner of quoting (cf. Severinson-Eklundh and Macdonald 1994).

The final medium factor "message format" describes how messages are displayed on users' computer screens. This includes the order of the messages, whether and how additional information is appended, and what happens when users' computer screens become filled with messages. Studying the effect of message ordering, Herring (1999) has, for instance, found out that a chronological order of messages leads to a disrupted turn adjacency and interleaved exchanges.

Having dealt with the medium factors of Herring's scheme, the focus now turns to the eight social factors she incorporates. A list of these social factors is given in Table 3.2 which, similar to the table of medium factors, is also open to complementation.

Table 3.2: The social factors of Herring's classification scheme (Herring 2007: 18f.).

S1	Participation structure	• One-to-one, one-to-many, many-to-many • Public/private • Degree of anonymity/pseudonymity • Group size; number of active participants • Amount, rate and balance of participation
S2	Participant characteristics	• Demographics: gender, age, occupation, etc. • Proficiency: with language/computers/CMC • Experience: with addressee/group/topic • Role/status: in "real life"; of online personae • Pre-existing sociocultural knowledge and interactional norms • Attitudes, beliefs, ideologies, and motivations
S3	Purpose	• Of group, e.g. professional, social, fantasy/role-playing, aesthetic, experimental • Goal of interaction, e.g. get information, negotiate consensus, develop professional/social relationships, impress/entertain others, have fun
S4	Topic or Theme	• Of group, e.g. politics, linguistics, feminism, soap operas, sex, science fiction, South Asian culture, medieval times, pub • Of exchanges, e.g., the war in Iraq, pro-drop languages, the project budget, gay sex, vacation plans, personal information about participants, meta-discourse about CMC
S5	Tone	• Serious/playful • Formal/casual • Contentious/friendly • Cooperative/sarcastic, etc.
S6	Activity	• E.g., debate, job announcement, information exchange, phatic exchange, problem solving, exchange of insults, joking exchange, game, theatrical performance, flirtation, virtual sex
S7	Norms	• Of organisation • Of social appropriateness • Of language
S8	Code	• Language, language variety • Font

As Table 3.2 illustrates, the first social factor "participant structure" relates to the number of active participants, their amount of participation, and whether participation is evenly distributed. Furthermore, this factor addresses if users' discourse takes place in a private or public manner as well as the extent to which participants hide their real-life identities in the online world (cf. Myers 1987). The degree of anonymity/pseudonymity must be differentiated from the medium factor "anonymous messaging", since it refers to participants' deliberate choice to interact anonymously/pseudonymously independent of the options a CMC system may give them with regard to anonymous messaging. As studies on participant structure have shown, this factor has, among other things, an effect on the politeness level participants use, since interactants tend to be more polite in private than public CMD (cf. Herring 2002) and "flame" more when hidden behind an anonymous online identity (cf. Donath 1999).

"Participant characteristic" is associated with a number of aspects, including participants' demographic background, their proficiency and experiences as well as their role and status in real life in contrast to their online identities. Furthermore, "participant characteristic" refers to the knowledge, norms, attitudes, beliefs, ideologies, and motivations users possess and bring along when communicating online. Research has also observed that participant gender conditions politeness and contentiousness among users of a social MUD (cf. Cherny 1994) as well as among participants of two academic discussion lists which only differed with respect to 'participant gender' (cf. Herring 1996).

Regarding the "purpose" of an online discourse, one must distinguish between "group purpose", i.e. an officially proclaimed reason for the existence of this online group, and "goals of interaction" which refer to individuals' aims when taking part in CMD. The factor "purpose" clearly differs among different CMD types. It may, however, even vary when the same technologies are used as Herring and Nix (1997) have shown. In their data of pedagogical and social IRC, they have demonstrated that participants discussed different topics and also used various strategies for topic development.

Similar to the social factor "purpose", "topic" also has to be differentiated on two levels. On the one hand, there is the topic on the group level which broadly determines what is appropriate to talk about in this online group. Discussion forums, for instance, have defined topics and consequently attract users who are interested in them. On the other hand, the topic at the exchange level is the content of a specific interaction which may differ from the officially determined topic of the group. A distinction between these two levels of topic is crucial when analysing topical digression. In this respect, Herring (1999) has shown that topic digression is more common in large online groups whose participants engage in text-based CMD.

The "tone" of messages is associated with the manner in which a particular act of communication is performed. It can vary along different parameters, including the degree of seriousness, formality, contentiousness, and cooperation. For example, research has found that the pragmatic meaning of emoticons partially depends on the tone of the message (cf. Huls 2006).

The social factor "activity" describes "discursive means of pursuing interactional goals" (Herring 2007: 20), e.g. "flirting" which is used to build personal relationships and intimacy. To make the interpretation of an activity easier, it is accompanied by contextualisation cues (cf. Gumperz 1982). As research has shown, there are also computer-mediated contextualisation cues such as emoticons or usernames which help the addressee to infer the illocution of a message (cf. Bechar-Israeli 1995; Danet et al. 1997; Heisler and Crabill 2006; Herring 2001).

As far as the "norms" in CMD are concerned, three kinds can be distinguished, namely norms of organisation, of social appropriateness, and of language. "Norms of organisation" are thereby related to administrative protocols describing how new online groups can be established, how users register, whether there is a moderator, and how members are punished in case of unethical behaviour.

The second type of norms, "norms of social appropriateness", refer to behavioural standards of an online group. These may either be explicit and publicly available in form of a Netiquette (cf. Shea 1994) or Frequently Asked Questions (FAQs), or they may implicitly develop among members of a group without being fixed or officially acknowledged.

The "norms of language" relate to linguistic conventions which are characteristic of this online community, thus separating them from other groups. These include the use of specific acronyms, abbreviations, word formations or inside jokes (cf. Baym 1995; Cherny 1999).

Finally, "code" is associated with the language and language variety of participants as well as the font they use to type their messages. As Danet and Herring (2007) have demonstrated, the number of non-English-speaking Internet users has increased rapidly in recent years. Although this development has not yet balanced out the dominance of the English language on the Internet, it nonetheless reveals that this situation is definitely changing. The language variety which participants use thereby refers to the dialect and register of their messages. The latter are usually formulated in a standard, educated, written form of a language, although sometimes also regional, social class, or ethnic dialects can be found (cf. Androutsopoulos and Ziegler 2004). Differences in the linguistic code have thereby been shown to fulfil different discourse functions (cf. Androutsopoulos and Hinnekamp 2001).

It is important to note the relationship between the font participants use and the writing system of their language. In this respect, participants may employ a font such as ASCII text based on the Roman alphabet to type messages in languages based on this alphabet, or they make use of a font which transliterates a non-Roman writing system, such as those of Greek or Arabic, into Roman letters (cf. Berjaoui 2001; Tseliga 2007). A third possibility is the use of special non-ASCII fonts developed for languages such as Japanese, Chinese or Korean. With the innovation of a Unicode character encoding standard, it has clearly become easier for users of non-Roman writing systems to take part in communication on the Internet (cf. Danet and Herring 2007). However, sometimes transliteration into the Roman alphabet is still needed in certain contexts. In these cases script choice can serve different pragmatic functions (cf. Tseliga 2007).

Herring's classification scheme is very flexible because both lists of influential factors remain open to complementation and because no specific relationship is assumed between medium and situation nor between the specific features of the technological or situational context. This flexibility makes it applicable to a large variety of different CMD data and thus also allows for a comparison of them. As the Internet expands and new varieties of discourse emerge, future research is needed which reveals additional factors conditioning variation in computer-mediated language use, especially since Herring's scheme has so far been primarily based on findings of textual CMD (cf. Herring 2007: 27). More insight is also desirable with regard to possible correlations of factors which have not yet been systematically studied. Finally, as Herring (2007) herself points out, there is still need for research which supplements descriptive classifications with long-term ethnographic observations of online discourse communities. Ideally, the findings of these studies would be validated by participants of these online groups to get the most information possible about the context as well as for the analysis of CMD (cf. Herring 2007: 28).

Chapter 4: The methodology of the present study

After having given an overview of the underlying theoretical approach of this study, Chapter 4 turns to the conducted project itself, precisely to its methodology. It is first dealt with the data of the present study (4.1.) before the statistical analyses are briefly clarified (4.2.).

4.1. The data of the present study

Part 4.1. of this chapter comments on the data of this project, i.e. electronic complaints which have been downloaded from the British and German feedback forum of eBay. For a better understanding of this data type, this subchapter begins with a presentation of important background information about eBay (4.1.1.) which is followed by a description of the technical and social context of its feedback forum[25] (4.1.2.). Hereafter, an account of the data collection procedures is given (4.1.3.) before the advantages and disadvantages of the chosen data are finally discussed (4.1.4.).

4.1.1. eBay and its feedback forum

Founded by Pierre Omidyar in 1995, eBay has developed into the world's most popular online marketplace. To date, 233 million users are registered worldwide[26], including individuals as well as small businesses trading items in thousands of diverse categories (http://www.ebay.co.uk). While eBay is wellknown for its auction format, users can also buy and sell in fixed-price formats with a single mouse click. In contrast to that, buyers have the chance to outbid others until a set time is over in an auction. Similarly to conventional auctions, bidding on eBay works in two ways. Bidders may, on the one hand, make the lowest viable bid possible and wait until being outbid by someone else. Then they may place a new minimum bid or opt out of this auction. On the

---

[25] Since in the meantime eBay has improved its feedback system, the present description is not up-to-date anymore. However, it illustrates the regulations operating when the data was sent (2004-2006) (compare 4.1.3.). For a description of the changes of the regulations of eBay's feedback forum see, for instance, Kleinz and Götz (2008: 104ff.).

[26] Netratings: February 2008 (http://www.ebay.co.uk).

other hand, they can place a 'proxy' bid which is the maximum amount they are willing to pay. In this case, eBay acts as proxy bidder for them, i.e. eBay is bidding in their place until the item is 'won' or their specific maximum amount has been exceeded by another bidder. At the end of a 'won' auction both transactional partners receive an email from eBay providing them with each other's contact information. Additionally, the message informs them that this is now a binding contract between the two parties which not only means that the buyer is obliged to pay for the item even if s/he is no longer interested in it, but also that the seller has to send the item after having received the payment. Whereas bidding on an item and winning an auction is free, a seller has to pay an insertion fee for listing the item as well as a final value fee, i.e. a percentage of the final price, once an item has been sold. Therefore, a seller has to pay for an auction even if the buyer does not pay for the item. If this happens, the seller can issue a so-called 'non-paying bidder alert', often referred to as NPBA in feedback comments, which informs the highest bidder about the consequences in case s/he does not pay for the item. If the buyer still refuses to pay, the seller can further request a refund for the final value fee (FVF) from eBay. Nevertheless, the seller still loses the insertion fee. On the other hand, all trading partners who receive more than three NPBAs from different sellers are barred from eBay and their account is blocked. However, there is nothing to prevent disregistered members to reregister a new alias.
To further protect and build trust between their customers, eBay has created a feedback system and a feedback removal policy.[27] Given the focus of the present study on complaints exchanged on the British and German feedback forum of eBay, the specific contextual factors of this forum are described in the following.

[27] Knobel and Lankshear (2002: 19) stress in this respect that eBay's feedback system has had a powerful influence on other Internet-based social interactions in that numerous other interactive Internet sites also introduced feedback systems as public reputation markers, such as Plastic 2001 (http://www.plastic.com) or Yahoo! Geocities 2001 (http://www.us.geocities.yahoo.com).

4.1.2. The technical and social context of the present data

As mentioned in Chapter 3, CMC covers a large variety of different communicative situations. When analysing data from the Internet, it is hence crucial to outline the specific communicative context of the chosen database. The precision and flexibility of Herring's (2007) faceted classification scheme makes it a helpful tool in this respect. Furthermore, it is particularly suitable for an application to the present text-based data, since until now this scheme has primarily been based on research findings for textual CMD. In light of these advantages, Herring's scheme is used here in order to describe the contextual factors which potentially influence eBay members' linguistic choices when communicating on the feedback forum of eBay.

As explained in 3.3.2., Herring (2007) distinguishes between two types of influences on CMD, precisely medium (technological) and situation (social), whereby each type of influence consists of an open-ended list of categories or factors, whose realisations vary according to the specific online situation. The relevant medium factors and appropriate values of the chosen database are listed in Table 4.1. Due to the particulars of the feedback forum of eBay, some of the categories proposed in Herring's (2007) classification scheme have been left out while other medium factors have been added as they are likely to condition eBay traders' CMD. To highlight the latter, they are printed in italics in Table 4.1. Moreover, as there is no necessary order of the factors in this scheme, the order proposed by Herring (2007: 13) has been changed slightly to enable a coherent description of the chosen database.

Table 4.1: Medium factors that characterise the feedback forum of eBay.

No.	Medium factor	Realisation(s)
M1	*Message type*	• *Appraisal, neutral, complaint*
M2	*Rating system*	• *Appraisal (+1)* • *Neutral (+/- 0)* • *Complaint (-1)*
M3	Channel of communication	• Visual • Text-based messages
M4	*Length and structure of interaction*	• *Minimum: one feedback comment* • *Maximum: feedback comment followed by reply and follow-up or vice versa*
M5	Size of message buffer	• 80 characters
M6	Message transmission	• 1-way

M7	Synchronicity	• Asynchronous system
M8	Persistence of transcript	• Permanent part of user's feedback score • Viewable on the feedback forum for one year
M9	Filtering	• Controlled by eBay • Filtering of messages that are classified as feedback abuse
M10	Message format	• Symbols precede each feedback comment • New feedback comments added at top of list • Overview of feedback given on user's ID card
M11	Private messaging	• Members can choose a private profile, i.e. comments are hidden, but the feedback score remains viewable
M12	Anonymous messaging	• Username

Aiming at smooth and satisfactory trading among its customers, eBay has created a feedback system and a feedback removal policy. Feedback is a valuable indicator of users' reputations on eBay. It is made up of comments and ratings left by trading partners after a performed transaction. Sellers and buyers thereby have the choice between three different types of comments, namely an appraisal, neutral or a complaint. These types of feedback comments are connected with a rating system which is used to determine each member's feedback score. Precisely, an appraisal increases the feedback score by one point, a neutral rating leaves it the same, and a complaint results in a decrease of the feedback score by one point. These ratings, together with the amount of transactions an eBay member has conducted, make up the percentage of his/her overall feedback score. High percentages reveal trustworthiness and thus a good reputation on eBay. When choosing one of the three types of feedback comments, a user has to click the appropriate box after which s/he can type his/her comment in the space provided. All feedback comments consist of text only and are preceded by a symbol illustrating which type of feedback was chosen. After having received a feedback comment, a member has the opportunity to leave a reply. Additionally, the initiator of the interaction has the option to send a follow-up comment which may be used to complement his/her original feedback, comment on a received reply, or give some further information about events that are relevant to the conducted business transaction but happened after the original feedback had been sent. Whether to leave a feedback, reply, or follow-up is optional. The size of the message buffer, however, is fixed. All comments are restricted to a maximum length of 80 characters.

In minimum, an interaction therefore consists of one feedback comment only, but can maximally reach a length of three comments in a row: a feedback comment which is followed by a reply and follow-up or vice versa. In contrast to feedback comments though, replies and follow-ups have no effect on recipients' overall feedback score.

Regarding message transmission, all comments on this feedback system are sent as a whole, i.e. in form of 1-way transmission (cf. Cherny 1999) which clearly makes any spontaneous interruption of a sender impossible.

As far as synchronicity of the participants is concerned, the feedback system of eBay can clearly be classified as asynchronous, because messages are stored at the receiver's site. Thereby it is important to mention that once a feedback has been left, it can neither be edited nor removed but will be a permanent part of a trader's feedback score and viewable on the website for one year. The persistence of transcripts and their permanent influence on user's overall feedback score enables members to carefully inform themselves about potential trading partners. Since bad reputation on eBay is likely to scare off other traders, the permanence of feedback comments clearly increases the pressure on users to behave in a fair and honest way. However, if a sender contacts eBay and explicitly asks for the removal of his/her comment, or if the feedback comment falls under eBay's removal policy, exceptions to the permanence of feedback comments can be made. eBay classifies all comments as feedback abuse which fulfil any of the criteria below:

- The feedback is slanderous, libellous, defamatory or otherwise illegal.
- The feedback comment contains profane, vulgar, obscene, or racist language or adult material. Inflammatory language, such as "fraud, liar, cheater, scam artist, con man" etc., are strongly discouraged but will not be removed.
- The feedback comment contains personal identifying information about another member, including real name, address, phone number, or email address.
- The feedback comment contains links or scripts.

These kinds of comments are filtered and removed by eBay. However, before their removal, the eBay member is first asked whether s/he wants to rephrase her/his comment. In respect to eBay's filter, it is further important to note that it neither contains a comprehensive list of swear words, nor does it detect swear words that are spelled differently. Thus, this filter can easily be circumvented.

The next category 'message format' refers to different aspects of the visual presentation of messages on the computer screen. Regarding the chosen database, it is important to mention that a particular symbol revealing the type of comment and thus assisting interpretation always precedes a feedback comment. As far as the order of the messages is concerned, new feedback comments and related replies are always added to the top of the list, so that the most recent messages are presented first. If a member's homepage on eBay becomes filled with feedback messages, older ones are stored on a second page which can be accessed by clicking on a link presented on the former.

An overview of a user's reputation is given on his/her ID card which can also be found on her/his homepage on eBay. Displayed on this card is the amount of feedback comments this member received during the past year. These are classified according to the type of feedback given. In addition to this, the overall feedback score and percentage of positive feedback, a member's eBay username, his/her date of membership and location can be learned from this card.

All users can thereby choose whether they want to leave their feedback profile public or make it private. With a public profile, a member's ID card as well as his/her comments remain viewable to anyone visiting the website, even if they are not registered on eBay. A private profile means that a member's feedback comments are hidden from the audience. At the same time though, the number of positive, neutral and negative feedback this user has received can still be seen. Given that public profiles increase the transparency and hence build trust between eBay members, eBay strongly encourages its users to keep their feedback profile public (http://www.ebay.co.uk).[28]

[28] To increase the incentive to leave one's feedback profile public, eBay changed the conditions of a private feedback profile in September 2006. Since then a private profile bans a member from selling items on eBay, leaving only the option to buy them (http://www.ebayco.uk).

Yet, in order to protect their privacy, members choose a user name when they register. Hence, instead of their real names, only their aliases appear on the screen. However, in order to prevent that this anonymity attracts swindlers to this online market, eBay verifies all information given on a new member's user agreement form shortly after registration procedures.

Having dealt with the relevant medium factors, the focus now turns to the situational factors which potentially condition variation in the chosen database. An overview of the important social categories and their appropriate values is given in Table 4.2. As with the medium factors, the order of the situation factors proposed by Herring (2007: 18f.) has been changed slightly and another significant factor has been added, which is again highlighted by italics in the following Table 4.2.

Table 4.2: Situation factors that characterise the feedback forum of eBay.

No.	Situation factor	Realisation(s)
S1	Participation structure	• Group size: ever-growing eBay community • One-to-one, one-to-many • Mainly public feedback profiles • Amount of participation: varies
S2	Participant characteristics	• Demographic factors: over 18, gender possibly revealed by username • Different nationalities; focus of this study on British and German traders • Pre-existing cultural norms • Pre-existing interactional norms: common knowledge of communicative norms of this feedback forum • Experience with e-commerce and eBay's feedback forum: varies • Proficiency with CMC on eBay's feedback forum: varies
S3	*Relations among participants*	• *Social relations: for the most part characterised by high social distance and equal power relations* • *Personal relations: depend on experience made with trading partner*
S4	Topic or Theme	• Previous transaction
S5	Purpose	• Group purpose: smooth and safe trading • Goal of interaction: varies according to the type of feedback comment
S6	Tone	• Depends on the type of feedback comment
S7	Activity	• Complaining • Appraising

S8	Norms	• Of organisation: registration form, feedback removal policy, rules for punishment of misconduct • Of social appropriateness: Netiquette, implicit norms of eBay community • Of language: linguistic conventions of eBay community
S9	Code	• Different languages; focus of this study on British English and German • Font: ASCII text (with and without umlaut)

After a performed transaction, anyone who is registered on eBay and thus belongs to the ever-growing eBay community can leave a feedback comment which is thus always sent from one eBay user to his/her trading partner. Yet, a sender's message may also seem to be addressed to the whole community. This ambiguity in address is likely to result from the fact that feedback comments are usually public as long as members have not intentionally hidden their feedback profile. Therefore, all comments do not only aim at telling one's trading partner one's opinion about the previous transaction but also informing the whole eBay community about one's previous trading experience. Participants thereby contribute to the communication on this feedback forum to varying degrees, since participation depends on the frequency of their e-commerce on this online marketplace. In other words, active traders leave more comments than those rarely doing business on eBay.

The second category, 'participant characteristics', describes "participants' backgrounds, skills and experiences, as well as their real life knowledge, norms, and interactional patterns they bring to bear when they engage with others online" (Herring 2007: 19). Given eBay's priority to protect its customers' privacy, many of the participants' characteristics remain unknown. With regard to participants' demographics, it is only certain that all eBay members have to be at least 18 years old. Furthermore, users' gender may be revealed by their username which, however, may also be misleading. All other demographic variables such as participants' social class, status, or occupation remain undefined. Yet, given that computers have become such a pervasive feature of most people's lives, regardless of their status or social class (cf. Collot 1991: 19), it is reasonable to assume that these unknown demographic factors vary greatly among members of the eBay community.

While eBay members are from all over the world, the present study focuses on British and German eBay users (see. 4.1.3.). Given this cross-cultural approach, it will be interesting to investigate whether and how participants' pre-existing British and German cultural norms influence their communicative behaviour in CMC. On the other hand, all chosen subjects belong to the eBay community and thus share the knowledge of the specific communicative norms developed among the members of this feedback forum. This shared knowledge may result in a uniform communicative behaviour which may cover up other possibly existing cultural differences.

Other participants' characteristics include the experience users have made in previous transactions and in communicating on eBay's feedback forum as well as the proficiency they have developed with leaving comments. In light of traders' different rates of e-commerce on eBay both aspects clearly differ among members of the eBay community, spanning from very experienced traders, who are also highly proficient in communicating on this feedback forum, to beginners leaving a comment for the first time. However, it is important to recognise that many of these beginners are at least familiar with the publicly available communicative norms on this feedback forum and have also gained experience by reading comments left by other traders. Absolute beginners are hence an exception.

The third social category, 'Relations among participants', has been adopted from Biber (1988) and embraces both the social role relations and the particular personal relations among interlocutors. With respect to the social role relations among interlocutors, text-based CMC fundamentally differs from communicative situations in which interlocutors can see and hear each other. Such relations, in which the person's age, gender or social status are known, are clearly non-existent in text-based CMC (cf. Collot 1991: 19). With regard to the feedback forum of eBay, traders are for the most part strangers who lack all knowledge about their interlocutor's age, gender, or status in "real life". Their relationship is hence mainly characterised by a high social distance accompanied by equal power relations. This equality among eBay members is further supported by the fact that all users belong to the eBay *community* and are regarded as trading *partners* in the "online world". Apart from these highly anonymous relations, it is also possible that an eBay members' username may reveal their gender, or that trading partners may "know" each other from previous transactions, or may even be friends. Furthermore, they may have had email, telephone, or personal contact during their trading process. In these instances, the relationship among trading partners has certainly become a different one than the anonymous relationship described above.

With regard to the particular personal relations among eBay users, it can be said that they primarily depend on the course of the preceding transaction and thus become obvious in the type of feedback comment one of the partners submits. Since the present study focuses on complaints, the personal relations among the chosen subjects can clearly be regarded as hostile, specifically because in many messages dislike of one's trading partner is overtly expressed.

The category 'topic' can be described on two levels: firstly, the topic of the online group, i.e. of the feedback forum of eBay, and secondly, the topic of the exchange, i.e. what these eBay traders are actually talking about. Regarding the present data, the topics of these two levels coincide as both deal with the traders' previous transactions.

Closely related to 'topic' is the category 'purpose' which describes the outcome eBay members intend from communicating on the feedback forum. Here again two levels have to be distinguished, namely 'group purpose' and 'goal of interaction'. The group purpose on this feedback forum is to judge the previous transaction and hence contribute to one's trading partner's reputation on eBay. This, in turn, aims at enabling safe trading and protects all eBay members. On the other hand, the goals of interaction, i.e. what an individual sender hopes to achieve through his/her comment, varies according to the type of comment s/he formulates. Regarding complaints, the main aim is to get forbearance for the unsatisfactory trading process. In addition to that, a complaint enables the release of one's anger and thereby warns other eBay members against unfair trading partners.

The 'tone' participants use to formulate their comments clearly depends on the type of feedback comment they leave. While in positive feedback comments their tone is very cooperative, it varies in neutral comments from a cooperative to a contentious style of speaking, and becomes angry and hostile in complaints. Yet, independent of the type of comment that is left, the communicative style on this feedback forum is characterised by a casual tone.

The 'activity types' on eBay's feedback forum are both appraising and complaining. However, in light of the focus of the present study, the 'activity type' of the collected database is obviously complaining which is further underlined by members' use of computer-mediated contextualisation cues such as frownies.

The norms of eBay's feedback forum can be described in terms of organisation, appropriateness, and language. The first of them includes registration regulations on eBay, its feedback removal policy, as well as regulations of punishments in case of unfair trading behaviour. Specific to the chosen database is the fact that members' behaviour is always controlled by eBay's security system and that users can report any other trader's misconduct. Regarding the norms of appropriateness, it can be distinguished between explicitly written and publicly available behavioural standards, i.e. the Netiquette on eBay and the norms which have implicitly developed among members of the eBay community. These implicit norms include, for instance, standards prescribing what kind of misconduct justifies the choice of a negative feedback comment and how overtly one's dislike may be expressed. The third types of norms are norms of language. They refer to linguistic conventions which are specifically used by members of the eBay community thereby differentiating them from other online groups. Examples include specific abbreviations, signs, or inside words.

Finally, the 'code' of the present data signifies the language and font participants use when formulating their comments. As far as the present corpus is concerned, all selected complaints are formulated in British English or German (see 4.1.3.), so that all subjects made use of the ASCII[29] character set based on the Roman alphabet. Thereby it is important to mention that the Germans have additional signs, namely umlaut, at their disposal (cf. Hentschel 1998: 17).

Moreover, Herring (2007) claims that medium and situation factors may correlate with one another. Regarding the present data, it is, for instance, likely that the limited message buffer has had an impact on the language norms which have developed among eBay users.

---

[29] ASCII is an acronym for „American Standard Code for Information Interchange (cf. Danet and Herring 2007: 2).

4.1.3. Data collection procedures

Having outlined the technical and social context of the feedback forum of eBay, the focus now turns to the data collection procedures of the present study. Linguists have distinguished between two different ways the Internet can be employed in research. These are referred to as 'Web as corpus' and 'Web for corpus building' (cf. Fletcher 2004, 2007; Hundt et al. 2007; De Schryver 2002). While in the former approach commercial crawlers or Internet-based search engines are used to create corpora from the Web directly, the latter signifies that researchers manually select the data to build offline monitor corpora. The present study falls under the 'Web for corpus building' approach, since its data has been collected manually from the feedback forum of the online auction house eBay, precisely the British and German websites (http://www.ebay.co.uk, http://www.ebay.de). To increase the comparability between the two data sets, specific criteria for the data collection procedures were set. First of all, the language of the complaints as well as the location displayed on the subjects' ID cards was controlled. Hence, only British English and German complaints which had been exchanged between eBay users who had registered on the British or German eBay domain respectively were selected. All subjects' feedback profiles had thereby obviously been public. Furthermore, all complaints had been sent within a comparable period of time, namely in the years 2004-2006. This is especially important, since language is always subject to change, especially in rather new communicative mediums such as text-based CMC (cf. Claridge 2007: 89).

In addition to that, all comments were preserved exactly as typed, which is important, since any "incorrect" spelling, grammar and/or punctuation can have a special meaning in electronic discourse and is thus worth analysing.

Another significant criterion in the data collection process was that the content of all complaints was controlled. Thereby it was decided to focus on the most common reasons for complaining on eBay. To find out which reasons are in fact the most common ones, a pilot study was conducted. Precisely, a total of 200 British English and 200 German complaints were randomly selected. To enhance comparability between the two data sets, the amount of senders and addressees was held similar between the two sets, i.e. it was made sure that the

British English and German complaints had been sent by 200 different eBay users to 80 complainees in each group. Furthermore, both the British English and German complaints had all been sent within a set timeframe of one month, namely August 2005. After the collection procedure, the data sets of the pilot study were analysed according to the reasons for complaining. The results are outlined in percentages below. While the exact findings are displayed in Table 4.3, Figure 4.1 illustrates the results figuring 3% or more.

Table 4.3: Distribution of the occurring reasons for complaining on eBay in per cent (%).

Reason for complaining	**BrE complaints**	**German complaints**
Item was different than expected	28	28,5
Item was different than expected (D)	17,5	19,5
Item has not been received	17,5	13,5
Item has not been received (D)	16,5	13
Delivery time was too long	0,5	7
Delivery time was too long (D)	1,5	2,5
Seller was rude	4,5	3,5
Seller did not reply to attempts to contact him/her	4	3
Seller did not reply to attempts to contact him/her (D)	0,5	0,5
Postage was too high	3	3
Item was different than expected (T)	3	0,5
No refund was given	0	2,5
Buyer never paid for the item	1	1
Bad service	1	0
Buyer never paid for the item (D)	0	0,5
Item has never been received (T)	0,5	0
?	1	1,5
Total	100	100

Abbreviations:
BrE: British English
Item NR: Item has not been received
Item DIFF: Item was different than expected
D: 'double-complaint', i.e. the sender complained for two reasons in one comment.
T: 'triple-complaint', i.e. the sender complained for three reasons in one comment.
?: The reason for complaining could not be identified.

Figure 4.1: Graphic representation of the occurring reasons for complaining on the British and German eBay domain. Results figuring less than 3% are not illustrated.

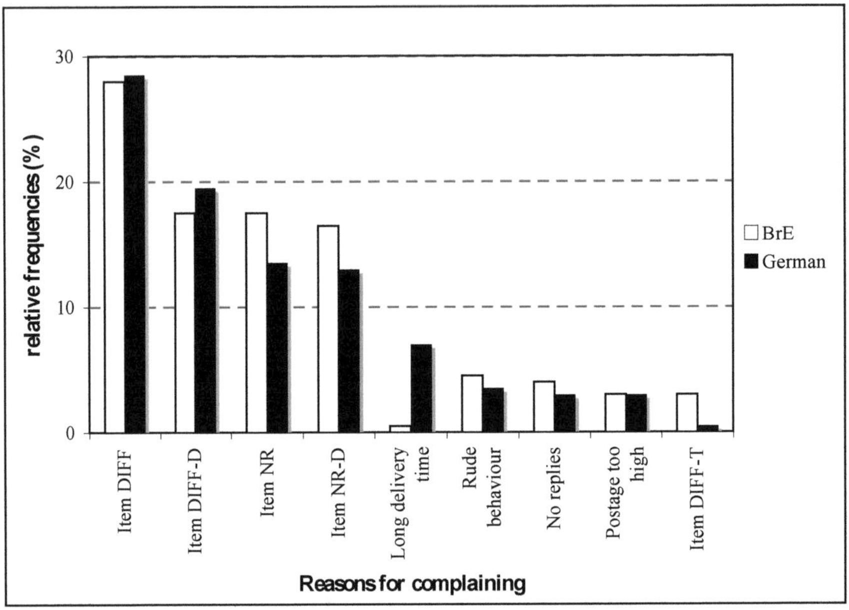

The findings clearly show that on both the British and German eBay domain the most common reasons for complaining are as follows:

- the item was different than expected (Item DIFF),
- it was different in addition to another reason for complaining (Item DIFF-D),
- the item has not been received (Item NR),
- and finally, that the item has never been received in addition to some further reason for complaining (Item NR-D).

In all of these four main reasons for complaining, the complainer is always the buyer and the complainee the seller of the previous transaction. In addition to that, it is worth noting that the Germans complain significantly more often about a long delivery time. Here p reveals a highly significant difference between the British and German data set ($p = 0.001^{**}$) (see Table 4.4, compare also 4.2.). Comparing the sum of single and double complaints concerning the delivery time, the difference between the two data sets is still highly significant ($p = 0.002^{**}$) (see Table 4.4, compare also 4.2.).

Table 4.4: Relative frequencies regarding complaints about a long delivery time. Significant differences are highlighted by bold print.

Reason for complaining	**BrE data set relative frequencies (%)**	**German data set relative frequencies (%)**	**Significance (p)**
Long delivery time	0.5	7	**0.001****
Long delivery time (single and double complaints)	2	9.5	**0.002****

The reason for the extreme difference between British and German users complaining about a long delivery time, may either be that German eBay users are often late in sending the item or that punctuality is more important in German culture, which may result in Germans being less patient.

Let us now return to the data of the main study. Since the pilot study revealed that the above mentioned four reasons are by far the most common ones on the British and German feedback forum of eBay, it was decided to focus on these four reasons in the main study. To build the corpus of the main study, a total of 100 British English and 100 German complaints for each of the four most common reasons for complaining were collected. Thereby it was made sure that all complaints had been sent by different complainers to different complainees, which is crucial to rule out the possibility that the complaining habits of one particular subject can influence the results.

The data collection for the main study thus resulted in eight data sets, four British English and four German ones, each of them consisting of 100 complaints. As all collected complaints were complete in themselves, i.e. had not been complemented by a follow-up, the data of the main study resulted in a total of 400 British English and 400 German complaints sent by 400 complainers to 400 complainees in each group (see Tables 4.5 and 4.6).

Table 4.5: Overview of the British English data of the present study.

	BrE complainers	**BrE complaints**	**BrE complainees**
Item DIFF	100	100	100
Item DIFF-D	100	100	100
Item NR	100	100	100
Item NR-D	100	100	100
Total	**400**	**400**	**400**

Table 4.6: Overview of the German data of the present study.

	German complainers	German complaints	German complainees
Item DIFF	100	100	100
Item DIFF-D	100	100	100
Item NR	100	100	100
Item NR-D	100	100	100
Total	**400**	**400**	**400**

4.1.4. Choice of data: advantages and disadvantages

In contrast to data collected by other data eliciting instruments such as role-play or discourse-completion task (DCT) (cf. Beebe and Cummings 1996), a major advantage of Internet data is their authenticity. Complainers and complainees are not aware of the fact that their comments are subject to linguistic research so that the "'Observers' Paradox' that has traditionally plagued research in the social sciences" (Herring 1996: 5) can be avoided. Thus, neither subjects' awareness of being the focus of research nor the presence of a researcher or an audio- or videotape can have an impact on subjects' behaviour.

Furthermore, the chosen database can be easily accessed and the collection of a large amount of data is not too time-consuming, as comments can simply be collected via the options 'copy' and 'paste'. This data collection procedure therefore not only allows for qualitative but also quantitative analysis.

In addition to that, the procedure of 'copy' and 'paste' bears the advantage that the original comment can be preserved exactly as typed, which is significant for data analysis in CMC (see 4.1.3.). What is more, the effort of transcription or copying needed by other data collection methods is not necessary.

A major advantage of the chosen 'Web for corpus building' approach is that, in contrast to studies in which data is collected via Internet-based search engines, it enables the control of at least some situational variables. This clearly enhances the comparability of data sets in contrastive studies such as the present one.

However, not only the 'Web for corpus building' approach but also the particular choice of eBay as database adds to the comparability of the collected British and German data set. Given that all eBay domains are designed in a similar way, the communicative situations on their feedback forums are alike. Precisely, no matter on which eBay domain members registered and take part in business transactions, they all face similarly structured websites, can use the same links, and are subject to the same eBay rules. Additionally, they all have the same amount of background information about their interlocutors, since members' ID cards display the same facts on all eBay domains. As far as the exchange of feedback comments is concerned, they are always addressed to one trading partner only but are viewable to an audience, namely anyone visiting the website. Furthermore, on all eBay domains the feedback comments are restricted to the same maximum length of 80 characters and can always be complemented by a follow-up of the same maximum length.

The controllability of the present data does not only make the collected British and German data set very alike but also enables a "reproducibility of results by repeating the experiment on a different corpus that has been compiled according to the same criteria" (Lüdeling et al. 2007: 10).

A final noteworthy advantage is what Hundt et al. (2007) call "accessibility". Data is considered accessible if it can be analysed using "the standard software tools we like working with" (Hundt et al. 2007: 3) after being saved offline. Regarding the present study, this enabled statistical analysis via SPSS 16.0.

Of course, there are also some drawbacks to the chosen approach. Herring (1996), for instance, claims that electronic research brings about "ethical dilemmas" (cf. Herring 1996: 5) as one can use electronic data for research without informing participants about one's purpose. Researchers further face the question of how much information about the data sources they should actually reveal in their scientific publication. One extreme position in this respect advocates "that researchers should avoid mention of any specifics concerning the messages or their sources altogether, including the name of the discussion group, so as not to violate the 'perceived privacy' of the participants" (Herring 1996: 5). Researchers in favour of the opposite extreme argue that quoting computer-mediated material without its source is a violation of copyright laws (cf. Cavazos 1995). So far there has been no general agreement about this issue. In the present study it can, however, be argued that feedback forums, in contrast to other forms of CMC, are designed for the public. All eBay users are aware of the fact that their feedback is viewable to anyone visiting the website. As a consequence, they can decide whether they wish to leave a comment at all, as well as whether they want their own feedback profile to be public or private (see

4.1.2.). Regarding the present study, only those subjects were chosen who had made the choice to leave their feedback profile public and were thus aware of the fact that it is open to everyone online. Moreover, eBay members use an alias instead of their real name, which also protects their privacy. However, given that a member's username may display their real name or may be known to others, they have been left out in the present report so that the preservation of all subjects' privacy can be guaranteed.

Another disadvantage of the present data is the limited amount of background information available about the chosen complainers and complainees. The only information known about the subjects is the location displayed on their ID card and that both seller and buyer are at least 18 years of age. Any further background information about participants' characteristics remains unknown (see 4.1.2.).

In light of the cross-cultural focus of the present study, there arises of course the problem that the location displayed on each member's ID card is not always equivalent to this member's nationality and mother tongue. Attempts were made to contact a sample of the chosen subjects to ask them about this background information. However, these messages were blocked because eBay bans any contact which does not concern trading issues, since it may violate a member's privacy. Therefore, the British and German eBay customer service was contacted to find out more about the location given on users' ID card. Yet, again for the sake of protection, eBay does not give away any statistical information about its customers. Nonetheless, they revealed that the location displayed on users' ID card signifies the country they live in and that this information must be genuine, since eBay checks new members' name and address shortly after registration.

On the other hand, eBay members' place of residence need not always be equivalent to their nationality. However, as the following Table 4.7 and Figure 4.2 illustrate, the vast majority of the British and German population consist of native people. The numbers are taken from the year 2005, since this is the year in which the majority of the collected complaints were sent. Table 4.7 and Figure 4.2 reveal that in 2005 91.2% of the population in Germany were natives (cf. Albrecht et al. 2007: 119, Federal Statistical Office and the Statistical

Offices of the Länder (D_Statis) 2007b), and up to 96% in the UK (cf. Albrecht et al. 2007: 200).

Table 4.7: The ratio of native and foreign population in the UK and Germany in 2005.

	UK	Germany
Native population	96%	91.2%
Foreign population	4%	8.8%

Figure 4.2: Graphic representation of the ratio of native and foreign population in the UK and Germany in 2005.

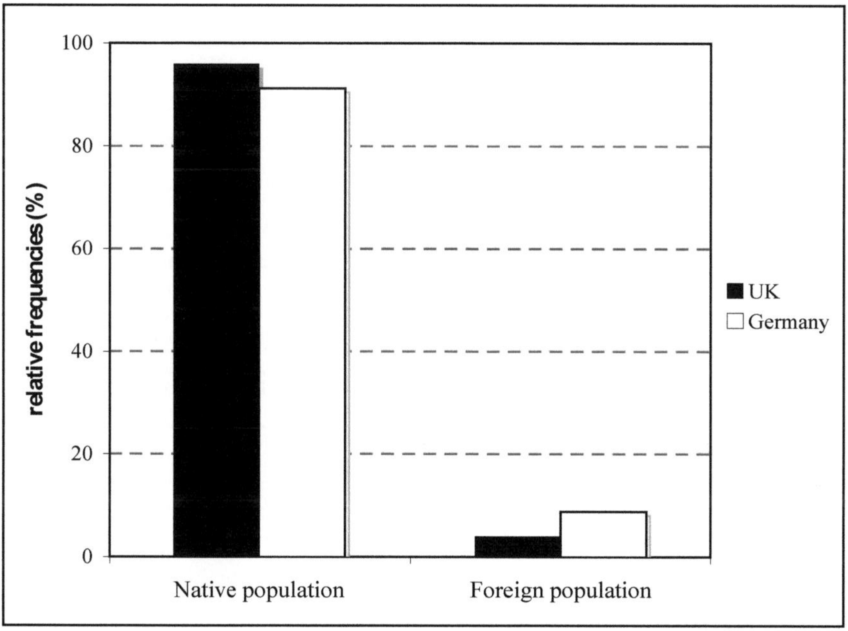

Due to these figures and the fact that the data of the present study were randomly selected, it is very likely that the overall results of this study do in fact mirror British and German native speakers' behaviour.

Nonetheless, since it cannot be guaranteed that all chosen subjects are native speakers, the term "native" is avoided in the present report. The labels "British speakers" and "German speakers" are employed instead.

4.2. Statistical analysis

As mentioned in the introduction, the collected data was analysed with respect to the following categories: the use of complaint strategies, level of directness, means of modification, use of pronouns, and features of CMC. Since typing errors, non-standard spelling of words, and missing spaces frequently occur in the collected complaints, automatic coding via electronic search engines would have been inaccurate. Thus all coding was done manually.
After the data sets were coded, frequency counts and statistical analyses were conducted via SPSS 16.0. The frequency counts include absolute as well as relative frequencies and are displayed in terms of percentages below. When absolute frequencies clarify the received results, they are additionally given.
To find answers to the research questions of the present study the following data sets were statistically compared. Regarding research question 1, i.e. to find out whether British and German eBay traders' online complaints differ with regard to the five categories under investigation, the four British English and four German data sets were compared (see Table 4.8).

Table 4.8: The data sets which were compared for investigation of research question 1.

Data sets which were compared to investigate whether BrE and German complaints differ with regard to the five categories of analysis
BrE Item NR versus German Item NR
BrE Item DIFF versus German Item DIFF
BrE Item NR-D versus German Item NR-D
BrE Item DIFF-D versus German Item DIFF-D

As far as research question 2 is concerned, namely whether the reason for complaining has an impact on British and German eBay traders' linguistic choices, the British English data set *Item has not been received* was compared with the British English data set *Item was different than expected*, and the British English data set *Item has not been received (double complaint)* with the British English data set *Item was different than expected (double complaint)*. The data sets consisting of single and double complaints were thereby separately treated to avoid that the number of reasons for complaining may influence the results. The same comparisons were conducted for the German data sets (see Table 4.9).

Table 4.9: The data sets which were compared for investigation of research question 2.

Data sets which were compared to investigate whether the reason for complaining impacts BrE and German eBay traders' linguistic choices.
BrE Item NR versus BrE Item DIFF
BrE Item NR-D versus BrE Item DIFF-D
German Item NR versus German Item DIFF
German Item NR-D versus German Item DIFF-D

Finally, for the investigation of research question 3, that is whether it makes a difference if British and/or German traders have one or two reasons for complaining, the data sets consisting of single complaints, i.e. *Item has not been received* and *Item was different than expected*, were compared with the data sets of double complaints, namely *Item has not been received (double complaint)* and *Item was different than expected (double complaint)* (see Table 4.10). With regard to these comparisons it was crucial that the reason for complaining was held constant between data sets under investigation to rule out that different reasons may impact the results.

Table 4.10: The data sets which were compared for investigation of research question 3.

Data sets which were compared to investigate whether it makes a difference if British and/or German traders have one or two reasons for complaining
BrE Item NR versus BrE Item NR-D
BrE Item DIFF versus BrE Item DIFF-D
German Item NR versus German Item NR-D
German Item DIFF versus German Item DIFF-D

To examine whether there are statistical differences between the data sets, three kinds of statistical tests were conducted, depending on the measurement level of data under investigation. Specifically, nominal data were analysed by the use of the Qui-square Test, ordinal data by the means of the Mann-Whitney U-Test, and the Independent-Samples T-Test was applied to interval data.

In the present report significant results are presented in terms of probability levels (p) and significant differences marked by asterisks. The common critical values for linguistic projects are assumed, i.e. a $p = 0.05$ level for significant and a $p = 0.01$ level for highly significant differences (cf. Wray and Bloomer 2006: 213f.).

Chapter 5: Data analysis

In Chapter 5 the focus turns to the analysis of the collected data. Specifically, the five categories of analysis are explained and clarified by using examples from the present data sets. As mentioned in 4.2., these include: the use of complaint strategies, the chosen level of directness, the employment of modification, the presence of pronouns as well as of features of CMC. The reasons for choosing these categories are described in the following.

As cross-cultural studies on complaints in spoken interaction have revealed, speakers of different cultural backgrounds differ with regard to the first four categories, which often results in misunderstandings and the formation of stereotypes. More precisely, cross-cultural differences have become apparent regarding the range of complaint strategies that are used, the frequencies with which the strategies are employed, the directness level that is chosen, the extent with which the complaints are modified and whether they are oriented towards self, the content, or the addressee (cf. House and Kasper 1981; Möhl 1996; Trosborg 1995). As House and Kasper (1981) have demonstrated, these differences also hold true when comparing British and German speakers, who are the focus of the present study. Given that the cultural differences regarding the first four categories of analysis have only been proven to exist in complaining situations in spoken interaction, it is certainly worth analysing whether these differences can also be found in other language modalities such as CMC. Diverging findings in online complaints may thereby imply that contextual factors of CMC influence users' linguistic choices.

Moreover, when dealing with data from the Internet, it is certainly crucial to investigate linguistic features which typically occur in this language modality, thus making the last category of analysis, i.e. the handling of features of CMC, a matter of importance. However, researchers investigating such features in different types of CMC such as email, chat, or weblog systems (cf. Baron 2000; Beißwenger 2001, 2007; Claridge 2007; Lewin and Donner 2002; Werry 1996), have so far neither looked at their use in online feedback forums nor cross-culturally compared their handling in online complaints. Regarding this research gap, the investigation of these features in the present data is thus highly significant to fill existing deficiencies in this research field.

When illustrating the categories of analysis by examples from the present data, the attempt was made to represent all data sets evenly to give a detailed account of the data under investigation. All examples are therefore preceded by a reference in brackets, which enables the reader to find them in the appendix of the present report. These references always begin with an abbreviation revealing whether the example is a British English or German complaint. This is followed by the information about the specific data set the presented example is taken from as well as the position it takes in the data list of the appendix.[30] The first reference (BrE, NR-D 50), thus demonstrates that the example is taken from the British English data set "Item has not been received (double complaints)" and that it is complaint number 50 in the list of complaints of this specific data set.
Moreover, an English translation of the German complaints is always given in brackets behind each German example. Due to language specificity, unconventional abbreviations and non-standard spellings of German words are, however, lost in the English translation.
In this chapter each category of analysis is explained and illustrated using examples from the present data sets (5.1. to 5.5.). This is always followed by a description of data analysis, i.e. an account of the coding procedures and the statistical tests which were employed (5.1.1. to 5.5.1.). For a more detailed analysis of the present data, sum variables were also coded which are explained in 5.6. As for the other categories of analysis, this is followed by a description of the procedures of data analysis (5.6.1.).

5.1. Complaint strategies

Similar to previous studies on complaints in spoken communication (cf. Geluykens and Kraft 2003; House and Kasper 1981; Kraft and Geluykens 2002, 2004; Olshtain and Weinbach 1987, 1993; Trenchs 1994; Trosborg 1995), the present analysis investigated the different complaint strategies speakers use to formulate their complaints.[31] On the basis of the present data eight strategies

[30] For a clarification of the abbreviations used in these references, see the list of abbreviations.
[31] As a synonym for the term 'strategy' scholars also use the expression 'realisation pattern' (cf. Laforest 2002). However, since the term 'strategy' is more common in this research field, it is also used in the present report.

have been differentiated and are presented below. As it becomes obvious from the given examples, eBay members either use a single strategy or combinations of them to formulate their electronic complaints. For the sake of clarity, the strategy to be illustrated is always underlined in the given example.

Strategy 1: Expression of disappointment

In order to avoid conflict, complainers who use Strategy 1 refrain from mentioning the complainable or the complainee in the proposition. Instead they express their disappointment about the state of affairs, thereby focusing on their own feelings only. However, in sending their electronic complaint to a particular trading partner, they nonetheless reveal their accusation against the complainee.

Examples:

(BrE, NR-D 50) item never received and no refund given by seller <u>very disappointing</u>

(G, DIFF-D 33) die sim karte geht nicht verküfer antwortet nicht <u>schade</u>
(sim card doesn't work seller doesn't reply <u>what a pity</u>)

Strategy 2: Expression of anger or annoyance

In case of Strategy 2, complainers still avoid mentioning the offensive act or the addressee as the guilty person but rather express their general anger and annoyance about the situation. In doing so, they concentrate on their own feelings which, however, reveal a heightened negative attitude towards the complainable than Strategy 1.

Examples:

(BrE, NR 71) <u>too useless for words</u>

(G, DIFF 30) <u>einfach nicht wundern</u>, bei halbem Preis=halbe Beutelgröße
(<u>simply no wonder</u>, half price=half size of bag)

Strategy 3: Explicit complaint

In an explicit complaint, complainers mention the offensive act, the hearer, or both. They, however, refrain from explicitly judging the addressee's behaviour as well as from instigating any sanctions.

Examples:

(BrE, DIFF-D 2) <u>item was water damaged tried to contact seller no replay to emails</u>

(G, NR-D 59) !!!!!!!!!!!!!!!!!!!!!!!!!!!KEINE WARE UND KEIN GELD ZURÜCK !!!!!!!!!!!!!!!!!!!!!!
(!!!!!!!!!!!!!!!!!!!!!!!!!!!ITEM NOT RECEIVED AND NO MONEY BACK !!!!!!!!!!!!!!!!!!!!!!!)

Strategy 4: Negative judgement

In using Strategy 4, complainers explicitly state that the offensive act for which they hold the complainee responsible is bad.

Examples:

(BrE, DIFF-D 66) problem with bike no reply from seller thumbs down

(G, NR 36) Nach 3 Wochen immer noch nicht da!!! Echt peinliche Aktion!
(after 3 weeks still not received!!! What a pathetic thing to do!)

Strategy 5: Drawing one's own conclusion

Having had a bad experience with the transactional partner, complainers may also choose Strategy 5, in which case they draw a conclusion for their future action. Specifically, they decide to avoid any further business transactions with the complainee.

Examples:

(BrE, NR-D 1) didn't recieve items bought. no responce to e-mails. Will not buy from again

(G, DIFF 78) Luxus Taschenuhr ! ? Mehr als Schrott ! Einmal und nie wieder !!!!!!!!!!!!!!!!!!
(Luxurious pocket watch ! ? More than rubbish ! once and never again !!!!!!!!!!!!!!!!!!)

Strategy 6: Warning others

Complainers employing Strategy 6 explicitly warn the whole eBay community against the complainee.

Examples:

(BrE, NR 1) NO GOODS RECEIVED.... REPORTED TO EBAY.... AVOID!!!

(G, NR-D 41) Geld am 31.05. überwiesen; keine Ware erhalten; Kontakt abgebrochen;VORSICHT!!!
(Money transferred on 5/31; no item received; broken off contact; BEWARE!!!)

Strategy 7: Threat

In case complainers aim at stronger sanctions than only worsening the complainee's reputation, they may threaten the addressee with higher authorities such as lawyers or eBay's security system. Possible sanctions are thus not carried out by the complainers themselves but by these authorities, resulting in sanctions such as fines or a ban from eBay.

Examples:

(BrE, DIFF 24) I am reporting you to ebay the good's you sold me are scrap.

(G, DIFF-D 67) falsche Patronen bis heute kein Geld zurück Rechtsanwalt ist eingeschaltet frech
(wrong cassettes as of today still no refund lawyer is informed cheeky)

Strategy 8: Insult

In using insults, complainers explicitly condemn the accused as a person, whereby they often call them names.

Examples:

(BrE, NR-D 99) NEVER RECEIVED ITEM.DID NOT REPLY TO
E MAILS..ROBBERS

(G, NR 11) Voll die Zecke . Ware nicht angekommen !!Ein Großer Lügner
(An absolute parasite . Item didn't arrive !!A big liar)

5.1.1. Data analysis

The complaint strategies which were used to formulate the collected complaints were analysed according to several aspects which were statistically compared between data sets using the Qui-square or Independent Samples T-Test, depending on the measurement level of the data under investigation (see 4.2.). Specifically, the analysis included the frequencies with which the different strategies were chosen as well as whether a combination of strategies was employed. Furthermore, to get an idea of the prototypical British English and German complaint on the feedback forum of eBay[32], both the amount of strategies which were employed to formulate each online complaint as well as

[32] In this study the prototypical complaint signifies the type of complaint which is most frequently employed.

their specific order were taken into account. Strategy sequences which figured 5% or more in one of the two data sets were statistically compared. The final aspect of analysis concerned the number of different strategy sequences British English and German eBay traders used to formulate their complaints in each data set, as it gives a more accurate impression of how diverse or formulaic their online complaints are. While the amount of different strategy sequences are nominal data and were hence statistically compared between data sets using the Qui-square Test, the other aspects of analysis consist of interval data, so the Independent Samples T-Test was conducted.

The coding procedures are illustrated by two examples of the present data sets. An overview of the coding of the first example with regard to the use of complaint strategies is given in Table 5.1. However, the number of different strategy sequences cannot be illustrated, since its calculation depends on the whole data set.

Example:

(BrE, NR 1) NO GOODS RECEIVED.... REPORTED TO EBAY.... AVOID!!!

Table 5.1: Overview of the coding of the online complaint (BrE, NR 1) with regard to the use of complaint strategies.

Variables	Coding
Strategy 1: Expression of disappointment	0
Strategy 2: Expression of anger or annoyance	0
Strategy 3: Explicit complaint	1
Strategy 4: Negative judgement	0
Strategy 5: Drawing one's own conclusion	0
Strategy 6: Warning others	1
Strategy 7: Threat	1
Strategy 8: Insult	0
Presence of a strategy combination	1
Amount of strategies per complaint	3
Strategy sequence[33]	316273

As Table 5.1 shows, the electronic complaint (BrE, NR 1) consists of a Strategy 3 (*explicit complaint*), a Strategy 6 (*warning others*), and a Strategy 7 (*threat*). Accordingly, this online complaint is made up of a combination of strategies, precisely of a total of three strategies. The sequence of these strategies is thereby

[33] The coding of strategy sequences within each complaint does not illustrate frequencies. The order of the numerals mirrors the order of the strategies within the complaint.

Strategy 3 (*explicit complaint*), followed by Strategy 7 (*threat*), followed by Strategy 6 (*warning others*).

With regard to data sets consisting of double complaints, it is important to mention that the two different reasons for complaining were not coded as distinct strategies, since it is the nature of double complaints that traders complain about two reasons at the same time. This procedure also has the great advantage that it makes data sets of single and double complaints comparable. Accordingly, the following example of a double complaint was coded to consist of one strategy, precisely Strategy 3 (*explicit complaint*).

Example:

(BrE, NR-D 9) No item recived .no response to e mail..

Given that the example (BrE, NR-D 9) consists only of one strategy, no combination of strategies is employed (see the following Table 5.2).

Table 5.2: Overview of the coding of the online complaint (BrE, NR-D 9) with regard to the use of complaint strategies.

Variables	Coding
Strategy 1: Expression of disappointment	0
Strategy 2: Expression of anger or annoyance	0
Strategy 3: Explicit complaint	1
Strategy 4: Negative judgement	0
Strategy 5: Drawing one's own conclusion	0
Strategy 6: Warning others	0
Strategy 7: Threat	0
Strategy 8: Insult	0
Presence of a strategy combination	0
Amount of strategies per complaint	1
Strategy sequence	31

5.2. Level of directness

The second aspect of analysis concerns the directness level eBay members choose to formulate their complaint, whereby the term 'directness' signifies the degree of face-threat for the complainee. Similar to prior studies on complaints in oral communication (cf. House and Kasper 1981; Olshtain and Weinbach 1987, 1993; Trosborg 1995) the complaint strategies of the present study are in an order of increasing directness: Strategy 1 being the least and Strategy 8 the most direct one. The number of each strategy thus signifies its directness level, whereby a higher directness level represents more serious threats and hence more 'conflict potential' of the complaint (cf. Rubino and Bettoni 2006: 346; Trosborg 1995: 314). The different levels of directness were determined by the following factors which to a large extent correspond to those set up in House and Kaspers's (1981: 159) as well as Trosborg's study (1995: 315). Precisely, they depend on:

1. the intensity of negative feelings a speaker expresses towards the complainable,
2. whether the complainable and/or the addressee's involvement is/are mentioned,
3. whether a negative evaluation of the addressee's action is explicitly expressed,
4. whether sanctions are implicitly/explicitly manifested,
5. the severity of the negative consequences likely to follow the complaint,
6. and finally, whether the addressee is condemned as a person.

Using Strategy 1 and 2 complainers focus on their own feelings. There is a focus on self in that speakers send messages about themselves, called "Ich-Botschaften" (cf. Schulz von Thun 1996: 28, 1998: 131ff.), which makes their complaints very indirect. Strategy 2 is more direct than Strategy 1, since senders' negative feelings towards the complainable are more intense. When using Strategy 3, the focus shifts from the complainer to the complainable and complainee, making at least the complainable explicit, which clearly increases the face-threat involved. Strategy 4 presents a further rise in face-threat and hence directness, because, in contrast to Strategy 3, it involves an explicit negative judgement of the addressee's behaviour thereby enhancing the threat against the complainee's positive face (see 2.3.2.). Strategy 5 is the first strategy in this increasing order of directness in which the complainer makes additional sanctions explicit that go beyond a mere worsening of the complainee's overall feedback score and reputation on eBay. Specifically, the complainer decides to refrain from doing further business with the addressee, which is likely to affect other eBay traders, hence reducing the complainee's options for future business transactions. The amount of eBay users who are scared off, however, is lower when Strategy 5 is used than with Strategy 6 where the whole eBay community is warned against the complainee. The explicitness of this warning makes this strategy a stronger deterrent than Strategy 5, therefore resulting in a larger reduction of trading partners at the complainee's disposal. As a consequence, the amount of eBay members bidding for a complainee's item is decreased remarkably which in turn is likely to result in a price cut and therefore financial losses for the complainee. Strategy 7 leads to even more severe negative consequences for the complainee than Strategy 5 and 6, since it involves the consultation of higher authorities such as eBay's security system or lawyers, who have a wider range of options to hold the complainee legally liable for their misconduct. Finally, Strategy 8 is the most direct strategy complainers can choose, since it not only condemns the complainee's behaviour but also degrades them as a person.

5.2.1. Data analysis

When analysing the present data, the directness level of each comment was coded and statistically compared between data sets using the Mann-Whitney U-Test (see 4.2.). In case a comment consisted of a combination of strategies, the directness level of the most direct strategy was counted. The coding procedures are illustrated by the following examples.

Examples:

(BrE, DIFF 19) wrong size was sent

(G, NR 13) VORSICHT! WARE BEZAHLT UND KEINE ERHALTEN - NIE WIEDER!!
(BEWARE! ITEM PAID FOR BUT NEVER RECEIVED – NEVER AGAIN!!)

The first example (BrE, DIFF 19) consists of one strategy, namely Strategy 3 (*explicit complaint*). The directness level of this comment was hence coded as 3. In the second example (G, NR 13), a strategy combination is employed which is made up of Strategy 6 (*warning others*), Strategy 3 (*explicit complaint*), and Strategy 5 (*drawing one's own conclusion*). Since the most direct strategy of this online complaint is *warning others*, the directness level of this complaint was coded as 6.

5.3. Modification

In addition to classifying complaint strategies according to directness level, it has proven useful to analyse whether and how speakers modify their complaints (cf. House and Kasper 1981; Trosborg 1995). With modification of complaints, it is possible to distinguish between internal and external modification. While internal modification functions on the sentence level, external modification is achieved by the use of supportive moves to justify the complainer's "right" to place blame for something on the complainee or to provide face-saving arguments. Modifiers of both categories can thereby either intensify or mitigate the face-threatening nature of complaints.

Since only the effect of modification is important for the present investigation, i.e. whether it increases or softens the impact a complaint is likely to have on the complainee, it is only distinguished between upgrading and downgrading modification, thereby leaving out its relation to syntax.

The following means of up- and downgrading modification were obtained from the present data sets. They have been ordered into three categories, namely upgrading modifiers, downgrading modifiers, and intensifiers used to aggravate the softening effect of downgrading modifiers. The different means of modification are again illustrated using examples from the present data set. For the sake of clarity they are underlined in the given examples.

Category 1: Upgrading modifiers

Upgrading modifiers denote all modifiers which are used to increase the face-threatening effect a complaint is likely to have on the complainee. Relevant categories are explained below.

Intensifier:

'Intensifiers' are adverbials, adjectives or numerals which strengthen certain parts of the proposition (cf. House and Kasper 1981: 169; Trosborg 1995: 328).

Examples:

(BrE, DIFF 95) Item case scratched. can not give as a pressent. <u>very</u> disapointed.

(BrE, NR-D 27) Nothing received and no reply to <u>numerous</u> emails. Have they stopped trading ?

(BrE, DIFF-D 6) Faulty item <u>6</u> emails asking for details to return no response. Shysters don't by

(G, NR 5) Ich habe die Ware noch immer nicht erhalten !!!
(I still haven't received the item !!!)

(G, NR-D 90) ACHTUNG Gezahlt und kein Artikel, jeder Kontakt unbeantwortet !!! ACHTUNG
(BEWARE Paid and no item, all contact remained unanswered !!! BEWARE)

(G, DIFF-D 62) Ware entsprach nicht Artikelbeschreibung; keine Antwort auf mehrere Nachfragen
(Item didn't correspond to description; no answer to several inquiries)

Aggressive interrogative:

The 'aggressive interrogative' signifies the use of the interrogative mood to explicitly involve the addressee and thereby intensify the impact of the complaint (cf. House and Kasper 1981: 170).

Examples:

(BrE, DIFF 41) rare vintage shirts? More like cheap market copies! Not what I was expecting!

(G, DIFF-D 74) keine übereinstimmende Artikelbeschreibung-Kontakt???ungeklärt-sehr enttäuscht
(Item doesn't correspond to description – contact???unresolved-very disappointed)

Time reference:

A 'time reference' is employed to stress the length of time a complainer has been waiting for the addressee to abolish the complainable or provide some sort of repair, and thus to emphasise the negative consequences of the state of affairs a complainer has had to bear. Specifically, the complainer either states the exact date s/he ordered or paid for the item, or s/he makes the period of time s/he has been waiting explicit.

Examples:

(BrE, NR 65) Purchased and paid 4 August 2005, not received and now 11 August 2005

(BrE, NR-D 18) ignores messages & hasn't sent goods 11days after payment

(G, NR-D 21) Am 10.04. bezahlt - keine Ware - keine Erstattung des Kaufpreises !!!
(Paid on 10 April – no item – no refund !!!)

(G, DIFF-D 99) Kette Kaputt und sollte eine neue kriegen und warte schon 4 wochen
(Necklace broken and should have received a new one and have already been waiting for 4 weeks)

Sarcasm[34]:

A sarcastic utterance is an obviously false statement meant to express the opposite of what is literally said. In using this modifier a complainer stresses his/her negative social attitude towards the addressee.

Examples:

(G, NR 40) hab jetzt 2 Monate gewartet und keine Ware bekommen, schönen Dank
(have waited for 2 months and have not received any item, thanks a lot)

(G, DIFF-D 72) devekte ware erhalten! reklamiert und warte noch immer auf ersatz echt super!!!
(faulty item! Complained and still waiting for compensation really great!!!)

Category 2: Downgrading modifiers

Downgrading modifiers have the opposite function than upgrading ones. Accordingly, they reduce the face-threat involved when voicing a complaint. Relevant categories of the present study are again illustrated below.

Expression of regret:

By the use of adverbials a complainer shows that s/he regrets making the complaint and ruining the addressee's name on eBay.

Examples:

(BrE, NR-D 49) unfortunatly i have not recieved this item and no response to emails

(G, NR 46) Leider keine CD erhalten
(unfortunately haven't received the CD)

(G, DIFF 6) leider nicht die bestellte Ware geliefert
(unfortunately has not send the ordered item)

---

[34] Following Culpeper (1996) the term *sarcasm* was preferred to *irony*, since *irony* can refer to enjoyment or comedy, while *sarcasm* is always employed as a means to achieve social disharmony (see 2.3.6.).

Play down:

The 'play down' describes syntactical devices that tone down the negative effects of the complaint (cf. Kasper and House 1981: 166). Examples include, for instance, the use of the interrogative mood or negation.

Examples:

(BrE, NR 43) can you send me my vinyl pleaseeeeeeeeeee.

(BrE, DIFF 80) paints coming of the bowls. not very good

(G, DIFF 66) Schuhe waren nicht so gut, vorne direkt eingerissen
(shoes weren't that good, immediately torn in the front)

Understater:

'Understaters' are modifiers that under-represent certain parts of the proposition (cf. Trosborg 1995: 328). Since there is no understater in the German data of this study, only a British English example is given.

Example:

(BrE, NR 21) hi thankyou just one little things what have i won and when will it be here jay

Politeness marker:

'Politeness markers' are optional elements used to show deference and to bid for cooperative behaviour (cf. Kasper and House 1981: 166).

Examples:

(BrE, NR 43) can you send me my vinyl pleaseeeeeeeeeee.

(G, NR-D 77) Keine Ware da - keine Reaktion ! Bei dem Betrag - mehr Zuverlässigkeit bitte !
(no item – no reply ! Regarding the price – more reliability please!)

Disarmer:

Disarmers function on the interpersonal level and prepare for the face-threat at hand (cf. Trosborg 1995: 329f.). With regard to the present data, they are either apologies for voicing such a harmful speech act or face-saving arguments to partly counterpart the negative effects of the complaint.

Examples:

(BrE, DIFF 12) item has been received but very dissapointed with it so negative feedback sorry

(BrE, DIFF-D 38) Item delivery was quick but, CD was not sent as per ad; not response to e-mail

(G, NR 71) Tut mir leid ... aber ich habe die Ware nie bekommen !!
(I'm sorry … but I have never received the item !!)

(G, DIFF 82) SCHNELLE LIEFERUNG ABER PASST NICHT
(FAST DELIVERY BUT DOESN'T FIT)

Category 3: Intensifiers used to aggravate the softening effect of downgrading modifiers

The different up- and downgrading modifiers may also be used simultaneously to influence the effect of one another. As far as the present data is concerned, intensifiers are, for instance, employed in combination with downgrading modifiers to aggravate their softening effect. Due to their mitigating effect, they have been treated as a separate category from the other upgrading modifiers. In the following examples intensifiers are, for instance, used to increase the effect of disarmers.

Examples:

(BrE, NR-D 2) Item not received, no response from seller, very surprised as feedback is good

(G, DIFF 38) ware sehr schnell angekommen, leider gefälscht, vorsicht!!!!!!!!!!
(item arrived very fast, unfortunately a fake, beware!!!!!!!!!!)

5.3.1. Data analysis

To analyse the data, the absolute frequencies with which the different up- and downgrading modifiers occurred were coded and statistically compared between data sets using the Independent Samples T-Test (see 4.2.). As for the previously explained categories of analysis, the coding procedures are again illustrated by an example from the present data sets. An overview of the coding of this example with regard to the use of modification is given in Table 5.3.

Example:

(BrE, NR-D 64) Brought on 11/11/05,paid instantly with P/P.Still not received,no answer to emai

Table 5.3: Overview of the coding of the online complaint (BrE, NR-D 64) with regard to the use of modification.

Categories	Variables	Coding
Category 1: Upgrading modifiers	Intensifier	2
	Aggressive interrogative	0
	Time reference	1
	Sarcasm	0
Category 2: Downgrading modifiers	Expression of regret	0
	Play down	0
	Understater	0
	Politeness marker	0
	Disarmer	0
Category 3: Intensifiers used to aggravate the softening effect of downgrading modifiers	Intensifiers (downgrading)	0

As Table 5.3 reveals, the complainer uses three modifiers in the given example. These are all *upgrading modifiers*, precisely a *time reference* and two *intensifiers*, mentioned in the order of their occurrence. *Downgrading modifiers* as well as *intensifiers used to aggravate the softening effect of devices* are not employed in this complaint, and thus coded as zero in the analysis.

5.4. Use of pronouns

The use of pronouns reveals complainers' personal involvement and attitude towards the proposition of their utterance (cf. Claridge 2007: 97; Hatipoğlu 2007: 769). In doing so, they may be used as a means to intensify or mitigate the face-threat of speech acts and are thus another significant aspect when investigating complaints (cf. Trosborg 1995: 322ff.).

Due to the contextual factors of the present data, the following categories of pronouns have been investigated. They are again underlined in the given examples.

First person pronouns (singular and plural, all cases):

The use of first person pronouns marks the personal involvement of complainers. On the one hand, senders thereby identify themselves as the complainer and thus take on the responsibility for issuing the face-threatening act (cf. Trosborg 1995: 323). In doing so, they threaten their own positive face. On the other hand though, they also stress that they have had to bear the negative effects of the complainable, which increases the attack against the complainee who is thought to be responsible for it.

Examples:

(BrE, NR 74) i've never received the item

(BrE, DIFF-D 31) Sent me fake not 'Faith' boots then offered me refund and didn't do it.

(G, NR 5) Ich habe die Ware noch immer nicht erhalten !!!
(I still haven't received the item !!!)

(G, NR 96) Bis heute noch nichts bei mir angekommen
(Until today still has not arrived at my place)

Second person pronouns (singular and plural, all cases):

By using second person pronouns, complainers directly approach the complainee and hence explicitly establish the addressee as the agent of the complainable (cf. Claridge 2007: 97; Trosborg 1995: 325).

Examples:

(BrE, DIFF 24) I am reporting you to ebay the good's you sold me are scrap.

(BrE, NR-D 74) readn ur feedbak, u aint answern me either, wheres my bloody dvd, bin waitn 14 d

(G, DIFF-D 52) Lange Lieferzeit,Falsche Ware,Nie wieder bei Euch
(Long delivery time,Wrong item,Never again from you)

Third person pronouns (singular and plural, all cases):

Another means to stress the complainee's guilt and thereby enhance the face-threat of the complaint is the use of third person pronouns referring to the complainee (cf. Claridge 2007: 98).

Examples:

(BrE, DIFF-D 8) TOTTALY IGNORANT PEOPLE, THEY SELL FAULTY GOODS THEN MESS YOU ABOUT FOR REFUND—

(BrE, DIFF-D 83) I sent the item bak cuz it was damaged & she still wudn't giv refund total CON!!

(G, NR 84) habe das geld am 4.3.2005 an ihn überwiesen und die ware kam bis heute nicht.
(transfered the money to him on 3/4/2005 and as of today, item still hasn't arrived.)

(G, DIFF-D 75) Habe nur die Hülle erhalten. Er war nicht bereit, Ersatz zu leisten. nie wieder!
(Only received the cover. He wasn't willing to compensate for it. never again!)

Third person pronouns which do not stand for the complainee were not included in this category, since they do not enhance the face-threat at hand. For illustration see the following examples.

Examples of a third person pronouns which were NOT included in the analysis:

(BrE, DIFF8) item listed as cream but no mention of the fact that they're patterned too.

(G, DIFF 98) Laut Bezeichnung soll die Ware neu sein, war sie aber nicht.
(According to description item is supposed to be new, however it is not.)

Demonstrative pronouns followed by nouns denoting the complainee:

A third option to emphasise one's belief that the addressee is responsible for the complainable and hence to increase one's attack, is the use of demonstrative pronouns which are followed by nouns denoting the complainee (cf. Hiltrop 2003: 35).

Examples:

(BrE, NR 11) item never received from this seller

(BrE, NR-D 66) its been 2 weeks i paid still no film . no message nothing this person rips you

(G, NR 86) ware nie angekommen. hände weg von diesem verkäufer!
(Item has never arrived. keep away from this seller!)

Given that the effect of this category is also to stress the complainee's involvement in the state of affairs, demonstrative pronouns followed by nouns which do not stand for the addressee were excluded from this category. For illustration see the following examples.

Examples of a demonstrative pronouns which were NOT included in the analysis:

(BrE, NR 38) I have still not recieved this item

(G, NR-D 75) KEINE WARE UND KEIN GELD ZURÜCK SEHR SCHADE BEI DIESEM BETRAG !!!!!!!
(NO ITEM AND NO REFUND WHAT A PITY AT THIS PRICE !!!!!!!)

Pronouns addressing the eBay community:

Since the feedback forum of eBay is public and its purpose is to reveal eBay users' reputation, complaints may not only be addressed to the complainee but similarly, and sometimes even solely, to the rest of the eBay community. Complainers may hence use pronouns which directly address the other eBay traders.

Examples:

(BrE, NR 51) I DID NOT RECEIVE MY ITEM FROM THIS SELLER, BEFORE YOU BUY THINK TWICE!

(G, NR 39) Habe bislang keine Ware erhalten! Ist doch absurd.Kannste inne Pfeife rauchen!!
(Haven't received the item! That's absurd. He's a washout.[35])

Indefinite pronouns:

To reduce direct accusation and blame of the complainee, i.e. to reduce the face-threat at hand, complainers may also use indefinite pronouns to formulate their comment (cf. Trosborg 1995: 326).

Examples:

(BrE, DIFF-D 15) lingerie is a lot smaller than sizes state and you cannot return unlike shops

(G, DIFF 14) Das Telfon Ist nicht ISDN fähig. Man sollte es auch nicht als dieses Verkaufen!!
(The telephone does not work with ISDN. One should not sell it as such!!)

However, it is important to mention that despite the softening effect of these indefinite pronouns, the online complaint is still sent to a specific eBay user, thereby revealing him/her as the accused person. Furthermore, the complaint also retains its negative effect on the addressee's overall feedback score.

[35] As 'Kannste inne Pfeife rauchen' is an idiomatic expression, it cannot be literally translated. The second person pronoun 'te' (dialectal form) is therefore lost in the English translation.

5.4.1. Data analysis

The absolute frequencies with which the different types of pronouns occurred in each complaint were coded and their usage statistically compared between data sets using the Independent Samples T-Test (see 4.2.). Given that complainers may use three types of pronouns to stress the complainee's guilt in the state of affairs, namely *second person pronouns, third person pronouns*, and *demonstrative pronouns followed by nouns denoting the complainee*, they were not only separately analysed but also added to form the variable *pronouns referring to the complainee*, whose usage was again statistically compared using the Independent Samples T-Test. This procedure has the advantage that it enables better insight into the frequency with which the complainee is personally accused and hence his/her positive face threatened.

The coding procedures are again illustrated by an example from the present data sets. An overview of the coding of this example with regard to the use of pronouns is illustrated in Table 5.4.

Example:

(BrE, NR 51) I DID NOT RECEIVE MY ITEM FROM THIS SELLER, BEFORE YOU BUY THINK TWICE!

Table 5.4: Overview of the coding of the online complaint (BrE, NR 51) with regard to the use of pronouns.

Variables	Coding
First person pronouns	2
Second person pronouns	0
Third person pronouns	0
Demonstrative pronouns followed by nouns denoting the complainee	1
Pronouns referring to the complainee	1
Pronouns addressing the eBay community	1
Indefinite pronouns	0

As Table 5.4 illustrates, the example (BrE, NR 51) was coded to contain two first person pronouns, a demonstrative pronoun followed by a noun denoting the complainee, and a pronoun addressing the other eBay members. Since the pronouns referring to the complainee is the sum of the use of second person pronouns, third person pronouns and demonstrative pronoun followed by a noun denoting the complainee it also counts as 1 in the given example.

5.5. Features of CMC

In CMC, the expression of senders' attitudes and feelings cannot only be lexically expressed by the use of specific complaint strategies, modifiers or pronouns, but also by the use of elements which have (often) only been regarded as genre-specific or as indicative of the creative nature of CMC (cf. Androutsopoulos 2006; Bader 2002; Bays 1998; Claridge 2007; Collot and Belmore 1996; Crystal 2001; Danet et al. 1997; Herring 1996, 2001; Hundt et al. 2007; Raymond 1993; Reid 1991; Schiano 1997; Siever 2006; Wenz 1998; Werry 1996; Yates 1996). Given their effect on the expressiveness of electronic language, they clearly need to be integrated into the feature pool for linguistic investigation. The following features have therefore been analysed with regard to the present data. They have been classed into three groups, namely emoticons, intensifying features of CMC which are used to increase the face-threat of the complaint, and intensifying features of CMC which are employed to intensify the softening effect of downgrading modifiers. In the illustrating examples the specific feature of CMC which is explained is always underlined.

Category 1: Emoticons

Emoticons are graphic representations of the senders' facial expression and thus the mood attributed to them (cf. Bader 2002: 93f., 106f.; Höflich 1997: 212; Herring 2001: 623; Raettig 1999: 19f.; Sanderson 1997: 307f.; Wenz 1998: 5; Wiest 1997: 236; Wilson 1992: 42). The emoticons in the present data sets are all frownies. As the following examples show, they occur either with or without "nose", and can be intensified by a repetition of the round bracket symbolising an eBay member's pouting mouth.

Examples:

(BrE, DIFF 68) Poor quality, advert suggest items is of a product other than cheep plastic :-(

(BrE, DIFF-D 67) Not model shown in picture. No reply to email :(

(G, DIFF 58) verkratztes, passungenaues nokia cover, sieht nach b-ware aus!!! :-(
(scratched, non-fitting nokia cover, looks like second-hand item!!! :-()

(G, DIFF-D 86) Nein danke! Erst paßt nix und dann ewig auf Antwort/ Rückzahlung warten;o(((
(No thanks! First nothing fits and then you have to wait ages for reply/refund ;o((()

Category 2: Intensifying features of CMC

To intensify their online complaints, the subjects of the present study use different features of CMC. These embrace the use of visual signs, capitalisation, exclamation marks, as well as the repetition of punctuation marks and letters. These intensifying features are explained below.

Visual signs:

When visual signs are used, complaints are highlighted, so that they hit users' eyes who browse the list of eBay users' feedback comments. Complaints in which visual signs are used are thus more frequently read and can be remembered more easily due to their striking appearance (cf. Edelmann 1996: 251; Zimbardo and Gerrig 1999: 233). In addition to that, asterisks are, as in chat communication, used to signalise action (cf. Raettig 1999: 13).

Examples:

(BrE, NR-D 77) 2 WEEKS STIL AWAITIN ITEM, NO REPLIES, ##### bad ebayer #####

(G, DIFF-D 41) Echt dreiste Abzocke*Bilder ausgeschnitten*Seiten fehlen-Unfreundlicher Kontakt
(Really bold rip-off*pictures cut out*pages are missing-unfriendly contact)

Capitalisation:

If senders make use of capitalisation to intensify their online complaint, they may either capitalise specific words of a message or the message as a whole (cf. Bader 2002: 104f.; Herring 2001: 617; Raettig 1999: 10ff.; Wenz 1998: 2; Werry 1996: 57; Wiest 1997: 236). Capital letters in comments on eBay's feedback forum are, in contrast to chat communication, not only used as a mean to signal an increase in volume[36] which expresses complainers' heightened negative attitude towards the state of affairs and their increased emotional involvement. The use of capitalisation also has an eye-catching effect. Thus, similar to visual signs they increase the frequency with which the complaints are

[36] For the use of capitalisation in chats to signal shouting, see for instance Bader (2002: 104f.), Raettig (1999: 13f.).

looked at and the efficiency with which they are remembered (cf. Edelmann 1996: 251; Zimbardo and Gerrig 1999: 233). For illustration see the following examples.

Examples:

(BrE, NR 51) I DID NOT RECEIVE MY ITEM FROM THIS SELLER, BEFORE YOU BUY THINK TWICE!

(BrE, DIFF 57) trainers came quick but ended up being size 9. BEWARE!!!

(G, NR 29) habe leider mein spiel NICHT erhalten
(Unfortunately have NOT received my game)

Exclamation mark(s):

As in writing, the use of an exclamation mark indicates utterance type (cf. Claridge 2007: 99). In deliberately formulating the online complaint as an exclamation, complainers show their arousement to achieve an intensifying effect. This effect is even more prevalent if more than one exclamation mark is employed. As it becomes obvious from the following examples, both types, i.e. single exclamations marks and repeated ones may occur within online complaints at the same time.

Examples:

(BrE, DIFF-D 16) Not as described! Seller doesnt reply to emails! Avoid at all costs!

(BrE, NR-D 13) ink not recieved after 15 days!! no contact from seler even after i emailed um!

(G, NR-D 17) Achtung !!!!!!!!! Bezahlt aber keine Ware! Kein E-mail Kontakt. Keine Reaktion !
(Beware !!!!!!!!! Paid but no item! No e-mail contact. No reaction !)

(G, NR 23) ware bezahlt nie erhalten!!
(Paid item have never received it!!)

Repetition of punctuation marks other than exclamation marks:

In addition to exclamation marks, complainers may also repeat other types of punctuation marks to convey their emotional attitude and hence to aggravate their online complaint (cf. Bader 2002: 105f.; Raettig 1999: 10ff.; Wiest 1997: 236). For illustration see the following examples.

Examples:

(BrE, NR 20) did not get the pants, wre are they?????

(G, DIFF 40) 100% kein Original, Ärmel viel zu kurz, Kindergröße???
(100% no original, sleeves much too short, children's wear???)

(G, DIFF-D 86) Nein danke! Erst paßt nix und dann ewig auf Antwort/ Rückzahlung warten;o(((
(No thanks! First nothing fits and then waiting ages for reply/refund;o((()

Since the repetition of periods is not employed to intensify the face-threat of the complaint but rather to hint at aspects which are left unspoken, they have NOT been included in this category. For illustration see the following examples:

Examples of a repeated punctuation marks which have NOT been included in the analysis:

(BrE, NR-D 98) i still didnt receive my item and they dont respond to my emails....

(G, DIFF-D 100) unvollständige lieferung und sehr lange wartezeit nach rücksendung...........
(incomplete delivery and very long period of waiting after return...........)

Repetition of letters:

To convey the lengthening in pronunciation of particular phonemes, Internet users repeat letters of words (cf. Bader 2002: 105f.; Herring 2001: 617). In online complaints this is also used for the sake of intensification. Since this feature does not occur in the British English data sets, only a German example is given.

Examples:

(G, NR-D 51) Bezahlte Wahre nie angekommen, Nachfrage nicht erhört, bloooooß nicht!!!!!
(Item which was paid for has never arrived, inquiries haven't been heard, neeeever deal with them!!!!![37])

Category 3: Intensifying features of CMC used to aggravate the softening effect of downgrading modifiers

The different means of intensification may also be used in combination with downgrading modifiers, in order to intensify the softening effect of these

[37] The German expression 'blooooß nicht' cannot be translated literally. However, the English translation expresses its meaning.

downgrading devices. In light of their function to further mitigate the face-threat of the complaint rather than aggravating it, the intensifying features of CMC which occurred in combination with downgrading devices have been treated as a distinct category. For illustration of these features see the following examples.

Examples:

(BrE, NR 43) can you send me my vinyl pleaseeeeeeeeeee.

(BrE, DIFF 67) post was fast, but shoes were awful, dirty, sequins missing, sole faulty, Sorry!

(G, NR 33) Sorry ! Habe nie die Ware erhalten,17€ für nichts !!!!!!!!!!!!!!!!!!!!!!!!!!!!!!!
(Sorry ! Never received the item,17€ for nothing !!!!!!!!!!!!!!!!!!!!!!!!!!!!!!!)

While in the first example the politeness marker ‘please’ is intensified by a repetition of the letter ‘e’, the other two examples illustrate the use of an exclamation mark to aggravate the mitigating effect of the preceding disarmer ‘sorry’.

5.5.1. Data analysis

The different features of CMC were coded with regard to their absolute frequencies and compared between data sets using the Independent Samples T-Test (see 4.2.). For the sake of accuracy, two variables were coded regarding the use of capitalisation: the employment of *capitalisation of particular words* within a complaint and the use of *capitalisation of the whole message*. Similarly, the coding procedures of the use of exclamation marks included two variables, namely the use of *single exclamation marks* and the employment of *more than one exclamation mark.* Consequently, the analysis of the repetition of punctuation marks was split into two variables: the *repetition of exclamation marks* and the *repetition of punctuation marks other than exclamation marks.*

These coding procedures have several major advantages. First, they enable a very precise analysis of eBay traders’ handling of capitalisation as well as the use of exclamation marks in their online complaints. Secondly, the twofold coding of the repetition of punctuation marks, namely the use of *repeated exclamation marks* on the one hand, and the *repetition of punctuation marks other than exclamation marks* on the other, makes a more accurate analysis of the repetition of punctuation marks possible.

The coding procedures are again illustrated by an example from the present data sets. An overview of the coding of this example with regard to the use of features of CMC is given in Table 5.5.

Example:

(G, NR 49) Geld überwiesen, KEINE WARE ERHALTEN!!! Finger weg! BETRÜGER!!!!
(Money transferred, NO ITEM RECEIVED!!! Keep away! SWINDLER!!!!)

Table 5.5: Overview of the coding of the online complaint (G, NR 49) with regard to the use of features of CMC.

Categories	Variables	Coding
Category 1: Emoticons	Emoticons	0
Category 2: Intensifying features of CMC	Visual signs	0
	Capitalisation of words	1
	Capitalisation of the message	0
	Single exclamation marks	1
	Repetition of exclamation marks	2
	Repetition of punctuation marks other than exclamation marks	0
	Repetition of letters	0
Category 3: Intensifying features of CMC used to aggravate the softening effect of downgrading modifiers	Intensifying features of CMC (downgrading)	0

As Table 5.5 reveals, the example (G, NR 49) shows a complaint in which capitalisation is used, precisely the *capitalisation of words* within this complaint. Furthermore, this online complaint is intensified by the use of exclamation marks, namely a *single exclamation mark* and two *repetitions of them*. The remaining features of CMC are all absent.

5.6. Sum variables

In addition to analysing the different categories separately, two sum variables have been coded which are all-embracing in that they unite variables of different analytical categories. These include the *total use of mitigating features* as well as the *total use of intensifying features*. For an overview of these sum variables see the following Table 5.6.

Table 5.6: Overview of the sum variables and the variables incorporated in them.

All-embracing sum variables	Variables which make up each sum variable
Total use of mitigating features	**Downgrading modifiers:** Expression of regret Play down Understater Politeness marker Disarmer
	Intensifier (downgrading)
	Intensifying features of CMC (downgrading)
	Indefinite pronouns
Total use of intensifying features	Presence of a strategy combination
	Upgrading modifiers: Intensifier Aggressive interrogative Time reference Sarcasm
	Pronouns referring to the complainee: Second person pronouns Third person pronouns Demonstrative pronouns followed by nouns denoting the complainee
	Intensifying features of CMC: Capitalisation of words Capitalisation of the message Visual signs Exclamation marks (single and repeated) Repetition of punctuation marks Repetition of letters

As it becomes obvious from Table 5.6 the sum-variable *total use of mitigating features* unites all variables which soften the face-threat of the complaint. This sum variable hence includes *the different types of downgrading modifiers, the intensifier or intensifying features of CMC used to aggravate the softening effect of downgrading devices,* as well as *the use of indefinite pronouns*. The sum variable *total use of intensifying features*, on the other hand, incorporates all variables which aggravate the face-threat involved. In other words, it is made up of the following variables: *the presence of strategy combinations, the different types of upgrading modifiers, the pronouns referring to the complainee*, and the *intensifying features of CMC*.

With regard to the *intensifying features of CMC*, which are incorporated in the sum variable *total use of intensifying features*, it is worth mentioning that the use of more than one exclamation mark intensifies a complaint in two ways. Firstly, due to the fact that exclamation marks signify the complaint as the utterance type 'exclamation', and secondly through its repetition. To take this twofold intensification into account, the sum variable *total use of intensifying features* includes the variable *exclamation marks* which embraces single and repeated ones, as well as the variable *repetition of punctuation marks* in which the use of more than one exclamation mark is again incorporated.

5.6.1. Data analysis

As for the other categories of analysis, the absolute frequencies at which the two sum variables occurred within each complaint were coded and statistically compared between data sets using the Independent Samples T-Test (see 4.2.). The coding procedures are again illustrated by an example. An overview of the coding of this example concerning the use of the sum variables is given in Table 5.7.

Example:

(G, DIFF-D 82) UNSERIÖS! Verkauft Gebrauchtware als Neuware! Reagiert nicht! Ganz mies!!!
(SHADY! Sells second hand items as new! Doesn't respond! Absolutely terrible!!!)

Table 5.7: Overview of the coding of the online complaint (G, DIFF-D 82) with regard to the use of the sum variables.

Sum variables	Coding
Total use of mitigating features	0
Total use of intensifying features	8

As Table 5.7 illustrates, *mitigating features* do not occur in the given example. The *total use of the intensifying features* figures 8, as one strategy combination is used, one *upgrading modifier*, i.e. the intensifier 'ganz' (absolutely), as well as six *intensifying features of CMC*, which embrace the use of capitalisation of words, four uses of exclamation marks, and one repetition of them.

Chapter 6: Results

In Chapter 6 the results of the present study are illustrated in form of tables and diagrams. Significant differences between data sets under investigation are highlighted in tables by bold print. If the standard deviations of both groups are 0, p cannot be calculated. In such cases, p is thus missing in particular cells of the table.

The findings of the present study are displayed in the following order. It begins with an illustration of the results with regard to the comparison of the British English and German complaints (6.1.). This is followed by a presentation of the findings concerning the comparison of the British English data sets (6.2.). Finally, the results of the comparison of the German data sets are demonstrated (6.3.). Within each subchapter the results are shown in the order the different categories of analysis have been introduced in Chapter 5. Thus, it is first dealt with the use of complaint strategies which is related to the choice of the level of directness, the employment of strategy combinations, and the amount of strategies and particular strategy sequences which are used to formulate the online complaints. What follows are the findings of the use of modification, pronouns, and features of CMC, as well as the occurrence of the two sum variables in the collected data sets.

This chapter concludes with a summary of the results, whereby the research questions of this study are answered (6.4.).

6.1. Comparison of British English versus German complaints

For investigation of research question 1, i.e. whether British and German traders differ with regard to their complaining behaviour on the feedback forum of eBay, the four different British English and German data sets were statistically compared (see 4.2.). The findings of these comparisons are illustrated in the following order: data set *Item has not been received* (6.1.1.), data set *Item was different than expected* (6.1.2.), data set *Item has not been received (double complaints)* (6.1.3.), and data set *Item was different than expected (double complaints)* (6.1.4.).

6.1.1. Data set: Item has not been received

Table 6.1 and Figure 6.1 illustrate the results of the comparison of the British English and German eBay traders' use of complaint strategies, level of directness, and amount of strategy combinations in the data set *Item has not been received (Item NR).*

Table 6.1: British English (BrE) and German traders' use of complaint strategies, level of directness, and amount of strategy combinations in the data set *Item NR*.

Data set: *Item NR* Complaint strategies	**BrE complaints relative frequencies (%)**	**German complaints relative frequencies (%)**	**Significance (p)**
Expression of disappointment	4	4	1.000
Expression of anger or annoyance	2	3	0.653
Explicit complaint	97	99	0.315
Negative judgement	12	14	0.676
Drawing one's own conclusion	3	8	0.122
Warning others	15	20	0.324
Threat	**3**	**11**	**0.024***
Insult	7	11	0.449
Level of directness			**0.005****
Strategy combination	**34**	**50**	**0.022***

Figure 6.1: Graphic representation of BrE and German eBay traders' use of complaint strategies and combinations of them in the data set *Item NR*.

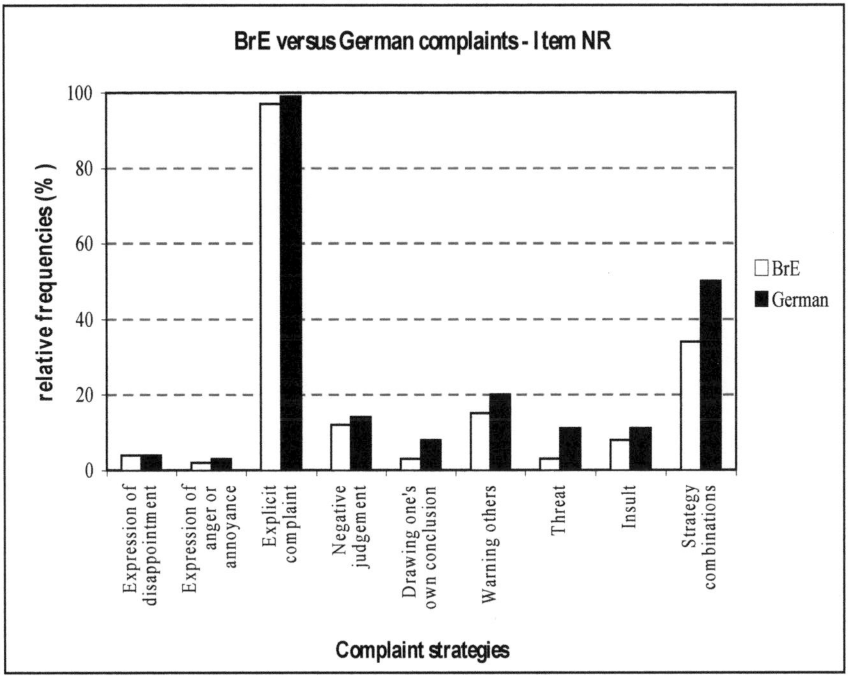

As Table 6.1 and Figure 6.1 illustrate, the British English and German eBay traders use the same range of complaint strategies, whereby the strategy *explicit complaint* is by far the most common strategy in both data sets. Furthermore, while the first strategies are used almost similarly often, the Germans employ the more direct strategies: *drawing one's own conclusion, warning others, threat*, and *insult* to a larger extent. However, only regarding the strategy *threat* a significant difference can be observed (p = 0.024*, see Table 6.1). When statistically comparing the *directness levels* British English and German eBay traders use to formulate their complaints, the results reveal a highly significant difference between them (p = 0.005**, see Table 6.1), in that the Germans are significantly more direct than their British English counterparts. In addition to that, the Germans employ significantly more often *combinations of strategies* to formulate their online complaints (p = 0.022*, see Table 6.1).

The following Table 6.2 and Figure 6.2 present the results regarding the amount of strategies British English and German traders typically employ to formulate the complaints in the data set *Item NR.*

Table 6.2: The amount of strategies BrE and German eBay traders use to formulate their complaints in the data set *Item NR.*

Data set: *Item NR* Amount of strategies per complaint	**BrE complaints relative frequencies (%)**	**German complaints relative frequencies (%)**	**Significance (p)**
Use of one strategy	**66**	**50**	**0.022***
Use of a combination of two strategies	23	29	0.336
Use of a combination of three strategies	10	18	0.104
Use of a combination of four strategies	1	2	0.563
Use of a combination of five strategies	0	1	0.320

Figure 6.2: Graphic representation of the amount of strategies BrE and German traders use to formulate their complaints in the data set *Item NR.*

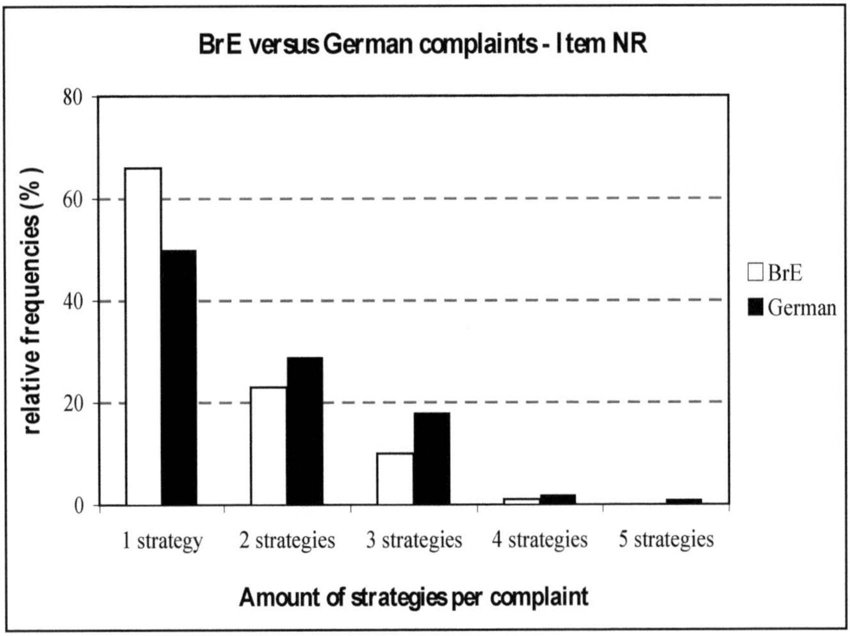

As becomes obvious from Table 6.2 and Figure 6.2, the complaints in the data set *Item NR* are minimally made up of one and maximally of five strategies. The use of one strategy is thereby most frequently employed by both the British English and German eBay traders. Despite this similarity, Table 6.2 also reveals that there is a significant difference in the frequency with which one strategy is used (p = 0.022*, see Table 6.2). However, this difference only exists, since the Germans use more strategy combinations consisting of two or three strategies, resulting in a different distribution of the number of strategies each online complaint is made of. Moreover, a combination of five strategies can only be found in the German data set, however, just once.

Table 6.3 and Figure 6.3 illustrate the strategy sequences which British English or German eBay traders use in at least 5% of the complaints in the data set *Item NR*.

Table 6.3: The strategy sequences BrE or German eBay traders use in at least 5% of the complaints in the data set *Item NR*.

Data set: *Item NR* Strategy sequences (minimum 5%)	**BrE complaints relative frequencies (%)**	**German complaints relative frequencies (%)**	**Significance (p)**
Explicit complaint	**65**	**49**	**0.022***
Explicit complaint/negative judgement	7	7	1.000
Explicit complaint/warning others	4	6	0.519

Figure 6.3: Graphic representation of the strategy sequences BrE or German eBay traders use in at least 5% of the complaints in the data set *Item NR*.

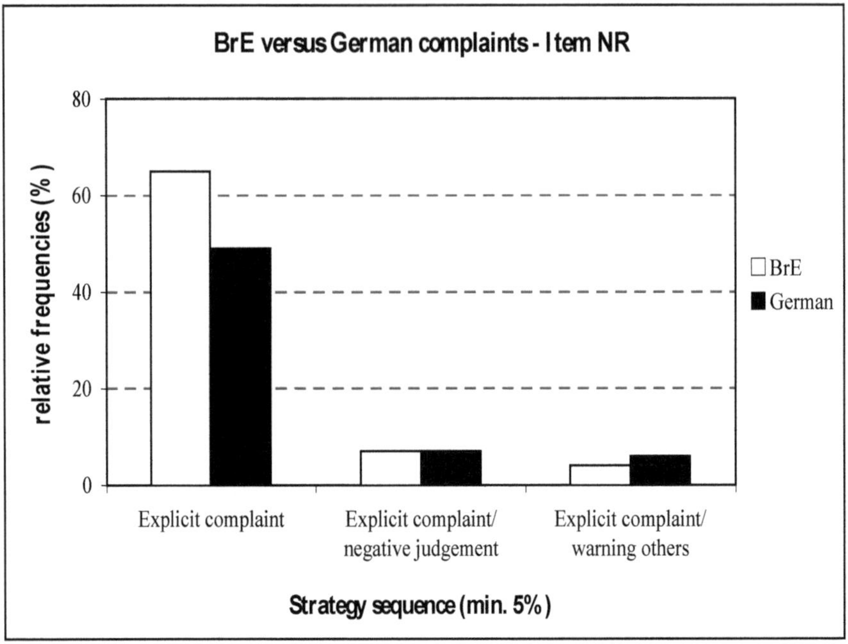

Table 6.3 and Figure 6.3 again show that the British English and German complaints in the data set *Item NR* are most frequently made up of only one strategy. When comparing the results of Table 6.2 and Table 6.3, it further becomes obvious that this strategy is in almost all cases an *explicit complaint*. Consequently, the prototypical complaint British English and German eBay traders use if they have not received the item is a complaint which consists of only one strategy, namely the strategy *explicit complaint*.

The following Table 6.4 and Figure 6.4 reveal the amount of different strategy sequences British English and German traders employ in their online complaints in the data set *Item NR*.

Table 6.4: The amount of different strategy sequences BrE and German eBay traders use to formulate their complaints in the data set *Item NR*.

Data set: *Item NR*	BrE complaints absolute frequencies	German complaints absolute frequencies	Significance (p)
Amount of different strategy sequences	23	31	0.276

Figure 6.4: Graphic representation of the amount of different strategy sequences BrE and German eBay traders use to formulate their complaints in the data set *Item NR*.

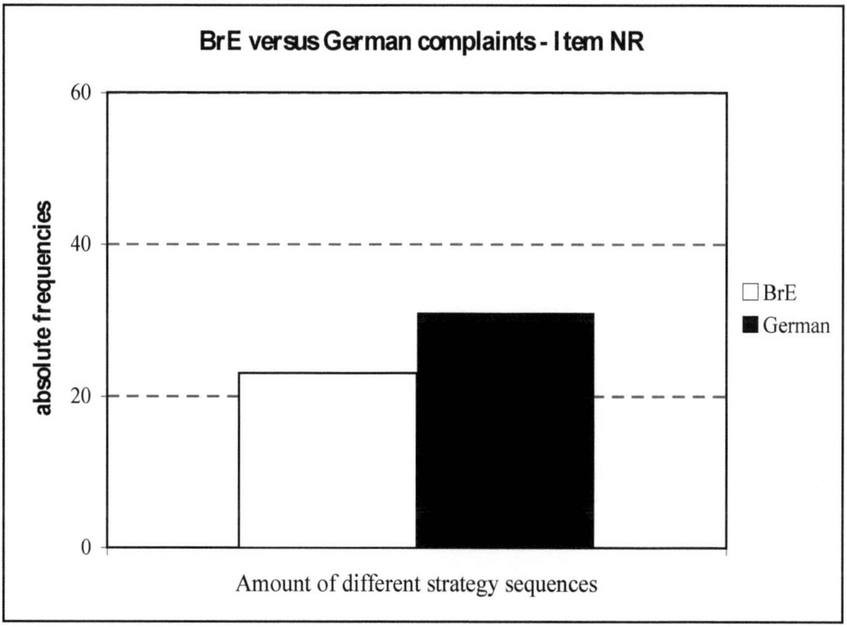

As becomes apparent from Table 6.4 and Figure 6.4, the German traders use a higher frequency of different strategy sequences. Their complaints are hence more diverse in this respect, however, without a significant difference (p = 0.276, see Table 4.6).

What follows are the results of the use of modification. It begins with an illustration of the results of the use of upgrading modifiers (see Table 6.5 and Figure 6.5), before the results of the use of downgrading modifiers are shown (see Table 6.6 and Figure 6.6).

Table 6.5: BrE and German eBay traders' use of upgrading modifiers in their complaints in the data set *Item NR.*

Data set: *Item NR* Upgrading modifiers	**BrE complaints relative frequencies (%)**	**German complaints relative frequencies (%)**	**Significance (p)**
Intensifier	31	34	0.322
Aggressive interrogative	6	2	0.151
Time reference	15	22	0.486
Sarcasm	0	2	0.158

Figure 6.5: Graphic representation of BrE and German eBay traders' use of upgrading modifiers in their complaints in the data set *Item NR.*

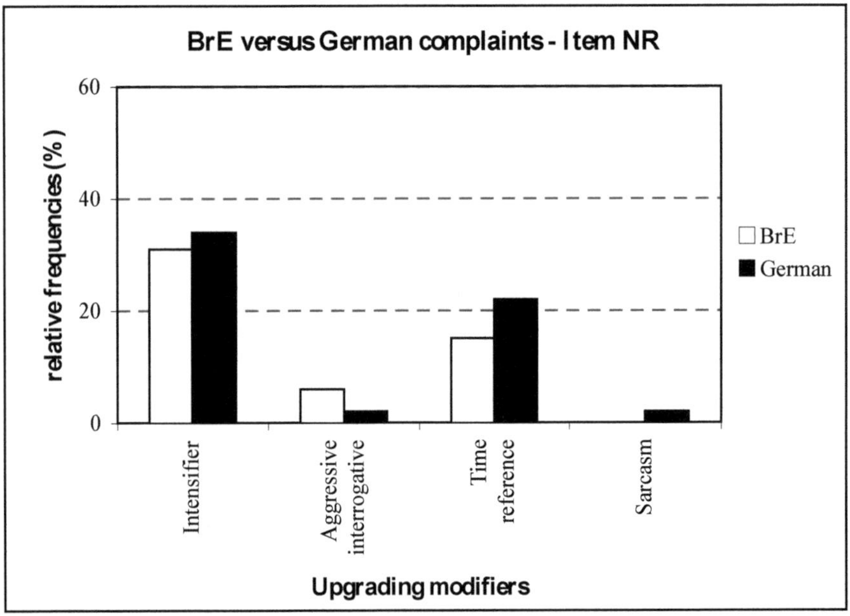

Regarding the use of upgrading modification, Table 6.5 and Figure 6.5 demonstrate that there are no significant differences in the use of upgrading modifiers between the British English and German data set *Item NR.* Specifically, the *intensifier* is the most frequently used upgrading modifier in both the British English and German complaints, followed by the *time reference*. Both types of upgrading modifiers are thereby more often employed by German traders but, as mentioned, without significant differences. The *aggressive interrogative* is, on the other hand, slightly more common in the British English complaints and *sarcasm* only occurs in the German data set, yet only very rarely.

Table 6.6: BrE and German eBay traders' use of downgrading modifiers in their complaints in the data set *Item NR*.

Data set: *Item NR* Downgrading modifiers	**BrE complaints relative frequencies (%)**	**German complaints relative frequencies (%)**	**Significance (p)**
Expression of regret	**0**	**5**	**0.025***
Play down	1	0	0.320
Understater	1	0	0.320
Politeness marker	1	0	0.320
Disarmer	0	3	0.083
Intensifier (downgrading)	0	0	

Figure 6.6: Graphic representation of BrE and German eBay traders' use of upgrading modifiers in their complaints in the data set *Item NR*.

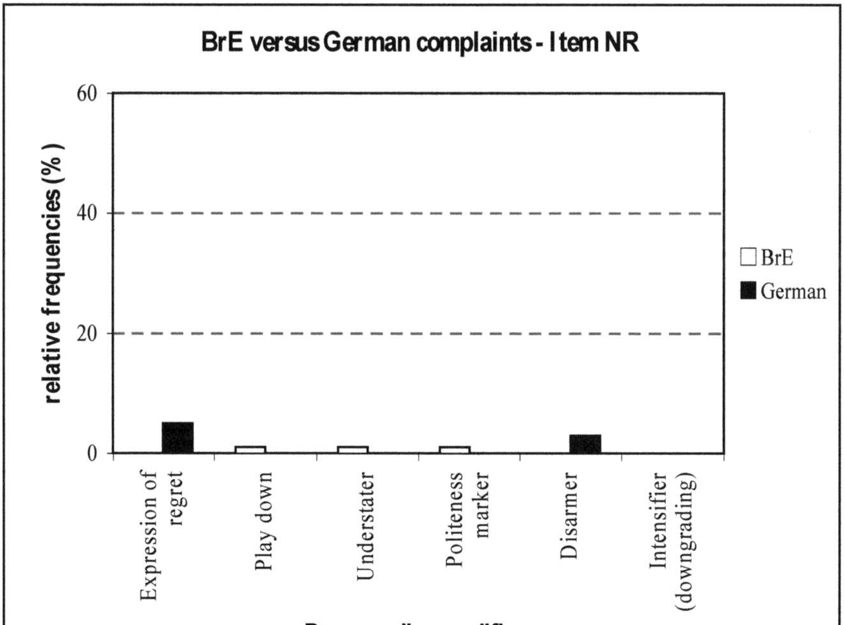

Abbreviation: Intensifier (downgrading) = Intensifier used to aggravate the mitigating effect of downgrading modifiers.

As far as the use of downgrading modifiers is concerned, Table 6.6 and Figure 6.6 show that these modifiers can only rarely be observed in the British English and German data set. While the British English traders employ the *play down, understater* and *politeness marker*, the Germans use *expressions of regret* and *disarmer*. With regard to the use of *expressions of regret*, a significant difference is found (p = 0.025*, see Table 6.6). However, in light of the infrequent use of this downgrading modifier, this result is not expressive. A simultaneous use of up- and downgrading modifiers, i.e. *intensifier which are used to aggravate the softening effect of downgrading devices*, cannot be found at all.

Turning to the use of pronouns, Table 6.7 and Figure 6.7 illustrate their occurrence in the British English and German data set *Item NR*.

Table 6.7: BrE and German eBay traders' use of pronouns in the complaints in the data set *Item NR*.

Data set: *Item NR* Use of pronouns	**BrE complaints relative frequencies (%)**	**German complaints relative frequencies (%)**	**Significance (p)**
First person pronouns	**35**	**15**	**0.001****
Second person pronouns	**4**	**0**	**0.045***
Third person pronouns	5	1	0.099
Demonstrative pronouns	9	3	0.075
Pronouns (complainee)	**16**	**4**	**0.004****
Pronouns (eBay community)	3	1	0.255
Indefinite pronouns	2	2	1.000

Figure 6.7: Graphic representation of BrE and German eBay traders' use of pronouns in the complaints in the data set *Item NR*.

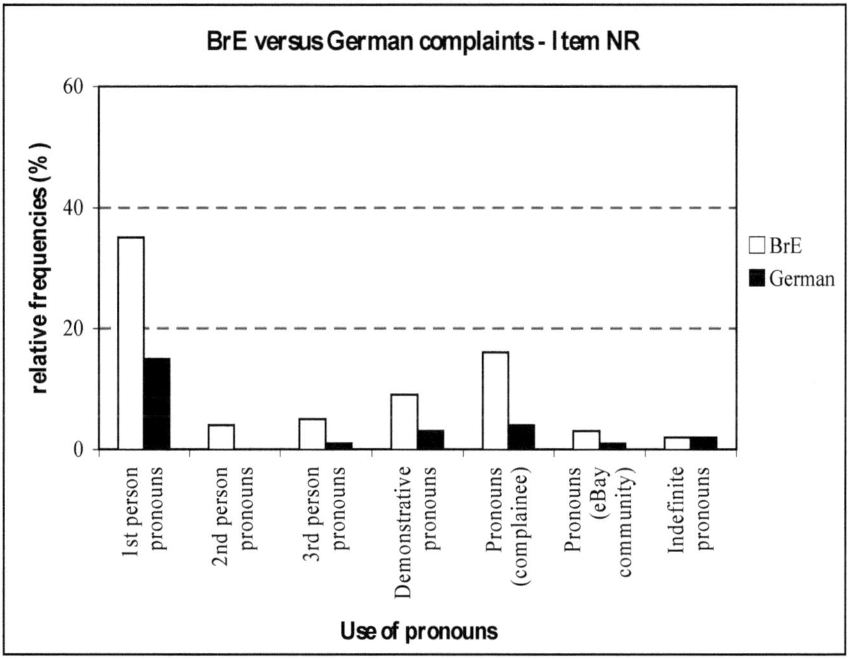

Abbreviations:
Demonstrative pronouns = Demonstrative pronouns followed by nouns denoting the complainee,
Pronouns (complainee) = Pronouns referring to the complainee,
Pronouns (eBay community) = Pronouns addressing the eBay community.

Table 6.7 and Figure 6.7 reveal that the use of pronouns is on the whole more common in the British English complaints. The category of pronouns which is most frequently employed by both the British English and German traders, is the category of *first person pronouns*. Despite this similarity, these pronouns are significantly more often used by British English speakers, whereby p reveals a highly significant difference (p = 0.001**, see Table 6.7). In addition to that, the British English traders show a tendency to use the *second person pronouns*, *third person pronouns* and *demonstrative pronouns followed by nouns denoting the complainee* more often. Yet, only the comparison of the British English and German data set with regard to the use of *second person pronouns* shows a significant difference (p = 0.045*, see Table 6.7), while the differences in use of *third person pronouns* and *demonstrative pronouns followed by nouns denoting the complainee* are less severe. On the whole though, the British English eBay members use significantly more often *pronouns referring to the complainee*, whereby p even reveals a highly significant difference between both data sets (p = 0.004**, see Table 6.7). In light of these findings, it can hence be said that in the data set *Item NR* the British English speakers do not only significantly more often stress their personal involvement by the use of pronouns but also the complainee's guilt in the state of affairs.

As far as the remaining categories of pronouns are concerned, i.e. the *pronouns addressing the eBay community* and *indefinite pronouns*, Table 6.7 and Figure 6.7 reveal that they occur only rarely in both data sets and also to an almost similar extent.

What follows is a presentation of the British English and German traders' use of features of CMC in their online complaints in the data set *Item NR*.

Table 6.8: BrE and German eBay traders' use of features of CMC in the complaints in the data set *Item NR*.

Data set: *Item NR* Use of features of CMC	**BrE complaints relative frequencies (%)**	**German complaints relative frequencies (%)**	**Significance (p)**
Emoticons	0	1	0.320
Visual signs	0	0	
Capitalisation (words)	4	10	0.098
Capitalisation (message)	11	7	0.325
Ex. m. (single)	**5**	**22**	**0.000321****
Ex. m. (repeated)	**15**	**41**	**0.000015****
Repet. other punct. m.	4	1	0.176
Repet. letters	0	0	
Intensifying features CMC (downgrading)	1	1	1.000

Figure 6.8: Graphic representation of BrE and German eBay traders' use of features of CMC in the complaints in the data set *Item NR*.

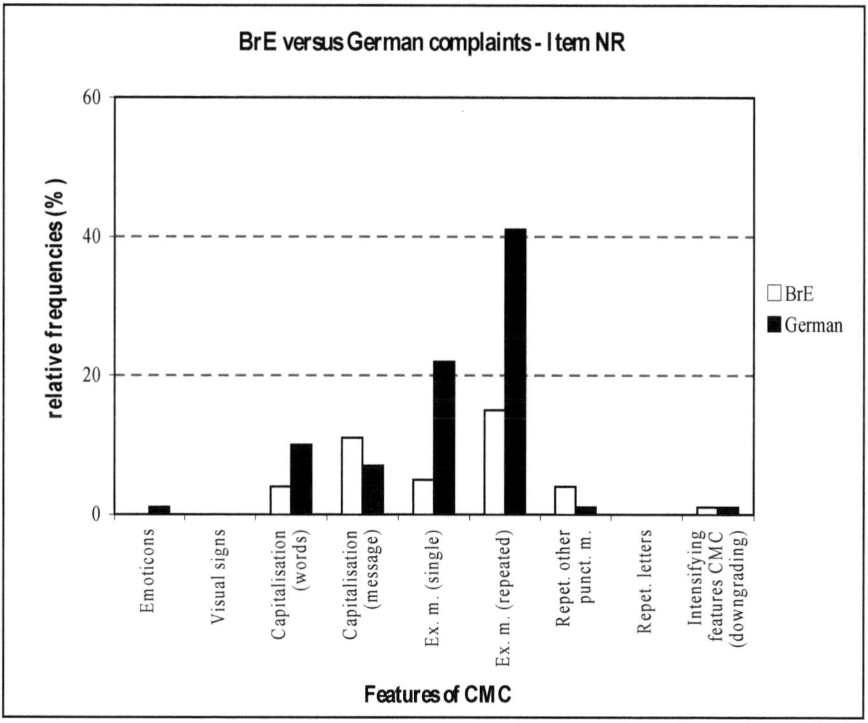

Abbreviations:
Capitalisation (words) = Capitalisation of words,
Capitalisation (message) = Capitalisation of the whole message,
Ex.m. (single) = Single exclamation marks,
Ex.m. (repeated) = Repetition of exclamation marks,
Repet. other punct. m. = Repetition of punctuation marks other than exclamation marks,
Intensifying features CMC (downgrading) = Intensifying features of CMC used to aggravate the softening effect of downgrading modifiers.

As Table 6.8 and Figure 6.8 demonstrate, *emoticons* occur only once in the German data set and *visual signs* cannot be found at all. With regard to the use of capitalisation, Table 6.8 and Figure 6.8 further reveal that *capitalisation of words* occurs more frequently in the German and *capitalisation of the whole message* more often in the British English data set, however, without significant differences.

Vast differences can, on the other hand, be found with regard to the use of exclamation marks: the Germans do not only use *single exclamation marks* but also *repeated ones* significantly more often than their British English counterparts, whereby p shows in both cases highly significant differences (*single exclamation marks* p = 0.000321**, *repetition of exclamation marks* p = 0.000015**, see Table 6.8).

Other types of punctuation marks are only rarely repeated by both British English and German traders, and the *repetition of letters* cannot be found at all. The last category, the use of *intensifying features of CMC which are used to aggravate the softening effect of downgrading modifiers,* occurs only once in each data set.

Finally, the results of the use of sum variables in the data set *Item NR* are presented (see Table 6.9 and Figure 6.9).

Table 6.9: The results of the sum variables in the BrE and German data set *Item NR.*

Data set: *Item NR* Sum variables	**BrE complaints relative frequencies (%)**	**German complaints relative frequencies (%)**	**Significance (p)**
Total use of mitigating features	4	10	0.439
Total use of intensifying features	**71**	**89**	**0.000072****

Figure 6.9: Graphic representation of the results of the sum variables in the BrE and German data set *Item NR.*

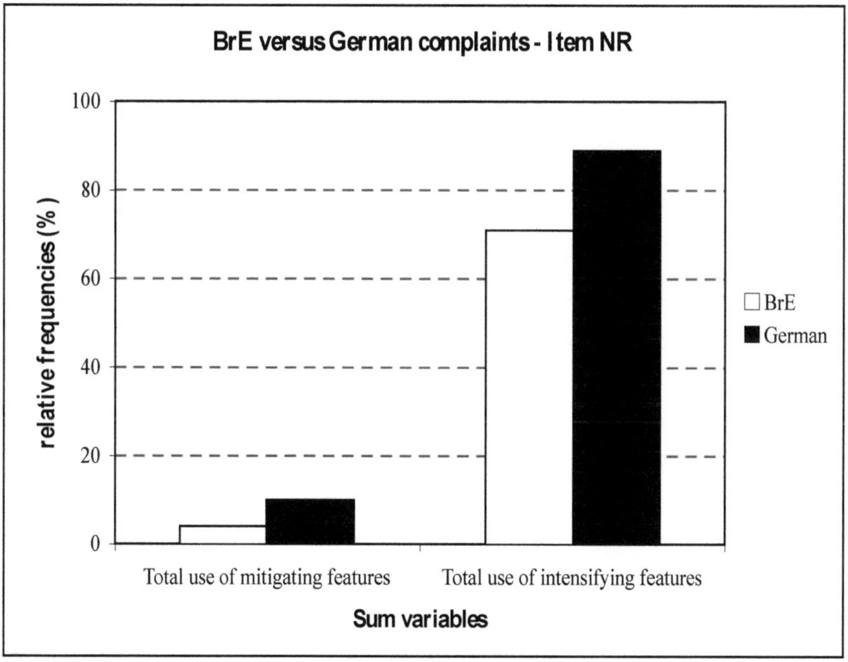

Table 6.9 and Figure 6.9 show that both the British English and German traders use by far less *mitigating features* than *intensifying features* in their online complaints in the data set *Item NR.* Furthermore, the Germans use slightly more *mitigating features*. At the same time though, they employ significantly more often *intensifying features*, whereby p even reveals a highly significant difference between the British English and German data set ($p = 0.0000072^{**}$, see Table 6.9).

6.1.2. Data set: The item was different than expected

Having outlined the results of the comparison between the British English and German data set *Item NR*, this subchapter deals with the results of the comparison of the British English and German data set *Item was different than expected (Item DIFF)*. It again begins with the findings concerning the use of complaint strategies, level of directness, and amount of strategy combinations (see Table 6.10 and Figure 6.10).

Table 6.10: British English (BrE) and German traders' use of complaint strategies, level of directness, and amount of strategy combinations in the data set *Item DIFF*.

Data set: *Item DIFF* **Complaint strategies**	**BrE complaints relative frequencies (%)**	**German complaints relative frequencies (%)**	**Significance (p)**
Expression of disappointment	13	8	0.703
Expression of anger or annoyance	2	3	0.653
Explicit complaint	100	99	0.320
Negative judgement	6	12	0.111
Drawing one's own conclusion	1	5	0.099
Warning others	13	11	0.854
Threat	1	2	0.563
Insult	5	3	0.473
Level of directness			0.721
Strategy combination	35	37	0.770

Figure 6.10: Graphic representation of BrE and German eBay traders' use of complaint strategies and combinations of them in the data set *Item DIFF*.

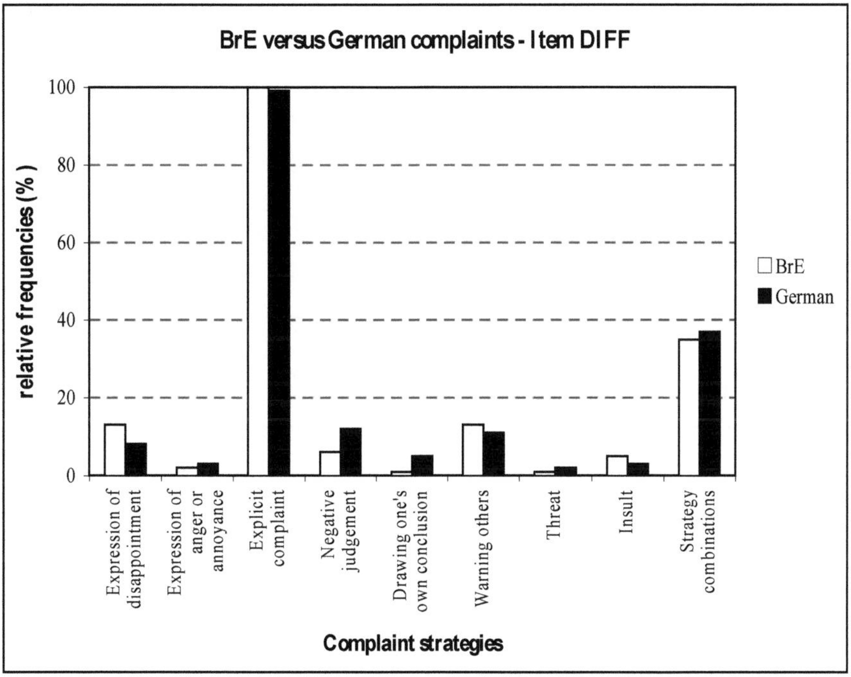

Table 6.10 and Figure 6.10 reveal that, as in the data set *Item NR*, the British English and the German speakers use the same range of complaint strategies, whereby the strategy *explicit complaint* is again by far the most frequently employed strategy in both the British English and German data set *Item DIFF*. In contrast to the results of the data set *Item NR* though, all different types of complaint strategies are used to an almost similar extent by both the British English and German eBay traders. Thus, no significant differences in this respect can be found. As a consequence, also the statistical comparison of the *level of directness* used in the British English and German complaints in the data set *Item DIFF* does not result in a significant difference. Furthermore, Table 6.10 and Figure 6.10 show that British English and German eBay traders also employ *combinations of strategies* to an almost similar extent.

The following Table 6.11 and Figure 6.11 display the amount of strategies British English and German eBay traders use in the data set *Item DIFF*.

Table 6.11: The amount of strategies BrE and German eBay traders use to formulate their complaints in the data set *Item DIFF*.

Data set: *Item DIFF* Amount of strategies per complaint	**BrE complaints relative frequencies (%)**	**German complaints relative frequencies (%)**	**Significance (p)**
Use of one strategy	65	63	0.770
Use of a combination of two strategies	30	26	0.531
Use of a combination of three strategies	4	10	0.098
Use of a combination of four strategies	0	1	0.320
Use of a combination of five strategies	1	0	0.320

Figure 6.11: Graphic representation of the amount of strategies BrE and German traders use to formulate their complaints in the data set *Item DIFF*.

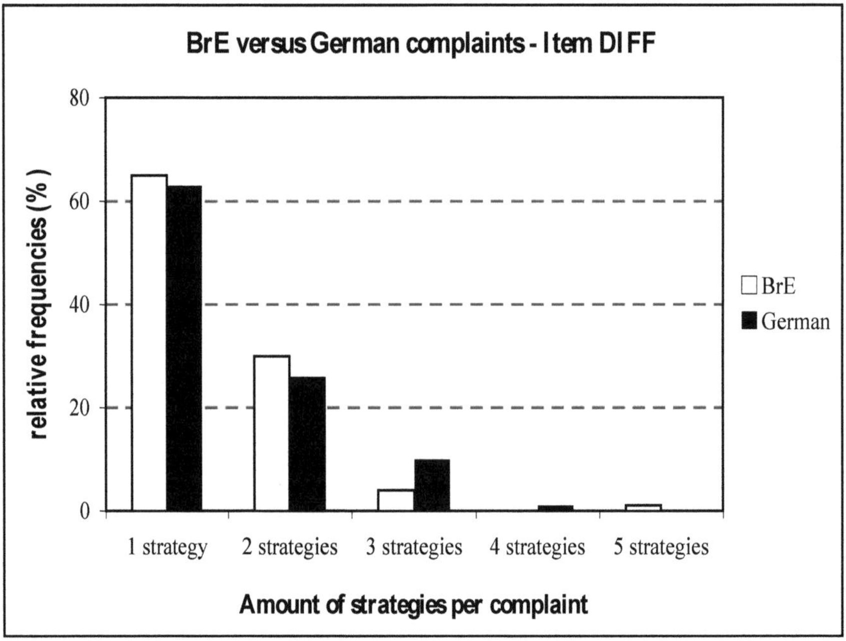

Table 6.11 and Figure 6.11 reveal that, similar to the data set *Item NR*, the complaints in the data set *Item DIFF* are minimally made up of one and maximally of five strategies. Again the use of one strategy is most common to formulate the British English and German online complaint. A combination of

four strategies occurs only in the German, a combination of five strategies only in the British English data set, in both cases, however, just once.

The following Table 6.12 and Figure 6.12 illustrate the use of strategy sequences British English or German eBay traders use in at least 5% of the complaints in the data set *Item DIFF*.

Table 6.12: The strategy sequences BrE or German eBay traders use in at least 5% of the complaints in the data set *Item DIFF*.

Data set: *Item DIFF* **Strategy sequences (minimum 5%)**	**BrE complaints relative frequencies (%)**	**German complaints relative frequencies (%)**	**Significance (p)**
Explicit complaint	65	62	0.661
Explicit complaint/ expression of disappointment	7	4	0.355
Explicit complaint/ warning others	7	4	0.355
Explicit complaint/ negative judgement	4	6	0.519

Figure 6.12: Graphic representation of the strategy sequences BrE or German eBay traders use in at least 5% of the complaints in the data set *Item DIFF*.

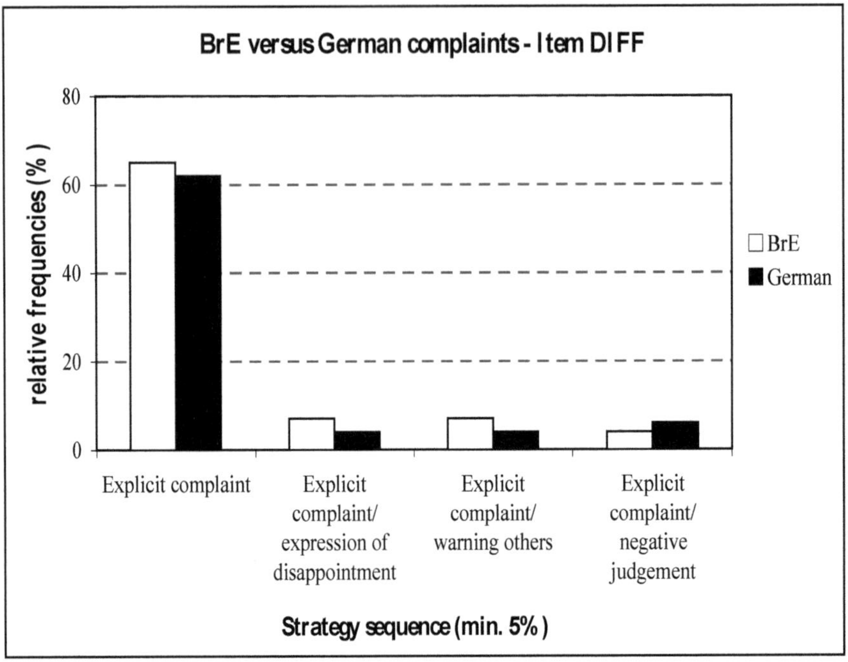

Table 6.12 and Figure 6.12 again demonstrate the dominance of the use of one strategy to formulate one's online complaint in the data set *Item DIFF*. As it is the case in the data set *Item NR*, this strategy is in almost all cases an *explicit complaint*. The prototypical complaint British English and German eBay traders thus formulate if the item was different than expected is once more a complaint consisting of one strategy which is an *explicit complaint*. Table 6.12 and Figure 6.12 further show that the use of a combination of two strategies is more diverse in that the strategy *explicit complaint* is combined with different types of strategies including, among others, the ones displayed in Table 6.12 and Figure 6.12, i.e. *expression of disappointment, warning others*, and *negative judgement*. What follows are the results of the amount of different strategy sequences British English and German eBay members employ in the complaints in the data set *Item DIFF* (see Table 6.13 and Figure 6.13).

Table 6.13: The amount of different strategy sequences BrE and German eBay traders use to formulate their complaints in the data set *Item DIFF*.

Data set: *Item DIFF*	**BrE complaints absolute frequencies**	**German complaints absolute frequencies**	**Significance (p)**
Amount of different strategy sequences	16	21	0.411

Figure 6.13: Graphic representation of the amount of different strategy sequences BrE and German eBay traders use to formulate their complaints in the data set *Item DIFF*.

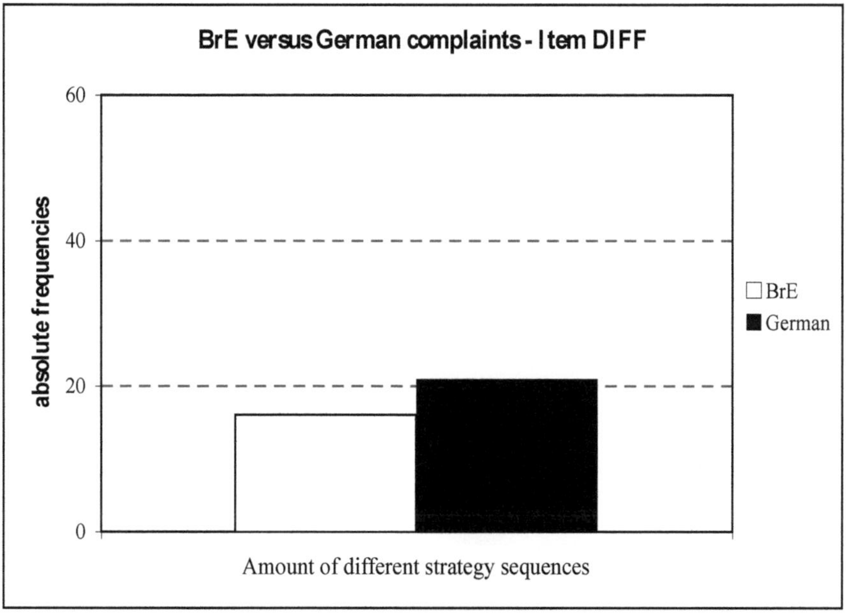

With regard to the amount of different strategy sequences, Table 6.13 and Figure 6.13 present that, as in the data set *Item NR*, the German traders show a tendency to use more different strategy sequences than their British English counterparts. This tendency is, however, even weaker than in the data set *Item NR*, and hence also does not result in any significant difference between the British English and German data set *Item DIFF*.

Turning to the results of the use of modification in the British English and German complaints in the data set *Item DIFF*, the following Table 6.14 and Figure 6.14 display the results of the use of upgrading modifiers.

Table 6.14: BrE and German eBay traders' use of upgrading modifiers in their complaints in the data set *Item DIFF*.

Data set: *Item DIFF* Upgrading modifiers	**BrE complaints relative frequencies (%)**	**German complaints relative frequencies (%)**	**Significance (p)**
Intensifier	28	25	0.712
Aggressive interrogative	3	3	0.737
Time reference	0	1	0.320
Sarcasm	0	1	0.320

Figure 6.14: Graphic representation of BrE and German eBay traders' use of upgrading modifiers in their complaints in the data set *Item DIFF*.

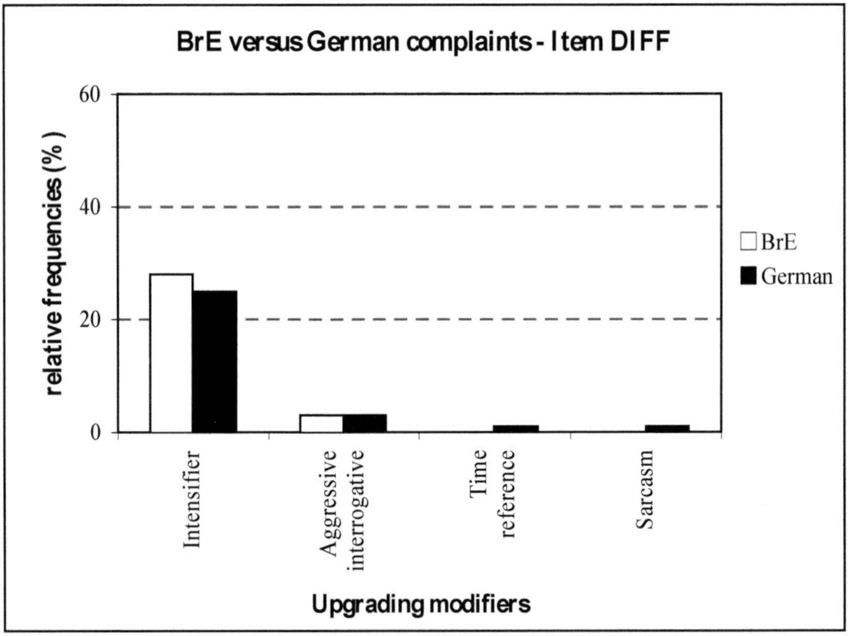

Similar to the results of the data set *Item NR*, Table 6.14 and Figure 6.14 also reveal for the data set *Item DIFF* that there are no significant differences in the use of upgrading modifiers between the British English and German data set. Furthermore, the *intensifier* is again the most frequently employed upgrading modifier in both data sets under investigation. All other types of upgrading modifiers are, however, only rarely employed, the *time reference* and *sarcasm* even only once by the Germans.

Shifting the focus to the use of downgrading modifiers the results are presented in Table 6.15 and Figure 6.16 below.

Table 6.15: BrE and German eBay traders' use of downgrading modifiers in their complaints in the data set *Item DIFF*.

Data set: *Item DIFF* Downgrading modifiers	**BrE complaints relative frequencies (%)**	**German complaints relative frequencies (%)**	**Significance (p)**
Expression of regret	**0**	**5**	**0.025***
Play down	2	4	0.410
Understater	0	0	
Politeness marker	1	0	0.320
Disarmer	8	8	0.813
Intensifier (downgrading)	0	1	0.320

Figure 6.15: Graphic representation of BrE and German eBay traders' use of upgrading modifiers in their complaints in the data set *Item DIFF*.

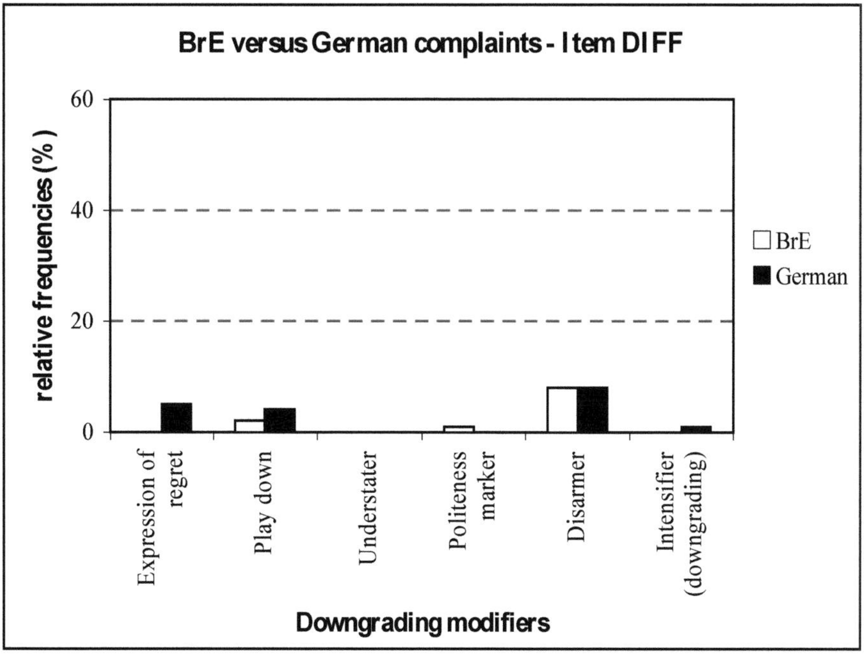

Regarding the use of downgrading modifiers, Table 6.15 and Figure 6.15 reveal that also in the data set *Item DIFF* these modifiers are only rarely used by both the British English and German eBay traders. Only the *disarmer* and *play down* can be found in both data sets. All other types of downgrading modifiers occur either in the British English or German data set. Specifically, *politeness marker* are only present in the British English and the *expression of regret* and *intensifier used to aggravate the mitigating effect of downgrading modifiers* only in the German complaints. With regard to the use of *expressions of regret* a significant difference between the British English and German data set *Item DIFF* is present (p = 0.025*, see Table 6.15). However, in the light of their infrequent occurrence, this result is not expressive.

The following Table 6.16 and Figure 6.16 display the British English and German eBay traders' use of pronouns in the data set *Item DIFF*.

Table 6.16: BrE and German eBay traders' use of pronouns in the complaints in the data set *Item DIFF*.

Data set: *Item DIFF* Use of pronouns	**BrE complaints relative frequencies (%)**	**German complaints relative frequencies (%)**	**Significance (p)**
First person pronouns	**20**	**5**	**0.001****
Second person pronouns	3	0	0.103
Third person pronouns	1	0	0.320
Demonstrative pronouns	2	1	0.414
Pronouns (complainee)	**6**	**1**	**0.050***
Pronouns (eBay community)	1	0	0.320
Indefinite pronouns	1	1	1.000

Figure 6.16: Graphic representation of BrE and German eBay traders' use of pronouns in the complaints in the data set *Item DIFF*.

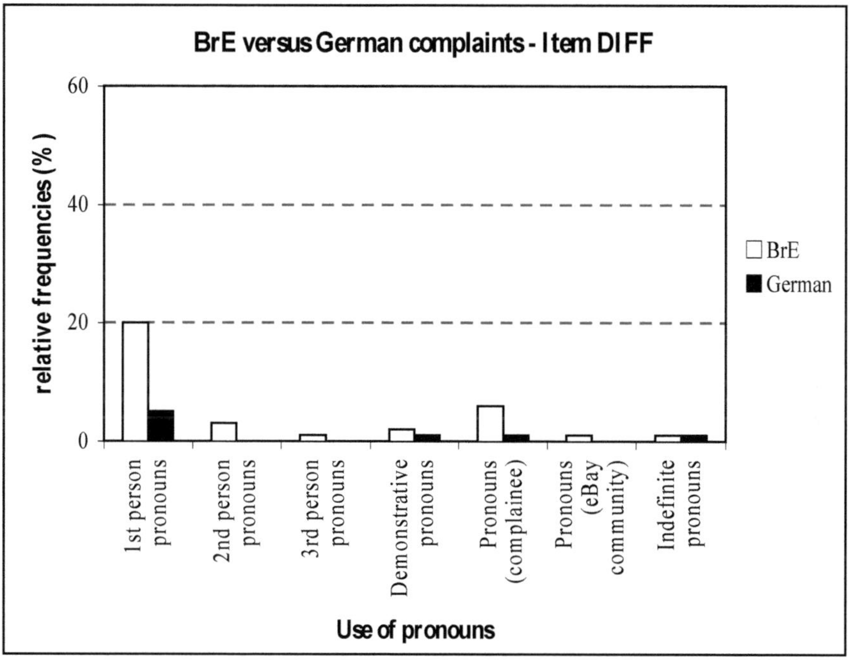

Table 6.16 and Figure 6.16 demonstrate that pronouns, as in the data set *Item NR*, are more frequently employed by the British English traders, who particularly favour the use of the *first person pronouns*, which they also employ significantly more often than their German counterparts. The value of p thereby even reveals a highly significant difference (p = 0.001**, see Table 6.16). All other types of pronouns are only rarely employed. Nevertheless, the comparison of the British English and German data set with regard to the use of *pronouns referring to the complainee* shows a significant difference (p = 0.050*, see Table 6.16) in that these pronouns are significantly more often employed by the British English traders. Given the overall infrequent occurrence of these pronouns, this finding is not very expressive. Yet, it points at the stronger tendency of British English speakers to use these types of pronouns to stress the complainee's guilt in the state of affairs.

Turning to the features of CMC, Table 6.17 and Figure 6.17 display the results.

Table 6.17: BrE and German eBay traders' use of features of CMC in the complaints in the data set *Item DIFF*.

Data set: *Item DIFF* **Use of features of CMC**	**BrE complaints relative frequencies (%)**	**German complaints relative frequencies (%)**	**Significance (p)**
Emoticons	1	1	1.000
Visual signs	1	0	0.320
Capitalisation (words)	11	6	0.207
Capitalisation (message)	5	3	0.473
Ex.m. (single)	16	22	0.236
Ex.m. (repeated)	**8**	**23**	**0.003****
Repet. other punct. m.	0	1	0.320
Repet. letters	0	0	
Intensifying features CMC (downgrading)	1	0	0.320

Figure 6.17: Graphic representation of BrE and German eBay traders' use of features of CMC in the complaints in the data set *Item DIFF*.

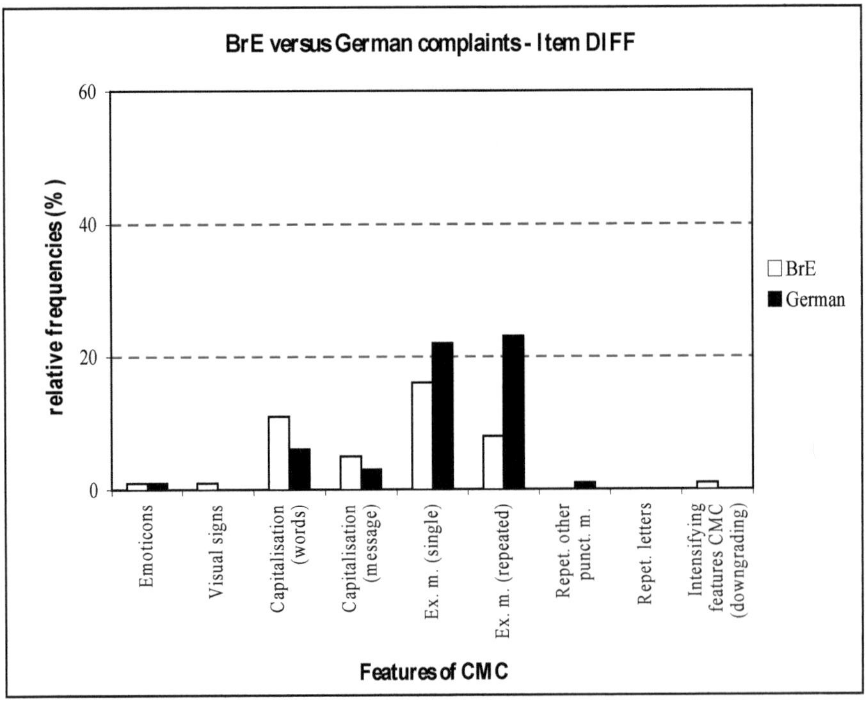

As Table 6.17 and Figure 6.17 show, *emoticons* and *visual signs* can again only rarely be traced. Furthermore, *capitalisation of words* and *capitalisation of the whole message* are more common in the British English complaints, however, without significant differences.

As far as the use of exclamation marks is concerned, once more differences between the British English and German data set become apparent. Specifically, the Germans use both *single* and *repeated exclamation marks* more often. Yet, only the *repetition of exclamation marks* is significantly more often employed, whereby p reveals a highly significant difference (p = 0.003**, see Table 6.7). With regard to the use of *single exclamation marks*, the differences are less striking and thus remain above the level of significance[38].

Table 6.17 and Figure 6.17 further illustrate that *punctuation marks other than exclamation marks* occur just once in the German complaints, while *letters* are not *repeated* at all. Last but not least, the *intensifying features of CMC which aggravate the mitigating effect of downgrading modifiers* can be traced just once in the British English complaints.

Finally, the results of the use of sum variables in the British English and German data set *Item DIFF* are illustrated in Table 6.18 and Figure 6.18.

Table 6.18: The results of the sum variables in the BrE and German data set *Item DIFF*.

Data set: *Item DIFF* **Sum variables**	**BrE complaints relative frequencies (%)**	**German complaints relative frequencies (%)**	**Significance (p)**
Total use of mitigating features	12	17	0.429
Total use of intensifying features	56	66	0.161

[38] The expression "above the level of significance" means that p > 0.05, and thus alpha > 5%.

Figure 6.18: Graphic representation of the results of the sum variables in the BrE and German data set *Item DIFF*.

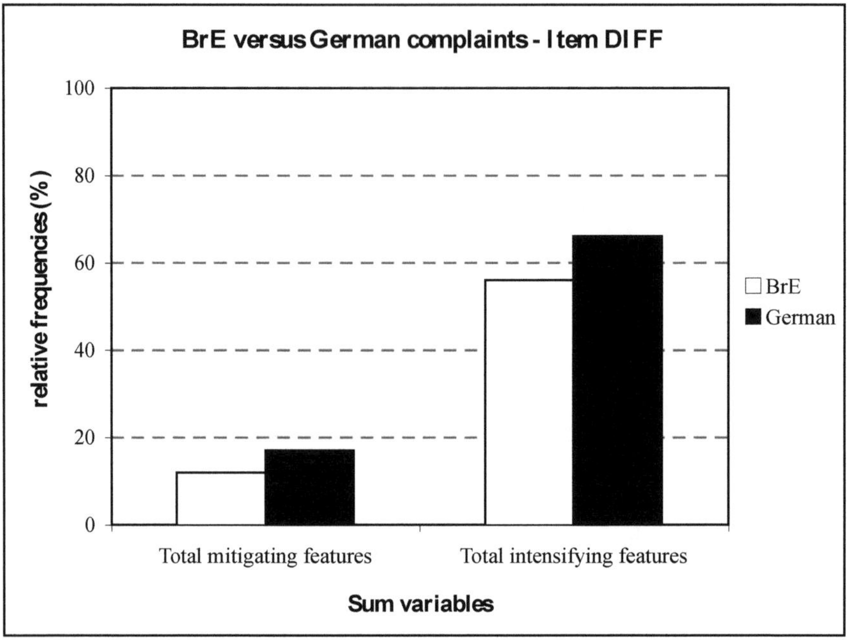

Similar to the results of the data set *Item NR*, both the British English and German traders use clearly less *mitigating features* than *intensifying features* in their complaints in the data set *Item DIFF* (see Table 6.18 and Figure 6.18). Furthermore, the Germans show a slight tendency to use more *mitigating* as well as *intensifying features* than the British English traders, yet without significant differences.

6.1.3. Data set: Item has not been received (double complaints)

In this subchapter the results of the statistical comparison of the British English and German data set *Item has not been received (double complaints) (Item NR-D)* are presented. As mentioned in 6.1., the received results are always illustrated in the same order. Therefore, it is first dealt with the results of the comparison of the British English and German eBay traders' use of complaint strategies, level of directness, and amount of strategy combinations (see Table 6.19 and Figure 6.19).

Table 6.19: British English (BrE) and German traders' use of complaint strategies, level of directness, and amount of strategy combinations in the data set *Item NR-D.*

Data set: *Item NR-D* Complaint strategies	**BrE complaints relative frequencies (%)**	**German complaints relative frequencies (%)**	**Significance (p)**
Expression of disappointment	7	4	0.355
Expression of anger or annoyance	1	1	1.000
Explicit complaint	100	100	
Negative judgement	10	13	0.328
Drawing one's own conclusion	2	6	0.126
Warning others	26	27	0.781
Threat	2	8	0.052
Insult	**14**	**3**	**0.005***
Level of directness			0.950
Strategy combination	54	55	0.888

Figure 6.19: Graphic representation of BrE and German eBay traders' use of complaint strategies and combinations of them in the data set *Item NR-D.*

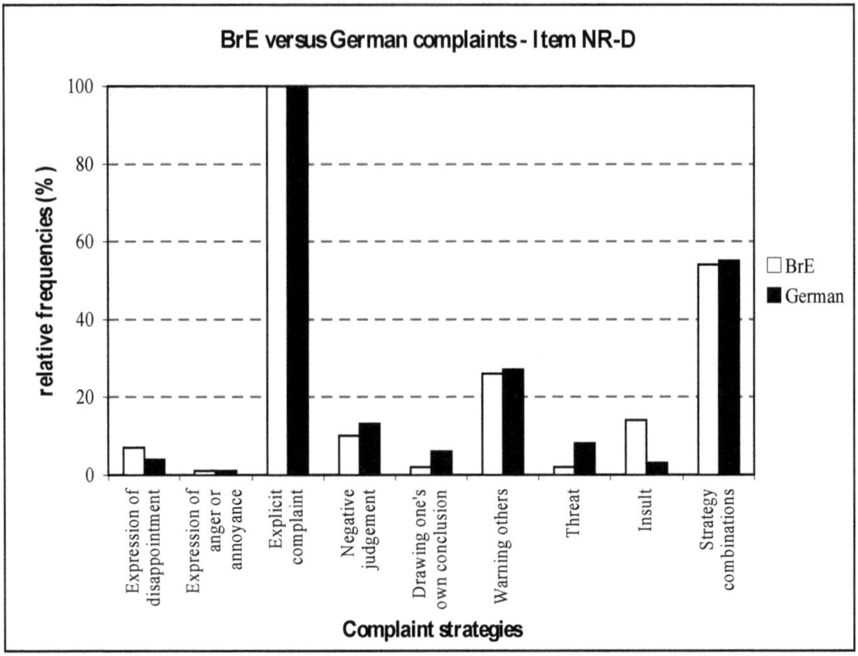

As Table 6.19 and Figure 6.19 reveal, the British English and German eBay traders again use the same range of complaint strategies, whereby the strategy *explicit complaint* is by far the most common strategy in both the British English and German data set *Item NR-D.* Regarding the frequency with which the different strategies are employed, it further becomes apparent that *insults* are significantly more often used by British English speakers, whereby p reveals a highly significant difference between the British English and German data set ($p = 0.005^{**}$, see Table 6.19). The Germans, on the other hand, show a tendency to use the strategies *drawing one's own conclusion* and *threat* to a larger extent, however, without significant differences. All other types of strategies as well as *combinations of them* are used to an almost similar extent. Regarding the *directness level* British English and German traders choose, no significant difference can be found.

The following Table 6.20 and Figure 6.20 display the amount of strategies British English and German eBay traders use to formulate their complaints in the data set *Item NR-D*.

Table 6.20: The amount of strategies BrE and German eBay traders use to formulate their complaints in the data set *Item NR-D*.

Data set: *Item NR-D* Amount of strategies per complaint	**BrE complaints relative frequencies (%)**	**German complaints relative frequencies (%)**	**Significance (p)**
Use of one strategy	46	45	0.888
Use of a combination of two strategies	46	42	0.571
Use of a combination of three strategies	**5**	**13**	**0.049***
Use of a combination of four strategies	3	0	0.083
Use of a combination of five strategies	0	0	

Figure 6.20: Graphic representation of the amount of strategies BrE and German traders use to formulate their complaints in the data set *Item NR-D*.

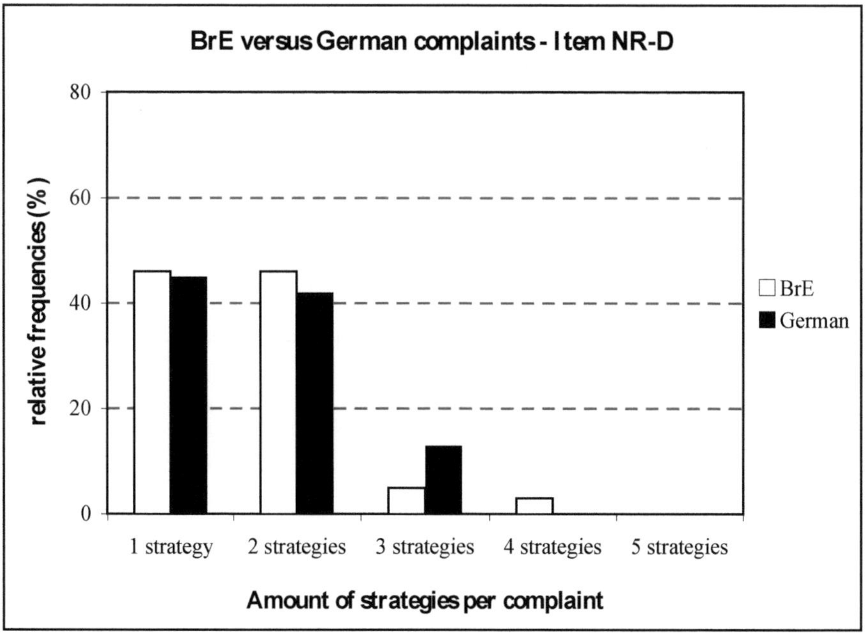

Table 6.20 and Figure 6.20 illustrate that the complaints in the data set *Item NR-D* are minimally made up of one and maximally of a combination of four strategies. In contrast to the results of the data set *Item NR* and *Item DIFF*, not only complaints consisting of one but also a combination of two strategies are most common in both the British English and German data set *Item NR-D*. With regard to the use of a combination of three strategies, this is significantly more often employed by German traders (p 0.049*, see Table 6.20), while a combination of four strategies is only present in the British English data set.

Turning to the strategy sequences British English and German eBay traders employ to formulate their complaints in the data set *Item NR-D*, the results are presented in Table 6.21 and Figure 6.21. Again the focus is thereby on those strategy sequences which either the British English or German traders use in at least 5% of the cases.

Table 6.21: The strategy sequences BrE or German eBay traders use in at least 5% of the complaints in the data set *Item NR-D*.

Data set: *Item NR-D* Strategy sequences (minimum 5%)	**BrE complaints relative frequencies (%)**	**German complaints relative frequencies (%)**	**Significance (p)**
Explicit complaint	46	45	0.888
Explicit complaint/ warning others	14	10	0.387
Explicit complaint/ negative judgement	7	7	1.000
Warning others/ explicit complaint	4	7	0.355
Explicit complaint/ insult	**6**	**1**	**0.050***
Explicit complaint/ threat	**0**	**6**	**0.014***

Figure 6.21: Graphic representation of the strategy sequences BrE or German eBay traders use in at least 5% of the complaints in the data set *Item NR-D*.

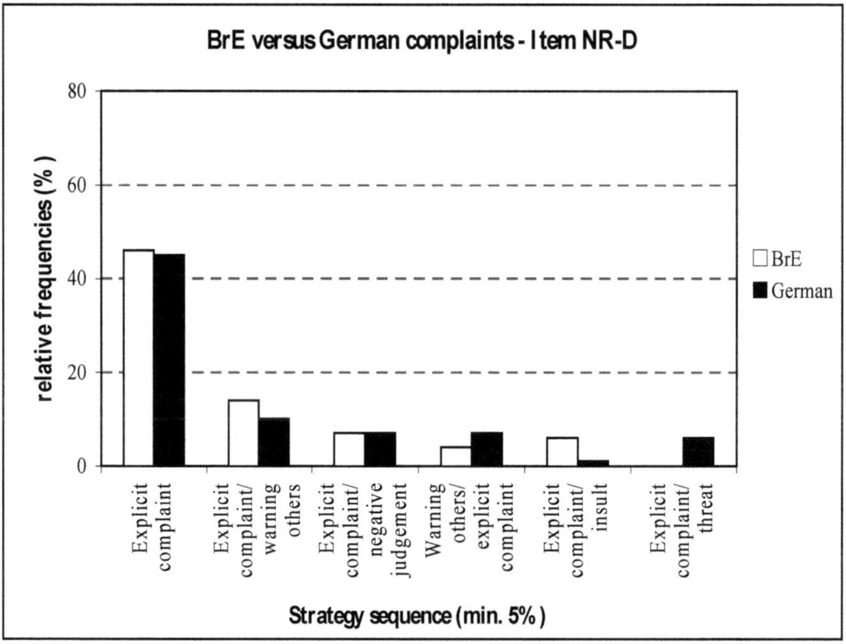

Table 6.21 and Figure 6.21 reveal that in cases where British English and German speakers use only one strategy to formulate their online complaint, they always choose the strategy *explicit complaint*. It hence becomes apparent that also in the data set *Item NR-D* the prototypical complaint British English and German eBay traders use is a complaint consisting of the strategy *explicit complaint*. The combinations of two strategies used within a complaint are more diverse, in that the strategy *explicit complaint* is combined with different types of strategies including, among others, the ones illustrated in Table 6.21 and Figure 6.21. These are the strategies *warning others, negative judgement, insult* or *threat*. As far as the combinations of the strategy *explicit complaint* and the strategy *threat* or *insult* are concerned, significant differences between the British English and German data set are obtained (*explicit complaint/insult* p = 0.050*, *explicit complaint/threat* p = 0.014*, see Table 6.21), which are, however, not expressive in light of their overall infrequent occurrence.

In the following Table 6.22 and Figure 6.22 the amount of different strategy sequences British English and German traders use in the data set *Item NR-D* are illustrated.

Table 6.22: The amount of different strategy sequences BrE and German eBay traders use to formulate their complaints in the data set *Item NR-D*.

Data set: *Item NR-D*	**BrE complaints absolute frequencies**	**German complaints absolute frequencies**	**Significance (p)**
Amount of different strategy sequences	20	21	0.876

Figure 6.22: Graphic representation of the amount of different strategy sequences BrE and German eBay traders use to formulate their complaints in the data set *Item NR-D*.

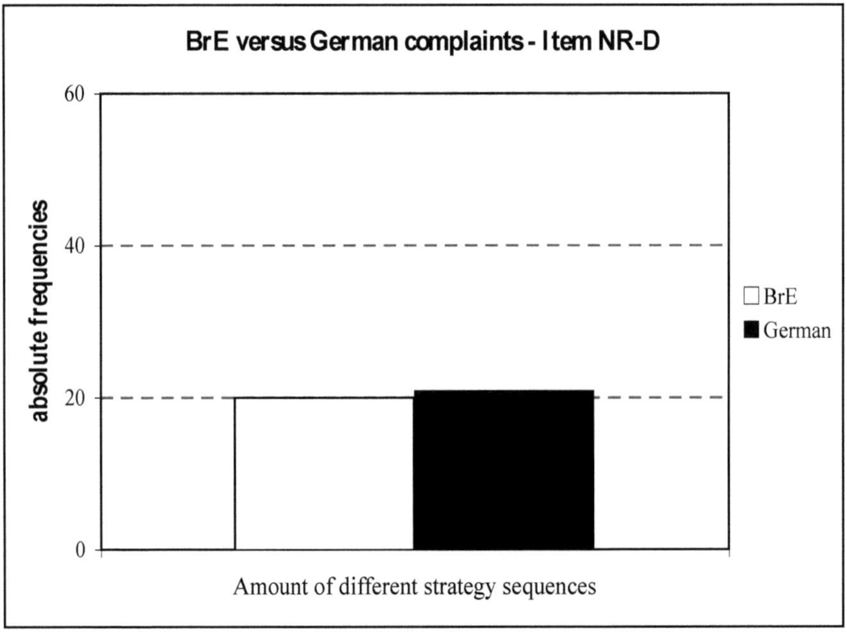

Table 6.22 and Figure 6.22 demonstrate that the British English and German eBay members use almost the same amount of strategy sequences in the data set *Item NR-D*. Thus, no significant difference is obtained.

Turning to the use of modification, the results of the use of upgrading modifiers are presented in Table 6.23 and Figure 6.23.

Table 6.23: BrE and German eBay traders' use of upgrading modifiers in their complaints in the data set *Item NR-D*.

Data set: *Item NR-D* Upgrading modifiers	**BrE complaints relative frequencies (%)**	**German complaints relative frequencies (%)**	**Significance (p)**
Intensifier	**45**	**30**	**0.033***
Aggressive interrogative	5	2	0.251
Time reference	23	20	0.632
Sarcasm	0	0	

Figure 6.23: Graphic representation of BrE and German eBay traders' use of upgrading modifiers in their complaints in the data set *Item NR-D*.

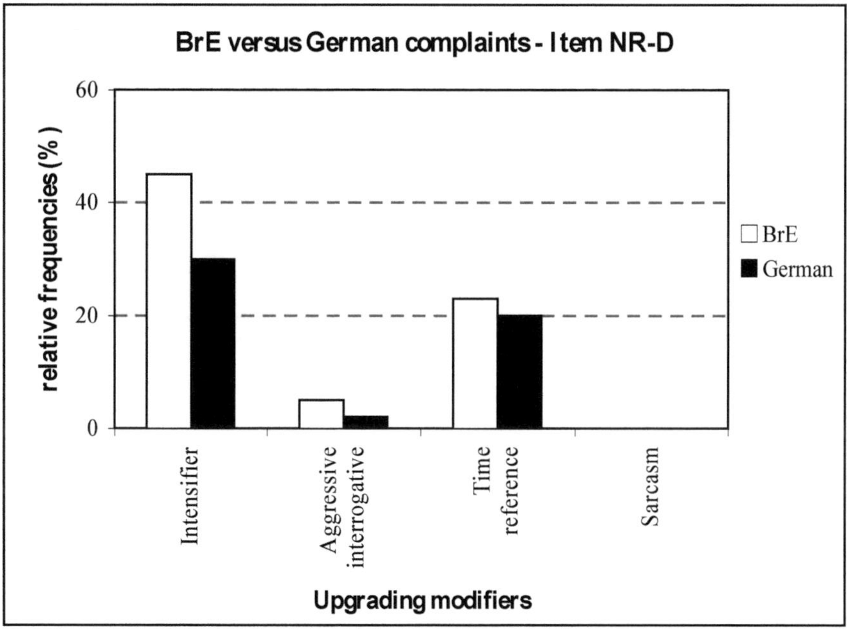

Table 6.23 and Figure 6.23 show that, similar to the results of the data sets *Item NR* and *Item DIFF*, the *intensifier* is the most frequently employed upgrading modifier in both the British English and German eBay data set *Item NR-D*. At the same time, Table 6.23 reveals that *intensifiers* are significantly more often employed by British English eBay members ($p = 0.033^*$, see Table 6.23). The use of *intensifiers* is followed by the employment of the *time reference*, whose frequent usage equals the findings of the data set *Item NR*. Last but not least, the

aggressive interrogative can only rarely be traced in the British English and German complaints and *sarcasm* is not present at all.

What follows are the results of the use of downgrading modifiers (see Table 6.24 and Figure 6.24).

Table 6.24: BrE and German eBay traders' use of downgrading modifiers in their complaints in the data set *Item NR-D*.

Data set: *Item NR-D* Downgrading modifiers	**BrE complaints relative frequencies (%)**	**German complaints relative frequencies (%)**	**Significance (p)**
Expression of regret	1	2	0.563
Play down	3	0	0.083
Understater	0	0	
Politeness marker	1	1	1.000
Disarmer	2	1	0.563
Intensifier (downgrading)	1	0	0.320

Figure 6.24: Graphic representation of BrE and German eBay traders' use of upgrading modifiers in their complaints in the data set *Item NR-D*.

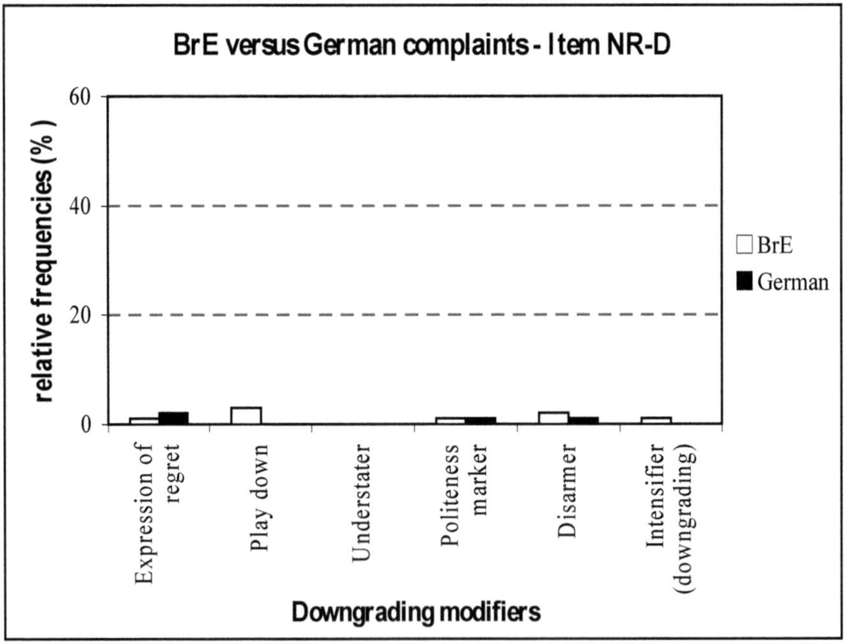

As far as the use of downgrading modification is concerned, Table 6.24 and Figure 6.24 illustrate that, similar to the findings of the data sets *Item NR* and *Item DIFF*, these modifiers occur only rarely in the British English and German data set. While the *expression of regret*, *politeness marker* and *disarmer* can be found in both the British and German complaints, the *play down* and *intensifiers used to aggravate the mitigating effect of downgrading modifiers* are only present in the British English data set. Last but not least, the *understater* does not occur at all.

The following Table 6.25 und Figure 6.25 display British English and German eBay traders' use of pronouns in the data set *Item NR-D*.

Table 6.25: BrE and German eBay traders' use of pronouns in the complaints in the data set *Item NR-D*.

Data set: *Item NR-D* Use of pronouns	**BrE complaints relative frequencies (%)**	**German complaints relative frequencies (%)**	**Significance (p)**
First person pronouns	**29**	**5**	**0.000021****
Second person pronouns	1	0	0.320
Third person pronouns	**11**	**0**	**0.001****
Demonstrative pronouns	**7**	**0**	**0.008****
Pronouns (complainee)	**18**	**0**	**0.0000023****
Pronouns (other eBay members)	2	0	0.181
Indefinite pronouns	0	0	

Figure 6.25: Graphic representation of BrE and German eBay traders' use of pronouns in the complaints in the data set *Item NR-D*.

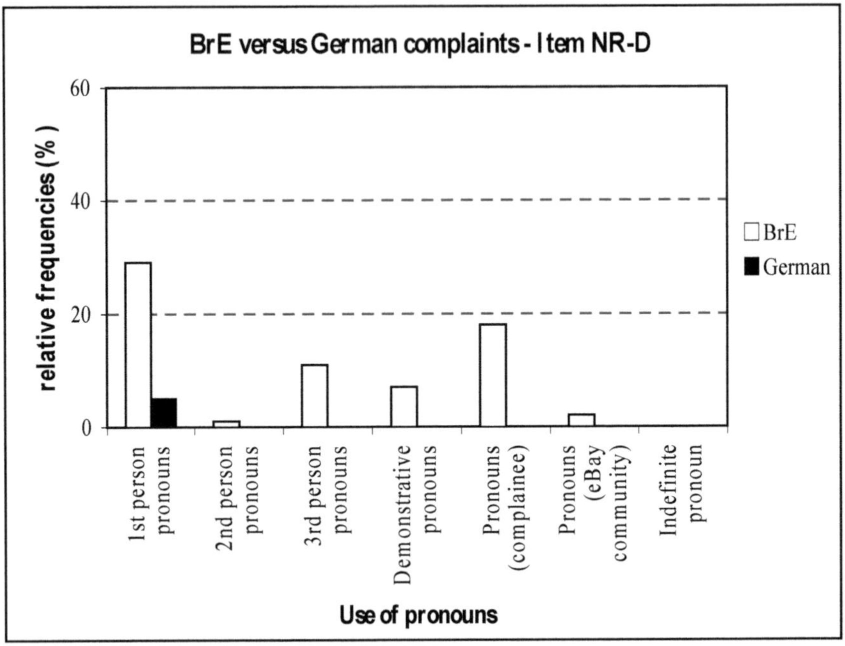

As becomes obvious from Table 6.25 and Figure 6.25, pronouns are again more common in the British English than in the German complaints, this time even very clearly. The only types of pronouns the Germans employ are the *first person pronouns* which are again particularly favoured by the British English traders, who use them significantly more often than their German counterparts. The value of p thereby again reveals a highly significant difference between the British English and German data set (p = 0.000021**, see Table 6.25).

At the same time, the British English traders also employ the *third person pronouns* as well as the *demonstrative pronouns followed by nouns denoting the complainee* significantly more often than the German speakers who do not use them at all. The value of p again reveals a highly significant difference with regard to both categories of pronouns (*third person pronouns* p = 0.001**, *demonstrative pronouns* p = 0.008**, see Table 6.25). Based on these findings, the British English eBay members certainly also use *pronouns which refer to the complainee* significantly more often, whereby p shows a highly significant

difference which is even more severe (p = 0.0000023**, see Table 6.25). In light of these findings it can hence be said that, as in the data set *Item NR*, also in the data set *Item NR-D* the British English traders do not only significantly more often stress their personal involvement by the use of pronouns, but also the complainee's guilt as far as the offensive act is concerned.
With regard to the two remaining categories of pronouns, Table 6.25 and Figure 6.25 further reveal that the *pronouns addressing the eBay community* occur just twice in the British English data set while the *indefinite pronouns* are not employed at all.
Turning to the use of features of CMC, Table 6.26 and Figure 6.26 demonstrate the results of the data set *Item NR-D*.

Table 6.26: BrE and German eBay traders' use of features of CMC in the complaints in the data set *Item NR-D*.

Data set: *Item NR-D* Use of features of CMC	**BrE complaints relative frequencies (%)**	**German complaints relative frequencies (%)**	**Significance (p)**
Emoticons	1	1	1.000
Visual signs	1	0	0.320
Capitalisation (words)	14	10	0.387
Capitalisation (message)	14	9	0.270
Ex.m. (single)	**11**	**26**	**0.004***
Ex.m. (repeated)	**15**	**39**	**0.000055****
Repet. other punct. m.	2	1	1.000
Repet. letters	0	1	0.320
Intensifying features CMC (downgrading)	0	0	

Figure 6.26: Graphic representation of BrE and German eBay traders' use of features of CMC in the complaints in the data set *Item NR-D*.

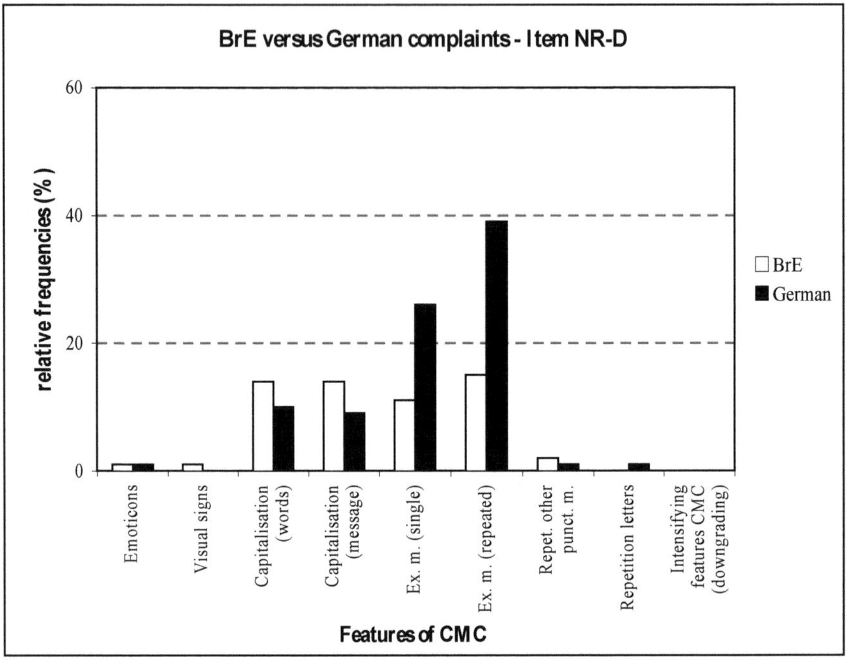

As Table 6.26 and Figure 6.26 reveal, *emoticons* and *visual signs* again occur extremely rarely in both the British English and German data set. Furthermore, as in the data set *Item DIFF*, the British English traders show a tendency to use the *capitalisation of words* and *capitalisation of the whole message* more often than their German counterparts, however, without significant differences.

The *use of exclamation marks* reveals, on the other hand, once more vast differences between the British English and German complaints. As in the data set *Item NR*, *single* and *repeated exclamation marks* are significantly more often used by German traders, whereby p shows highly significant differences with regard to both features (*single exclamation marks* p = 0.004**, *repetition of exclamation marks* p = 0.000055**, see Table 6.26). *Punctuation marks other than exclamation marks* are again very rarely *repeated* and to an almost similar extent, whereas *letters* are only *repeated* once in the German complaints.

The last category, *intensifying features of CMC which are used to aggravate the mitigating effect of downgrading modifiers,* cannot be found at all.

Finally, the results of the statistical comparison of the occurrence of sum variables in the British English and German complaints in the data set *Item NR-D* are presented (see Table 6.27 and Figure 6.27).

Table 6.27: The results of the sum variables in the BrE and German data set *Item NR-D.*

Data set: *Item NR-D* Sum variables	**BrE complaints relative frequencies (%)**	**German complaints relative frequencies (%)**	**Significance (p)**
Total use of mitigating features	5	4	0.365
Total use of intensifying features	89	86	0.159

Figure 6.27: Graphic representation of the results of the sum variables in the BrE and German data set *Item NR-D.*

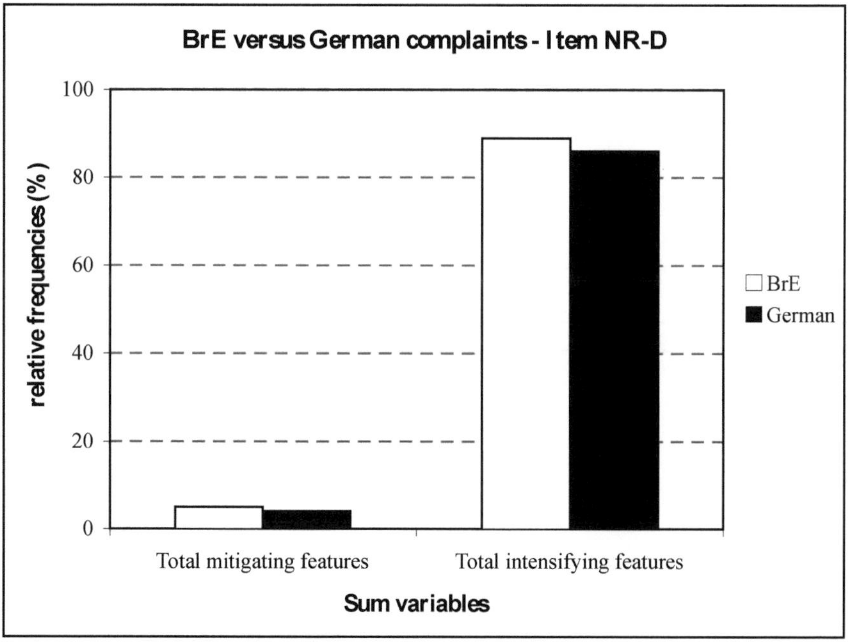

Similar to the results of the data sets *Item NR* and *Item DIFF*, Table 6.27 and Figure 6.27 show for the data set *Item NR-D* that both the British English and German traders use by far less *mitigating features* than *intensifying features* in their online complaints. Both types of features are thereby used to an almost similar extent.

6.1.4. Data set: Item was different than expected (double complaints)

Finally, the results of the statistical comparison of the British English and German data set *Item was different than expected (double complaint) (Item DIFF-D)* are illustrated. The following Table 6.28 and Figure 6.28 show the results of the comparison of the use of complaint strategies, level of directness, and amount of strategy combinations.

Table 6.28: BrE and German traders' use of complaint strategies, level of directness, and amount of strategy combinations in the data set *Item DIFF-D.*

Data set: *Item DIFF-D* Complaint strategies	**BrE complaints relative frequencies (%)**	**German complaints relative frequencies (%)**	**Significance (p)**
Expression of disappointment	12	7	0.230
Expression of anger or annoyance	1	0	0.320
Explicit complaint	100	100	
Negative judgement	11	13	0.542
Drawing one's own conclusion	**2**	**13**	**0.003****
Warning others	18	18	1.000
Threat	4	3	0.702
Insult	7	2	0.089
Level of directness			0.824
Strategy combination	50	48	0.779

Figure 6.28: Graphic representation of BrE and German eBay traders' use of complaint strategies and combinations of them in the data set *Item DIFF-D*.

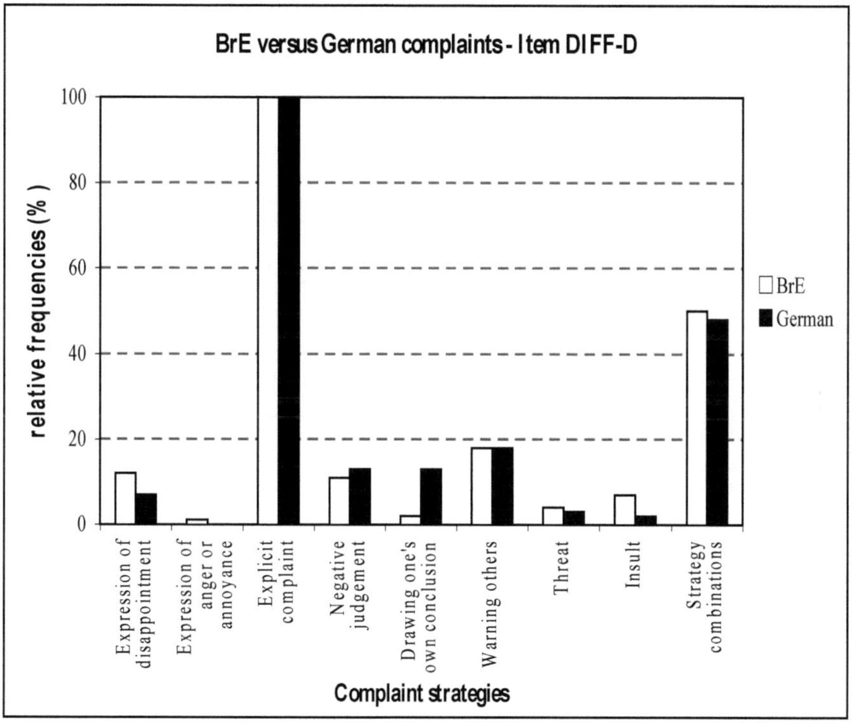

Similar to the results of the other data sets, Table 6.28 and Figure 6.28 reveal that again the strategy *explicit complaint* is by far the most frequently employed strategy by both British English and German eBay traders. In contrast to the other data sets, British English and German traders do not use the same range of strategies, because the *expression of annoyance* is only present in the British English data set *Item DIFF-D*. However, since it occurs just once, this finding is not expressive. Table 6.28 and Figure 6.28 further show that the British speakers show a tendency to use the *expression of disappointment* and *insult* to a larger extent, however, without significant differences. On the other hand, the German speakers use the strategy *drawing one's own conclusion* significantly more often than their British English counterparts, whereby p reveals highly significant differences between them (p = 0.003**, see Table 6.28). The remaining strategies as well as *strategy combinations* are used to an almost similar extent and also the *directness level* British English and German eBay members choose to formulate their online complaint is very similar.

What follows are the results of the amount of strategies British English and German traders use to formulate their complaints in the data set *Item DIFF-D* (see Table 6.29 and Figure 6.29).

Table 6.29: The amount of strategies BrE and German eBay traders use to formulate their complaints in the data set *Item DIFF-D*.

Data set: *Item DIFF-D* Amount of strategies per complaint	**BrE complaints relative frequencies (%)**	**German complaints relative frequencies (%)**	**Significance (p)**
Use of one strategy	50	52	0.779
Use of a combination of two strategies	44	38	0.391
Use of a combination of three strategies	6	10	0.300
Use of a combination of four strategies	0	0	
Use of a combination of five strategies	0	0	

Figure 6.29: Graphic representation of the amount of strategies BrE and German traders use to formulate their complaints in the data set *Item DIFF-D.*

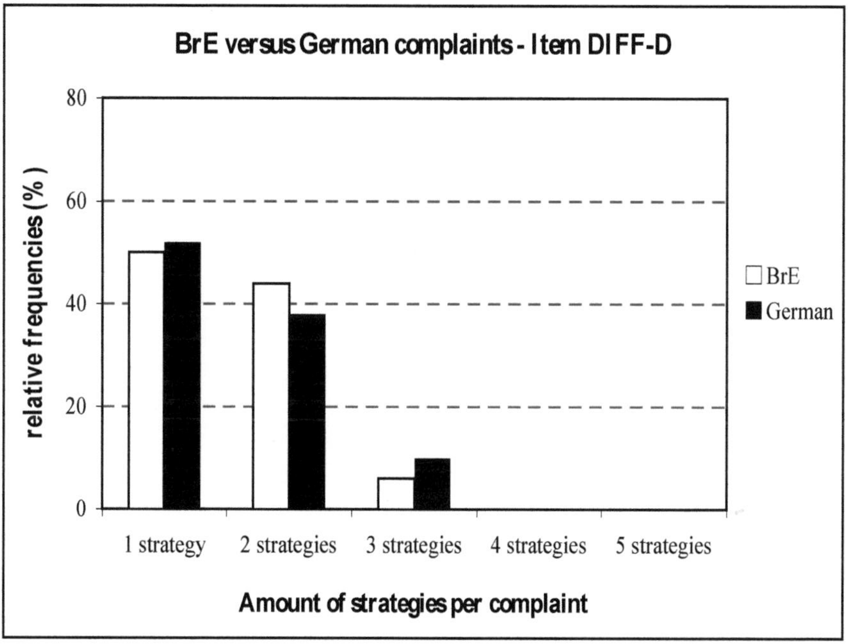

As Table 6.29 and Figure 6.29 reveal, the British English and German eBay traders use minimally one and maximally three strategies to formulate their online complaints in the data set *Item DIFF-D*. In this regard, no significant differences are obtained. The use of one strategy is favoured by both the British English and German speakers, which is, however, closely followed by the use of a combination of two strategies. The frequent occurrence of both a single strategy and a combination of two strategies is thereby similar to the results of the data set *Item NR-D*.

What follows are the results of the strategy sequences British English or German eBay traders use in at least 5% of the complaints in the data set *Item DIFF-D* (see Table 6.30 and Figure 6.30).

Table 6.30: The strategy sequences BrE or German eBay traders use in at least 5% of the complaints in the data set *Item DIFF-D*.

Data set: *Item DIFF-D* Strategy sequences (minimum 5%)	**BrE complaints relative frequencies (%)**	**German complaints relative frequencies (%)**	**Significance (p)**
Explicit complaint	50	52	0.779
Explicit complaint/ warning others	13	7	0.159
Explicit complaint/ drawing one's own conclusion	**1**	**11**	**0.003***
Explicit complaint/ expression of disappointment	7	5	0.554
Explicit complaint/ negative judgement	5	4	0.735
Warning others/ explicit complaint	1	6	0.055

Figure 6.30: Graphic representation of the strategy sequences BrE or German eBay traders' use in at least 5% of the complaints in the data set *Item DIFF-D*.

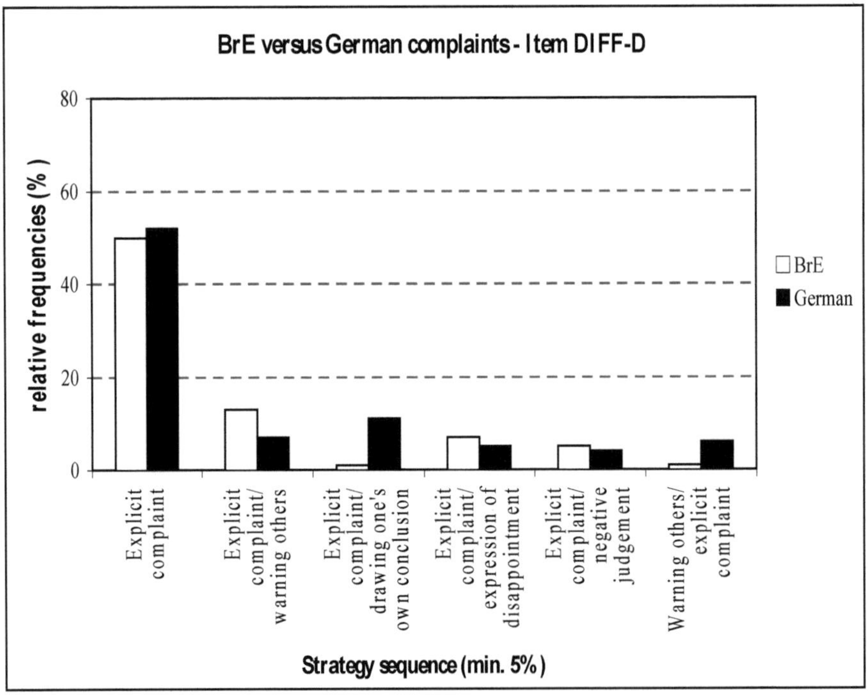

Table 6.30 and Figure 6.30 show that, as in the data set *Item NR-D*, the use of one strategy goes along with the strategy *explicit complaint*. The use of a combination of two strategies is, on the other hand, again more variable in that the strategy *explicit complaint* is combined with different types of strategies, including among others the ones illustrated in Table 6.30 and Figure 6.30, i.e. *warning others, drawing one's own conclusion, expression of disappointment,* or *negative judgement*. When comparing the results displayed in Table 6.28 and Table 6.30, it becomes apparent that the strategy *drawing one's own conclusion* is in almost all cases combined with the strategy *explicit complaint*. It is hence not surprising that not only the use of the strategy *drawing one's own conclusion* but also the use of the combination of the strategy *drawing one's own conclusion* with the strategy *explicit complaint* results in a highly significant difference between the British English and German data set (p = 0.003**, see Table 6.30). Specifically, it occurs significantly more often in the German complaints.

Turning to the amount of different strategy sequences British English and German eBay traders use to formulate their complaints in the data set *Item DIFF-D*, the results are presented in the following Table 6.31 and Figure 6.31.

Table 6.31: The amount of different strategy sequences BrE and German eBay traders use to formulate their complaints in the data set *Item DIFF-D*.

Data set: ***Item DIFF-D***	**BrE complaints absolute frequencies**	**German complaints absolute frequencies**	**Significance (p)**
Amount of different strategy sequences	20	18	0.746

Figure 6.31: Graphic representation of the amount of different strategy sequences BrE and German eBay traders use to formulate their complaints in the data set *Item DIFF-D*.

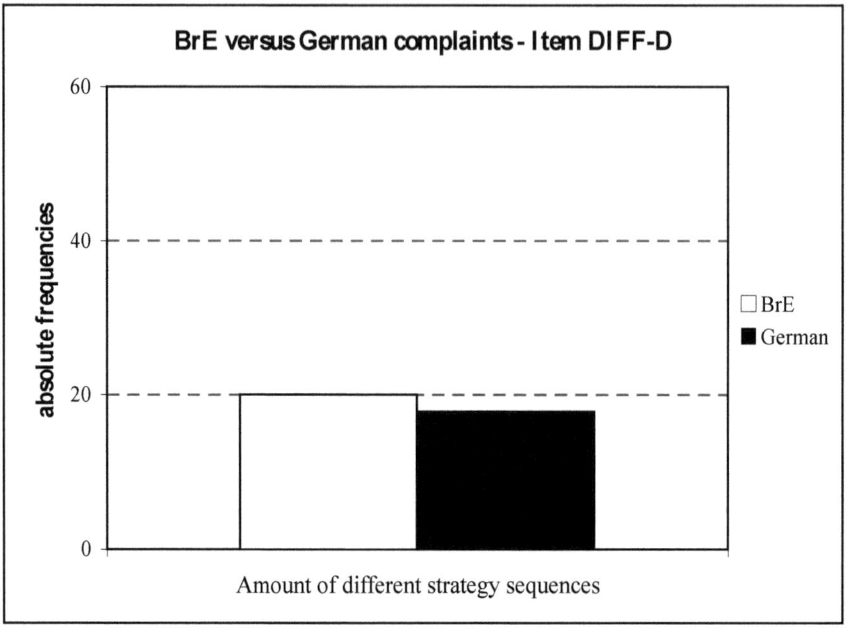

As Table 6.32 and Figure 6.31 demonstrate, the British English and German eBay traders use almost the same amount of different strategy sequences. Consequently, no significant difference is observed, which is similar to the results of all other data sets.

Shifting the focus to the use of modification, the following Table 6.32 and Figure 6.32 illustrate the use of upgrading modifiers in the data set *Item DIFF-D*.

Table 6.32: BrE and German eBay traders' use of upgrading modifiers in their complaints in the data set *Item DIFF-D*.

Data set: *Item DIFF-D* Upgrading modifiers	**BrE complaints relative frequencies (%)**	**German complaints relative frequencies (%)**	**Significance (p)**
Intensifier	30	31	0.708
Aggressive interrogative	0	2	0.158
Time reference	5	7	0.554
Sarcasm	0	1	0.320

Figure 6.32: Graphic representation of BrE and German eBay traders' use of upgrading modifiers in their complaints in the data set *Item DIFF-D*.

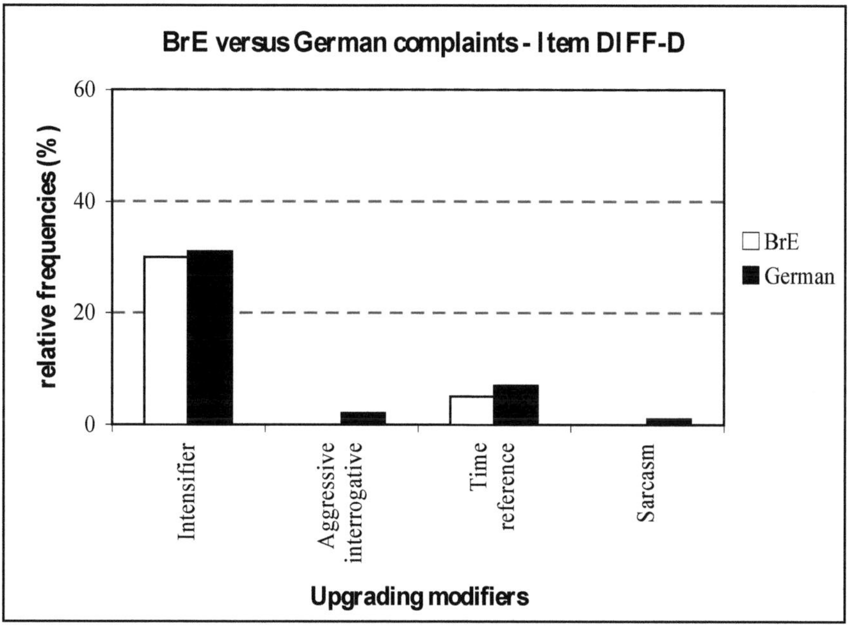

As far as the use of modification is concerned, Table 6.32 and Figure 6.32 show that there are no significant differences in the use of upgrading modifiers between the British English and German data set. Similar to the results of all other data sets, the *intensifier* is the most frequently used upgrading modifier in both the British English and German complaints.

All other types of upgrading modifiers are, as in the data set *Item DIFF*, only rarely used. The *time reference* can thereby be found in both the British English and German data set, while the *aggressive interrogative* and *sarcasm* occur only in the German complaints, but only once.

The results of the use of downgrading modifiers in the complaints in the data set *Item DIFF-D* are shown in Table 6.33 and Figure 6.33.

Table 6.33: BrE and German eBay traders' use of downgrading modifiers in their complaints in the data set *Item DIFF-D*.

Data set: *Item DIFF-D* Downgrading modifiers	**BrE complaints relative frequencies (%)**	**German complaints relative frequencies (%)**	**Significance (p)**
Expression of regret	0	3	0.083
Play down	1	2	0.563
Understater	0	0	
Politeness marker	1	0	0.320
Disarmer	**4**	**0**	**0.045***
Intensifier (downgrading)	0	0	

Figure 6.33: Graphic representation of BrE and German eBay traders' use of upgrading modifiers in their complaints in the data set *Item DIFF-D*.

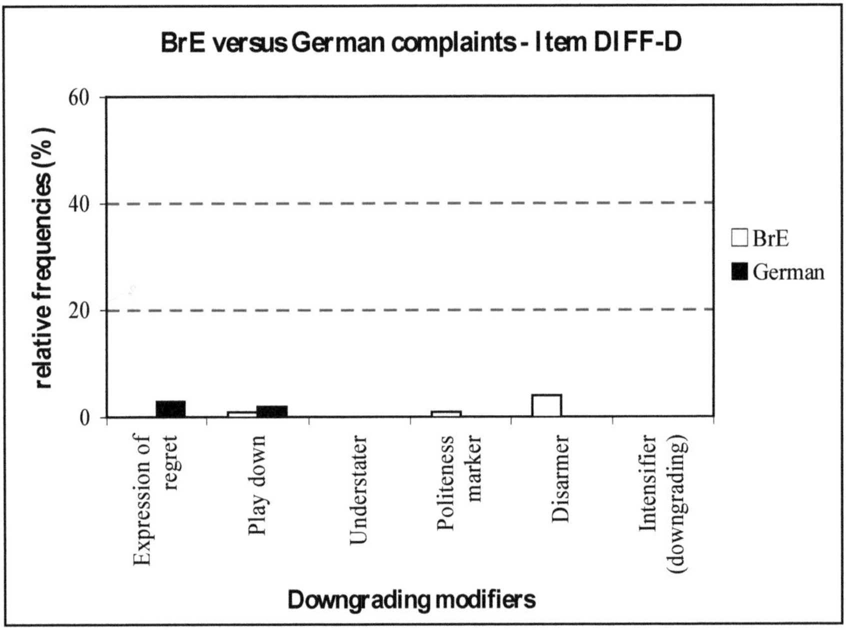

Regarding the use of downgrading modification, Table 6.33 and Figure 6.33 demonstrate that they are, as in all other data sets, only used very rarely. Furthermore, only the *play down* is used by both the British English and German eBay traders. In contrast to that, the *expression of regret* occurs only in the German and the *politeness marker* and *disarmer* only in the British English data set. With regard to the use of *disarmers* p reveals a significant difference between the British English and German complaints (p = 0.045*, see Table 6.33). However, due to the infrequent occurrence of this downgrading modifier, this significance is not expressive. Last but not least, Table 6.33 and Figure 6.33 show that *understater* and *intensifier used to aggravate the softening effect of downgrading devices* are not employed at all.

Shifting the focus to the use of pronouns, Table 6.34 and Figure 6.34 illustrate the results of the data set *Item DIFF-D*.

Table 6.34: BrE and German eBay traders' use of pronouns in the complaints in the data set *Item DIFF-D*.

Data set: *Item DIFF-D* Use of pronouns	**BrE complaints relative frequencies (%)**	**German complaints relative frequencies (%)**	**Significance (p)**
First person pronouns	**18**	**4**	**0.001****
Second person pronouns	1	1	1.000
Third person pronouns	6	1	0.055
Demonstrative pronouns	1	0	0.320
Pronouns (complainee)	8	2	0.052
Pronouns (eBay community)	2	0	0.158
Indefinite pronouns	1	0	0.320

Figure 6.34: Graphic representation of BrE and German eBay traders' use of pronouns in the complaints in the data set *Item DIFF-D*.

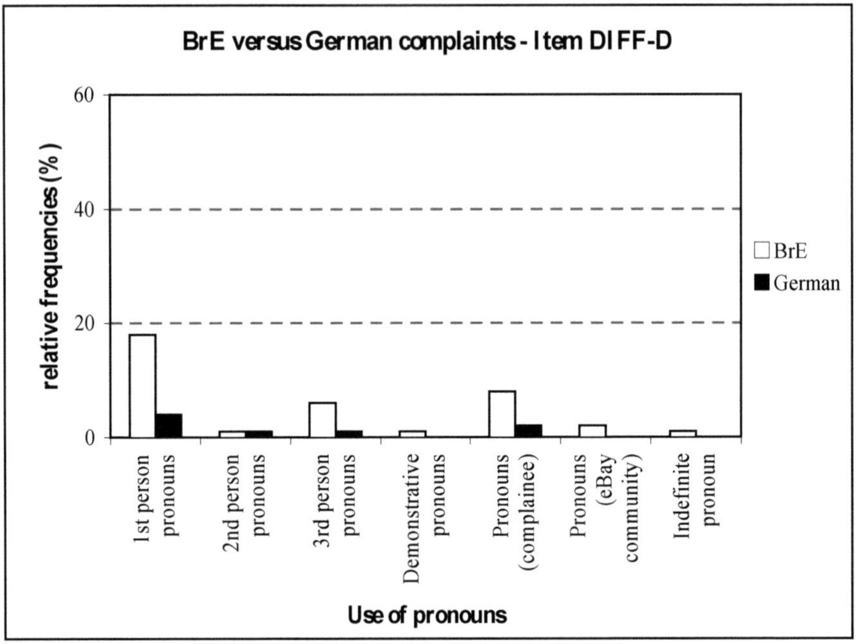

Table 6.34 and Figure 6.34 reveal that, similar to all other data sets, the British English speakers use more pronouns than the German traders, whereby they clearly favour the use of the *first person pronouns*. The statistical comparison with regard to the use of the *first person pronouns* hence again results in a significant difference, whereby p, as in all other data sets, reveals a highly significant difference between the British English and German data set (p = 0.001**, see Table 6.34). It further becomes apparent that the British English traders use the *third person pronouns* slightly more often than the Germans. Consequently, also the *pronouns referring to the complainee* occur more often in the British English than German complaints, however, without a significant difference. All other types of pronouns can only rarely be found.

The following Table 6.35 and Figure 6.35 display British English and German eBay traders' use of features of CMC in the data set *Item DIFF-D*.

Table 6.35: BrE and German eBay traders' use of features of CMC in the complaints in the data set *Item DIFF-D*.

Data set: *Item DIFF-D* Use of features of CMC	**BrE complaints relative frequencies (%)**	**German complaints relative frequencies (%)**	**Significance (p)**
Emoticons	1	1	1.000
Visual signs	0	1	0.320
Capitalisation (words)	15	9	0.194
Capitalisation (message)	7	2	0.089
Ex. m. (single)	**15**	**35**	**0.003***
Ex. m. (repeated)	20	21	0.900
Repet. other punct. m.	2	2	1.000
Repet. letters	0	0	
Intensifying features CMC (downgrading)	0	0	

Figure 6.35: Graphic representation of BrE and German eBay traders' use of features of CMC in the complaints in the data set *Item DIFF-D*.

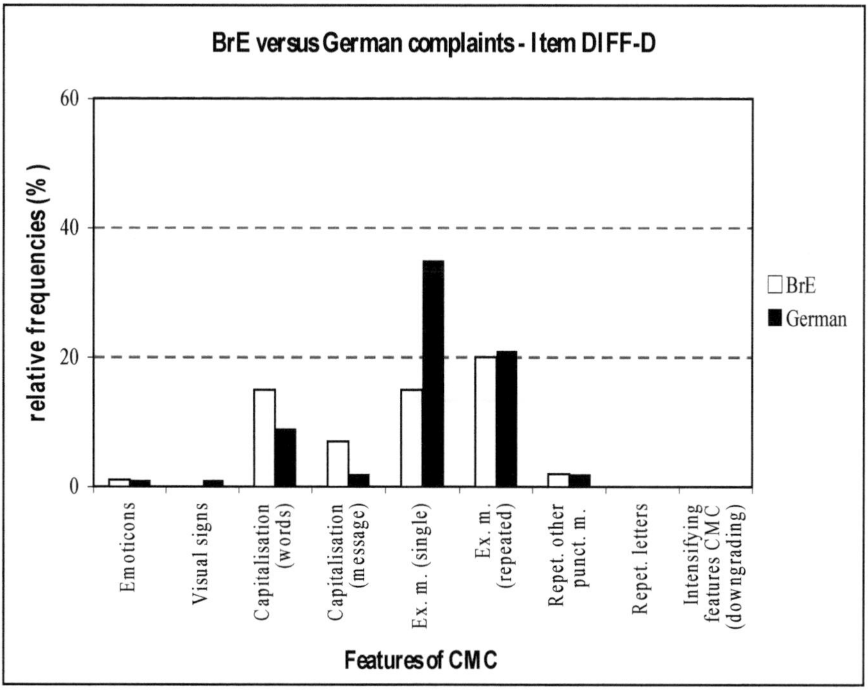

Turning to the features of CMC, Table 6.35 and Figure 6.35 demonstrate that also in the data set *Item DIFF-D, emoticons* and *visual signs* can only rarely be found. As in the data sets *Item DIFF* and *Item NR-D*, *capitalisation of words* or *the whole message* are more frequently employed by the British English traders, however, without significant differences.

As far as the *use of single exclamation marks* is concerned, the results once more reveal clear differences between the British English and German complaints. Specifically, the Germans use *single exclamation marks* significantly more often, whereby p reveals a highly significant difference between the British English and German data set (p = 0.003**, see Table 6.35). In contrast to that, *exclamation marks* are almost similarly often *repeated* by both the British English and German speakers.

Punctuation marks other than exclamation marks are again only rarely *repeated*, thereby almost similarly often. Finally, the *repetition of letters* as well as *intensifying features of CMC used to aggravate the softening effect of downgrading modifiers* are not employed at all.

Finally, the results of the occurrence of sum variables in the British English and German data set *Item DIFF-D* are presented in Table 6.36 and Figure 6.36.

Table 6.36: The results of the sum variables in the BrE and German data set *Item DIFF-D*.

Data set: *Item DIFF-D* Sum variables	**BrE complaints relative frequencies (%)**	**German complaints relative frequencies (%)**	**Significance (p)**
Total use of mitigating features	7	4	0.585
Total use of intensifying features	73	77	0.394

Figure 6.36: Graphic representation of the results of the sum variables in the BrE and German data set *Item DIFF-D*.

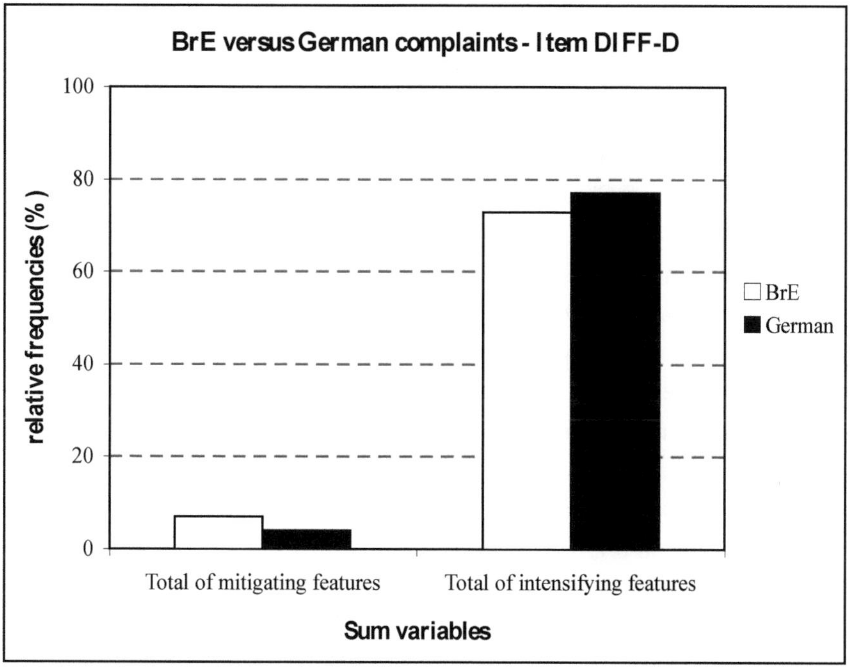

As in all other data sets, the British English and German traders also in the data set *Item DIFF-D* use by far less *mitigating features* than *intensifying features* (see Table 6.36 and Figure 6.36). Both types of features are thereby almost similarly often employed, which equals the results of the data set *Item NR-D*.

6.2. Comparison of the British English data sets

For the investigation of the research questions 2 and 3, i.e. whether the reason for complaining has an impact on British English and/or German traders' linguistic choices, and whether it makes a difference if British English and German traders have one or two reasons for their online complaint, the British English data sets were statistically compared, as well as the German ones (see 4.2.). In this part of Chapter 6 it is dealt with the results of the statistical comparison of the British English data sets before the focus shifts to the results of the comparison of the German data sets in 6.3. For a clearer overview of the different data sets, the word 'item' has been left out in tables, figures and texts within brackets, so that only the following abbreviations occur:

NR = Item has never been received, DIFF = Item was different than expected, NR-D = Item has not been received (double complaint), and DIFF-D = Item was different than expected (double complaint).

The findings of the comparison of the British English data sets are presented in the same order as in 6.1. Therefore, it begins with an illustration of the British English traders' use of complaint strategies, level of directness, and amount of strategy combinations (see Table 6.37, Table 6.38, Figure 6.37).

Table 6.37: BrE eBay traders' use of complaint strategies and combinations of them in the four different data sets.

	BrE complaints relative frequencies (%)			
Complaint strategies	**NR**	**DIFF**	**NR-D**	**DIFF-D**
Expression of disappointment	4	13	7	12
Expression of anger or annoyance	2	2	1	1
Explicit complaint	97	100	100	100
Negative judgement	12	6	10	11
Drawing one's own conclusion	3	1	2	2
Warning others	15	13	26	18
Threat	3	1	2	4
Insult	7	5	14	7
Strategy combination	34	35	54	50

Figure 6.37: Graphic representation of BrE eBay traders' use of complaint strategies and combinations of them in the four different data sets.

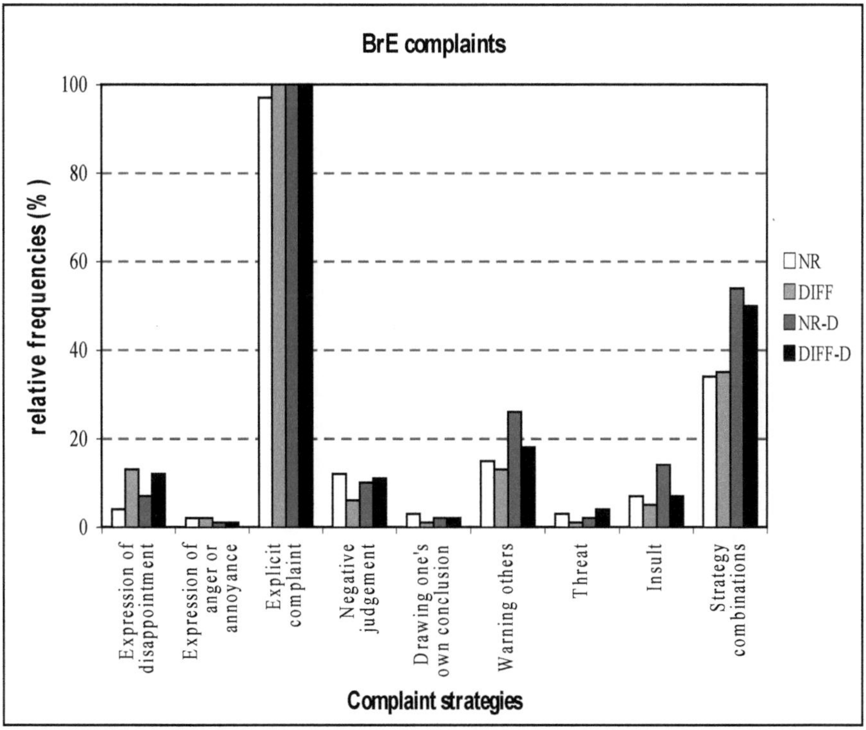

Table 6.38: Statistical comparison of BrE traders' use of complaint strategies, level of directness and strategy combinations in the four different data sets.

	BrE complaints Significance (p)			
	Different reason for complaining		**One or two reasons for complaining**	
Complaint strategies	**NR versus DIFF**	**NR-D versus DIFF-D**	**NR versus NR-D**	**DIFF versus DIFF-D**
Expression of disappointment	**0.023***	0.230	0.355	0.832
Expression of anger or annoyance	1.000	1.000	0.563	0.563
Explicit complaint	0.083		0.083	
Negative judgement	0.140	0.819	0.653	0.207
Drawing one's own conclusion	0.315	1.000	0.653	0.563
Warning others	0.714	0.166	0.059	0.376
Threat	0.315	0.410	0.653	0.176
Insult	0.335	0.086	0.251	0.554
Level of directness	0.397	0.125	**0.032***	**0.006****
Strategy combination	0.882	0.574	**0.004****	**0.032***

As Tables 6.37 and Figure 6.37 reveal, the British English traders use the same range of complaint strategies in all data sets, whereby the strategy *explicit complaint* is always by far the most frequently employed strategy.

Regarding research question 2, Table 6.38 shows that the reason for complaining has an influence on strategy choice, since British English traders significantly more often use *expressions of disappointment* in the data sets *Item DIFF* compared to the data set *Item NR* (p = 0.023*, see Table 6.38). This tendency can also be found in the double complaints, i.e. the comparison of the data set *Item DIFF-D* and the data set *Item NR-D*, however, without a significant difference. At the same time, British English traders show a tendency to choose more direct strategies in case they have *not received the item*, in that they use the strategies *negative judgement, drawing one's own conclusion, threat* and *insult* to a larger extent in the data set *Item NR* than in the data set *Item DIFF*, and the strategies *warning others* and *insult* clearly more often in the data set *Item NR-D* compared to the data set *Item DIFF-D*. However, all these tendencies are not strong enough to result in significant differences between the data sets under investigation.

Shifting the focus to the investigation whether it makes a difference if British English traders complain about one or two reasons at the same time, clear differences become apparent. Specifically, the British English traders choose a significantly higher *level of directness* in the double complaints (*NR* versus *NR-D* p = 0.032*, *DIFF* versus *DIFF-D* p = 0.006**) and also significantly more often use *strategy combinations* when they have two reasons for their online complaint (*NR* versus *NR-D* p = 0.004**, *DIFF* versus *DIFF-D* p = 0.032*) (see Table 6.38).

The following Tables 6.39 and 6.40, as well as Figure 6.38, illustrate the amount of strategies British English speakers use to formulate their complaints in the different data sets.

Table 6.39: The amount of strategies BrE eBay traders use to formulate their complaints in the four different data sets.

	BrE complaints relative frequencies (%)			
Amount of strategies per complaint	**NR**	**DIFF**	**NR-D**	**DIFF-D**
Use of one strategy	66	65	46	50
Use of a combination of two strategies	23	30	46	44
Use of a combination of three strategies	10	4	5	6
Use of a combination of four strategies	1	0	3	0
Use of a combination of five strategies	0	1	0	0

Figure 6.38: Graphic representation of the amount of strategies BrE eBay traders use to formulate their complaints in the four different data sets.

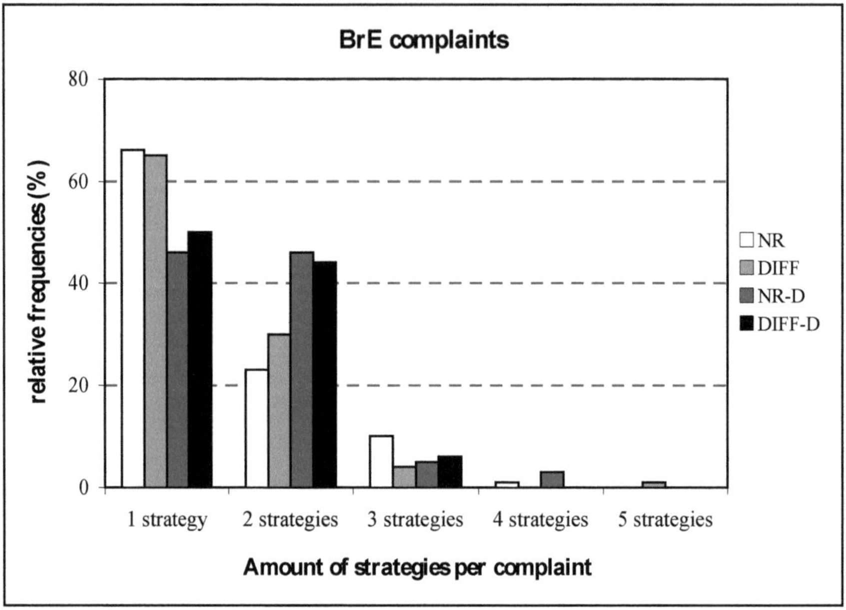

Table 6.40: Statistical comparison of the amount of strategies BrE eBay traders use to formulate their complaints in the four different data sets.

	BrE complaints Significance (p)			
	Different reason for complaining		**One or two reasons for complaining**	
Amount of strategies per complaint	**NR versus DIFF**	**NR-D versus DIFF-D**	**NR versus NR-D**	**DIFF versus DIFF-D**
Use of one strategy	0.882	0.574	**0.004****	**0.032***
Use of a combination of two strategies	0.264	0.778	**0.001****	**0.041***
Use of a combination of three strategies	0.098	0.758	0.181	0.519
Use of a combination of four strategies	0.320	0.083	0.315	
Use of a combination of five strategies	0.320			0.320

As it becomes obvious from Table 6.39 and Figure 6.38, the complaints of all British English data sets are minimally made up of one and maximally of three strategies. In the data sets *Item NR* and *Item NR-D* the British English speakers also use a combination of four strategies, but rarely, and in the data set *Item DIFF* they once employ the combination of five strategies to formulate their online complaint (see Table 6.39).

A different reason for complaining thereby does not have an influence on the amount of strategies British English speakers use. In contrast to that, the number of reasons British English traders have for their online complaint has a clear impact on the amount of strategies they employ to formulate them. Precisely, the British English speakers significantly more often use combinations of two strategies in double complaints than in single complaints (*NR* versus *NR-D* p = 0.001**, *DIFF* versus *DIFF-D* p = 0.041*, see Table 6.40). In the latter, however, they significantly more often favour the use of one strategy (*NR* versus *NR-D* p = 0.004**, *DIFF* versus *DIFF-D* p = 0.032*, see Table 6.40). Regarding the comparison of the data sets *Item NR* versus *Item NR-D*, these differences are even highly significant (*use of one strategy* p = 0.004**, *use of a combination of two strategies* p = 0.001**, see Table 6.40).

What follows are the results of the strategy sequences British English traders use in at least 5% in one of the data sets under investigation.

Table 6.41: The strategy sequences BrE traders use in at least 5% in one of the data sets under investigation.

	BrE complaints relative frequencies (%)			
Strategy sequences (min. 5%)	**NR**	**DIFF**	**NR-D**	**DIFF-D**
Explicit complaint	65	65	46	50
Explicit complaint/warning others	4	7	14	13
Explicit complaint/negative judgement	7	4	7	5
Explicit complaint/expression of disappointment	2	7	4	7
Explicit complaint/insult	0	2	6	3

Figure 6.39: Graphic representation of the strategy sequences BrE traders use in at least 5% in one of the data sets under investigation.

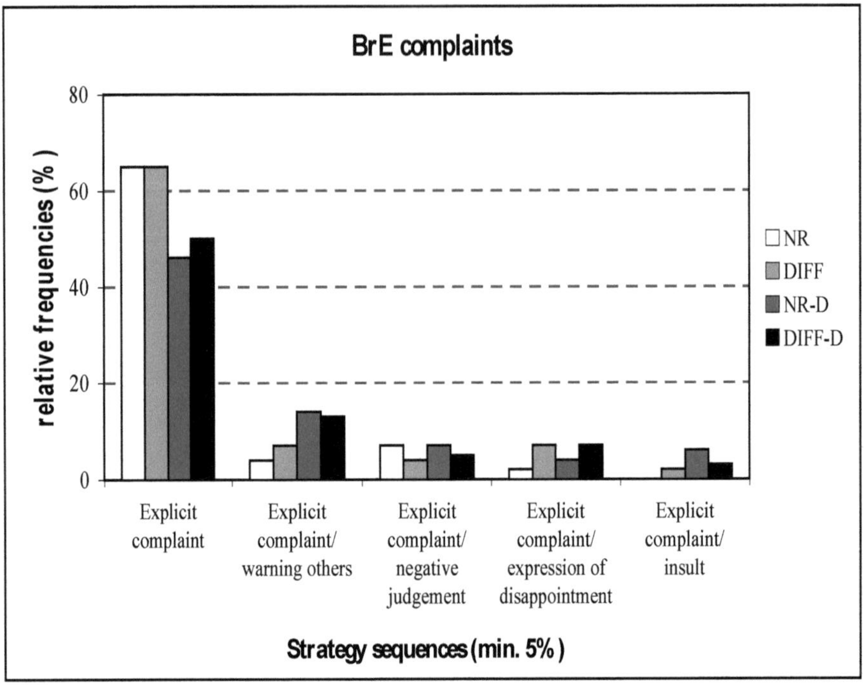

Table 6.42: Statistical comparison of the strategy sequences BrE traders use in at least 5% in one of the data sets under investigation.

	BrE complaints Significance (p)			
	Different reason for complaining		**One or two reasons for complaining**	
Strategy sequences (min. 5%)	**NR versus DIFF**	**NR-D versus DIFF-D**	**NR versus NR-D**	**DIFF versus DIFF-D**
Explicit complaint	1.000	0.574	**0.007****	**0.032***
Explicit complaint/warning others	0.355	0.837	**0.014***	0.159
Explicit complaint/ negative judgement	0.355	0.554	1.000	0.735
Explicit complaint/ expression of disappointment	0.089	0.335		
Explicit complaint/insult		0.309	**0.014***	

Table 6.41 and Figure 6.39 show that in cases where British English traders use one strategy to formulate their online complaint, this strategy is in almost all

cases an *explicit complaint*. Given that the use of one strategy occurs significantly more often in the single complaints (*NR* versus *NR-D* p = 0.004**, *DIFF* versus *DIFF-D* p = 0.032*, see Table 6.42), also the use of the strategy *explicit complaint* results in significant differences between the data sets consisting of single and double complaints (*NR* versus *NR-D* p = 0.007**, *DIFF* versus *DIFF-D* p = 0.032*, see Table 6.42). The value of p thereby once more shows a highly significant difference with regard to the comparison of the data sets *Item NR* and *Item NR-D*.

Given that the strategy combinations British English speakers formulate are diverse in that different strategies are combined, the most common type of complaint British English speakers employ in all data sets is a complaint consisting of one strategy, namely the strategy *explicit complaint*. This type of complaint is accordingly the prototypical complaint. Since it is the same in all data sets, it can be said that neither a different reason for complaining nor a different number of reasons British English traders complain about leads to differences in the prototypical complaint they use.

On the other hand, the number of reasons British English eBay users have for their online complaints impacts which strategies they combine to formulate a complaint consisting of two strategies. Specifically, the British English traders significantly more often use combinations of the strategy *explicit complaint* with either the strategy *warning others* or *insult* in the data set *Item NR-D* than *Item NR* (*explicit complaint/warning others* p = 0.014*, *explicit complaint/insult* p = 0.014*, see Table 6.42). This finding suggests that in double complaints British English speakers prefer the combination of an *explicit complaint* with more direct strategies over single complaints in order to enhance the face-threat of their double complaints. This proposition is also supported by the fact that the combination of the strategy *explicit complaint* and *warning others* is also more frequent in the data set *Item DIFF-D* compared to the data set *Item DIFF*, however, without a significant difference. This weaker tendency may in turn result from the fact that British English traders complain for a different reason in these data sets. Hence, both the number of reasons British English traders have for their complaints as well as the type of reason they complain about seem to impact which types of strategies British English speakers combine in complaints consisting of two strategies.

Shifting the focus to the amount of different strategy sequences British English eBay traders use to formulate their complaints, the following Tables 6.43 and 6.44 as well as Figure 6.40 reveal the results.

Table 6.43: The amount of different strategy sequences BrE eBay traders use to formulate their complaints in the four different data sets.

	BrE complaints absolute frequencies			
	NR	DIFF	NR-D	DIFF-D
Amount of different strategy sequences	23	16	20	20

Figure 6.40: Graphic representation of the amount of different strategy sequences BrE eBay traders use to formulate their complaints in the four different data sets.

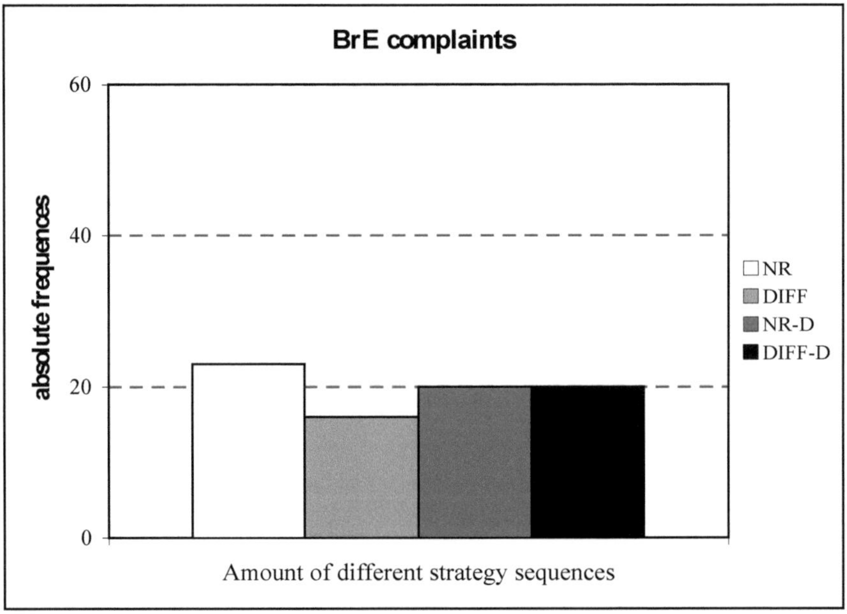

Table 6.44: Statistical comparison of the amount of different strategy sequences BrE eBay traders use to formulate their complaints in the four different data sets.

	BrE complaints Significance (p)			
	Different reason for complaining		**One or two reasons for complaining**	
	NR versus DIFF	**NR-D versus DIFF-D**	**NR versus NR-D**	**DIFF versus DIFF-D**
Amount of different strategy sequences	0.262	1.000	0.647	0.505

Table 6.43 and Figure 6.40 show that the British English speakers in the data set *Item NR* use slightly more and in the data set *Item DIFF* slightly less strategy sequences than in the data sets consisting of double complaints. However, the differences are only small so that no significant differences can be found (see Table 6.44). Therefore, neither the type of reason nor the difference whether British English speakers have one or two reasons for complaining has an influence on the amount of different strategy sequences they employ.

Turning to the use of modification, the following Tables 6.45, 6.46 and Figure 6.41 illustrate the results of the use of upgrading modifiers.

Table 6.45: BrE eBay traders' use of upgrading modifiers in their complaints in the four different data sets.

	BrE complaints relative frequencies (%)			
Upgrading modifiers	**NR**	**DIFF**	**NR-D**	**DIFF-D**
Intensifier	31	28	45	30
Aggressive interrogative	6	3	5	0
Time reference	15	0	23	5
Sarcasm	0	0	0	0

Figure 6.41: Graphic representation of BrE eBay traders' use of upgrading modifiers in their complaints in the four different data sets.

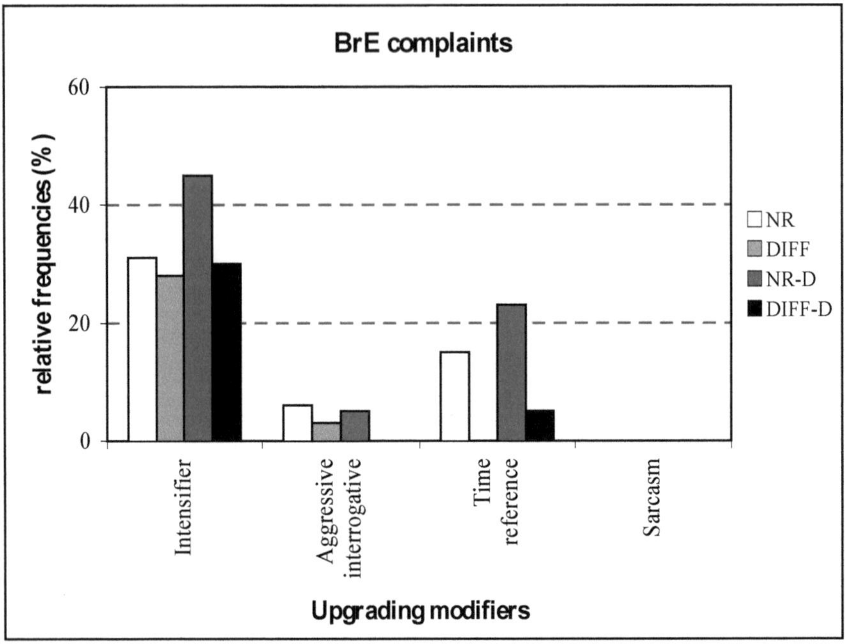

Table 6.46: Statistical comparison of BrE eBay traders' use of upgrading modifiers in their complaints in the four different data sets.

	BrE complaints Significance (p)			
	Different reason for complaining		**One or two reasons for complaining**	
Upgrading modifiers	**NR versus DIFF**	**NR-D versus DIFF-D**	**NR versus NR-D**	**DIFF versus DIFF-D**
Intensifier	0.677	**0.010****	**0.009****	0.683
Aggressive interrogative	0.558	**0.025***	0.758	0.103
Time reference	**0.000174****	**0.000228****	0.559	**0.025***
Sarcasm				

As Table 6.45 and Figure 6.41 illustrate, *intensifiers* are the most frequently employed type of upgrading modifiers in all four British English data sets. At the same time, the British English traders particularly favour their usage in the data set *Item NR-D*. Therefore, both the comparison of their presence in the data set *Item NR-D* with the data set *Item DIFF-D* and the comparison of the data set

Item NR with the data set *Item NR-D* result in highly significant differences (*NR-D* versus *DIFF-D* p = 0.010**, *NR* versus *NR-D* p = 0.009**, see Table 6.46), revealing an influence of both factors under investigation.

Furthermore, British English speakers' use of the *time reference* is clearly influenced by the type of reason they complain about, as they particularly favour this type of upgrading modifier if they have *not received their item*, regardless of whether they have one or two reasons for their online complaint. The comparison of the data set *Item NR* with the data set *Item DIFF* as well as the comparison of the data set *Item NR-D* with the data set *Item DIFF-D* even reveal in both cases highly significant differences (*NR* versus *DIFF* p = 0.000174**, *NR-D* versus *DIFF-D* p = 0.00028**, see Table 6.46). The number of reasons British English speakers have for their complaint additionally impacts their use of the *time reference* if they complain about the fact that the *item was different than expected.* Specifically, they significantly more often employ *time references* in the data set *Item DIFF-D* compared to the data set *Item DIFF* (p = 0.025*, see Table 6.46). Yet, due to the infrequent occurrence of this modifier in the data sets *Item DIFF* and *Item DIFF-D*, this result is not very expressive. It can hence be said that mainly the type of reason British English traders complain about influences their employment of the upgrading modifier *time reference*.

In addition to that, Table 6.46 illustrates that also the *aggressive interrogative* occurs significantly more often in the data set *Item NR-D* compared to the data set *Item DIFF-D* (p = 0.025*, see Table 6.46), hinting at an influence of the type of reason British English traders complain about. This influence, however, has to be judged as only weak given the overall infrequent occurrence of the *aggressive interrogative* in the data sets.

Last but not least, it is worth mentioning that *sarcasm* is not employed in any of the four British English data sets. An influence of the factors under investigation is thus clearly absent.

The following Table 6.47, 6.48 and Figure 6.42 illustrate the results of British English eBay traders' use of downgrading modifiers in their complaints in the four different data sets.

Table 6.47: BrE eBay traders' use of downgrading modifiers in their complaints in the four different data sets.

	BrE complaints relative frequencies (%)			
Downgrading modifiers	**NR**	**DIFF**	**NR-D**	**DIFF-D**
Expression of regret	0	0	1	0
Play down	1	2	3	1
Understater	1	0	0	0
Politeness marker	1	1	1	1
Disarmer	0	8	2	4
Intensifier (downgrading)	0	0	1	0

Figure 6.42: Graphic representation of BrE eBay traders' use of downgrading modifiers in their complaints in the four different data sets.

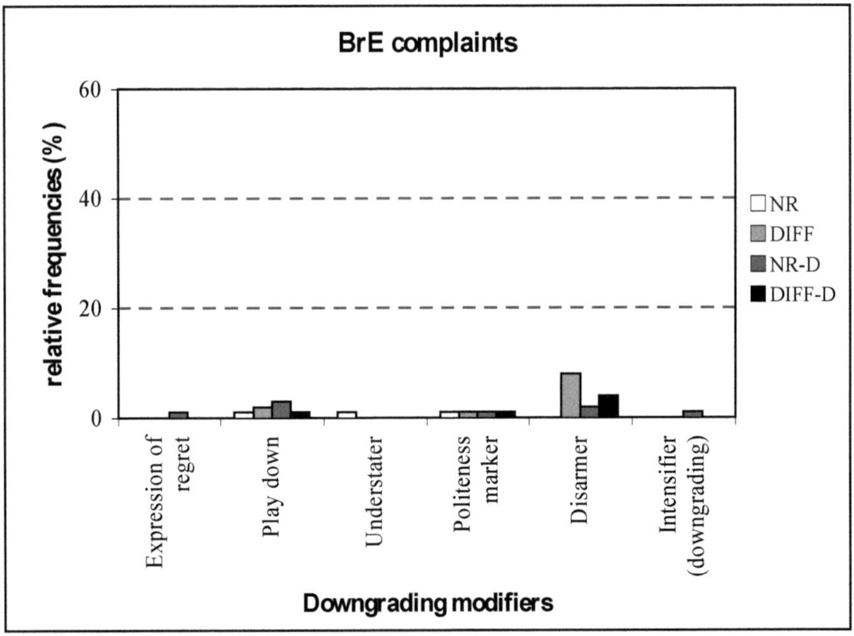

Table 6.48: Statistical comparison of BrE eBay traders' use of downgrading modifiers in their complaints in the four different data sets.

	BrE complaints Significance (p)			
	Different reason for complaining		One or two reasons for complaining	
Downgrading modifiers	**NR versus DIFF**	**NR-D versus DIFF-D**	**NR versus NR-D**	**DIFF versus DIFF-D**
Expression of regret		0.320	0.320	
Play down	0.563	0.315	0.315	0.563
Understater	0.320		0.320	
Politeness marker	1.000	1.000	1.000	1.000
Disarmer	**0.006****	0.410	0.158	0.186
Intensifier (downgrading)		0.320	0.320	

Table 6.47 and Figure 6.42 demonstrate that the downgrading modifiers are used only very rarely in all British English data sets. Nevertheless, *disarmer* occur significantly more often in the data set *Item DIFF* compared to the data set *Item NR*, whereby p reveals a highly significant difference ($p = 0.006^{**}$, see Table 6.48). This result points at an influence of the type of reason for complaining on British traders' use of *disarmer*, which however cannot be observed when comparing the data sets consisting of double complaints, i.e. *Item NR-D* and *Item DIFF-D*. The fact that the British English traders have to complain about two things at the same time is thus likely to prevent them from using *disarmer*.

Turning to the use of pronouns the results are presented in the following Tables 6.49 and 6.50 as well as Figure 6.43.

Table 6.49: BrE eBay traders' use of pronouns in the complaints in the four different data sets.

	BrE complaints relative frequencies (%)			
Use of pronouns	**NR**	**DIFF**	**NR-D**	**DIFF-D**
First person pronouns	35	20	29	18
Second person pronouns	4	3	1	1
Third person pronouns	5	1	11	6
Demonstrative pronouns	9	2	7	1
Pronouns (complainee)	16	6	18	8
Pronouns (eBay community)	3	1	2	2
Indefinite pronouns	2	1	0	1

Figure 6.43: Graphic representation of BrE eBay traders' use of pronouns in the complaints in the four different data sets.

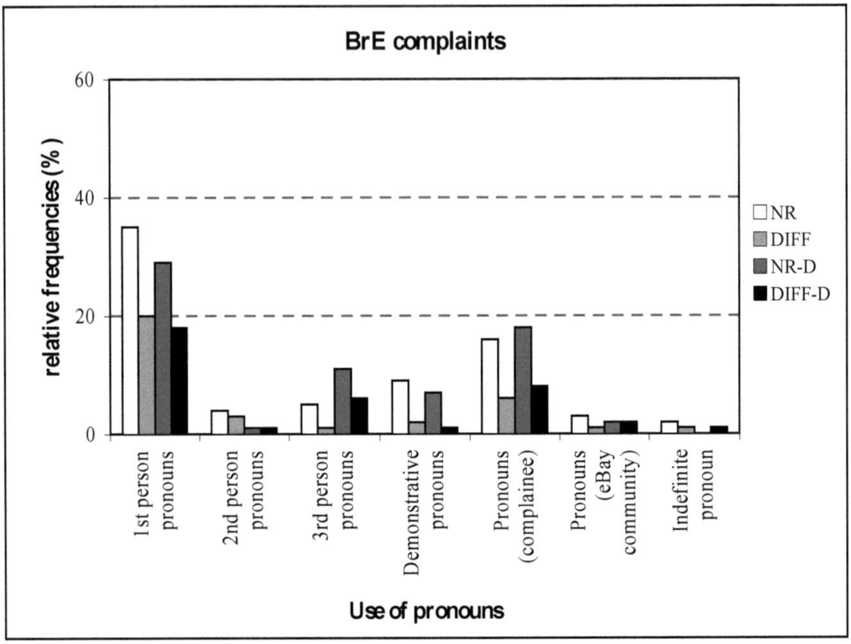

Table 6.50: Statistical comparison of BrE eBay traders' use of pronouns in the complaints of the four different data sets.

	BrE complaints Significance (p)			
	Different reason for complaining		**One or two reasons for complaining**	
Use of pronouns	**NR versus DIFF**	**NR-D versus DIFF-D**	**NR versus NR-D**	**DIFF versus DIFF-D**
First person pronouns	**0.016***	0.069	0.276	0.685
Second person pronouns	1.000	0.655	0.477	0.255
Third person pronouns	0.099	0.207	0.119	0.055
Demonstrative pronouns	0.101	**0.031***	0.604	0.414
Pronouns (complainee)	0.071	**0.024***	0.750	1.000
Pronouns (eBay community)	0.255	0.705	0.762	0.563
Indefinite pronouns	0.563	0.320	0.158	1.000

As Table 6.49 and Figure 6.43 reveal, the British English traders favour the use of *first person pronouns* in all data sets. The type of reason thereby has an impact on their use of these pronouns, since they employ them more often if they have *not received the item*. The comparison of the single complaints in the data sets *Item NR* and *Item DIFF* results in a significant difference (p = 0.016*, see Table 6.50), whereas the impact of the factor 'type of reason' is weaker regarding double complaints. Therefore, *first person pronouns* occur more frequently in the data set *Item NR-D* compared to the data set *Item DIFF-D*, however, without a significant difference.

In addition to that, the reason for complaining also impacts British English traders' use of *third person pronouns* as well as *demonstrative pronouns followed by nouns denoting the complainee*, since the British English speakers similarly show a tendency to use these types of pronouns more often if they have *not received the item* in single and double complaints. Yet, only the comparison of the use of *demonstrative pronouns followed by nouns denoting the complainee* in the data set *Item NR-D* compared to the data set *Item DIFF-D* results in a significant difference (p = 0.031*, see Table 6.50). Given these findings, the category *pronouns referring to the complainee* reveals an even stronger effect of the particular type of reason for complaining on the British English traders' use of these pronouns, as it brings together the results of the British English speakers' use of *second person pronouns, third person pronouns* and *demonstrative pronouns followed by nouns denoting the complainee*. Table 6.49 and 6.50 as well as Figure 6.43 thus show that if British English speakers have *not received the item*, they employ the *pronouns referring to the complainee* more often than if they have to complain about the fact that the *item was different than expected*. Despite this stronger effect, it nevertheless does not result in a significant difference with regard to the comparison of the single complaints *Item NR* versus *Item DIFF*. Accordingly, only the comparison of the data sets *Item NR-D* versus *Item DIFF-D* reveals a significant difference (p = 0.024*, see Table 6.50). Noteworthy in this respect is that the category *second person pronouns*, which also belong to the group of *pronouns referring to the complainee*, is not affected by the factor 'type of reason', in contrast to *third person pronouns* and *demonstrative pronouns followed by a noun denoting the complainee*. They are only rarely used and to an almost similar extent in single and double complaints respectively.

Regarding the remaining categories of pronouns, i.e. the use of *pronouns addressing the eBay community* as well as the use of *indefinite pronouns*, Table

6.49 and 6.50 as well as Figure 6.43 show that these types of pronouns also occur only rarely in all data sets and without significant differences in their usage.

What follows are the results of British English traders' use of features of CMC in the four different data sets (see Table 6.51, 6.52 and Figure 6.44).

Table 6.51: BrE eBay traders' use of features of CMC in the complaints in the four different data sets.

	BrE complaints relative frequencies (%)			
Use of features of CMC	**NR**	**DIFF**	**NR-D**	**DIFF-D**
Emoticons	0	1	1	1
Visual signs	0	1	1	0
Capitalisation (words)	4	11	14	15
Capitalisation (message)	11	5	14	7
Ex. m. (single)	5	14	11	15
Ex. m. (repeated)	15	8	15	20
Repet. other punct. m.	4	0	2	2
Repet. letters	0	0	0	0
Intensifying features CMC (downgrading)	1	1	0	0

Figure 6.44: Graphic representation of BrE eBay traders' use of features of CMC in the complaints in the four different data sets.

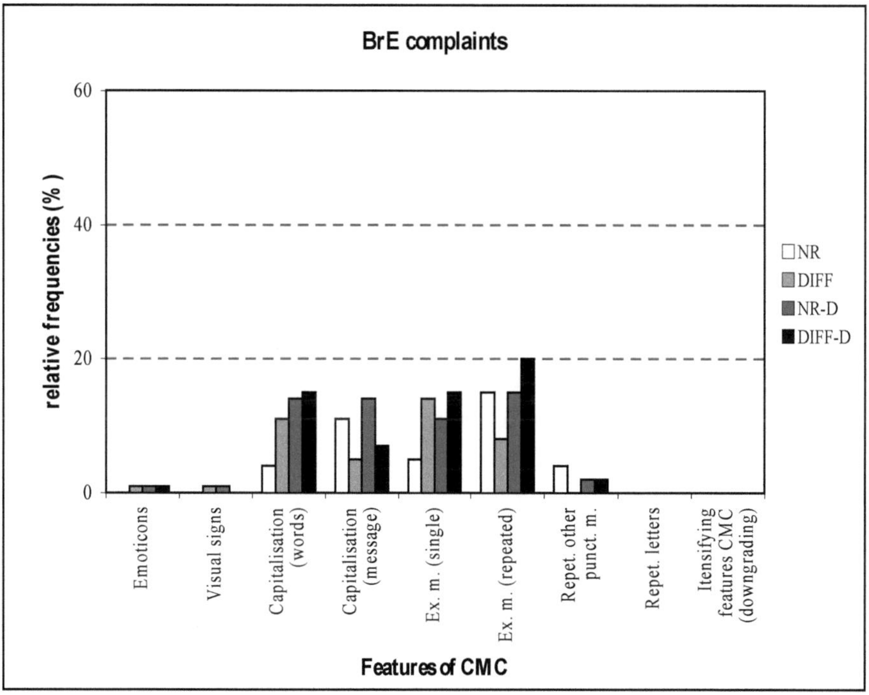

Table 6.52: Statistical comparison of BrE eBay traders' use of features of CMC in the complaints in the four different data sets.

	BrE complaints Significance (p)			
	Different reason for complaining		**One or two reasons for complaining**	
Use of features of CMC	**NR versus DIFF**	**NR-D versus DIFF-D**	**NR versus NR-D**	**DIFF versus DIFF-D**
Emoticons	0.320	1.000	0.320	1.000
Visual signs	0.320	0.320	0.320	0.320
Capitalisation (words)	0.061	0.842	**0.014***	0.403
Capitalisation (message)	0.119	0.108	0.524	0.554
Ex. m. (single)	**0.018***	0.200	0.077	0.496
Ex. m. (repeated)	0.097	0.199	1.000	**0.008****
Repet. other punct. m.	**0.045***	1.000	0.410	0.158
Repet. letters				
Intensifying features CMC (downgrading)	1.000		0.320	0.320

As Table 6.51 and Figure 6.44 show, *emoticons* and *visual signs* are only rarely used in the different British English data sets. The statistical comparison does not result in significant differences (see Table 6.52), illustrating that the factors under investigation do not impact their usage.

It further becomes apparent that the use of *capitalisation of words* seems to be influenced by both factors, the number of reasons British English traders complain about as well as the particular reason they have for their online complaint. Specifically, they *capitalise specific words* within their complaints significantly more often in the data set *Item NR-D* compared to the data set *Item NR* (p = 0.014*, see Table 6.52). The tendency to use more *capitalisation of words* in double complaints than single complaints can also be found if British English traders complain about the fact that the *item was different than expected*, however, without a significant difference. The weaker differentiation between the data sets *Item DIFF* and *Item DIFF-D* results from the fact that British English traders also show a tendency to use *capitalisation of words* more often if they have to complain about the fact that the *item was different than expected*, thus pointing at an additional influence of the reason for complaining. This influence is, however, again not strong enough to result in a significant difference between the data sets.

The particular reason British English speakers complain about also influences their use of *capitalisation of the whole message*. In contrast to the use of *capitalisation of words* though, British English traders favour the use of *capitalisation of the whole message* if they have *not received the item*. Yet, this tendency remains again above the level of significance.

As for British English speakers' use of *capitalisation of words*, also their *use of exclamation marks* is influenced by both factors, i.e. the type of reason and the number of reasons they complain about, whereby the influence is once more rather complex. Specifically, the type of reason British English traders complain about has a clear impact on their use of *single exclamation marks*, since they significantly more often employ them in the data set *Item DIFF* compared to the data set *Item NR* (p = 0.018*, see Table 6.52). This tendency to particularly use *single exclamation marks* if the *item was different than expected* can also be found when comparing the data sets consisting of double complaints, i.e. *Item DIFF-D* versus *Item NR-D*, however, without a significant difference. At the same time, Table 6.51 and Figure 6.44 reveal that also the number of reasons British English traders have for their online complaint has some impact on their use of *single exclamation marks* but only if they have *not received the item*. Precisely, they tend to intensify their complaint more often by the use of *single exclamation marks* in the data set *Item NR-D* compared to the data set *Item NR*. This tendency cannot be traced if they complain about the fact that the *item was different than expected*, i.e. in the comparison of the data sets *Item DIFF* versus *Item DIFF-D*.

On the other hand, the comparison of the data sets *Item DIFF* and *Item DIFF-D* results in an even highly significant difference with regard to British English traders' use of *repeated exclamation marks*, in that they favour their usage in the double complaints *Item DIFF-D* rather than the single complaints *Item DIFF* (p = 0.008**, see Table 6.52). At the same time, also the *repeated exclamation marks* are not only influenced by one factor, i.e. the amount of reasons for complaining, but similarly by the particular type of reason British English eBay members have for their online complaint. In other words, if they only have one reason for complaining they show a tendency to *repeat the exclamation marks* more often if they have *not received the item* than if the *item was different than expected*. The contrary can be found with regard to the use of *repeated exclamation marks* in the double complaints *Item NR-D* versus *Item DIFF-D*. Here they tend to *repeat their exclamation marks* more often if they complain about the fact that the *item was different than expected* and have an additional reason for complaining than if they have *not received the item* and have a second reason for their complaint. All these tendencies are, however, not strong enough to result in a significant difference.

Regarding the *repetition of punctuation marks other than exclamation marks*, Table 6.51 and Figure 6.44 illustrate that they occur clearly less often than the *repetition of exclamation marks*. Nonetheless, a significant difference can be found with regard to the comparison of the data sets *Item NR* and *Item DIFF* (p = 0.045*, see Table 6.52), in that the British English speakers significantly more often *repeat punctuation marks other than exclamation marks* if they have *not received the item*. However, in light of the infrequent occurrence of this variable, this finding is not very expressive. Yet, it again points at the tendency of British English traders to *repeat punctuation marks* in single complaints more often if they complain about the fact that they have *not received the item*.

Last but not least, Table 6.44a and Figure 6.44 show that the *repetition of letters* as well as the *intensifying features of CMC used to aggravate the softening effect of downgrading modifiers* are not employed at all. There is thus no influence of any of the factors under investigation observable.

Finally, it is turned to the results of the sum variables *total use of mitigating features* and *total use of intensifying features* which are illustrated in the following Tables 6.53, 6.54 and Figure 6.45.

Table 6.53: The occurrence of the sum variables in the four different BrE data sets.

	BrE complaints							
	NR		**DIFF**		**NR-D**		**DIFF-D**	
Sum variables	**#**	**%**	**#**	**%**	**#**	**%**	**#**	**%**
Total use of mitigating features	7	4	14	12	8	5	7	7
Total use of intensifying features	167	71	127	56	236	89	192	73

Symbols: % = relative frequencies, # = absolute frequencies

Figure 6.45: Graphic representation of the occurrence of the sum variables in the four BrE data sets.

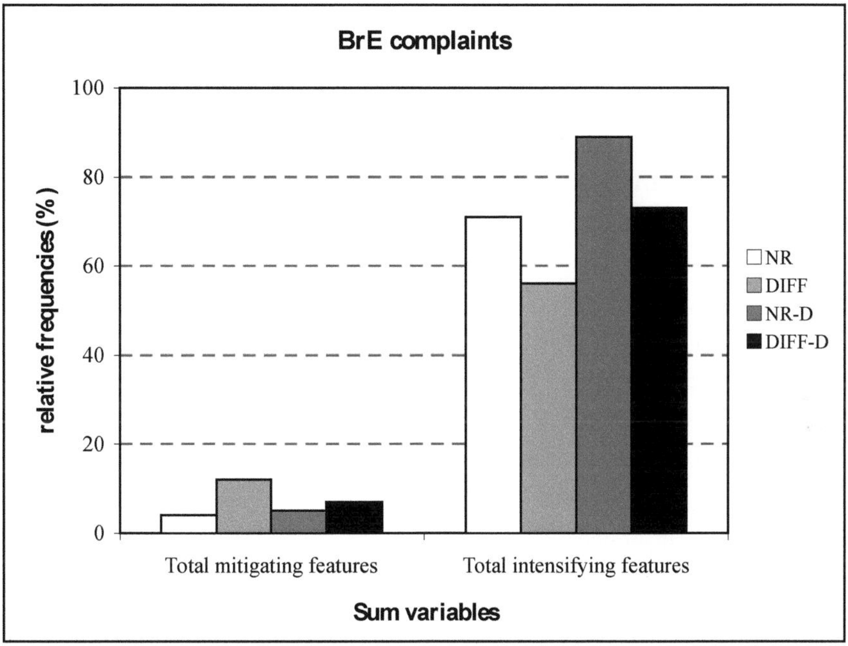

Table 6.54: Statistical comparison of the occurrence of the sum variables in the four BrE data sets.

	BrE complaints Significance (p)			
	Different reason for complaining		One or two reasons for complaining	
Sum variables	**NR versus DIFF**	**NR-D versus DIFF-D**	**NR versus NR-D**	**DIFF versus DIFF-D**
Total use of mitigating features	0.224	0.832	0.856	**0.046***
Total use of intensifying features	0.075	0.091	**0.003****	**0.010****

As Table 6.53 and Figure 6.45 reveal, the *total use of mitigating features* occurs clearly less often in the British English data sets than the *total use of intensifying features*.

On the whole, the British English speakers show a tendency to mitigate particularly the single complaints of the data set *Item DIFF*, pointing at an influence of both the type of reason as well as the number of reasons British

English eBay members have for their online complaint. With regard to the comparison of the data sets *Item DIFF* and *Item DIFF-D* the result even shows a significant difference (p = 0.046*, see Table 6.54).
Also as far as the *total use of intensifying features* is concerned, both factors, the particular type of reason and the amount of reasons British English traders have for their online complaint, have an impact.
Specifically, the British English speakers tend to use more *intensifying features* if they complain about the fact that they have *not received the item*. This tendency is, however, not strong enough to result in a significant difference. On the other hand, they show a clear tendency to particularly intensify their double complaints, so that both the comparison of the data sets *Item NR* and *Item NR-D* as well as the comparison of the data sets *Item DIFF* and *Item DIFF-D* result in highly significant differences (*NR* versus *NR-D* p = 0.003**, *DIFF* versus *DIFF-D* p = 0.010**, see Table 6.54). In light of these findings it is reasonable to assume that the difference whether British English traders have one or two reasons for their online complaint has a stronger impact on their use of *intensifying features* than the particular type of reason they complain about. This is also underlined by the absolute frequencies with which these features are employed (see Table 6.53).

6.3. Comparison of the German data sets

Having outlined the results of the statistical comparison of the British English data sets, it is now turned to the findings of the comparison of the German data sets, which shed further light on the research questions 2 and 3.

Once more it begins with an illustration of the results of the use of complaint strategies and combinations of them (see Table 6.55, 6.56 and Figure 6.46).

Table 6.55: German eBay traders' use of complaint strategies and combinations of them in the four different data sets.

	German complaints relative frequencies (%)			
Strategies	**NR**	**DIFF**	**NR-D**	**DIFF-D**
Expression of disappointment	4	8	4	7
Expression of anger or annoyance	3	3	1	0
Explicit complaint	99	99	100	100
Negative judgement	14	12	13	13
Drawing one's own conclusion	8	5	6	13
Warning others	20	11	27	18
Threat	11	2	8	3
Insult	11	3	3	2
Strategy combination	50	37	55	48

Figure 6.46: Graphic representation of German eBay traders' use of complaint strategies and combinations of them in the four different data sets.

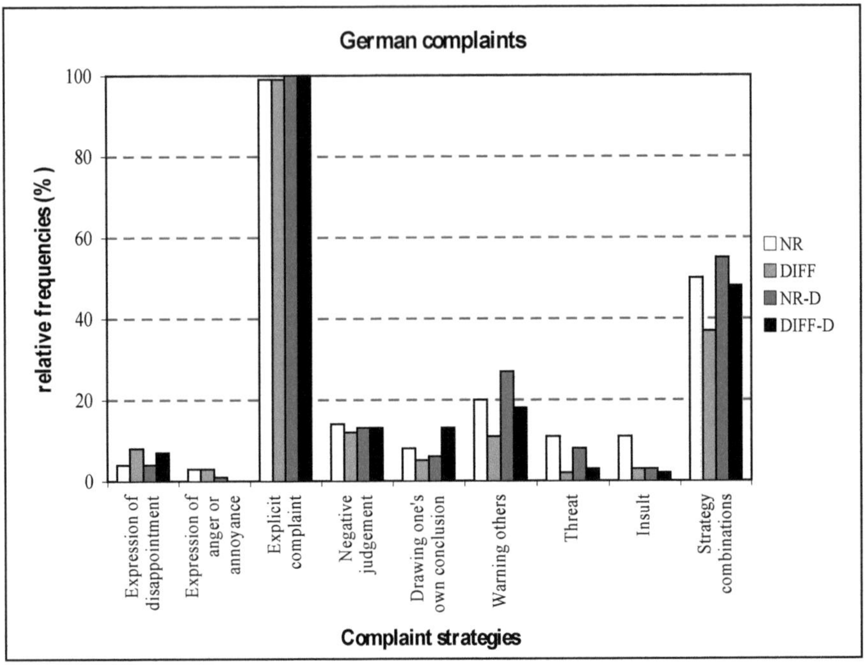

Table 6.56: Statistical comparison of German traders' use of complaint strategies, level of directness and strategy combinations in the four different data sets.

	German complaints Significance (p)			
	Different reason for complaining		One or two reasons for complaining	
Complaint strategies	**NR versus DIFF**	**NR-D versus DIFF-D**	**NR versus NR-D**	**DIFF versus DIFF-D**
Expression of disappointment	0.118	0.355	1.000	0.401
Expression of anger or annoyance	1.000	0.320	0.315	0.083
Explicit complaint	1.000	1.000	0.320	0.319
Negative judgement	0.844	0.858	0.853	0.849
Drawing one's own conclusion	0.392	0.181	0.803	**0.049***
Warning others	0.140	0.102	0.253	0.298
Threat	**0.010****	0.122	0.374	0.653
Insult	**0.021***	0.653	**0.021***	0.653
Level of directness	**0.001****	0.123	0.850	**0.024***
Strategy combination	0.064	0.324	0.481	0.117

As Table 6.55 and Figure 6.46 demonstrate, the German eBay traders use the same range of complaint strategies in almost all data sets. Only in the data set *Item DIFF-D* the strategy *expression of anger or annoyance* is missing. Due to the overall infrequent occurrence of this strategy, this finding is, however, not expressive. Table 6.55 and Figure 6.46 further show that, similar to the results of the British English speakers, also in the German data sets the strategy *explicit complaint* is by far the most common strategy employed.

Regarding research question 2, the reason for complaining seems to influence German traders complaining behaviour in that they show a clear tendency to use the more direct strategies *warning others, threat* and *insult* more often in the data set *Item NR* than *Item DIFF*. As far as the strategies *threat* and *insult* are concerned, this tendency results in a highly significant and a significant difference respectively (*threat* p = 0.010**, *insult* p = 0.021*, see Table 6.56). Accordingly, also the statistical comparison of the *level of directness* shows a highly significant difference between the data sets *Item NR* and *Item DIFF* in that the Germans choose a significantly higher *level of directness* when they have *not received the item* (p = 0.001**, see Table 6.56). The same tendency can also be found when comparing the double complaints, i.e. *Item NR-D* and *Item DIFF-D*, which is however weaker, since no significant difference can be found.

Moreover, the reason for complaining also seems to have some impact on the amount of *strategy combinations* German speakers use, since they also show a tendency to use more *strategy combinations* if they have *not received the item*, however, again without significant differences.

Turning to the investigation of research question 3, the findings reveal that also the number of reasons German eBay members have for their online complaint influences their use of complaint strategies. Specifically, if they complain about the fact that the *item was different than expected*, they also tend to use more direct strategies and *strategy combinations* in the double compared to the single complaints. To be more precise, they not only employ the strategy *drawing one's own conclusion* significantly more often in the data set *Item DIFF-D* compared to the data set *Item DIFF* (p = 0.049*, see Table 6.56), but also *warn the other eBay members* more often against the complainee, however, without a significant difference. When statistically comparing the *directness level* in the data sets *Item DIFF* and *Item DIFF-D* a significant difference is found in that the Germans are more direct in the double complaints compared to the single complaints (p = 0.024*, see Table 6.56). The statistical comparison of the amount of *strategy combinations* the German traders use in the single and double complaints does, on the other hand, not result in a significant difference, hence revealing that the tendency to use more *strategy combinations* in the double complaints *Item DIFF-D* is not that strong.

When looking at the findings of the comparison of the single and double complaints if the *item has not been received*, the findings show that the Germans significantly more often employ *insults* in the single complaints in the data set *Item NR* than in the double complaints in the data set *Item NR-D* (p = 0.021*, see Table 6.56). The chosen *level of directness* is, however, on the whole the same in the data sets *Item NR* and *Item NR-D*, and the tendency to use more *strategy combinations* in the double complaints than in the single complaints is only very weak.

Shifting the focus to the amount of strategies the German eBay traders use to formulate their complaints in the four different data sets the following Tables 6.57, 6.58 and Figure 6.47 illustrate the results.

Table 6.57: The amount of strategies German eBay traders use to formulate their complaints in the four different data sets.

	German complaints relative frequencies (%)			
Amount of strategies per complaint	**NR**	**DIFF**	**NR-D**	**DIFF-D**
Use of one strategy	50	63	45	52
Use of a combination of two strategies	29	26	42	38
Use of a combination of three strategies	18	10	13	10
Use of a combination of four strategies	2	1	0	0
Use of a combination of five strategies	1	0	0	0

Figure 6.47: Graphic representation of the amount of strategies German eBay traders use to formulate their complaints in the four different data sets.

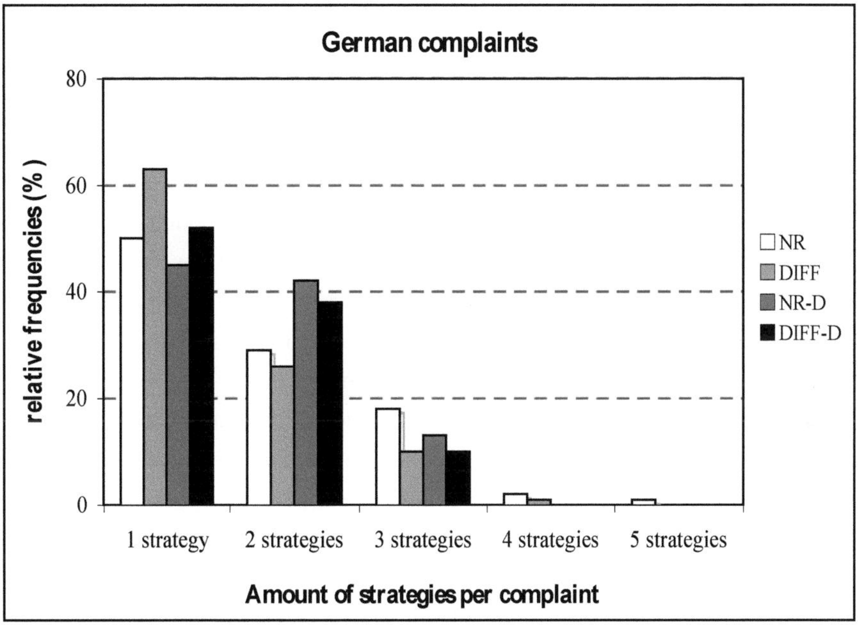

Table 6.58: Statistical comparison of the amount of strategies German eBay traders use to formulate their complaints in the four different data sets.

	German complaints Significance (p)			
	Different reason for complaining		One or two reasons for complaining	
Amount of strategies per complaint	**NR versus DIFF**	**NR-D versus DIFF-D**	**NR versus NR-D**	**DIFF versus DIFF-D**
Use of one strategy	0.064	0.324	0.481	0.360
Use of a combination of two strategies	0.637	0.566	0.055	0.117
Use of a combination of three strategies	0.104	0.509	0.331	0.070
Use of a combination of four strategies	0.563		0.158	1.000
Use of a combination of five strategies	0.320		0.320	0.320

As it becomes obvious from Table 6.57 and Figure 6.47, the complaints in all German data sets are minimally made up of one and maximally of three strategies. In the data sets *Item NR* and *Item DIFF* the German traders also employ a combination of four strategies, though only rarely, and in the data set *Item NR* they once use the combination of five strategies to formulate their online complaint (see Table 6.58).

In contrast to the British English speakers, the German traders' use of one strategy is influenced by the type of reason they complain about, since they tend to use one strategy more often if the *item was different than expected* than if they have *not received the item*. This difference is, however, not significant.

As far as the German traders' use of combinations of two strategies is concerned, the results reveal, as in the comparison of the British English data sets, an influence of the number of reasons they complain about. Specifically, also the Germans tend to use more combinations of two strategies in the double complaints. In contrast to the British English eBay members though, this tendency is too weak to result in any significant difference between the data sets.

The following Tables 6.59 and 6.60 as well as Figure 6.48 demonstrate the results of the strategy sequences the Germans use in the complaints in the four different data sets. The focus is again on the strategy sequences which occur at least 5% in one of the data sets under investigation.

Table 6.59: The strategy sequences German traders use in at least 5% in one of the data sets under investigation.

	German complaints relative frequencies (%)			
Strategy sequences (min. 5%)	**NR**	**DIFF**	**NR-D**	**DIFF-D**
Explicit complaint	46	62	45	52
Explicit complaint/drawing one's own conclusion	3	4	4	11
Explicit complaint/warning others	6	4	10	7
Explicit complaint/negative judgement	7	6	7	4
Warning others/explicit complaint	4	2	7	6
Explicit complaint/expression of disappointment	1	4	3	6
Explicit complaint/threat	4	1	6	0

Figure 6.48: Graphic representation of the strategy sequences German traders use in at least 5% in one of the data sets under investigation.

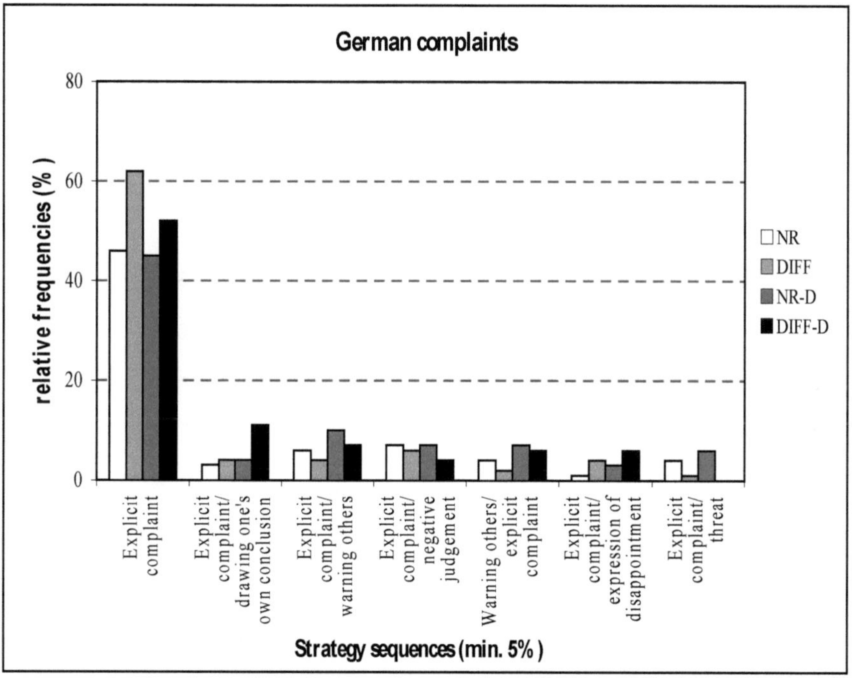

Table 6.60: Statistical comparison of the strategy sequences German traders use in at least 5% in one of the data sets under investigation.

	German complaints Significance (p)			
	Different reason for complaining		One or two reasons for complaining	
Strategy sequences (min. 5%)	**NR versus DIFF**	**NR-D versus DIFF-D**	**NR versus NR-D**	**DIFF versus DIFF-D**
Explicit complaint	0.064	0.324	0.573	0.155
Explicit complaint/ drawing one's own conclusion		0.061		0.061
Explicit complaint/ warning others	0.519	0.449	0.300	0.355
Explicit complaint/ negative judgement	0.776	0.355	1.000	0.519
Warning others/ explicit complaint		0.776	0.355	0.151
Explicit complaint/ expression of disappointment		0.473		0.735
Explicit complaint/threat		**0.014***	0.519	

Table 6.59 and Figure 6.48 reveal that, similar to the British English speakers, the Germans' use of one strategy in almost all cases goes hand in hand with the strategy *explicit complaint.* The employment of one strategy to formulate one's online complaint is thus again very uniform, while the use of combinations of strategies is more diverse. In light of these findings, it can thus be said that also in German the prototypical complaint in all data sets is a complaint which consists of one strategy, namely the strategy *explicit complaint.* Accordingly, as for the British English speakers, neither a difference in the type of reason nor in the number of reasons German traders complain about results in differences in the prototypical complaint they use. They, however, tend to use the prototypical complaint more often if they complain about the fact that the *item was different than expected,* particularly in the single complaints, but without significant differences.

Furthermore, the German eBay members tend to favour the use of the strategy sequence *explicit complaint* followed by *drawing one's own conclusion* in the data set *Item DIFF-D,* yet again without a significant difference. On the other hand, a significant difference can be found with regard to the use of the strategy combination *explicit complaint* and *threat* in the data set *Item NR-D* compared to the data set *Item DIFF-D* (p = 0.014*, see Table 6.60). Due to the overall infrequent occurrence of this strategy sequence though, this finding lacks expressiveness.

Shifting the focus to the amount of different strategy sequences German eBay traders use to formulate their complaints in the four different data sets, the following Tables 6.61 and 6.62 as well as Figure 6.49 reveal the results.

Table 6.61: The amount of different strategy sequences German eBay traders use to formulate their complaints in the four different data sets.

	German complaints relative frequencies (%)			
	NR	DIFF	NR-D	DIFF-D
Amount of different strategy sequences	31	21	21	18

Figure 6.49: Graphic representation of the amount of different strategy sequences German eBay traders use to formulate their complaints in the four different data sets.

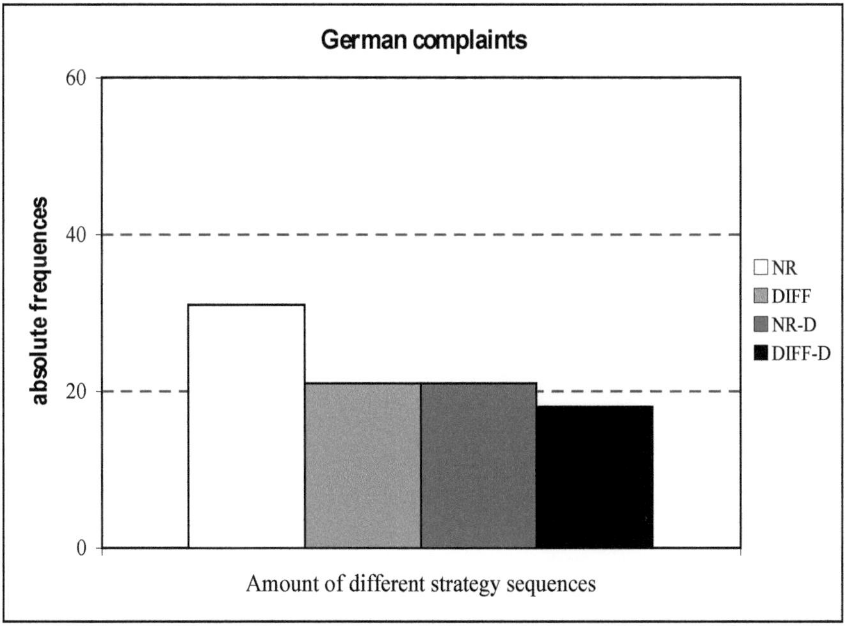

Table 6.62: Statistical comparison of the amount of different strategy sequences German eBay traders use to formulate their complaints in the four different data sets.

	German complaints Significance (p)			
	Different reason for complaining		**One or two reasons for complaining**	
	NR versus DIFF	**NR-D versus DIFF-D**	**NR versus NR-D**	**DIFF versus DIFF-D**
Amount of different strategy sequences	0.166	0.631	0.166	0.631

As becomes obvious from Table 6.61 and Figure 6.49, the German speakers use more different strategy sequences in the data set *Item NR* and slightly less in the data set *Item DIFF-D*. However, similar to the comparison of the British English data sets, also in the German data sets no significant differences can be found. It is thus reasonable to assume that once more neither the type of reason nor the number of reasons German speakers complain about has a real impact on the amount of different strategy sequences they employ.

Turning to the use of modification, the following Tables 6.63, 6.64 and Figure 6.50 illustrate the results of the use of upgrading modifiers.

Table 6.63: German eBay traders' use of upgrading modifiers in their complaints in the four different data sets.

	German complaints relative frequencies (%)			
Upgrading modifiers	**NR**	**DIFF**	**NR-D**	**DIFF-D**
Intensifier	34	25	30	31
Aggressive interrogative	2	3	2	2
Time reference	22	1	20	7
Sarcasm	2	1	0	1

Figure 6.50: Graphic representation of German eBay traders' use of upgrading modifiers in their complaints in the four different data sets.

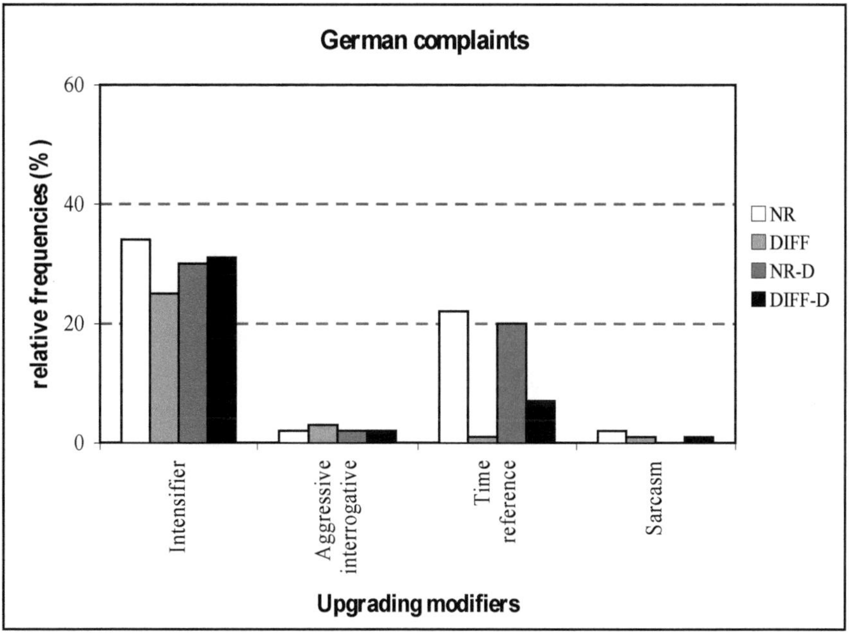

Table 6.64: Statistical comparison of German eBay traders' use of upgrading modifiers in their complaints in the four different data sets.

	German complaints Significance (p)			
	Different reason for complaining		One or two reasons for complaining	
Upgrading modifiers	NR versus DIFF	NR-D versus DIFF-D	NR versus NR-D	DIFF versus DIFF-D
Intensifier	0.369	1.000	0.567	0.731
Aggressive interrogative	0.653	1.000	1.000	0.653
Time reference	**0.000008****	**0.006****	0.546	**0.031***
Sarcasm	0.563	0.320	0.158	1.000

Table 6.63 and Figure 6.50 show that, as in all British English data sets, the *intensifier* is also in all German data sets the most frequently employed type of upgrading modifier. In contrast to the results of the British English data sets though, this type of modifier is used to an almost similar extent throughout the four different German data sets. Thus, neither the number of reasons nor the

type of reason the German speakers complain about impacts their use of *intensifiers*.

Regarding the use of the *time reference* a comparison of Table 6.46 and Table 6.64 reveals that the British English and German speakers show very similar behaviour in this respect. Precisely, the type of reason for the online complaint has a clear influence on both British English and German traders' use of the *time reference*, in that British English speakers and German speakers particularly employ this type of upgrading modifier if they have *not received the item*. Thus, also the comparison of the German data sets *Item NR* and *Item DIFF* as well as the comparison of the German data sets *Item NR-D* and *Item DIFF-D* result in highly significant differences (*NR* versus *DIFF* p = 0.000008**, *NR-D* versus *DIFF-D* p = 0.006**, see Table 6.64). In addition to that, *time references* also occur in the German data set *Item DIFF-D* significantly more often compared to the data set *Item DIFF* (p = 0.031*, see Table 6.64). Yet again, the overall infrequent occurrence of the *time reference* in the data sets *Item DIFF* and *Item DIFF-D* clearly reduces the expressiveness of this finding.

Finally, Table 6.63 and 6.64 as well as Figure 6.50 illustrate that the *aggressive interrogative* and *sarcasm* are only rarely used in all data sets and without significant differences between them. An influence of the factors under investigation is hence absent.

The following Tables 6.65 and 6.66 as well as Figure 6.51 illustrate the results of the German eBay traders' use of downgrading features in the complaints in the four different data sets.

Table 6.65: German eBay traders' use of downgrading modifiers in their complaints in the four different data sets.

	German complaints relative frequencies (%)			
Downgrading modifiers	**NR**	**DIFF**	**NR-D**	**DIFF-D**
Expression of regret	5	5	2	3
Play down	0	4	0	2
Understater	0	0	0	0
Politeness marker	0	0	1	0
Disarmer	3	8	1	0
Intensifier (downgrading)	0	1	0	0

Figure 6.51: Graphic representation of German eBay traders' use of downgrading modifiers in their complaints in the four different data sets.

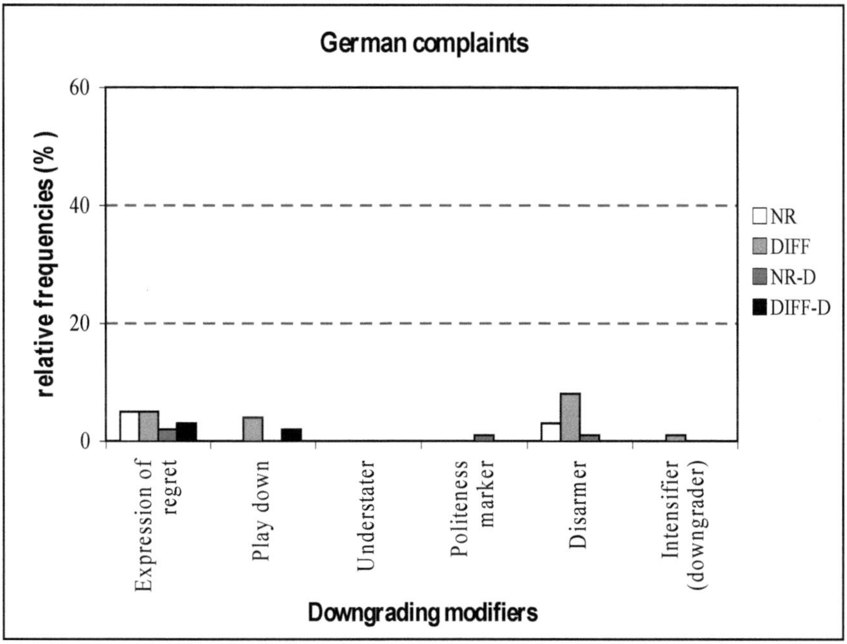

Table 6.66: Statistical comparison of German eBay traders' use of downgrading modifiers in their complaints in the four different data sets.

	German complaints Significance (p)			
	Different reason for complaining		One or two reasons for complaining	
Downgrading modifiers	**NR versus DIFF**	**NR-D versus DIFF-D**	**NR versus NR-D**	**DIFF versus DIFF-D**
Expression of regret	1.000	0.653	0.251	0.473
Play down	**0.045***	0.158		0.410
Understater				
Politeness marker		0.320	0.320	
Disarmer	0.122	0.320	0.315	**0.004****
Intensifier (downgrading)	0.320			0.320

As Table 6.65 and Figure 6.51 illustrate, the different types of downgrading modifiers are used, also in the German data sets, only very rarely. Nevertheless, the Germans do not only use the *play down* in the data set *Item DIFF* significantly more often compared to the data set *Item NR* (p = 0.045*, see Table 6.66), but also significantly more often *disarmer* in the data set *Item DIFF* compared the data set *Item DIFF-D* (p= 0.004**, see Table 6.66), whereby in the latter comparison p even reveals a highly significant difference. These findings point to an influence of both the type of reason and number of reasons German speakers have for their online complaint. Precisely, they particularly use downgrading devices if they only complain about the fact that the *item was different than expected*. An additional reason for complaining or the fact that the *item has not been received*, on the other hand, prevents the use of downgrading modifiers. On the whole it is, however, important to mention that in light of the overall infrequent occurrence of downgrading devices, these tendencies can only be regarded as weak.

What follows are the results of German eBay traders' use of pronouns in the complaints in the four different data sets (see Table 6.67, 6.68 and Figure 6.52).

Table 6.67: German eBay traders' use of pronouns in the complaints in the four different data sets.

	German complaints relative frequencies (%)			
Use of pronouns	**NR**	**DIFF**	**NR-D**	**DIFF-D**
First person pronouns	15	5	5	4
Second person pronouns	0	0	0	1
Third person pronouns	1	0	0	1
Demonstrative pronouns	3	1	0	0
Pronouns (complainee)	4	1	0	2
Pronouns (eBay community)	1	0	0	0
Indefinite pronouns	2	1	0	0

Figure 6.52: Graphic representation of German eBay traders' use of pronouns in the complaints in the four different data sets.

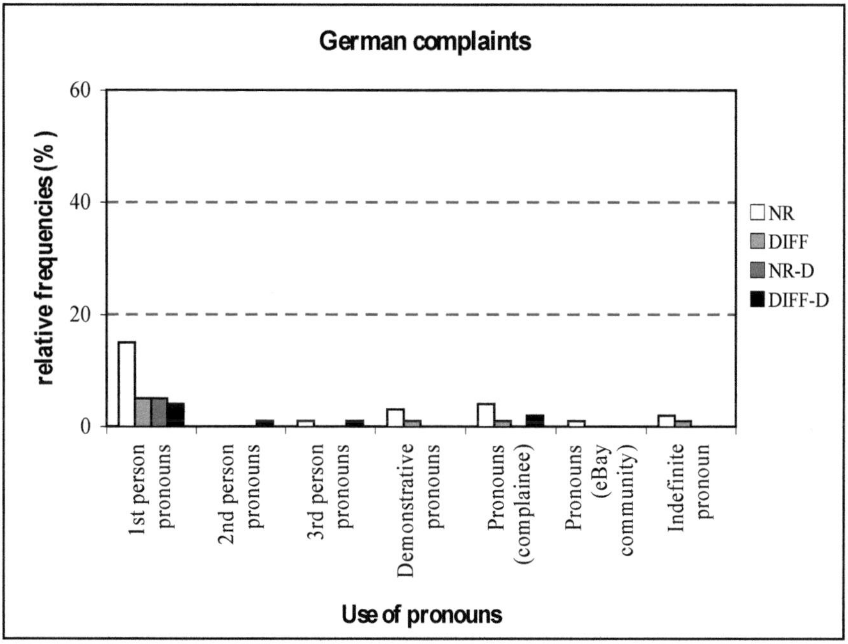

Table 6.68: Statistical comparison of German eBay traders' use of pronouns in the complaints in the four different data sets.

	German complaints Significance (p)			
	Different reason for complaining		One or two reasons for complaining	
Use of pronouns	**NR versus DIFF**	**NR-D versus DIFF-D**	**NR versus NR-D**	**DIFF versus DIFF-D**
First person pronouns	**0.014***	0.558	**0.032***	0.735
Second person pronouns		0.320		0.320
Third person pronouns	0.320	0.320	0.320	0.320
Demonstrative pronouns	0.315		0.083	0.320
Pronouns (complainee)	0.176	0.158	**0.045***	0.563
Pronouns (eBay community)	0.320		0.320	
Indefinite pronouns	0.563		0.158	0.320

Table 6.67 and Figure 6.52 demonstrate that the German speakers particularly favour the use of *first person pronouns* in their complaints in the data set *Item NR*. As a consequence, both the comparison of the data sets *Item NR* and *Item*

DIFF as well as of the data sets *Item NR* and *Item NR-D* result in significant differences (*NR* versus *DIFF* $p = 0.014*$, *NR* versus *NR-D* $p = 0.032*$, see Table 6.68), which reveals an influence of both the type of reason as well as the number of reasons German traders have for their online complaint. In other words, an additional reason for complaining or the fact that the *Item was different than expected*, rather than that the *item has not been received*, leads to a reduced employment of *first person pronouns*.
As Table 6.67 and Figure 6.52 further demonstrate, all other types of pronouns are very rarely used. Nonetheless, the comparison of the *pronouns referring to the complainee* in the data set *Item NR* versus the data set *Item NR-D* results in a significant difference ($p = 0.045*$, see Table 6.68) in that the German speakers favour the use of these pronouns in the data set *Item NR*. However, due to the overall infrequent occurrence of these pronouns, this finding is not very expressive. Yet it hints at the fact that German traders use pronouns particularly to intensify the face-threat of the complaint if they complain about the fact that they have *not received the item* and do not have an additional reason for their online complaint.
Shifting the focus to the German eBay users' handling of features of CMC, the following Tables 6.69 and 6.70 as well as Figure 6.53 illustrate the results.

Table 6.69: German eBay traders' use of features of CMC in the complaints in the four different data sets.

	German complaints relative frequencies (%)			
Use of features of CMC	**NR**	**DIFF**	**NR-D**	**DIFF-D**
Emoticons	1	1	1	1
Visual signs	0	0	0	1
Capitalisation (words)	10	6	10	9
Capitalisation (message)	7	3	9	2
Ex. m. (single)	22	22	26	35
Ex. m. (repeated)	41	23	39	21
Repet. other punct. m.	1	1	1	2
Repet. letters	0	0	1	0
Intensifying features CMC (downgrading)	1	0	0	0

Figure 6.53: Graphic representation of German eBay traders' use of features of CMC in the complaints in the four different data sets.

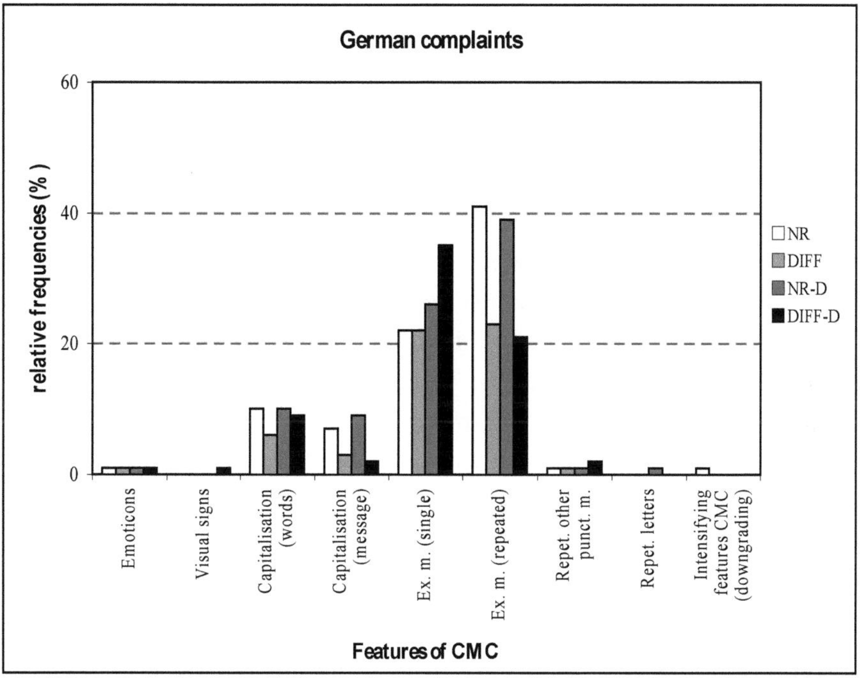

Table 6.70: Statistical comparison of German eBay traders' use of features of CMC in the complaints in the four different data sets.

	German complaints Significance (p)			
	Different reason for complaining		One or two reasons for complaining	
Use of features of CMC	**NR versus DIFF**	**NR-D versus DIFF-D**	**NR versus NR-D**	**DIFF versus DIFF-D**
Emoticons	1.000	1.000	1.000	1.000
Visual signs		0.320		0.320
Capitalisation (words)	0.300	0.811	1.000	0.423
Capitalisation (message)	0.196	**0.030***	0.604	0.653
Ex. m. (single)	0.890	0.155	0.218	**0.005****
Ex. m. (repeated)	**0.001****	**0.008****	0.842	0.664
Repet. other punct. m.	1.000	1.000	0.655	0.563
Repet. letters		0.320	0.320	
Intensifying features CMC (downgrading)	0.320		0.320	

As it becomes obvious from Table 6.69 and Figure 6.53, the Germans also use *emoticons* only rarely in all data sets and *visual signs* occur only once in the data set *Item DIFF-D*. Accordingly, significant differences cannot be found (see Table 6.70), which demonstrates that the Germans' use of these features of CMC is not influenced by the factors under investigation.
With regard to German traders' use of *capitalisation of words* only a very weak influence of both factors, the particular type of reason as well as the number of reasons German speakers have for their online complaint, can be found. Specifically, they *capitalise words* within their message the least if they only complain about the fact that the *item was different than expected.* The differences between data sets are, however, only small and certainly do not result in any significant differences.
With regard to the use of *capitalisation of the whole message*, the Germans are, as the British English speakers, influenced by the type of reason they complain about in that they *capitalise the whole message* more often if they have *not received the item,* regardless of whether they have one or two reasons for their online complaint. The difference in the use of the *capitalisation of the whole message* is thereby smaller in the comparison of the data sets *Item NR* and *Item DIFF*, since only the comparison of the data sets *Item NR-D* and *Item DIFF-D* results in a significant difference ($p = 0.030$*, see Table 6.70).
As far as the Germans' use of *exclamation marks* is concerned, the employment of *single* as well as *repeated ones* are influenced in different ways. To be more precise, the Germans particularly favour the use of *single exclamation marks* in their complaints in the data set *Item DIFF-D*. This finding points at an impact of both factors under investigation in that the German speakers only make a difference between single and double complaints if they have to complain about the fact that the *item was different than expected.* The statistical comparison between the data sets *Item DIFF* and *Item DIFF-D* thereby even reveals a highly significant difference ($p = 0.005$**, see Table 6.70).
As far as the use of the *repetition of exclamation marks* is concerned, a clear influence of the type of reason German traders complain about becomes apparent. Precisely, the German speakers particularly *repeat exclamation marks* if they have *not received the item*, regardless of whether they have one or two reasons to complain about. Accordingly, both the comparison of the data sets

Item NR and *Item DIFF* as well as the comparison of the data sets *Item NR-D* and *Item DIFF-D* result in highly significant differences (*NR* versus *DIFF* p = 0.001**, *NR-D* versus *DIFF-D* p = 0.008**, see Table 6.70).

Turning the focus to the *repetition of punctuation marks other than exclamation marks*, Table 6.69 and Figure 6.53 reveal that they occur only rarely in all data sets and to an almost similar extent. *Letters* are only *repeated* once in the data set *Item NR-D* and an *intensifying feature of CMC used to aggravate the mitigating effect of downgrading modifiers* occurs once in the data set *Item NR*. The factors under investigation thus do not impact the use of these features of CMC.

Last but not least, it is dealt with the results of the occurrence of the sum variables in the four different German data sets (see Tables 6.71, 6.72 and Figure 6.54).

Table 6.71: The occurrence of sum variables in the four different German data sets.

	German complaints							
	NR		DIFF		NR-D		DIFF-D	
Sum variables	#	%	#	%	#	%	#	%
Total use of mitigating features	11	10	19	17	4	4	5	4
Total use of intensifying features	272	89	157	66	273	86	216	77

Figure 6.54: Graphic representation of the occurrence of sum variables in the four German data sets.

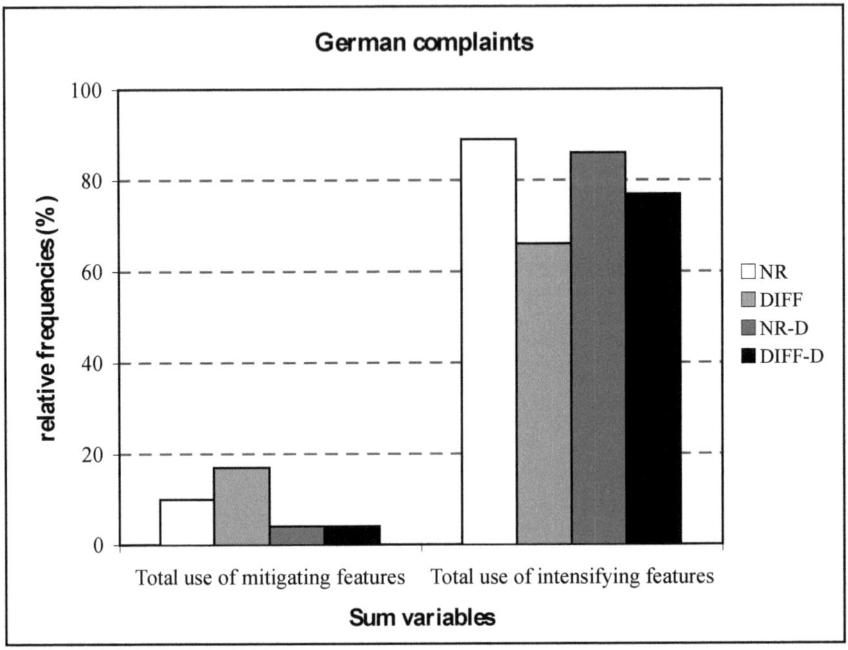

Table 6.72: Statistical comparison of the occurrence of sum variables in the four German data sets.

	German complaints Significance (p)			
	Different reason for complaining		**One or two reasons for complaining**	
Sum variables	**NR versus DIFF**	**NR-D versus DIFF-D**	**NR versus NR-D**	**DIFF versus DIFF-D**
Total of mitigating features	0.169	0.760	0.080	**0.008****
Total of intensifying features	**0.000008****	**0.046***	0.972	**0.018***

With regard to the total use of *mitigating features*, the German traders show a similar behaviour as the British English ones. Accordingly, Table 6.71 and Figure 6.54 reveal that *mitigating features* occur also in all German data sets clearly less often than *intensifying features*. Furthermore, the Germans show, similar to their British English counterparts, the tendency to mitigate their complaints particularly in the data set *Item DIFF*, whereby the comparison of the data sets *Item DIFF* and *Item DIFF-D* results in a significant difference, which in the case of the German speakers is even highly significant (p = 0.008**, see Table 6.72). In light of these findings, the presence of *mitigating features* in the German data sets seems, as in the British English ones, to be influenced by both the type of reason as well as the number of reasons the German eBay members have for their online complaint.

Shifting the focus to the German traders' *total use of intensifying features*, Table 6.71 and Figure 6.54 further illustrate that also the German speakers employ more *intensifying features* if they have *not received the item* than if they have to complain about the fact that the *item was different than expected*. In contrast to the British English speakers, the particular reason for complaining has a much stronger impact on German traders' *total use of intensifying features*, since both the comparison of the German data sets *Item NR* and *Item DIFF* as well as of the data sets *Item NR-D* and *Item DIFF-D* reveal a significant difference (*NR* versus *DIFF* p = 0.000008**, *NR-D* versus *DIFF-D* p = 0.046*, see Table 6.72). With regard to the comparison of the data sets *Item NR* and *Item DIFF*, p even reveals a highly significant difference. The comparisons of the British English data sets *Item NR* and *Item DIFF* as well as of the data sets *Item NR-D* and *Item DIFF-D* do, on the other hand, remains above the level of significance (see Table 6.54).

Focusing on the second influential factor, i.e. the number of reasons traders complain about, Table 6.71 and Figure 6.54 show that the fact whether German traders have one or two reasons for their online complaint has, in contrast to the British English speakers, no general influence on their *total use of intensifying features*. Precisely, only if the German speakers complain about the fact that the *item was different than expected* this factor has an impact in that they significantly more often intensify their double complaints in the data set *Item DIFF-D* (p = 0.018*, see Table 6.72). However, if they complain about the fact that they have *not received the item*, no differences between single and double complaints can be found.

6.4. Summary of the results

The comparison of British English and German complaining behaviour on the feedback forum of eBay reveals both similarities and differences. Due to the differences, research question 1, according to which it is asked whether British English and German traders' computer-mediated complaints differ with regard to the five categories of analysis, must be answered with a 'yes'.

With regard to the similarities, the results show that both the British English and German eBay traders use the same range of complaint strategies, whereby the strategy *explicit complaint* is by far the most common strategy employed in all data sets. Furthermore, the British English and German speakers use the same prototypical complaint in all four data sets, which is a complaint consisting of one strategy, namely an *explicit complaint*. Additionally, the amount of different strategy sequences British English and German traders use to formulate their complaints is also very similar, revealing that neither the British English nor the German complaints are more formulaic or diverse than the other. Finally it is worth mentioning the similarity that both the British English and German traders use many more *intensifying* than *mitigating features* in their complaints, whereby the amount of mitigation is approximately the same in all data sets.

On the other hand, the results also reveal differences. That is, although British English and German traders employ the same prototypical complaint in the four different data sets, the Germans nevertheless use significantly more *direct strategies* as well as *strategy combinations* in cases where they have *not received the item*. The German complaints in the data set *Item NR* are also significantly more often *intensified* than the British English ones. Furthermore, the German traders *threaten* their complainee significantly more often if they have *not received the item*, in single and double complaints. What is more, they are more in favour of the strategy *drawing one's own conclusion*, especially in the data set *Item DIFF-D*, in which a highly significant difference between the German and British English traders can be found. The British English traders, on the other hand, employ *insults* and the strategy combination *explicit complaint/insult* significantly more often in the data set *Item NR-D*.

Further obvious differences can be found in the way British English and German eBay members intensify their complaints. While the Germans use *exclamation mark(s)* significantly more often to express their anger in all data sets, the British English speakers favour the use of *pronouns which refer to the complainee* to stress the complainee's guilt in the state of affairs, and thus to aggravate their complaints. Only with regard to the data set *Item DIFF-D* no significant difference in the use of these pronouns can be traced.

Moreover, the British English traders use significantly more *first person pronouns* in all data sets to stress their personal involvement in the state of affairs. The value of p thereby even reveals a highly significant difference between all British English and German data sets.

In addition to these clear differences between the British English and German complaining behaviour on eBay, two weaker differing tendencies also become apparent. The first is the British English traders' bias to employ *capitalisation* as a means of intensification. Specifically, they use the *capitalisation of words* and *of the whole message* more often in the data sets *Item DIFF*, *Item NR-D* and *Item DIFF-D*, and the *capitalisation of words* more frequently in the remaining data set *Item NR*. However, these tendencies are not strong enough to result in significant differences between the British English and German data sets.

The second rather weak tendency, which nevertheless points at a difference between the British English and German complaints, concerns the use of the downgrading modifier *expression of regret*. Namely, this type of modifier is significantly more often favoured by the German speakers in the single complaints in the data sets *Item NR* and *Item DIFF*. However, since these significant differences are based on low frequencies only, this differing tendency has to be judged as only weak.

Shifting the focus to the investigation of whether the two factors, i.e. the particular type of reason and the number of reasons British English and German traders have for their online complaint, influence their complaining behaviour on the feedback forum of eBay, the findings illustrate as follows. The British English and the German speakers are influenced by both of these factors. The answers to research question 2 and 3 are thus also 'yes'.

When looking at how these factors affect British English and German speakers' use of *mitigating* and *intensifying features* in general, similarities as well as differences again become apparent.

Regarding the similarities, the two factors equally affect British English and German speakers' use of *mitigating features* in that they most frequently mitigate the single complaints of the data set *Item DIFF*. At the same time, both the British English and German traders use more *intensifying features* if they have *not received the item*, revealing a clear impact of the type of reason they complain about. This influence is even stronger with the German eBay members.

Another difference concerns the way in which British English and German traders' use of *intensifying features* is influenced by the number of reasons they have for their online complaint. The British English speakers are not only more strongly impacted but also more generally affected by this factor in that they use more *intensifying features* in double than in single complaints, regardless of the reason for their complaint. The influence on German speakers is, on the other hand, more specific. In other words, they are only sensitive to the number of reasons they complain about, i.e. they use more *intensifying features* in double than single complaints when they complain about the fact that the *item was different than expected.* In contrast to that, the complaints in the data sets *Item NR* and *Item NR-D* are intensified to an almost similar extent.

When taking a closer look at how the two influential factors impact the use of the different means that British English and German traders have at their disposal to mitigate and intensify the complaint, or to stress their personal involvement, the picture becomes very complex. Nonetheless, these influences reveal some tendencies regarding which of these means British English and German speakers favour in their complaints in one data set rather than the other due to an impact of the investigated factor(s). An overview of how the two factors under investigation influence the British English and German eBay members' use of the different features of mitigation, intensification, and of expressing their personal involvement is given in the following Tables 6.73, 6.74, 6.75 and Tables 6.76, 6.77, 6.78. For the sake of clarity, significant differences between data sets which are based on low frequencies only, and thus lack expressiveness, have been left out.[39] On the other hand, tendencies which

[39] An exception was made with regard to the use of mitigating features, due to their overall infrequent occurrence.

are weaker and remain above significance level, yet make the influence of factor(s) clearer, have been added to the tables but printed in brackets.

Table 6.73: Overview of how the two investigated factors influence the different features BrE traders may use to mitigate their complaints.

Means of mitigation	NR	DIFF	NR-D	DIFF-D	Influencing factor(s)
Downgrading modifiers		Disarmer			type, number

Table 6.74: Overview of how the two investigated factors influence the different features BrE traders may use to intensify their complaints.

Means of intensification	NR	DIFF	NR-D	DIFF-D	Influencing factor(s)
Level of directness			More direct in NR-D versus NR, mainly warning others and insult	More direct in DIFF-D versus DIFF	number
Strategy combinations	One strategy	One strategy	Combination of two strategies	Combina-tion of two strategies	number
Upgrading modifiers	Time reference		Time reference		type
			Intensifier		type, number
Pronouns	Pronouns referring to the complainee		Pronouns referring to the complai-nee, mainly (third person pronouns) and demonstra-tive pronouns		type
Intensifying features of CMC		(Capitali-sation of words)	Capitalisa-tion of words	(Capitalisa-tion of words)	type, number
	(Capitalisa-tion of the message)		(Capitalisa-tion of the message)		type
		Single exclamation marks	(Single exclamation marks)	(Single exclamation marks)	type, number
				Repetition of exclama-tion marks	type, number

Table 6.75: Overview of how the two investigated factors influence BrE traders' use of first person pronouns to express their personal involvement.

Means expressing one's personal involvement	NR	DIFF	NR-D	DIFF-D	Influencing factor(s)
Pronouns	First person pronouns		First person pronouns		type

Abbreviations:
type = the type of reasons speakers complain about,
number = the number of reasons speakers complain about,
for the remaining abbreviations see 6.2.

Table 6.73 illustrates that British English speakers' use of *disarmer* is influenced by both factors under investigation, i.e. the type of reason and the number of reasons they complain about. Specifically, they favour the use of *disarmer* in their complaints in the data set *Item DIFF*. An influence of the factors under investigation on the employment of other features of mitigation is absent.

Furthermore, although the prototypical British English complaint is a complaint consisting of the strategy *explicit complaint*, Table 6.74 reveals that the number of reasons British English traders have for their online complaint still has an impact on the *directness level* they choose as well as their use of *strategy combinations*. In other words, they choose a higher *level of directness* in double compared to single complaints, whereby in the data set *Item NR-D* this mainly results from a higher occurrence of the strategies *warning others* and *insult*. Furthermore, they more frequently employ a *combination of two strategies* in double than in single complaints, whereas in the latter they favour just one strategy.

British English speakers' use of *time references*, *pronouns referring to the complainee* as well as the *capitalisation of the whole message* are, on the other hand, influenced by the type of reason they complain about (see Table 6.74). Precisely, they particularly intensify their complaints by the use of *time references*, *pronouns referring to the complainee*, and the *capitalisation of the whole message* if they have *not received the item*. As far as the complaints in the data set *Item NR-D* are concerned, the *pronouns referring to the complainee* mainly consist of *third person pronouns* and *demonstrative pronouns followed by a noun denoting the complainee*.

Table 6.74 further reveals that British English traders' employment of *intensifiers*, the *capitalisation of words*, as well as of *single* and *repeated exclamation marks* are impacted by both factors under investigation, i.e. the type of reason and the number of reasons they complain about. Accordingly, they favour *intensifiers* in their complaints in the data set *Item NR-D* and *repeat exclamation marks* favourably in the data set *Item DIFF-D*. The influence on their employment of *capitalisation of words* and *single exclamation marks* is, on the other hand, rather complex. To be precise, they use the *capitalisation of words* more frequently in double rather than single complaints. Similarly though, the comparison of the single complaints shows that they use *capitalisation of words* more often if they complain about the fact that the *item was different than expected*. With regard to the use of *single exclamation marks*, British English traders employ them more frequently if they complain about the fact that the *item was different than expected*, regardless of whether they have one or two reasons to complain about. If British English eBay members, however, have *not received the item*, they use more *single exclamation marks* in double rather than single complaints.

Finally, Table 6.75 shows that the type of reason British English speakers complain about influences their use of *first person pronouns* in that they particularly stress their personal involvement if they have *not received the item*, regardless of whether they have one or two reasons for complaining.

Turning to the German eBay members, the following Tables 6.76, 6.77, 6.78 give an overview of how the two factors under investigation influence their use of the different features of mitigation, intensification, and of expressing their personal involvement.

Table 6.76: Overview of how the two investigated factors influence the different features German traders may use to mitigate their complaints.

Means of mitigation	**NR**	**DIFF**	**NR-D**	**DIFF-D**	**Influencing factor(s)**
Downgrading modifiers		Disarmer			type, number
		Play down			type, number

Table 6.77: Overview of how the two investigated factors influence the different features German traders may use to intensify their complaints.

Means of intensification	NR	DIFF	NR-D	DIFF-D	Influencing factor(s)
Level of directness	More direct in NR versus DIFF, mainly due to the use of warning others, threat, and insult			More direct in DIFF-D versus DIFF, mainly due to the use of drawing one's conclusion and warning others	type, number
Strategy combinations	(Combinations of strategies, amount more diverse)	(One strategy)	(Combination of two strategies)	(Combination of two strategies)	type, number
Upgrading modifiers	Time reference		Time reference		type
Intensifying features of CMC	(Capitalisation of the message)		Capitalisation of the message		type
				Single exclamation mark	type, number
	Repetition of exclamation mark		Repetition of exclamation mark		type

Table 6.78: Overview of how the two investigated factors influence German traders' use of first person pronouns to express their personal involvement.

Means expressing one's personal involvement	NR	DIFF	NR-D	DIFF-D	Influencing factor(s)
Pronouns	First person pronouns				type, number

Table 6.76 shows that the German traders' use of *disarmer* and *play down* is influenced by both factors under investigation in that they particularly favour their use if they complain about the fact that the *item was different than expected* and do not have an additional reason to complain about. Other features of mitigation do not display an influence of the factors under investigation.

As mentioned before, similar to the British English prototypical complaint also the German prototypical complaint is a complaint consisting of the strategy *explicit complaint* in all data sets. Nevertheless, Table 6.77 illustrates that, similar to the British English speakers, the factors under investigation also have an impact on the German traders' choice of the *directness level* they use as well as their employment of *strategy combinations*. The influences on the German speakers, however, differ from those on the British English ones. To be precise, the German's choice of *directness* and their use of *strategy combinations* are impacted by both factors, i.e. the type of reason and the number of reasons they complain about. For the *directness level*, Table 6.77 reveals that in single complaints the Germans are more direct if they have *not received the item*, which results mainly from the more frequent use of the strategies *warning others*, *threat*, and *insult*. If they complain about the fact that the *item was different than expected*, they become more direct in the double than the single complaints, which mainly results from a more frequent occurrence of the strategies *drawing one's own conclusion* and *warning others*.
Regarding the use of *strategy combinations*, there is a much weaker influence of the two investigated factors on the Germans than on the British English traders. Specifically, similar to the British English traders, the Germans also tend to use more *combinations of two strategies* in double rather than single complaints, however, without significant differences between data sets. In contrast to the British English traders, the Germans use one strategy only more frequently in the data set *Item DIFF* compared to the other data sets. However, if they have *not received the item* and do not have an additional reason for their online complaint they tend to employ more *strategy combinations* which are made up of more diverse numbers of strategies than their double complaints. Yet, also the influence of the factors on the German speakers' use of *strategy combinations* in the single complaints remains above the level of significance.
Furthermore, Table 6.77 shows that the type of reason they complain about influences their use of *time references*, the *capitalisation of the whole message*, and the *repetition of exclamation marks*. Similar to British English eBay members, the Germans particularly favour the use of *time references* and the *capitalisation of the whole message* if they have *not received the item*, regardless of whether they have one or two reasons for their online complaint. In

contrast to the British English speakers though, the German speakers additionally intensify their complaints in the data sets *Item NR* and *Item NR-D* by the *repetition of exclamation marks*.

German traders' use of *single exclamation marks* is, on the other hand, again influenced by both factors, i.e. the type of reason and the number of reasons they complain about, in that they favour *single exclamation marks* in their complaints in the data set *Item DIFF-D*.

Last but not least, Table 6.78 reveals that the German eBay members' use of *first person pronouns* is also impacted by both the type of reason and the number of reasons they complain about. Precisely, they mainly stress their personal involvement if they have *not received the item* and do not have an additional reason to complain.

To conclude, the results of this study show that the answers to all three research questions are positive. In other words, there are not only similarities but also differences in the way British English and German eBay traders formulate their online complaints. Furthermore, British English and German traders are influenced by both factors under investigation, i.e. the particular type of reason they complain about as well as the number of reasons they have for their online complaints. The way that these factors impact British English and German traders' linguistic choices is thereby complex and often differs with respect to distinct linguistic features.

Chapter 7: Discussion

Having outlined the results, they are now discussed with regard to previous research on complaining behaviour (7.1.) before they are interpreted in light of the famous theories of (im)politeness (7.2.) described above (see 2.3.).

7.1. Discussion in light of previous research on complaints

Given that studies often differ in their methodological approach even when focussing on the same phenomenon, such as complaints, it is difficult to compare their outcomes, since all the different factors involved in the data elicitation may influence the overall results. Some of these factors include the different composition of subjects, the use of different data eliciting instruments, and different situations described in these instruments, which in turn are accompanied by different contextual factors of these situations. Despite this complex picture of influencing factors, it is nonetheless useful to compare different studies on complaints, since it is these differences that may hint at factor(s) which will most likely have impacted participants' linguistic choices. Thus, when factors which seem to have caused a particular outcome are discussed, it is not to deny the complexity of other variables or combinations of them which may also have had a partial impact. The discussed factor(s), however, seem to be among the candidates for having an influence on subjects' linguistic behaviour. Of course, future research is needed to prove the hypothesised influences.

When looking at the complaint strategies British English and German eBay traders use in the present study, it becomes obvious that, in contrast to complaining behaviour in oral communication, both the British English and the German speakers are more direct in CMC. To be more precise, in studies on complaints in spoken communication (cf. Geluykens and Kraft 2003; House and Kasper 1981; Kraft and Geluykens 2002, 2004; Olshtain and Weinbach 1993; Trosborg 1995) the subjects quite frequently chose strategies which were less direct than any strategy defined in the present study, and at the same time avoided or only extremely rarely chose the most direct one(s). However, one must bear in mind that only House and Kasper's (1981) and Geluykens and

Kraft's (2003) study focused on the same nationalities as the present one. Kraft and Geluykens (2002, 2004), Olshtain and Weinbach (1993), and Trosborg (1995) compared British English or German native speakers to members of other nationalities. Their findings may hence be less valuable for a comparison with the results of the present study. Yet, both House and Kasper's (1981) as well as Geluykens and Kraft (2003) results confirm the above-mentioned findings of British English and German speakers less direct complaining behaviour in spoken interaction. Specifically, with regard to the most direct end of the continuum, House and Kasper (1981) found that their most direct level, which is similarly defined as the most direct strategy of the present study, namely *insult*, occurred just once (0.9%) in the German and never in the English data (House and Kasper 1981: 161). In contrast to that, *insults* are chosen in the present electronic data by both the British English and German native speakers, and even amount to a maximum of 14% in the British English data set *Item NR-D* and 11% in the German data set *Item NR*. These findings therefore demonstrate a greater directness in CMC compared to spoken discourse. This difference is likely to result from the particular communicative situation of this new language modality in which members remain anonymous and are less fearful of retribution than they would be in physical space. This assumption is supported by research showing that the anonymity in the Internet abets abusive behaviour (cf. Danet 1998; Gilboa 1996; Graham 2008; Herring 1994, 2002, 2004b; Hiltrop 2003). On eBay's feedback forum the anonymity is further enhanced by the employment of usernames, which work like masks behind which one can hide and hence protect one's real identity (cf. Danet 1998).
The liberating effect of the anonymity in CMC seems to be even stronger on British English speakers, since the difference between their complaining behaviour in spoken interaction and CMC is larger than that of the Germans. More precisely, studies on complaints in oral communication revealed that British English speakers avoided the use of not only the most direct strategy, but also of the second most direct one, which were both present in German spoken interaction (cf. House and Kasper 1981: 161). In contrast to that, the present findings show that both the British English and German speakers use the same range of strategies, including the most direct ones. As a consequence, the British traders are similar to the German speakers in their directness, with the exception

of the data set *Item NR*. Thus, House's (1996b, 2000) proposed dimension of 'directness versus indirectness' along which the British English and Germans habitually display different preferences, in that Germans are more direct than British English speakers, can only be confirmed if they have *not received the item,* revealing that the reason for complaining is also a crucial factor which impacts speakers' linguistic choices. However, the types of direct strategies British English and German traders favour to achieve their directness level show some differences. While the Germans prefer *threats* if they have *not received the item*, and *draw more conclusions* for their future action, especially in the data set *Item DIFF-D*, the British English speakers use *insults* significantly more often if they have *not received the item and have an additional reason* for their online complaint. The finding that Germans more often threaten their complainee is in line with Pierre Weitmann's observation, who works at the Sales Service in Munich, and also found that Germans more often threaten their trading partners on eBay with the involvement of higher authorities than French, Spanish, or Italian traders (Krieger 2008: 29). However, the present study further reveals that this is not generally the case, but depends on the particular reason for their complaint.

In addition to the specific communicative situation of CMC, which is likely to facilitate the use of extremely direct strategies such as *threats* and *insults*, the particular relationship between eBay traders may also contribute to this effect. Specifically, most eBay trading partners are strangers who have not met before and will never meet in the future, given their distant places of residence. Hence, they may not feel obliged to make face contributions to someone they do not know and to whom they will not develop any relationship, especially not after having been - from their point of view - treated unfairly. This assumption is in line with Wolfson's (1988, 1989) bulge theory which predicts that most face work is invested between acquaintances rather than between intimates and strangers (cf. Wolfson 1988: 33, 1989: 130).

Unlike Laforest's (2002: 1597) claim that there is no prototype of complaints, the analysis of the present data reveals that eBay traders have developed a prototypical complaint which is similar for both British English and German speakers, as well as for all four different data sets. This greater uniformity on the feedback forum of eBay compared to complaints in oral communication (cf.

House and Kasper 1981; Kraft and Geluykens 2002, 2004; Laforest 2002; Trosborg 1995) points at a norm which seems to have developed among members of the eBay community, which is regarded here as a CofP, since this approach allows one to address the dynamic and emergent nature of this online community. The norms which have developed in this CofP also seem to embrace the amount of different strategy sequences British English and German traders employ to formulate their complaints, since they are very similar in all British English and German data sets. The development of a communicative norm may have partly resulted from a very restricted communicative situation on eBay. Precisely, not only are the messages limited to a maximum length of 80 characters, but the amount of turns is also fixed. Hence, in contrast to spoken interaction, speakers on eBay's feedback forum cannot develop their complaint over several turns, or formulate it as long as they like. Instead they must immediately come to the point. Such focus is in fact in line with the main function of this forum, which is to enable eBay members, who browse other traders' feedback comments, to get an impression of other members' trading behaviour and reputation as quickly as possible. This is certainly easiest to achieve with short and pointed comments, so one may assume that not only the restricted communicative situation but also the function of eBay's feedback forum has led to the development of a short prototypical complaint. Due to this function it is also the case that the addressivity on this forum is more complex than in most spoken interactions, since one's online comment is not only addressed to one recipient, but also intended to be read by all other eBay members.

The function of eBay's feedback forum and the accompanied twofold form of address help to explain why the prototypical complaint on this forum particularly consists of the strategy *explicit complaint*. In fact, it is this strategy which most clearly provides information about other traders' misconduct and thus what to expect when dealing with them. The high frequency of *explicit complaints* consequently reveals that it is important for members of the eBay community to adhere to Grice's Maxims of Quality, Relation and Manner. In other words, speakers using the *explicit complaint* want to give other members the most truthful and relevant information in a perspicuous way. Furthermore, the fact that in the prototypical complaint the strategy *explicit complaint* is used on its own without being combined with another strategy reveals that Grice's Maxim of Quantity is also prevalent in this CofP. Any added strategy would make a comment more complex and the recipient's process of inference longer. This would in turn demand more effort from recipients, which traders want to avoid given their aim of providing concise and quick information about other traders' behaviour and reputation.

Moreover, there are additional reasons which may account for the fact that the strategy *explicit complaint* is not combined with another strategy in the prototypical complaint. When looking at Strategy 1: *expression of disappointment* and Strategy 2: *expression of anger or annoyance*, it can be said that their semantic contribution to the prototypical complaint is superfluous, since interactants are aware of the fact that complaints are accompanied by these feelings. Senders may hence avoid mentioning them to reduce typing effort. On the other hand, complainers may feel that these expressions are in fact not strong enough to express their real anger towards the state of affairs. This may also explain why frownies, which similarly express speakers' disappointment or disapproval, occur only rarely in the present complaints. In such cases, complainers may opt for more face-threatening strategies, such as the Strategies 4 to 8. These are, however, not as frequent as one might expect in an anonymous communicative situation like the feedback forum of eBay. This may be due to the fact that, as Edwards (2005) as well as Stokoe and Hepburn (2005) have shown, there is always also a 'subjective side' to complaints. In other words, by making a complaint speakers always express something about themselves, in that they may be heard as objective and reasonable, or as "moaning, whining, ranting, biased, prone to complaining, paranoid, invested, over-reacting, over-sensitive, or whatever other vernacular category might apply" (Edwards 2005: 5). Consequently, the danger of damaging one's own face may prevent complainers from using too face-threatening strategies and cause them to prefer the most objective category *explicit complaint*. This may especially be the case since not only the traders' face but also financial losses are at stake. The importance of adhering the subjective side of the complaint is even further enhanced given that eBay's feedback forum is public and that the feedback system lists all feedback comments a particular eBay member has written. Anyone who is online can thus easily get an impression of members' habits in leaving feedback, which is likely to deter traders from being too direct or from performing revengeful acts.

Another influential factor which might have led to the specific prototypical complaint found on both the British and German eBay domain is what Pöchhacker (1995) calls 'diaculture', i.e. constructs like 'engineering culture', 'science culture', or 'business culture', which are likely to share features across cultures. Part of the 'business diaculture' is the CBS communicative style (cf. Lanham 1983, cited in Scollon and Scollon 1995), which aims at 'clarity, brevity, and sincerity' (CBS). In order to conform to the CBS and thus to sound 'business-like', eBay members, regardless of their different cultural background, may opt for a short complaint consisting only of the most clear complaint strategy: an *explicit complaint.*

Turning to the use of modification, the findings again reveal a difference between the British English and German complaints in spoken interaction and in online settings. While in face-to-face situations, downgrading modification has been revealed to be prominent compared to upgrading modification (cf. House and Kasper 1981: 171ff.; Kraft and Geluykens 2002: 238, 2004: 261; Trosborg 1995: 358ff.), the opposite is the case in CMC. This result points again at an influence of the anonymous setting of the new medium. Furthermore, the findings of this study show that the British English and German speakers' use of modification in online complaints is much more similar than their behaviour in face-to-face situations. Specifically, in spoken discourse British speakers have been found to use more mitigating modifiers than the Germans (cf. House and Kasper 1981: 172f.), but the present results reveal that the British English and German traders use not only approximately the same amount of upgrading and downgrading modifiers in online complaints, but also employ them in a similar way. That is, both employ less downgrading than upgrading modifiers, and favour the upgrading modifier, *intensifier*, in all data sets, and *time reference* if they have *not received the item*. Thus, the latter modifier, *time reference*, seems to be bound to specific situations. This explains why it could only be found in very few previous studies on complaints, such as Stokoe and Hepburn's (2005) study on noise formulations in neighbour complaints. In Stokoe and Hepburn's (2005) study as well as in the present study, this modifier is often used to appeal to the subjective side of the complaint, since complainers using the modifier *time reference* want to stress the period of time they have had to bear the offensive act in order to prove that there is a strong reason for complaining and that they are not over-reacting. At the same time, the precision of the date and/or period of time gives the complaint the appearance of being more serious and objective, thereby increasing the possibility that the complainer is perceived as a serious and correct trader. On the whole, the similarities between British English and German eBay traders' use of modifiers hints at the fact that also with regard to modification, members of the eBay community seem to have developed a norm which covers up cultural differences which have been found to exist in spoken interaction (cf. House and Kasper 1981).

An exception to these norms is the fact that the Germans significantly more often employ the downgrading modifier *expression of regret* in single complaints of the data sets *Item NR* and *Item DIFF*. However, since these significant differences are based on low frequencies only, this differing tendency must be judged as a weak one. Furthermore, it is worth questioning whether this downgrading modifier expresses sincere regret. It may also be meant sarcastically or may have become a routinised expression in face-threatening speech acts like complaints. The latter assumption is in line with Leech's (2007) observation that "forms encoding politeness have often become highly conventionalised and therefore come to have a weakened force" (Leech 2007: 196).

In addition to the same prototypical complaint and a very similar behaviour regarding modification, it also seems to be the norm on both the British English and the German feedback forum of eBay to formulate elliptical comments which often contain typing errors and lack commas and punctuation marks. Ellipses and the omission of punctuation marks are likely to be attributed to the limited message buffer of 80 characters. However, in light of the fact that most of the British English and German eBay traders clearly use less than 80 characters to formulate their complaints, these features could also be explained by traders' wish to save typing effort. This postulation could also explain their lack of interest in correct spelling.

In contrast to the previously described similarities between British English and German traders' communicative behaviour on the feedback forum of eBay, the present results demonstrate more differences between British English and

German speakers as far as their use of pronouns and features of CMC is concerned. To be more precise, the use of pronouns is much more common among British English traders who not only particularly favour the use of *first person pronouns*, but also use *pronouns which address the complainee* significantly more often. British English speakers' frequent use of these types of pronouns is in line with Trosborg's (1995) findings in spoken interaction. However, her results differ from the present ones since in her face-to-face situations British English speakers used *pronouns addressing the complainee* even more (cf. Trosborg 1995: 357) than in the present online setting. Furthermore, the present results reveal that British English speakers' use of *first person pronouns* as well as *pronouns referring to the addressee* is influenced by the reason for their complaint, since their employment of these pronouns occurs more frequently if they have *not received the item* (in single and double complaints) than if the *item was different than expected* (in single and double complaints). The difference between Trosborg's (1995) results and the present results may thus have resulted from both the different reasons for complaining and the different language modality. Further research clarifying this supposition is definitely needed.

Germans' preference for other features to intensify their complaint rather than pronouns may be affected to some extent by the more complex pronominal system in German, which distinguishes between 'Du' and 'Sie'. To avoid having to decide which form to use, speakers may just leave them out. Furthermore, the suffix of German verbs clearly indicates its case and gender, making a pronoun more superfluous than in English. It may therefore only be due to the different structure of the German and the English language that British English speakers tend to use more pronouns than Germans, rather than an intent to stress their personal involvement in the state of affairs and depict the addressee as the guilty person. However, an argument against this assumption is that the shortness of the present complaints and the fixed addressivity, i.e. from one trader to his/her trading partner, makes pronoun usage unnecessary in the English as well, given that the omission of these pronouns would not result in any misunderstanding in the present online complaints. For illustration see the following examples.

(BrE, NR 11) item never received from <u>this seller</u>
(BrE, NR 100) item never recieved

(BrE, NR 74) i've never received the item
(BrE, NR 96) never recieved item

As examples (BrE, NR 96) and (BrE, NR 100) clearly demonstrate, complainers could have easily omitted the direct reference to themselves or the complainee without reducing the comprehensibility of their comments. Additionally, pronoun omission in the given examples cannot be explained by the fixed message buffer, since less than 80 characters are used in all examples above. Nonetheless, British English traders prefer the use of *first person pronouns* and *pronouns addressing the complainee* clearly more often than German traders, so it may not only be due to a structural difference of the British English and German language that British English and German speakers differ in their amount of pronoun usage, but also because of a stronger tendency of British English eBay traders to intensify their complaint by the use of pronouns. This assumption can further be backed by the finding that the British English speakers' use of *first person pronouns* and *pronouns addressing the complainee* in the present study is influenced by the reason for their complaint. Specifically, they favour the use of these types of pronouns if they have *not received the item*, in single and double complaints. If British English speakers' increased pronoun usage were simply a matter of the structure of the English language, such an influence would not exist. Instead, their use of pronouns would be equally distributed among all data sets.

When shifting the focus to the use of features of CMC, the findings reveal that the Germans greatly exceed the British English traders in their use of *exclamation marks*, *single* and *repeated* ones. The British English traders, on the other hand, show a tendency, though clearly weaker, to use *capitalisation* instead. In online communication *capitalisation* signals loudness of an utterance. At the same time, *exclamation marks* designate an utterance as exclamation, which is also associated with an increase in volume. So it may be the case that British English and German speakers have developed different norms to express an increase in volume and thereby to make up for missing acoustic means in CMC. With regard to the present data, *capitalisation* also has the effect of visually emphasising a complaint, so that it strikes the beholder's eye when browsing the comments. As a consequence, it is read more often and also more easily remembered (cf. Edelmann 1996: 251; Zimbardo and Gerrig 1999: 233).

By using *exclamation marks* this can only be achieved if they are strikingly often repeated, which Germans do more often than British English speakers. British English and German traders may thus use different means to achieve the same effects.

The investigation of whether British English and German traders' overall use of *intensifying* and *mitigating features* is influenced by the factors under investigation, namely the type and number of reasons for the online complaint, reveals an influence of both factors. Thus, the intensity with which these traders intensify or mitigate the complaints of the four different data sets differs. Such differences are likely to reveal how these traders judge the severity of the different complaints, which is in line with previous studies on complaints, which show cultural differences in complainers' perception of the offence (cf. Frescura 1995; Olshtain and Weinbach 1993; Rubino and Bettoni 2006). Given that complainers are likely to feel entitled to take more face-threatening actions in the case of more severe offences, it is reasonable to assume that the more *intensifying features* and the less *mitigating features* British English and German traders employ, the more severely they judge the misconduct of the complainee. From the findings that both factors, i.e. the type and number of reasons for traders' complaints, have an impact on their use of *intensifying* and *mitigating features*, it follows that both of these factors also influence British English and German speakers' judgement. Specifically, the present results demonstrate that the British English speakers are mainly influenced by the number of reasons they complain about, while the type of reason is more influential for the Germans.

Along these lines British English and German speakers' judgement of the severity of the different types of complaints can be visualised in Figures 7.1 and 7.2. Due to the fact that no statements can be made about specific values of severity, the illustrated severity scales do not show any particular dimensions. Nonetheless, the distance between the four different data sets is expressive. It is based on the amount of *mitigating* and *intensifying features* used in each data set. While the use of *mitigating features* leads to a reduction of severity and hence shifts a data set to the left on the scale, the presence of *intensifying features* has the opposite effect.

Figure 7.1: Graphic representation of the four British English data sets on a severity scale.

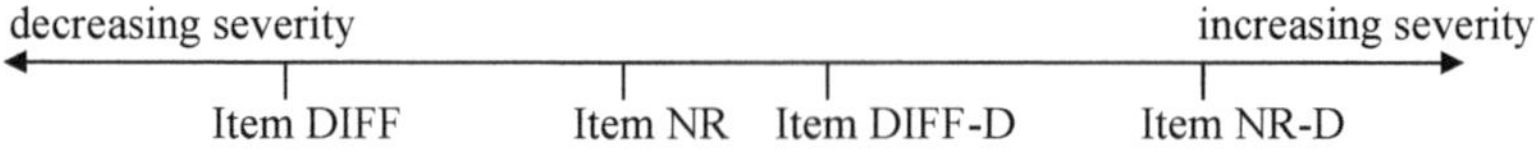

Figure 7.2: Graphic representation of the four German data sets on a severity scale.

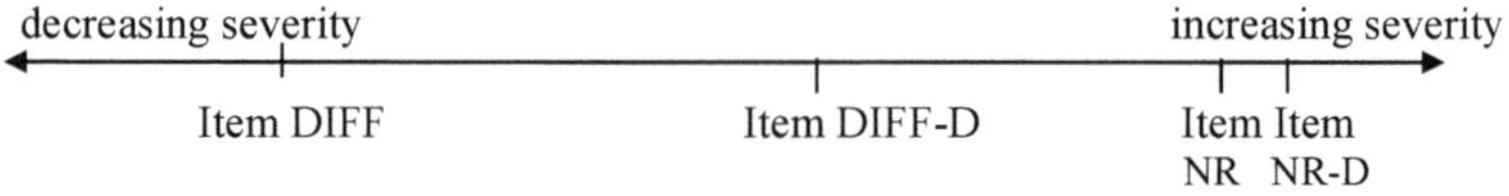

With regard to Figures 7.1 and 7.2, it becomes obvious that both the British English and German traders seem to regard the fact that the *item was different than expected* as the least severe and the fact that the *item had not been received plus an additional reason for complaining* as the most severe type of complaint. Furthermore, both appear to judge the fact that the *item was different than expected plus an additional reason for complaining* as more severe than the single complaint *Item DIFF*. On the other hand, a clear difference becomes obvious with regard to the complaints in the data set *Item NR*. While the Germans seem to judge their severity as similar to the double complaints *Item NR-D*, on the British English severity scale this data set is placed in between the complaints in the data sets *Item DIFF* and *Item DIFF-D*. The Germans' judgement of a high severity of the single complaints *Item NR* is further emphasised by the fact that the Germans are significantly more direct in this respect. However, they also regard the double complaints in the data set *Item NR-D* as more severe than the British English speakers, but the difference between the British English and German traders' evaluation is much smaller compared to their judgement of the single complaints *Item NR*. Given these findings, the question arises as to what might have led to such differences in evaluation. One explanation may be that there are cultural differences in the expectations British English and German traders have regarding business transactions, as they have had different cultural experiences in personal contact with trading partners and/or on their eBay domain. Regarding the latter, the results of the pilot study may provide a hint (see 4.1.3.). Specifically, its results reveal that it is more common on the British English domain of eBay that items are not received by traders than on the German domain. Traders on the British English forum may thus have become more used to such circumstances, which in turn may have led to their milder judgement. In light that German traders in the pilot study complain about a long delivery time significantly more often, one may also assume that the fact that an item does not arrive at all must clearly result in an increase in their anger and bring about a stricter judgement.

Moreover, the finding that British English and German traders' evaluation of the severity of the double complaints *Item NR-D* is more similar than their judgement of the severity of the single complaints *Item NR*, may result from the following. The Germans may believe that if they not only have to complain about the already severe offence that the *item has not been received*, but also for a second reason, their complaint is strengthened to such an extent that a further increase by a more frequent use of *intensifying features* is no longer needed. Yet, these explanations certainly remain mere hypotheses until research is conducted in this respect.

The results show a very complex picture when turning to the way the two factors under investigation influence which particular means of *intensification*, *mitigation* or *personal involvement* British English and German traders use in one type of complaint rather than the other. While the use of some features are influenced by either the type of reason or the number of reasons traders complain about, other features are impacted by a combination of these factors, or even none of them. Within these complex influences, cultural similarities and differences become apparent. Yet, much more research is definitely needed to ascertain when exactly these factors become influential and interact with each other, and which further factors may play a role in British English and German traders' choice of linguistic means in online complaints.

So on the whole, members of the entire eBay community seem to have developed particular norms on this forum with regard to the use of complaint strategies, modification, and language correctness, which cover up other potential cultural differences with regard to complaining behaviour. As a consequence, British English and German online complaints are more similar in this respect than in spoken interaction. Also, Graham (2007) found in her electronic data of messages sent to an online ChurchList that members of this list have developed communicative norms which they even openly discuss in case of violation (Graham 2007: 755). Discussions about behavioural norms do not take place on eBay's feedback forum, given the maximum length of all comments. However, Knobel and Lankshear's (2002) observations of the message board located on the US eBay website demonstrated that communicative norms are a topic on this discussion forum (cf. Knobel and Lankshear 2002: 24), whose communicative situation is much more alike to Graham's (2007) ChurchList data. Of course, one must take into account that Knobel and Lankshear (2002) only focused on the US domain of eBay. Yet, given that there are similar discussion forums on all eBay domains, it is very likely that communicative norms are similarly discussed on the British English and German message boards of eBay.

Apart from the communicative norms which concern both the British English and German eBay domain and may even refer to the entire eBay community, the present results also reveal communicative complaining behaviour which is specific to either the British English or German eBay domain, thus pointing at existing culturally-specific norms. These especially include the use of pronouns and features of CMC, and the way in which British English and German traders are influenced by the two factors under investigation. Hence, although the language modality of CMC seems to enforce the development of more uniform communicative behaviour among members of online communities regardless of their nationality, communicative differences between members of different cultural backgrounds still become apparent and definitely need further scholarly attention.

7.2. Discussion in light of (im)politeness theories

In situations of conflict, those in which FTAs like complaints are voiced, the question arises as to how interactants navigate relational work. Accordingly, it is worth investigating whether the present online complaints are intended and/or perceived as impolite, appropriate/politic, or even as polite. This section therefore focuses on how the different realisations of the present complaints have to be interpreted in light of the different frameworks of (im)politeness explained in 2.3.

In light of Leech's (1983) conversational maxim view, most of the British English and German complaints demonstrate a disregard of the PP. Specifically, since complaints belong to Searle's (1975) categorisation of expressives, they are closely related to Leech's (1983) Maxim of Approbiation, which operates along a directness scale (see 2.3.1.). Accordingly, speakers who most closely adhere to this maxim would not complain at all, since this would minimise disapproval of their addressee the most. Yet, there are also situations, like the present ones, in which complaints are acceptable, since complainers have had to suffer from the offensive act for which the complainee is responsible. The social balance between the interlocutors has thus been disturbed, but can be regained by a complaint (cf. Edmondson and House 1981). When voicing their complaints, speakers have then the choice of either adhering to Leech's (1983) Approbiation Maxim by formulating their complaint indirectly, or disregarding this maxim by formulating their complaint rather bluntly. Regarding the present data, the complaint strategies which reflect an adherence to the Approbiation Maxim are the two least direct strategies, i.e. Strategy 1: *expression of disappointmen*t and Strategy 2: *expression of anger or annoyance*, since speakers using these strategies focus on themselves to avoid mentioning the offensive act or the hearer and thus to minimise their disapproval of other. As mentioned in 7.1., the strategy *explicit complaint*, on the other hand, is a clear case in which speakers follow Grice's (1975) CP, whereby Leech's (1983) PP is neglected. Regarding the other strategies which exceed Level 3, it can be said that their employment represents a clear violation of the PP, given that, according to Leech's (1983) Approbiation Maxim, an increase in directness results in an increase in the dispraise of the other. Regarding Leech's (1983) theory, their occurrences are hence clear instances of speaker's being impolite. However, since Leech (1983) has been criticised for neglecting the impolite side of language, these more direct strategies fall outside the scope of the conversational-maxim view.

Prominent in Brown and Levinson's (1987 [1978]) face-saving view is the interlocutors' notion of face, whose maintenance is the aim of each interaction. As mentioned in 2.2.3.2., this theory states that complaints are clear threats against the addressee's positive face, but may similarly threaten his/her negative face if the addressee's freedom of action is impeded. Redressive actions in the form of positive and/or negative politeness are hence called for. This is especially the case since the relationship between most transactional partners on eBay is characterised by a large social distance which, according to Brown and

Levinson's (1987 [1978]) formula for calculating the weightiness of an FTA, leads to an increase in the weightiness involved.

With regard to the present complaints, some investment in saving the recipient's face wants can be found. Specifically, some complainers choose the less direct Strategies 1 and 2, which fall under Brown and Levinson's (1987 [1978]) off-record super strategy. In addition, the present subjects employ downgrading modifiers and indefinite pronouns to soften the face-threat at hand.

However, as the results of the present study reveal, both complaint strategies at the low end of the directness scale as well as mitigating features are only rarely used. Instead, complainers employ far more intensifying features to strengthen their complaints. These findings contradict the assumption one would make following Brown and Levinson's (1987 [1978]) theory which predicts a large amount of mitigating features in serious FTAs such as the present complaints. This is especially the case given Brown and Levinson's (1987 [1978]) belief of a direct relationship between increasing weight of contextual factors and increasing politeness. However, as studies have proven, this correlation is not only inaccurate, but their formula to calculate the weightiness of an FTA is also too simple to account for everyday interactions (cf. Wolfson 1988). Furthermore, Leech's (1983) as well as Brown and Levinson's (1987 [1978]) underlying assumption of a positive correlation between indirectness and politeness often does not hold true (cf. Culpeper 2008), and scholars have also convincingly argued that intent and context play a critical role in identifying (im)politeness (cf. Bousfield 2007, 2008; Culpeper 1996, 2005, 2008; Culpeper et al. 2003; Fraser and Nolen 1981; Haugh 2007; Locher and Watts 2005; Mills 2005, 2009; Schnurr et al. 2008; Tracy 2008). Thus, it is not surprising that the conversational-maxim and the face-saving view are not sufficient when analysing the present complaining behaviour, especially not given its occurrence in a complex situation such as CMC.

Indeed, when defining impoliteness Culpeper (1996, 2005, 2008), Culpeper et al. (2003), and Bousfield (2008) argue that, for impoliteness to occur, the speaker must intend to offend the addressee's face,[40] who must similarly perceive the speaker's behaviour as a face-attack. The perceptions of

[40] For an alternative view see Terkourafi (2008: 70).

(im)politeness are thereby varied and subjective, so the speaker's intent is open to differing interpretations by the speaker and hearer (cf. Locher and Watts 2005; Mills 2003; Spencer-Oatey 2005; Watts 2003). However, regarding the present data, it can be argued that the sender's intent to voice a complaint and attack the recipient's face becomes obvious by the particular symbol preceding each online complaint on eBay's feedback forum. So the recognition of intention is clearly simplified.

Regarding the importance of context, Smith (1999) and Graham (2007, 2008) have demonstrated that the parameters of the computer medium can have an enormous impact on the interpretation and enactment of (im)politeness and are thus critical in an analysis of (im)politeness within an online community. Therefore, they are discussed in more detail below with respect to the present eBay data.

Similar to other modes of communication, the expectations and norms of the CofP, here the British English and German eBay community, affect members' enactment and perception of e-(im)politeness. Accordingly, members of a given CofP do not only have to adhere to their individual face needs but also to norms and expectations of the group. Spencer-Oatey (2005) addresses this by distinguishing between group members' personal identity and social identity. In addition to the norms of the particular CofP, there are also the following influences on (im)politeness and politic behaviour in online settings: 1) the guidelines for Netiquette, 2) the limitations of the medium itself, and 3) the participant structure.

Regarding Netiquette, eBay has developed clear rules on how to leave feedback, which are similar on all eBay domains. Accordingly, eBay strongly encourages its members to leave only fair and factual comments and ratings which relate to the specific transaction with one's trading partner. Before leaving neutral or negative feedback, members are further urged to contact their transactional partner to try to resolve the issue first. Furthermore, eBay has formulated clear definitions of feedback abuse. As these comments are not permitted, they are filtered and removed by eBay. However, comments containing inflammatory language, such as *fraud*, *liar*, *cheater*, *scam artist*, *con man* etc., do not fall under eBay's removal policy. They are only strongly discouraged. On the whole, eBay's Netiquette can be seen as an authoritative guideline for appropriate behaviour (cf. Graham 2008: 283), which functions to make interactants "consciously aware of appropriate politic behaviour" (Watts 2003: 164). This is not to deny the subjectivity and variability of the perception of (im)polite and (non-)politic behaviour, but it is reasonable to assume that eBay's Netiquette is prominent within the community as an important guideline for behaviour and thus reflects what members of this CofP expect to be politic/appropriate. In line with Graham (2008), these expectations are considered to be more-or-less stable by the members.

Due to eBay's encouragement of fair and honest trading, Knobel and Lankshear (2002) regard eBay as "an 'educator' in that it 'teaches' people how they should act within this new cyber space; how they should act in relation to each other" (Knobel and Lankshear 2002: 20). However, whether members of the eBay community follow eBay's regulations of the 'right' kind of cyber practices will be investigated on the basis of the present data below.

The second factor influencing the enactment and interpretation of (im)politeness in online settings are the limitations of the medium, which relate to the lack of paralinguistic markers. As scholars have shown, prosody can be an important resource for identifying an utterance as impolite (cf. Beebe 1995; Culpeper et al. 2003; Locher and Watts 2008). In circumstances such as CMC, in which non-verbal cues and prosodic markers are missing, speaker intent (and impoliteness) may be difficult to determine. As a consequence, Internet users may employ alternative strategies, such as smileys or capitalisation. However, as Graham (2003, 2005, 2008) convincingly argued, these textual markers cannot meet the complexities involved in conveying speakers' intent. However, as mentioned above, the present feedback comments have additional interpretation cues in that they are preceded by a particular symbol illustrating the sender's intent to voice a complaint. The reader's interpretation of the writer's intent is thus facilitated. Another influential factor for the enactment and interpretation of (im)politeness which derives from the medium itself is the restriction of turns and the fixed message buffer within each interaction on eBay's feedback forum (see 4.1.2.). Consequently, face enhancement or damage cannot be developed over several turns or expressed by elaborated linguistic means, but must be short and concise. Moreover, computer-mediated interaction also has a particular participant structure which differs from other language modes, further influencing participants' handling of (im)politeness. Specifically, the eBay community is not only extremely large, but the number of registered members is also continually rising. All members who send their feedback comments to their particular trading partner are aware of the fact that their comments are similarly read by an audience. The presence of this audience clearly affects their practice of (im)politeness in that eBay members have to invest in relational work (cf. Locher and Watts 2005) or rapport management (cf. Spencer-Oatey 2000b, 2002, 2005) not only with their transactional partner, but also with an audience that is unknown. The notions of what constitutes polite behaviour may thereby differ between senders, the addressees of their messages, as well as members of the audience.

In addition to the specific context of the present CMC data, there is another relational aspect which is crucial when investigating (im)politeness, namely power. As Bousfield (2008) stresses: "the exercise of power is both ubiquitous and inescapable when dealing with any aspect of politeness and impoliteness" (Bousfield 2008: 129). However, in the same way that (im)politeness is not a concept upon which researchers have yet agreed upon, further difficulties arise because there has not been a definite account of power in the literature (cf. Bousfield and Locher 2008: 8). This certainly does not mean that power can be neglected in an investigation of (im)politeness, specifically not after numerous scholars have pointed at a close relation between power and (im)politeness (cf. Bousfield 2008; Brown and Levinson 1987 [1978]; Culpeper 2008; Harris 2003; Holmes and Stubbe 2003; Limberg 2008; Locher 2004; Mills 2003; Mullany 2004; Tiisala 2004; Watts 2003).

Fairclough (1989: 43) distinguishes between power *in* and power *behind* discourse. While power in discourse designates the exercise of power in language, power behind discourse refers to the constitution of social institutions and societies through power relations. Brown and Levinson (1987 [1978]) and other researchers in that tradition were mainly concerned with power behind discourse, such as interactant's role and status (cf. Brown and Levinson 1987 [1978]). Because of this, they reduced the notion of power to static, given values on a variable that provides input to a formula for calculating the weightiness of the FTA involved. Accordingly, they predicted that the higher the relative power of the speaker, the more politeness they tend to receive. Post-modern scholars, however, have shown that Brown and Levinson's (1987 [1978]) power variable does not reflect the complexity of how power works in interaction (cf. Bousfield 2008; Culpeper 2008; Graham 2008; Locher 2004; Watts 1991). For instance, they have demonstrated that "people with higher status can refrain from exercising power" while "interactants with low status can decide to exercise power over people with relatively greater status" (Locher 2004: 31), i.e. that power behind language need not go along with power in language. Thus, more recent studies have dealt with the notion of power in a more sophisticated way, and despite the fact that there has not been a single definition of power, post-modern approaches have nonetheless agreed upon a dynamic notion of power in the following manner: power is open to negotiation, it is (often) expressed through language, it presumes a conflict of interest, and it involves a restriction of the action-environment of at least one interlocutor (cf. van Dijk 1989; Locher 2004; Wartenberg 1990; Watts 1991).

With regard to the present data, power behind language concerns the fact that the complainers, being the customers of the transaction, are of higher status due to their possession of customer power, which is also expressed in the idiom 'the customer is always right'. Leaving a complaint on eBay's feedback forum can always be regarded as a customer's exercise of power, regardless of how the complaint is formulated, since it always involves a "latent conflict and clash of interests" (Locher 2004: 39) between the interlocutors and leads to a restriction of the target's action-environment. A serious clash of interests is assumed, since by leaving a complaint the speaker intends to cause face loss of the addressee and also wants it to be perceived as such. Accordingly, the sender wishes to damage the complainee's reputation, i.e. their "positive social value" (Goffman 1967: 5), which the latter wants to maintain or even enhance. Face-attacks are especially detrimental, in these situations where both traders' faces and financial losses are at stake.

In addition to the presence of a serious conflict, a complaint additionally restricts the target's action-environment, in that the recipient is forced to a reaction, which may involve a decision to defend themselves, to make a counter-attack, or not to reply at all. Furthermore, a complaint also impedes the target's freedom of action-environment because it leads to a reduction of the complainee's overall feedback score, which deters other traders from dealing with the complainee and thus reduces their amount of potential trading partners. The more face-threatening the complaint, the more eBay members are likely to avoid business transactions with the complainee. This reveals the expressiveness that power in language may have. The assumption that serious FTAs such as the present complaints are a powerful linguistic means of exercising power is in line with Locher's (2004) argumentation when discussing the connection between serious conflict and the issue of power in disagreements (cf. Locher 2004: 201).

Turning to the more detailed analysis of (im)politeness in the present data, some words of caution are important. Precisely, when analysing interpersonal and intersubjective constructs such as the interpretation of (im)polite and (non-) politic behaviour in complex situations, as is the case on eBay's feedback forum, determining intent and its recognition is certainly problematic (cf. Culpeper et al. 2003: 1552). Therefore, any of the following interpretations which have been tried to be supported by plausible evidence, must be regarded as suggestions.

As the present results reveal, both the British English and German eBay traders choose the same prototypical complaint in all data sets, namely a comment consisting of the strategy *explicit complaint*. Given that eBay's Netiquette, i.e. the authoritative guideline for appropriate behaviour (cf. Graham 2008: 283), dictates to its customers to leave not only honest and fair, but also factual comments in order to give other traders a good idea of what to expect when dealing with other members, this type of complaint is likely to be regarded as the most appropriate by members of the eBay community. The prototypical complaint can hence be regarded as the type of complaint which meets the expectations and norms of the CofP and thus goes unnoticed. In Fraser and Nolen's (1981) view, this constitutes polite behaviour. However, Locher and Watts' (2005) terminology is adopted in the present discussion (see 2.3.4.), which means that behaviour which is in line with the norms of the CofP is considered to be unmarked/politic/appropriate (see 2.3.4.). Thus, when using the prototypical complaint and thereby meeting the norms and expectations of the CofP they belong to, members stress their social identity (cf. Spencer-Oatey 2000b, 2002, 2005).

On the other hand, if complainers try to maintain the addressee's face by the use of the less direct Strategies 1 and 2, this comes at the expense of Grice's (1975)

CP. That is, they breach the Maxim of Relation, since they avoid mentioning the reason for complaining, i.e. the offensive act of the addressee. However, this information is crucial for the other eBay members to get an idea what to expect in business transactions with the complainee. As a consequence, it is likely that the speaker's communicative behaviour is negatively evaluated by the audience reading the comment, since they desire more accurate information. Given that the sender does not intend to cause damage against the audience, this instance is a case of over-politeness resulting from relational mismanagement, in that participants have different perceptions of what constitutes appropriate behaviour, which leads to communicative behaviour which is negatively evaluated from at least one perspective (cf. Culpeper 2008: 26). The fact that over-politeness can be taken negatively by interactants is in line with Locher's (2004), Watts' (2005), and Culpeper's (2008) assumption, which claims that over-politeness is perceived in a negative way when it "exceeds the boundary between appropriateness and inappropriateness" (Locher 2004: 90). However, while Locher (2004) and Watts (2005) did not cite any data in support of their claim, Culpeper (2008: 24ff.) was the first who also empirically underlined this assumption.

The recipient's judgement of the sender's effort to reduce the face-threat is, however, likely to differ from the audience's point of view. More precisely, they may either regard themselves as innocent and thus the complaint as inappropriate and impolite, or they see the complainer's point and are glad about the sender's investment in relational work, which helps them to save their reputation at least to some extent. These diverging evaluations of audience, sender and recipient again demonstrate how diverse the perceptions of (im)polite and (non-)politic behaviour may be, depending on whose point of view it is judged from.

On the other hand, over-politeness can also be used intentionally and perceived as an intentional attack on the addressee's face, in which case it is called 'sarcasm' (cf. Bousfield 2008: 148; Culpeper 2008: 28). In this respect, Bousfield (2008) speaks of insincere politeness and therefore categorises it as off-record impoliteness. In line with Bousfield (2008) it can be argued that the present instances of sarcasm can be identified as such, due to their occurrence in settings in which they are totally unexpected and unnecessary. For illustration see the following example.

(G, NR 40) hab jetzt 2 Monate gewartet und keine Ware bekommen, schönen Dank
(have waited for 2 months and have not received any item, thanks a lot)

Since the expression 'schönen Dank' (thanks a lot) is absolutely unexpected in FTAs, such as complaints, it is foregrounded and highly interpretable in this setting. As such it can only be interpreted as sarcasm, since it is opposite to the context, i.e. it violates the expected norms in that setting.

Shifting the focus to the use of Strategy 4, *negative judgement*, it can be argued that it is for users to make judgements about a previous event. Accordingly, Strategy 4 is also within the social norms and can hence be regarded as sanctioned behaviour, i.e. behaviour which is permissible given the roles and power relations of the interactants (cf. Culpeper 2005). However, not every *negative judgement* may be a sanctioned strategy, since senders may also choose lexical items which breach the guidelines of eBay's Netiquette. These clearly exceed the boundaries of appropriateness and shift the participants' perception into the impolite/inappropriate/marked area of Locher and Watts' (2005) scale of relational work.

Having had a bad experience with one's transactional partner, eBay members may also opt to explicitly express in their comment that they *draw a conclusion* for their future action in refraining from doing business with the complainee again. Because in business transactions it is the right of each participant to choose their transactional partners, this strategy also falls within sanctioned behaviour and thus within the boundaries of appropriateness. Given that speaker's using Strategy 5 focus on themselves, they stress their individual identity (cf. Spencer-Oatey 2000b, 2002, 2005). In contrast to that, Strategy 6, *warning others*, is clearly oriented towards members' social identity (cf. Spencer-Oatey 2000b, 2002, 2005), as complainers assume it is beneficial for the other group members to be warned against dishonest traders and thus to be saved a disappointment, which is even accompanied by the loss of money. When *warning* them, senders thus want to meet the social group's presumed interactional wants. Since *warnings* deter other eBay traders from doing business with the complainee and thereby restrict their action-environment, they are clear instances of senders' exercise of power. While both the senders and the audience may regard this strategy as appropriate, since it aims at supporting fair and honest trading on eBay, the addressee's judgement is again likely to differ. They may regard it as inappropriate and impolite that the complaint explicitly addresses the other eBay members instead of focusing on the previously conducted business transaction.

In this respect, *threats* are even worse, given that the sender *threatens* the addressee with the involvement of higher authorities, such as eBay's security system or lawyers. In light of these institutions' abilities to restrict the target's action-environment more severely, such as blocking the target from eBay or handing them over to be dealt with by the courts, *threats* are further instances of senders demonstrating their power. However, as Limberg (2008) has shown in his data of police-public discourses, even such powerful and highly face-attacking strategies as *threats* may fall into the category of sanctioned behaviour (Limberg 2008: 166). Specifically, with regard to the present data it can be argued that traders who have been treated unfairly in transactions in which a lot of of money is at stake, and who were unsuccessful in solving the issue with their trading partner are entitled to take more severe actions to demand their right. In these situations, *threatening* the addressee with the involvement of higher authorities can be seen as legitimate behaviour. However, if the threatener has never tried to contact his/her transactional partner to solve the problem, or if only a small amount of money is at stake, *threats* can be evaluated as overreactions and unfair trading habits. For the audience on eBay it is difficult to judge whether a *threat* to involve higher authorities is within the limits of the social norm or exceeds it, since the other eBay members lack the knowledge of whether an attempt to solve the issue has been made. Furthermore, it is only possible to find out more about the items traders dealt with in the past for a month, so eBay members are not able to get an idea of the amount of money that is at stake outside of this time span. Due to these circumstances, eBay members' evaluations of *threats* are likely to diverge. Their judgements are thereby presumably influenced by the frequency with which *threats* occur on the particular eBay domain. The present findings, for instance, show that if the *item has not been received*, *threats* are more common on the German eBay domain than on the British English one. As a consequence, the audience of the German feedback forum are likely to judge *threats* more mildly in this respect, i.e. more often as appropriate, than the British English audience. Similarly, each participant's own level of threatening is also likely to affect his/her judgement of other member's behaviour. In other words, a trader who often uses *threats* to demand his/her rights is more likely to evaluate a *threat* of another member as appropriate than a trader who uses *threats* only in very extreme cases. Moreover, there are also types of *threats* which clearly exceed sanctioned behaviour, such as *threats* of violence. Luckily, these kinds of *threats* do not occur in the present data sets.

Finally, *insults* must clearly be regarded as behaviour which violates eBay's Netiquette and is evaluated by members of the eBay community as impolite/inappropriate/marked. Regarding Bousfield's (2008) categorisation, it is a clear case of on-record impoliteness, which is employed to unambiguously attack the target's face. As the present findings reveal, there are situations in which traders are extremely frustrated and simply want to attack the complainee's face using this severe strategy despite being aware of the fact that it contradicts the 'cyber civic' goal of eBay. Similarly, Knobel and Lankshear (2002) as well as Hiltrop (2003) found in their eBay data that traders do not always follow eBay's Netiquette, but also engage in activities that include "nasty" and "hurtful acts toward others" (Knobel and Lankshear 2002: 26).

The aim these complainers seem to pursue is to release part of their anger and to exercise their power. This is in line with Beebe (1995) who argued that there are two functions of "instrumental power", which roughly corresponds to Culpeper's (1996, 2005, 2008) notion of impoliteness, namely 1) to vent negative feelings and 2) to get power, whereby 'getting power' can be understood as the exercise of power. Beebe (1995) mentions that one purpose of the second function is to appear superior by the use of "insults" and "putdowns" (Beebe 1995: 159f.).

In this respect it is also noteworthy that the speaker's intention to use the most direct strategy, *insult*, becomes particularly obvious if they make an effort to misspell their *insult* in order to avoid eBay's filter. Although not present in the data of this study, Hiltrop (2003) found instances of the *insults* "bulshi*er" (Hiltrop 2003: 28) and "WASRERB@St@D" (Hiltrop 2003: 29) in complaints on the British English eBay domain, which illustrate the senders' intent to spell the swear words differently in order to make sure that the *insults* reach the target and are not removed by eBay.

Having discussed how the different complaint strategies are likely to be judged by the participants of eBay's feedback forum, it is important to emphasise that the use of modification, pronouns, and/or features of CMC within these comments are likely to impact traders' evaluation of the appropriateness of the complainer's comment. As far as these linguistic features are concerned, eBay's Netiquette does not provide any guidelines for their appropriate usage, so it can be assumed that the norms and related expectations regarding their employment have developed among members of a CofP in communicative practice over time. As the present findings reveal, some of these norms have developed differently on the British English and German eBay domain. More precisely, while it is very common to use *exclamations marks* as a means of intensification on the German domain, their usage is significantly less frequent on the British English eBay marketplace. In contrast to Germans, British English traders favour the use of *pronouns* in their online complaints. In light of these different communicative practices which are accompanied by differing expectations of appropriateness, it is reasonable to predict that a British English trader who is less prone to the use of *exclamation marks* may regard a complaint consisting of the strategy *explicit complaint* as appropriate, the use of *repeated exclamation marks* at the end of it, however, as strange and inappropriate, which shifts his/her overall evaluation closer to the impolite/inappropriate/marked area of relational work. The same may hold true if Germans face complaints whose formulations contain too many *pronouns* compared to their own norm.

Moreover, since no interaction occurs in a vacuum, interlocutors of an interaction always use their prior experiences with the particular communicative partner to interpret the other's behaviour and intent (cf. Graham 2007). Regarding the present data, the complainer's and complainee's interpretations are shaped by the experiences they had with their trading partner during the previous business transaction and, if applicable, during the complainer's attempt to contact the complainee outside the feedback forum. These interactions, which precede the formulation of the complaint, remain unknown to the audience and thus do not impact the way they interpret the complaint. However, an aspect of a complainer's history which is likely to impact all eBay members' judgement of a particular complaint is their prior behaviour on eBay's feedback forum, i.e. the way traders phrased previous feedback comments and replied to them. For instance, if eBay members are known to be quarrelsome, other members' interpretations of their comments are affected by this negative image.

Moreover, Knobel and Lankshear (2002) showed that there is a social hierarchy on eBay in that PowerSellers[41] are regarded as 'wiser' than newcomers because of their experience in trading (Knobel and Lankshear 2002: 24). Accordingly, a PowerSeller's violation of the norms of CofP is likely to be regarded as less severe than a beginner's misconduct. Similarly, Graham (2007) found in her study on the negotiation of (im)politeness within ChurchList, an e-mail community, that the core members[42] were more powerful in that they could break the rules of the FAQ[43] and get away with it, while new users were reprimanded for it. Graham (2008) further revealed that (im)politeness and conflicts resulting from differing interpretations of (im)polite behaviour can lead to the (re)negotiation of the norms of interaction, which then alter the members' expectations for appropriate behaviour. Whether discussions about eBay traders' behaviour on the discussion forum of eBay (cf. Knobel and Lankshear 2002) may also result in alterations of the communicative norms on eBay is definitely worth investigating in future endeavours.

On the whole, the present discussion has shown that, if the context of the interaction as well as the communicative norms of the particular CofP are included in the investigation of (im)polite and (non-)politic behaviour, the analysis becomes much more complex. Accordingly, behaviour which constitutes impoliteness in the view of Brown and Levinson's (1987 [1978]) or Leech's (1983) politeness framework, must often be judged as appropriate given

---

[41] There is a PowerSeller Programme on eBay for very active and honest traders. Qualified PowerSellers can be recognised by a PowerSeller icon next to their user ID. Eligible to become a PowerSeller are those traders who, among other criteria, average a minimum of £ 750 (or the Euro exchange rate equivalent) in sales or 100 sold items per month, for three consecutive months and achieve an overall feedback rating of 100, of which 98% or more is positive (http://www.ebay.co.uk).

[42] Graham (2008) defined "core members [...] to be those who (1) post over 100 messages in one calender year, and (2) have the power (via the acceptance by the *other* 'core' members) to influence norms of interaction within the CofP" (Graham 2008: 289).

[43] The FAQ (Frequently Asked Questions) is sent to all members of the ChurchList when they subscribe. It provides technical guidelines as well as guidelines for appropriate interaction within the community (Graham 2008: 282).

the specific norms of the CofP. Examinations of the communicative practices of British English and German eBay members indicate that, on each particular eBay domain, specific norms for interaction have developed by a fusion of the norms for interaction prescribed by eBay and the norms eBay traders have developed during communicative practices. As a consequence, each eBay domain operates on a unique set of expectations for what constitutes (im)polite and (non-)politic behaviour. This certainly does not mean that the communicative behaviour on either the British English or German eBay domain is more polite than on the other, since following Pike's (1967: 37) 'emic standpoint', which is certainly favourable in cross-cultural investigations, it is argued here that behaviour must always be evaluated relative to the context and function in which it occurs. Yet deviations from norms operating in a CofP are likely to result in conflicts, which in turn negatively affect the relations between individuals within the group (cf. Graham 2007). Given that the results of this study reveal differences in the norms British English and German traders follow when complaining on their eBay domain, it is reasonable to assume that intercultural communicative settings between British English and German eBay traders are sources for miscommunication and conflicts. In light of eBay's aim to enable fair, honest and smooth trading on each of its platforms, not only between British English and German traders but between members from all over the world, further research on the communicative behaviour of traders on eBay's different domains must be a major concern, since it helps to find both the origins of conflicts as well as ways to avoid them.

Chapter 8: Implications and outlook

Having presented the results and discussed them in light of previous research, the final chapter aims at drawing conclusions for the improvement of cross-cultural communication as well as language pedagogy, and also points at areas which need future scholarly attention.

Given that the present study reveals differences in the way British English and German traders complain on their eBay domains, it is important to raise awareness of these differing communicative norms, since they are potential sources for conflicts in intercultural communicative settings. Such an awareness is not only significant to avoid miscommunication and/or the formation of stereotypes, but it may also lead to a better atmosphere between trading partners of different cultural backgrounds, and may help them to communicate more efficiently. Of course, not only British English and German speakers do business on the Internet, so that it is also crucial to find out more about the communicative behaviour of traders of other nationalities. Shaw (2000), for instance, revealed differences between the Spanish and Danish 'business culture'. While Danes were most 'function'-oriented, the Spaniards displayed a greater 'personality' orientation (cf. Shaw 2000: 189). Whether these differences also hold true in online settings is definitely worth investigating.

Since the Internet enables traders from all over the world to take part in business transactions, there are many instances in which speakers of different mother tongues become trading partners. To enable communication between them, at least one of them must often use a foreign language as communicative means. In this respect sales agent Pierre Weitmann observed that traders from France, Italy and Spain have problems communicating in English on eBay, which frequently results in misunderstandings (cf. Krieger 2008: 29). Accordingly, further cross-cultural, intercultural, as well as interlanguage studies are a pressing need. Cross-cultural studies thereby constitute a crucial precondition for an in-depth analysis of speakers' interlanguage, since they enable investigations of whether pragmalinguistic failure of speakers can be attributed to their reliance on their L1 in L2 contexts. As research in this line has demonstrated, pragmatic transfer even occurs at high proficiency levels (cf. Beebe at al. 1990; Blum-Kulka 1982,

1983; Cohen and Olshtain 1981; House 1989; Olshtain 1983; Olshtain and Cohen 1983; Takahashi and Beebe 1987).

Moreover, the present study is limited because of its sole focus on the speech act of complaining and neglect of traders' reactions to them as well as possibly occurring follow-up comments. Studies focusing on the complete exchanges, which in maximum consist of the complaint, a reply, and follow-up comment, may not only shed light on a complainee's perception of the complaint and thus its perlocutionary effect, but also enable scholars to investigate interlocutors' further investment in relational work and their struggle over power. Regarding reactions to complaints, Alicke et al. (1992) demonstrated that the type of response elicited by a complaint varied with the reason given for complaining. Similar investigations in online settings are definitely called for, which also embrace the examination of a wider range of reasons speakers complain than the present study covered.

An equally attractive and important alternative would clearly be the focus on other types of feedback comments, i.e. the appraisal and neutral comment, as well as their related turns. Furthermore, given that eBay has improved its feedback system since the conduction of the present study, it would be equally interesting to investigate whether these improvements have led to changes in traders' linguistic behaviour. Relatedly, studies comparing the behaviour on eBay's feedback forum with that of traders on other feedback systems may reveal factors of the systems itself which impact traders' linguistic choices. Such findings may point at ways the structure of feedback systems can be improved to support 'cyber civic' behaviour of its users.

A further limitation of the present study which needs improvement in future endeavours is the lack of demographic information about the present subjects. Specifically, knowledge about factors such as subjects' age, gender or social standing not only allows investigators to make data sets more comparable, but also opens up a wide sphere of further contrastive studies. Regarding for instance the gender of participants, studies on complaining behaviour in face-to-face situations revealed not only differences in the way men and women exhibited their complaints (cf. Geluykens and Kraft 2003; Kraft and Geluykens 2002, 2004; Trenchs 1994), but also with regard to the functions complaints were used for (cf. Alicke et al. 1992; Wolfe and Powell 2006). Equally, a growing body of literature has identified gender differences in CMC (cf. Brail 1996; O'Brian 1999; Brown 2000; Cherny 1994; Cohen 2001; Ess 1996; Gilboa 1996; Hall 1996; Harcourt 2000; Herring 2003, 2004b; Kiesler et al. 1984; Sutton 1994). These include a tendency of women to be more polite, supportive, emotionally expressive, and less verbose than men in public forums. Conversely, men were shown to be more likely to insult, challenge, express sarcasm, use profanity, and send long messages. However, Herring and Paolillo (2006) revealed in their investigation of the relationship between language, gender and genre in weblogs that it was genre rather than gender which significantly correlated with the use of stylistic features. These findings hence stress the importance of more fine-grained investigations of gender differences in online settings. Regarding eBay, economically oriented studies found gender differences in trading habits (Koch et al. 2007). Yet, research focusing on linguistic behaviour of male and female eBay traders is still missing.

A further aspect for future consideration includes the frustration level eBay traders need to achieve until they start complaining instead of opting out. In her study on the complaining behaviour of eBay users from the German-Swiss and traders from French-speaking Switzerland, Müller et al. (2007), for instance, revealed that if traders received electronic devices with little bugs, 71.1% of the German-Swiss users would complain, but only 28.0% of the traders from French-speaking Switzerland (Müller et al. 2007: 18). Likewise, Drew (1998) notes that "we do not complain to just anyone: we choose who to complain to and what kinds of complaints might appropriately be made to which kinds of recipients" (Drew 1998: 323f.). That kind of recipient orientation also remains a topic in need of investigation.

In addition, the present study takes first steps into the still largely undiscovered area of the analysis of speech acts in online settings. Further research that will fill this research gap is definitely called for.

Finally, in light of the immense increase in CMC, it has clearly become important that speakers from all over the world develop an awareness of language use on the Internet, which embraces all the different kinds of CMC modes, such as chats, emails, feedback forums or message boards. Accordingly, it is a pressing need that language pedagogy continually improves its frameworks, which are designed to enable students to become informed and

critical users of the Web, since the use of CMC will not only continue to spread, but also be accompanied by the invention of further technologies in this field.
To conclude, the present study has given initial insight into British English and German complaining behaviour on eBay. Hopefully, this will provide researchers with an incentive to further pursue these fascinating endeavours in the near future.

References

ABADI, ADINA (1990): "The speech act of apology in political life". *Journal of Pragmatics* 14: 467-487.

ABBOTT, CHRIS (2002): "Writing the visual: The use of graphic symbols in onscreen texts". In: Snyder, Ilana (Ed.): *Silicon Literacies: Communication, Innovation and Education in the Electronic Age*. London: Routledge, 31-46.

ALBRECHT, BIRGIT, BARATTA, MARIO, BRANDER, SYBILLE, CASPAR, OLDAG, ESCHENHAGEN, WIELAND, HARTMANN, CHRISTOF, JANSEN, SABINE, WOLFGANG, JUNG, KRAFT, EKKEHARD, KRäMER, HARALD, MANIG, BERT-OLIVER, PAESLER, REINHARD, ROTMANN, PHILIPP and UNGER-KUNZ, MARGIT (2007): *Der Fischer Weltalmanach 2008*. Frankfurt a.M.: Fischer Taschenbuch Verlag.

ALICKE, MARK D., BRAUN, JAMES C., GLOR, JEFFREY E., KLOTZ, M. L., MAGEE, JON, SEDERHOLM, HEATHER and SIEGEL, ROBIN (1992): "Complaining behavior in social interaction". *Personality and Social Psychology Bulletin* 18(3): 286-295.

ALLAN, KEITH (1998): "Speech act theory – an overview". In: Mey, Jakob L. (Ed.): *Concise Encyclopaedia of Pragmatics*. Amsterdam: Elsevier, 927-938.

ANDROUTSOPOULOS, JANNIS K. (2006): "Introduction: Sociolinguistics and computer-mediated communication". *Journal of Sociolinguistics* 10(4): 419-438.

ANDROUTSOPOULOS, JANNIS K. (2013): "Code-switsching in computer-mediated communication". In: Herring, Susan C., Stein, Dieter and Virtanen, Tuija (Eds.): *Pragmatics of Computer-mediated Communication*. Berlin/New York: Mouton de Gruyter, 667-694.

ANDROUTSOPOULOS, JANNIS K. and HINNEKAMP, VOLKER (2001): "Code-switching in der bilingualen Chat-Kommunikation: ein explorativer Blick auf #hellas and #turks". In: Beißwenger, Michael (Ed.): *Chat-Kommunikation. Sprache, Interaktion, Sozialität & Identität in synchroner computervermittelter Kommunikation. Perspektiven auf ein interdisziplinäres Forschungsfeld*. Stuttgart: Ibidem, 367-401.

ANDROUTSOPOULOS, JANNIS K. and ZIEGLER, EVELYN (2004): "Exploring language variation on the Internet: Regional speech in a chat community". In: Gunnarson, Britt-Louise, Bergström, Lena, Eklund, Gerd, Fridell, Staffan, Hansen, Lise H. and Karstadt, Angela (Eds.): *Language Variation in Europe: Papers from the Second International Conference on Language Variation in Europe, ICLaVE 2*. Uppsala: Uppsala University, 99-111.

ANIS, JACQUES (2007): "Neography: Unconventional spelling in French SMS text messages". In: Danet, Brenda and Herring, Susan C. (Eds.): *The Multilingual Internet: Language, Culture, and Communication Online*. Oxford/New York: Oxford University Press, 87-115.

ARNDT, HORST and JANNEY, RICHARD W. (1979): "Interactional and linguistic models for the analysis of speech data: An integrative approach". *Sociologia Internationalis* 17(1-2): 3-45.

AUSTIN, JOHN (1962): *How to Do Things with Words*. Oxford: Clarendon Press.

AUSTIN, PADDY (1990): "Politeness revisited – the dark side". In: Bell, Allan and Holmes, Janet (Eds.): *New Zealand Ways of Speaking English*. Clevedon: Multilingual Matters, 277 –293.

BADER, JENNIFER (2002): "Schriftlichkeit und Mündlichkeit in der Chat-Kommunikation". *Net.Worx. Die Online-Schriftreihe des Projekts Sprache@Web* 29, *http://www.mediensprache.net/networx/networx-29.pdf*, retrieved February 12, 2009.

BALKA, ELLEN (1993): "Women's access to on-line discussions about feminism". *Electronic Journal of Communication* 3, *http://www.cios.org/www/ejcmain.htm*, retrieved December 14, 2008.

BALLMER, THOMAS T. (1979): "Probleme der Klassifikation von Sprechakten". In: Grewendorf, Günther (Ed.): *Sprechakttheorie und Semantik*. Frankfurt a.M.: Suhrkamp, 247-274.

BALLMER, THOMAS T. and BRENNENSTUHL, WALTRAUD (1981): *Speech Act Classification: A Study in the Lexical Analysis of English Speech Activity Verbs*. Berlin: Springer.

BARON, NAOMI S. (1984): "Computer-mediated communication as a force in language change". *Visible Language* XVIII(2): 118-141.

BARON, NAOMI S. (2000): *Alphabet to Email*. London: Routledge.

BARRON, ANNE (2003): *Acquisition in Interlanguage Pragmatics. Learning How to Do Things with Words in a Study Abroad Content*. Amsterdam/Philadelphia: Benjamins.

BAYM, NANCY (1993): "Interpreting soap operas and creating community: Inside a computer-mediated fan culture". *Journal of Folklore Research* 30(2/3): 143-176.

BAYM, NANCY (1995): "The emergence of community in computer-mediated communication". In: Jones, Steve (Ed.): *Cybersociety: Computer-Mediated Communication and Community*. Thousand Oaks, CA: Sage, 138-163.

BAYM, NANCY (1996): "Agreements and disagreements in computer-mediated discussion". *Research on Language and Social Interaction* 29(4): 315-345.

BAYS, HILLARY (1998): "Framing and face in Internet exchanges: A socio-cognitive approach". *Linguistik Online* 1, *http://viadrina.euv-frankfurt-o.de/~wjournal/bays.htm*, retrieved June 15, 2008.

BECHAR-ISRAELI, HAYA (1995): "From (Bonehead) to (cLoNehEAd): Nicknames, play and identity on Internet Relay Chat". *Journal of Computer-Mediated Communication* 1(2), *http://jcmc.indiana.edu/vol1/issue2/bechar.html*, retrieved July 3, 2008.

BEEBE, LESLIE M. (1995): *Polite Fictions: Instrumental Rudeness as Pragmatic Competence*. Georgetown University Round Table on Languages and Linguistics. Georgetown, 154-168.

BEEBE, LESLIE M. and CUMMINGS, MARTHA C. (1996): "Natural speech act data versus written questionnaire data: How data collection method affects speech act performance". In: Gass, Susan M. and Neu, Joyce (Eds.): *Speech Acts Across Cultures. Communication in a Second Language*. Berlin/New York: Mouton de Gruyter, 65-86.

BEEBE, LESLIE M., TAKAHASHI, TOMOKO and ULISS-WELTZ, ROBIN (1990): "Pragmatic transfer in ESL refusals". In: Scracella, Robin C., Andersen, Elaine and Krashen, Stephen D. (Eds.): *Developing Communicative Competence in a Second Language*. Rowley, MA: Newbury House Publishers, 55-73.

BEIßWENGER, MICHAEL (Ed.) (2001): *Chat-Kommunikation*. Stuttgart: Ibidem.

BEIßWENGER, MICHAEL (2007): *Sprachhandlungskoordination in der Chat-Kommunikation*. Berlin/New York: Mouton de Gruyter.

BEIßWENGER, MICHAEL, HOFFMANN, LUDGER and STORRER, ANGELIKA (Eds.) (2004): *Internetbasierte Kommunikation*: Themenheft der Osnabrücker Beiträge zur Sprachtheorie (OBST 68), 5-9.

BENSON, THOMAS W. (1993): "Editor's introduction: Computer-mediated communication". *Electronic Journal of Communication* 3(2), *http://www.cios.org/www/ejcmain.htm*, retrieved September 4, 2007.

BERGS, ALEXANDER (1999): "Innovativer Sprachgebracuh bei computervermittelter Kommunikation", *http://www.linguistik.uni-bonn.de/downloads/ha01.html#5.%DFf*, retrieved December 3, 2008.

BERJAOUI, NASSER (2001): "Aspects of the Moroccan Arabic orthography with preliminary insights from Moroccan computer-mediated communication". In: Beißwenger, Michael (Ed.): *Chat-Kommunikation. Sprache, Interaktion, Sozialität & Identität in synchroner computervermittelter Kommunikation. Perspektiven auf ein interdisziplinäres Forschungsfeld*. Stuttgart: Ibidem, 431-465.

BIBER, DOUGLAS (1988): *Variation Across Speech and Writing*. Cambridge: Cambridge University Press.

BILBOW, GRAHAME (1995): "Requesting strategies in the cross-cultural business meeting". *Pragmatics* 5(1): 45-55.

BLOMMAERT, JAN (1998): *Different Approaches to Intercultural Communication: A Critical Survey*. Plenary lecture, Lernen und Arbeiten in einer international vernetzten und multikulturellen Gesellschaft, Expertentagung Universität Bremen, Institut für Projektmanagement und Wirtschaftsinformatik (IPMI). Universität Bremen, 27-28.

BLUM-KULKA, SHOSHANA (1982): "Learning to say what you mean in a second language: A study of speech act performance of learners of Hebrew as a second language". *Applied Linguistics* 3: 29-60.

BLUM-KULKA, SHOSHANA (1983): "Interpreting and performing speech acts in a second language: A cross-cultural study of Hebrew and English". In: Wolfson, Nessa and Judd, Elliot (Eds.): *Sociolinguistics and Language Acquisition.* Rowley, MA: Newbury House Publishers, 36-55.

BLUM-KULKA, SHOSHANA (1987): "Indirectness and politeness in requests: Same or different?" *Journal of Pragmatics* 11(1): 131-146.

BLUM-KULKA, SHOSHANA (1990): "You don't touch lettuce with your fingers: Parental politeness in family discourse". *Journal of Pragmatics* 14(2): 259-288.

BLUM-KULKA, SHOSHANA (1991): "Interlanguage pragmatics: The case of requests". In: Phillipson, Robert and Kellerman, Eric (Eds.): *Foreign/Second Language Pedagogy Research: A Commemorative Volume for Claus Faerch.* Clevedon: Multilingual Matters, 255-272.

BLUM-KULKA, SHOSHANA, HOUSE, JULIANE and KASPER, GABRIELE (1989): *Cross-cultural Pragmatics: Requests and Apologies*. Norwood, NJ: Ablex.

BOURDIEU, PIERRE (1990): *The Logic of Practice*. Stanford: Stanford University Press.

BOUSFIELD, DEREK (2006): "Beginnings, middles and ends: a biopsy of the dynamics of impolite exchanges". *Journal of Pragmatics*, *http://www.10.1016/j.pragma.2006.11.005*, retrieved May 3, 2007.

BOUSFIELD, DEREK (2007): "Impoliteness, preference organization and conductivity". *Multilingua* 26(1-2): 1-33.

BOUSFIELD, DEREK (2008): "Impoliteness in the struggle for power". In: Bousfield, Derek and Locher, Miriam A. (Eds.): *Impoliteness in Language*. Berlin/New York: Mouton de Gruyter, 127-153.

BOUSFIELD, DEREK and LOCHER, MIRIAM A. (2008): "Introduction: Impoliteness and power in language". In: Bousfield, Derek and Locher, Miriam A. (Eds.): *Impoliteness In Language. Studies on its Interplay with Power in Theory and Practice*. Berlin/New York: Mouton de Gruyter, 1-13.

BOXER, DIANA (1993a): *Complaining and Commiserating. A Speech Act View of Solidarity in Spoken American English.* New York: Peter Lang.

BOXER, DIANA (1993b): "Social distance and speech behavior: The case of indirect complaints". *Journal of Pragmatics* 19(2): 103-125.

BOXER, DIANA (1993c): "Complaining and commiserating: Exploring gender issues". *Text* 13(3): 371-395.

BRAIL, STEPHANIE (1996): "The price of admission: Harassment and free speech in the wild, wild west". In: Cherny, Lynn and Weise, Elizabeth R. (Eds.): *Wired_Women.* Seattle: Seal Press, 141-157.

BREWER, MARILYNN B. and GARDNER, WENDI (1996): "Who is this 'we'? Levels of collective identity and self representations". *Journal of Personality and Social Psychology* 71(1): 83-93.

BROWN, JANELLE (2000): "What happened to the Women's Web?" *http://www.salon.com/tech/feature/2000/08/25/womens_web.html*, retrieved September 14, 2005.

BROWN, PENELOPE and LEVINSON, STEPHEN (1978): "Universals in language usage: Politeness phenomena". In: Goody, Esther N. (Ed.): *Questions and Politeness: Strategies in Social Interaction*. Cambridge: Cambridge University Press, 256-289.

BROWN, PENELOPE and LEVINSON, STEPHEN (1987): *Politeness. Some Universals in Language Usage*. Reissued with corrections and new introduction. Cambridge: Cambridge University Press.

BUCHHOLTZ, MARY (1999): "'Why be normal?' Language and identity practices in a community of nerd girls". *Language and Society* 18(2): 203-223.

CASHMAN, HOLLY R. (2006): "Impoliteness in children's interactions in a Spanish/English bilingual community of practice". *Journal of Politeness Research* 2(2): 217-246.

CAVAZOS, EDWARD A. (1995): "Intellectual property in cyberspace: Copyright law in a new world". In: Cavazos, Edward A. and Morin, Gavino (Eds.): *Cyberspace and the Law: Your Rights and Duties in the On-line World*. Cambridge, MA: MIT Press, 47-65.

CHAFE, WALLACE L. and DANIELEWICZ, JANE (1987): "Properties of spoken and written language". In: Horowitz, Rosalind and Samuels, Jay S. (Eds.): *Comprehending Oral and Written Language*. San Diego/London: Academic Press, 83-113.

CHERNY, LYNN (1994): "Gender differences in text-based virtual reality". In: Buchholtz, Mary, Liang, Anita C., Sutton, Laurel A. and Hines, Caitlin (Eds.): *Cultural Performances: Proceedings of the Third Berkeley Women and Language Conference*. Berkeley: Berkeley Women and Language Group, 102-115.

CHERNY, LYNN (1999): *Conversation and Community: Chat in a Virtual World*. Stanford, CA: Center for the Study of Language and Information.

CHOU, CANDACE C. (1999): "From simple chat to virtual reality: Formative evaluation for synchronous communication systems to online learning". *WebNet 1999*: 225-230, *http://www2.hawaii.edu/~cchou/ppdla99/index.htm*, retrieved October 10, 2005.

CLARIDGE, CLAUDIA (2007): "Constructing a corpus from the web: Message boards". In: Hundt, Marianne, Nesselhauf, Nadja and Brewer, Carolin (Eds.): *Corpus Linguistics and the Web*. Amsterdam/New York: Rodopi, 87-108.

CLYNE, MICHAEL, BALL, MARTIN and NEIL, DEBORAH (1991): "Intercultural communication at work in Australia: Complaints and apologies in turns". *Multilingua* 10: 251-273.

COHEN, ANDREW D. and OLSHTAIN, ELITE (1981): "Developing a measure of sociolinguistic competence: The case of apology". *Language Learning* 31: 113-134.

COHEN, ANDREW D. and OLSHTAIN, ELITE (1993): "The production of speech acts by EFL learners". *TESOL Quarterly* 27(1): 33-56.

COHEN, JOYCE (2001): "He-mails, she-mails: Where sender meets gender". *New York Times* May 17, D1 and D9.

COLLOT, MILENA (1991): "Electronic language: A pilot study of a new variety of English". *CCE Newsletter* 5: 13-31.

COLLOT, MILENA and BELMORE, NANCY (1996): "Electronic language: A new variety of English". In: Herring, Susan C. (Ed.): *Computer-Mediated Communication: Linguistic, Social and Cross-Cultural Perspectives.* Amsterdam/Philadelphia: Benjamins, 13-28.

CONDON, SHERRI L. and CECH, CLAUDE, G. (1996): "Discourse management strategies in face-to-face and computer-mediated decision making interactions". *Electronic Journal of Communication* 6(3), http://www.cios.org/www/ejc/v6n396.htm, retrieved December 4, 2005.

CONDON, SHERRI L. and CECH, CLAUDE G. (2001): *Profiling Turns in Interaction.* Proceedings of the 34th Annual Conference of the Hawaii International Conference on System Sciences. Los Alamitos, CA, IEEE Computer Society Press.

COULMAS, FLORIAN (1981a): "Introduction: Conversational routine". In: Coulmas, Florian (Ed.): *Conversational Routine. Explorations in Standardized Communication Situations and Prepatterned Speech.* Berlin/New York: Mouton de Gruyter, 1-18.

COULMAS, FLORIAN (1981b): "'Poison to your soul.' Thanks and apologies contrastively viewed". In: Coulmas, Florian (Ed.): *Conversational Routine. Explorations in Standardized Communication Situations and Prepatterned Speech.* Berlin/New York: Mouton de Gruyter, 273-288.

CRAIG, ROBERT T., TRACY, KAREN and SPISAK, FRANCES (1986): "The discourse of requests: Assessment of a politeness approach". *Human Communication Research* 12(4): 437-468.

CRYSTAL, DAVID (1985): *A Dictionary of Linguistics and Phonetics.* Oxford/Malden: Blackwell Publishers.

CRYSTAL, DAVID (2001): *Language and the Internet.* Cambridge: Cambridge University Press.

CULPEPER, JONATHAN (1996): "Towards an anatomy of impoliteness". *Journal of Pragmatics* 25(3): 349-367.

CULPEPER, JONATHAN (1998): "(Im)politeness in drama". In: Culpeper, Jonathan, Short, Mick and Verdonk, Peter (Eds.): *Studying Drama. From Text to Context.* London: Routledge, 83-95.

CULPEPER, JONATHAN (2005): "Impoliteness and *The Weakest Link*". *Journal of Politeness Research* 1(1): 35-72.

CULPEPER, JONATHAN (2008): "Reflections on impoliteness, relational work and power". In: Bousfield, Derek and Locher, Miriam A. (Ed.): *Impoliteness in Language. Studies on its Interplay with Power in Theory and Practice.* Berlin/New York: Mouton de Gruyter, 17-44.

CULPEPER, JONATHAN, BOUSFIELD, DEREK and WICHMANN, ANNE (2003): "(Im)politeness revisited: With special reference to dynamic and prosodic aspects". *Journal of Pragmatics* 35(10-11): 1545–1579.

D'AMICO-REISNER, LYNNE (1983): "An analysis of the surface structure of disapproval exchanges". In: Wolfson, Nessa and Judd, Eliot (Eds.): *Sociolinguistics and Language Acquisition*. Rowley, MA: Newbury House Publishers, 102-115.

DANET, BRENDA (1998): "Text as mask: Gender, play and performance on the Internet". In: Jones, Steven G. (Ed.): *Cybersociety 2.0*. Thousand Oaks, CA: Sage, 129-158.

DANET, BRENDA and HERRING, SUSAN C. (2007): "Multilingualism on the Internet". In: Hollinger, Marlis and Pauwels, Anne (Eds.): *Language and Communication: Diversity and Change. Handbook of Applied Linguistics, vol. IX*. Berlin/New York: Mouton de Gruyter.

DANET, BRENDA, RUEDENBERG, LUCIA and ROSENBAUM-TAMARI, YEHUTI (1997): "'Hmmm... Where's that smoke coming from?' Writing, play and performance and Internet Relay Chat". In: Sheizaf, Rafaeli, Sudweeks, Fay and Mc Laughlin, Margaret (Eds.): *Network and Netplay: Virtual Groups on the Internet*. Cambridge, MA: MIT Press, 41-76.

DAVIS, BOYD, H. and BREWER, JEUTONNE P. (1997): *Electronic Discourse. Linguistic Individuals in Virtual Space*. Albany: State University of New York Press.

VAN DIJK, TEUN A. (1989): "Structures of discourse and structures of power". *Communication Yearbook* 12: 18-59.

DONATH, JUDITH (1999): "Identity and virtual community". In: Smith, Marc A. and Kollock, Peter (Eds.): *Communities in Cyberspace*. London: Routledge, 29-59.

DREW, PAUL (1998): "Complaints about transgressions and misconduct". *Research on Language and Social Interaction* 31: 295-325.

EBAY (2005): *http://www.ebay.co.uk*

EBAY (2005): *http://www.ebay.de*

ECKERT, PENELOPE and MCCONNELL-GINET, SALLY (1999): "New generalisations and explanations in language and gender research". *Language in Society* 28(2): 185-203.

EDELMANN, WALTER (1996): *Lernpsychologie*. Weinheim: Beltz Psychologie Verlags Union.

EDMONDSON, WILLIS (1981): *Spoken Discourse. A Model for Analysis*. London: Longman.

EDMONDSON, WILLIS and HOUSE, JULIANE (1981): *Let's Talk and Talk About it. A Pedagogic International Grammar of English*. München: Urban & Schwarzenberg.

EDWARDS, DEREK (2005): "Moaning, whining and laughing: The subjective side of complaints". *Discourse Studies: An Interdisciplinary Journal for the Study of Text and Talk* 7(1): 5-29.

EELEN, GINO (2001): *A Critique of Politeness Theories*. Manchester/Northampton: St. Jerome Publishing.

ESCANDELL-VIDAL, VICTORIA (1996): "Towards a cognitive approach to politeness". *Language Sciences* 18(3-4): 629-650.

ESS, CHARLES (1996): "Beyond false dilemmas: Men and women on the net - a plea for democracy and understanding". *Computer-Mediated Communication Magazine* 3(1), *http://www.december.com/cmc/mag/1996/jan/ess.html*, retrieved January 2, 2006.

FAIRCLOUGH, NORMAN (1989): *Language and Power*. London: Longman.

FEDERAL STATISTICAL OFFICE AND THE STATISTICAL OFFICES OF THE LäNDER (D_STATIS) (2007a): "Mobiltelefonieren im Jahr 2006 um 10,7% billiger als 2005", Press release No. 008 from January 8, 2007. *www.destatis.de*.

FEDERAL STATISTICAL OFFICE AND THE STATISTICAL OFFICES OF THE LäNDER (D_STATIS) (2007b): "Area and population - Foreign population", Press release from November 29, 2007. *www.destatis.de*.

FERRARA, KATHLEEN et al. (1991): "Interactive written discourse as an emergent register". *Written Communication* 8(1): 8-34.

FLETCHER, WILLIAM H. (2004): "Making the web more useful as a source for linguistic corpora". In: Connor, Ulla and Upton, Thomas A. (Eds.): *Corpus Linguistics in North America 2002. Selection from the Fourth North American Symposium of the American Association for Applied Corpus Linguistics*. Amsterdam/New York: Rodopi.

FLETCHER, WILLIAM H. (2007): "Concordancing the web: Promise and problems, tools and techniques". In: Hundt, Marianne, Nesselhauf, Nadja and Brewer, Carolin (Eds.): *Corpus Linguistics and the Web*. Amsterdam/New York: Rodopi, 25-46.

FRASER, BRUCE (1975): "The concept of politeness". NWAVE Meeting. Georgetown University: Pages.

FRASER, BRUCE (1981): "On apologizing". In: Coulmas, Florian (Ed.): *Conversational Routine. Explorations in Standardized Communication Situations and Prepatterned Speech*. Berlin/New York: Mouton de Gruyter, 259-271.

FRASER, BRUCE (1990): "Perspectives on politeness". *Journal of Pragmatics* 14(2): 219-236.

FRASER, BRUCE and NOLEN, WILLIAM (1981): "The association of deference with linguistic form". *International Journal of the Sociology of Language* 27: 93-109.

FRESCURA, MARINA (1995): "Face orientations in reacting to accusatory complaints: Italian L1, English L1, and Italian as a Community Language". *Pragmatics and Language Learning* 6: 79-108.

FRITZ, GERD and HUNDSNURSCHER, FRITZ (1975): "Sprechaktsequenzen. Überlegungen zur Vorwurf/Rechtfertigungs-Interaktion". *Der Deutschunterricht* 27: 81-103.

GASS, SUSAN M. (1997): *Input, Interaction and the Second Language Learner*. Mahwah, NJ: Erlbaum.

GATES, BILL (1993): "The Quotes & Saying Database", *http://www.quotesandsayings.com/gbillgates.htm*, retrieved December 10, 2008.

GEIS, MICHAEL L. (1995): *Speech Acts and Conversational Interaction*. Cambridge: Cambridge University Press.

GELUYKENS, ROLAND and KRAFT, BETTINA (2003): "Sociocultural variation in native and interlanguage complaints". In: Jaszcolt, Katarzyna M. and Turner, Ken (Eds.): *Meaning Through Language Contrast*. Amsterdam/New York: Benjamins, 251-261.

GILBOA, NETTA "GRAYAREA" (1996): "Elites lamers, narcs and whores: Exploring the computer underground". In: Cherny, Lynn and Weise, Elizabeth R. (Eds.): *Wired_Women*. Seattle: Seal Press, 98-113.

GILTROW, JANET (2013): "Genre and Computer-mediated Communication". In: Herring, Susan C., Stein, Dieter and Virtanen, Tuija (Eds.): *Pragmatics of Computer-mediated Communication*. Berlin/New York: Mouton de Gruyter, 717-738.

GILTROW, JANET and STEIN, DIETER (2009): *Genres in the Internet*. Amsterdam/Philadelphia: John Benjamins Publishing Company.

GOFFMAN, ERVING (1967): *Interactional Ritual: Essays on Face-to-Face Behavior*. Garden City, NY: Anchor Books.

GOFFMAN, ERVING (1971): *Relations in Public: Microstudies of the Public Order*. Harmondsworth: Penguin.

GOLDBARG, ROSALYN N. (2009): "Spanish-English codeswitcing in email communication". *Language@Internet* 6 (article 3), http://www.languageatinternet.org/articles/2009/2139, retrieved December 12, 2010.

GOODWIN, CHARLES and GOODWIN, MARJORIE H. (1990): "Interstitial argument". In: Grimshaw, Allen D. (Ed.): *Conflict Talk. Sociolinguistic Investigations of Arguments in Conversations*. Cambridge: Cambridge University Press, 85-117.

GRAHAM, SAGE L. (2003): *Cooperation, Conflict and Community in Computer-Mediated Communication*. Unpublished PhD Thesis, Georgetown University, Washington D.C.

GRAHAM, SAGE L. (2005): "A cyber-parish: Gendered identity construction in an online episcopal community". In: Allyson, Jule (Ed.): *Gender and the Language of Religion*. Basingstoke: Palgrave Macmillan, 133-150.

GRAHAM, SAGE L. (2007): "Disagreeing to agree: Conflict, (im)politeness and identity in a computer-mediated community". *Journal of Pragmatics* 39(4): 742-759.

GRAHAM, SAGE L. (2008): "A manual for (im)politeness?: The impact of the FAQ in an electronic community of practice". In: Bousfield, Derek and Locher, Miriam A. (Eds.): *Impoliteness in Language*. Berlin/New York: Mouton de Gruyter, 281-304.

GRICE, HERBERT P. (1975): "Logic and conversation". In: Cole, Peter and Morgan, Jerry (Eds.): *Syntax and Semantics. Vol. III: Speech Acts*. San Diego/London: Academic Press, 41-58.

GRICE, HERBERT P. (1989): "Reprint. Logic and conversation". In: Grice, Herbert P. (Ed.): *Studies in the Way of Words*. Cambridge, MA: Harvard University Press, 22-40.

GU, YUEGUO (1990): "Politeness phenomena in modern Chinese". *Journal of Pragmatics* 14: 237-257.

GUDYKUNST, WILLIAM B. (2000): "Methodological issues in conducting theory-based cross-cultural research". In: Spencer-Oatey, Helen (Ed.): *Culturally Speaking. Managing Rapport Through Talk across Cultures*. London/New York: Continuum, 293-315.

GUMPERZ, JOHN J. (1982): "Contextualization conventions". In: Gumperz, John J. (Ed.): *Discourse Strategies*. Cambridge: Cambridge University Press, 130-152.

GÜNTHER, SUSANNE (2000): "Argumentation and resulting problems in the negotiation of rapport in a German-Chinese conversation". In: Spencer-Oatey, Helen (Ed.): *Culturally Speaking: Managing Rapport Through Talk Across Cultures*. London/New York: Continuum, 217-239.

HAFNER, KATIE and LYON, MATTHEW (1996): *Where Wizards Stay Up Late: The Origins of the Internet*. New York: Simon and Schuster.

HALL, KIRA (1996): "Cyberfeminism". In: Herring, Susan C. (Ed.): *Computer-Mediated Communication: Linguistic, Social and Cross-Cultural Perspectives*. Amsterdam/Philadelphia: Benjamins, 147-170.

HALLIDAY, MICHAEL A.K. (1978): *Language as a Social Semiotic: The Social Interpretation of Language and Meaning*. London: Arnold.

HARCOURT, WENDY (2000): "World wide women and the web". In: Gauntlett, David (Ed.): *Web.Studies: Rewiring Media Studies for the Digital Age*. London: Arnold, 150-158.

HARRIS, SANDRA (1984): "The form and function of threats in court". *Language & Communication* 4(4): 247-271.

HARRIS, SANDRA (2001): "Being politically impolite: extending politeness theory to adversarial political discourse". *Discourse and Society* 12(4): 451-472.

HARRIS, SANDRA (2003): "Politeness and power: Making and responding to 'requests' in institutional settings". *Text* 23(1): 27-52.

HATIPOGLU, ÇILER (2007): "(Im)politeness, national and professional identities and context: Some evidence from emailed 'Call for Papers'". *Journal of Pragmatics* 39(4): 760-773.

HAUGH, MICHAEL (2007): "The discursive challenge to politeness research". *Journal of Politeness Research* 3: 295-317.

HEISLER, JENNIFER and CRABILL, SCOTT (2006): "Who are 'stinkybug' and 'packerfan4'? Email pseudonyms and participants' perceptions of demography, productivity, and personality". *Journal of Computer-Mediated Communication* 12(1): article 6, *http://jcmc.indiana.edu/vol12/issue1/heisler.html*, retrieved March 21, 2007.

HELD, GUDRUN (1996): *Verbale Höflichkeit. Studien zur linguistischen Theoriebildung und empirische Untersuchung zum Sprachverhalten französischer und italienischer Jugendlicher in Bitt- und Dankessituationen.* Tübingen: Narr.

HENTSCHEL, ELKE (1998): "Communication on IRC". *Linguistic Online* 1, *http://viadrina.euv-frankfurt-o.de/~wjournal/irc.htm*, retrieved August 4, 2006.

HERRING, SUSAN C. (1994): "Politeness in computer culture: Why women thank and men flame". In: Buchholtz, Mary, Liang, Anita C., Sutton, Laurel A. and Hines, Caitlin (Eds.): *Cultural Performances: Proceedings of the Third Berkeley Women and Language Conference*. Berkeley: Berkeley Women and Language Group, 278-294.

HERRING, SUSAN C. (Ed.) (1996): *Computer-Mediated Communication: Linguistic, Social and Cross-Cultural Perspectives*. Amsterdam/Philadelphia: Benjamins.

HERRING, SUSAN C. (1999): "Interactional coherence in CMC". *Journal of Computer-Mediated Communication* 4(4), *http://jcmc.indiana.edu/vol4/issue4/herring.html*, retrieved August 5, 2006.

HERRING, SUSAN C. (2001): "Computer-mediated discourse". In: Schiffrin, Deborah, Tannen, Deborah and Hamilton Heidi E. (Eds.): *The Handbook of Discourse Analysis*. Oxford/Malden: Blackwell Publishers, 612-634.

HERRING, SUSAN C. (2002): "Computer-mediated communication on the Internet". *Annual Review of Information Science and Technology* 36: 109-168.

HERRING, SUSAN C. (2003): "Gender and power in online communication". In: Holmes, Janet and Meyerhoff, Miriam (Eds.): *The Handbook of Language and Gender*. Oxford/Malden: Blackwell Publishers, 202-228.

HERRING, SUSAN C. (2004a): "Computer-mediated discourse analysis: An approach to researching online behavior". In: Barab, Sasha A., Kling, Rob and Gray, James H. (Eds.): *Designing for Virtual Communities in the Service of Learning*. Cambridge: Cambridge University Press, 338-276.

HERRING, SUSAN C. (2004b): "Computer-mediated communication and woman's place". In: Lakoff, Robin T. (Ed.): *Language and Woman's Place: Text and Commentaries*. Oxford/New York: Oxford University Press, 216-222.

HERRING, SUSAN C. (2007): "A faceted classification scheme for computer-mediated discourse". *Language@Internet* 1, *http://www.languageatinternet.de/articles/761*, retrieved April 2, 2008.

HERRING, SUSAN C., MARTISON, ANNA and SCHECKLER, REBECCA (2002): *Designing for Community: The Effects of Gender Representation in Videos on a Web Site*. Proceedings of the 35th Hawaii International Conference on System Sciences. Los Alamitos, CA, IEEE Press.

HERRING, SUSAN C. and NIX, CAROLE G. (1997): "Is 'serious chat' an oxymoron? Academic vs. social uses of Internet Relay Chat". Paper presented at the American Association of Applied Linguistics. Orlando, FL: Pages.

HERRING, SUSAN C. and PAOLILLO, JOHN C. (2006): "Gender and genre variation in weblogs". *Journal of Sociolinguistics* 10(4): 439-459.

HERRING, SUSAN C., STEIN, DIETER and VIRTANEN, TUIJA (2013): "Introduction to the pragmatics of computer-mediated communication". In: Herring, Susan C., Stein, Dieter and Virtanen, Tuija (Eds.): *Pragmatics of Computer-mediated Communication*. Berlin/New York: Mouton de Gruyter, 3-32.

HEYD, THERESA (2008): *Email Hoaxes*. Amsterdam/Philadelphia: John Benjamins Publishing Company.

HILTROP, SVENJA (2003): *British and American Complaints in Electronic Discourse*. Master Thesis. English Department. Rheinische Friedrich-Wilhelms-Universität, Bonn.

HÖFLICH, JOACHIM R. (1997): "Ansätze zu einer Theorie der technisch vermittelten Kommunikation". *Zeitschrift für Semiotik* 19(3): 203-228.

HOFSTEDE, GEERT (1993): *Interkulturelle Zusammenarbeit: Kulturen-Organisationen-Management*. Wiesbaden: Gabler.

HOLMES, JANET (1995): *Women, Men, and Politeness*. London: Longman.

HOLMES, JANET and MEYERHOFF, MIRIAM (1999): "The community of practice: Theories and methodologies in language and gender research". *Language in Society* 28(2): 173-183.

HOLMES, JANET and STUBBE, MARIA (2003): *Power and Politeness in the Workplace. A Sociolinguistic Analysis of Talk at Work*. London: Longman.

HOUSE, JULIANE (1986): "Cross-cultural pragmatics and foreign language teaching". In: Bausch, Karl-Richard, Königs, Frank G. and Kogelheide, Rainer (Eds.): *Probleme und Perspektiven der Sprachlehrforschung*. Frankfurt a.M.: Scriptor, 281-295.

HOUSE, JULIANE (1989): "'Oh excuse me please...' apologizing in a foreign language". In: Kettemann, Bernhard, Bierbaumer, Peter, Fill, Alwin and Karpf, Annemarie (Eds.): *Englisch als Zweitsprache*. Tübingen: Narr, 303-328.

HOUSE, JULIANE (1993): "Missverstehen im interkulturellen Diskurs". In: Timm, Johannes-Peter and Vollmer, Helmut J. (Eds.): *Kontroversen in der Fremdsprachenforschung*. Bochum: Brockmeyer, 178-192.

HOUSE, JULIANE (1996a): "Contrastive discourse analysis and misunderstanding: The case of German and English". In: Hellinger, Marlis and Ammon, Ulrich (Eds.): *Contrastive Sociolinguistics*. Berlin/New York: Mouton de Gruyter, 345-361.

HOUSE, JULIANE (1996b): "Missverstehen in interkulturellen Begegnungen". In: House, Juliane (Ed.): *Wie lernt man Sprachen - Wie lehrt man Sprachen? Zwanzig Jahre Sprachlehrforschung am Zentralen Fremdspracheninstitut der Universität Hamburg*. Hamburg: Zentrales Fremdspracheninstitut (ZFI), 154-169.

HOUSE, JULIANE (2000): "Understanding misunderstanding: A pragmatic-discourse approach to analyzing mismanaged rapport in talk across cultures". In: Spencer-Oatey, Helen (Ed.): *Culturally Speaking. Managing Rapport Through Talk Across Cultures*. London/New York: Continuum, 145-164.

HOUSE, JULIANE and KASPER, GABRIELE (1981): "Politeness markers in English and German". In: Coulmas, Florian (Ed.): *Conversational Routine. Explorations in Standardized Communication Situations and Prepatterned Speech*. Berlin/New York: Mouton de Gruyter, 157-185.

HULS, ERICA (2006): *The Communicative Functions of Emoticons in Computer-Mediated Communication*. Unpublished Manuscript.

HUNDT, MARIANNE, NESSELHAUF, NADJA and BREWER, CAROLIN (Eds.) (2007): *Corpus Linguistics and the Web*. Amsterdam/New York: Rodopi.

HYMES, DELL (1974): *Foundations in Sociolinguistics: An Ethnographic Approach*. Philadelphia: University of Pennsylvania Press.

IDE, SACHIKO (1982): "Japanese sociolinguistics: Politeness and women's language". *Lingua* 57: 357-385.

IDE, SACHIKO (1989): "Formal forms and discernment: Two neglected aspects of universals of linguistic politeness". *Multilingua* 8(2-3): 223-248.

IDE, SACHIKO (1993): "Preface: The search for integrated universals of linguistic politeness". *Multilingua* 12: 7-11.

INFANTE, DOMINIC and WIGLEY, CHARLES (1986): "Verbal aggressiveness: An interpersonal model and measure". *Communication Monographs* 53: 61-69.

KASPER, GABRIELE (1989): "Variation in interlanguage speech act realization". In: Gass, Susan M., Madden, Carolyn, Preston, Dennis and Selinker, Larry (Eds.): *Variation in Second Language Acquisition: Discourse and Pragmatics*. Clevedon: Multilingual Matters, 37-58.

KASPER, GABRIELE (1990): "Linguistic politeness: Current research issues". *Journal of Pragmatics* 14(2): 193-218.

KASPER, GABRIELE (1994): "Politeness". In: Asher, Ronald E. and Simpson, J.M.Y. (Eds.): *The Encyclopaedia of Language and Linguistics*. Oxford: Pergamon. Vol. 6, 3206-3211.

KASPER, GABRIELE and SCHMIDT, RICHARD (1996): "Developmental issues in interlanguage pragmatics". *Studies in Second Language Acquisition* 18(2): 149-169.

KATZ, ELIHU (1987): *Face Risk in the Expression of Censure: A Cross-Cultural Study.* Master Thesis. School of Education. Tel Aviv University.

KECSKES, ISTAVAN (2004): "Editorial: Lexical merging, conceptual blending, and cultural crossing". *Intercultural Pragmatics* 1(1): 1-26.

KERBRAT-ORECCHIONI, CATHERINE (1997): "A multilevel approach in the study of talk-in-interaction". *Pragmatics* 7(1): 1-20.

KIENPOINTNER, MANFRED (1997): "Varieties of rudeness: Types and functions of impolite utterances". *Functions of Language* 4(2): 251-287.

KIESLER, SARA, SIEGEL, JANE and MCGUIRE, TIMOTHY W. (1984): "Social psychological aspects of computer-mediated communication". *American Psychologist* 39: 1123-1134.

KLEINZ, THORSTEN and GÖTZ, SILJA (2008): "Wie man in den Wald hineinruft..." *eBay Magazin* 2: 104-107.

KNAPP, KARLFRIED and KNAPP-POTTHOFF, ANNELIE (1987): "Instead of an introduction: Conceptual issues in analyzing intercultural communication". In: Knapp, Karlfried, Enninger, Werner and Knapp-Potthoff, Annelie (Eds.): *Analyzing Intercultural Communication.* Berlin/New York: Mouton de Gruyter, 1-13.

KNOBEL, MICHELE and LANKSHEAR, COLIN (2002): "What am I bid? Reading, writing and ratings at eBay.com". In: Snyder, Ilana (Ed.): *Silicon Literacies: Communication, Innovation and Education in the Electronic Age.* London: Routledge, 15-30.

KO, KWANG-KYU (1996): "Structural characteristics of computer-mediated language: A comparative analysis of InterChange discourse". *Electronic Journal of Communication* 6(3), *http://www.cios.org/www/ejc/v6n396.htm*, retrieved November 12, 2005.

KOCH, MARTINA, GAUB, MAXIMILIAN, KRIEGER, TATJANA and AICHELE, MONIKA (2007): "Wie Frauen und Männer Einkaufen". *eBay Magazin* 3: 19-21.

KOCHMAN, THOMAS (1983): "The boundary between play and nonplay in black verbal dueling". *Language in Society* 12(3): 329-337.

KOOLE, TOM and TEN THIJE, JAN D. (1994): *The Construction of Intercultural Discourse: Team Discussion of Educational Advisers.* Amsterdam/New York: Rodopi.

KOUTLAKI, SOFIA A. (2002): "Offers and expressions of thanks as face enhancing acts: T□'arof in Persian". *Journal of Pragmatics* 34(12): 1733-1756.

KRAFT, BETTINA and GELUYKENS, ROLAND (2002): "Complaints in French L1 and L2: A cross-linguistic investigation". In: Foster-Cohen, Susan (Ed.): *Eurosla Yearbook Volume 2.* Amsterdam/Philadelphia: Benjamins, 227-242.

KRAFT, BETTINA and GELUYKENS, ROLAND (2004): "Beschwerdeverhalten in Muttersprache und Lernersprache: Eine kontrastive Analyse der Sprachen Deutsch und Französisch". In: Pittner, Karin, Pittner, Robert J. and Schütte, Jan C. (Eds.): *Beiträge zu Sprache und Sprachen 4. Vorträge der Bochumer Linguistik-Tage*. Munich: Lincom, 257-265.

KRIEGER, TATJANA (2008): "Der Kulturschock". *eBay Magazin* 3: 28-29.

KROEBER, ALFRED L. and KLUCKHOHN, CLYDE (1952): *Culture: A Critical Review of Concepts and Definitions*. Cambridge, MA: Peabody Museum.

LABOV, WILLIAM (1972): "Rules for ritual insults". In: Sudnow, David (Ed.): *Studies in Social Interaction*. New York: Free Press, 120-169.

LAFOREST, MARTY (2002): "Scenes of family life: Complaining in everyday conversation". *Journal of Pragmatics* 34: 1595-1620.

LAKOFF, ROBIN T. (1973): "The logic of politeness, or minding your p's and q's". *Chicago Linguistics Society* 9: 292-305.

LAKOFF, ROBIN T. (1975): *Language and Women's Place*. New York: Harper and Row.

LAKOFF, ROBIN T. (1977): "What you can do with words: Politeness, pragmatics, and performatives". In: Rogers, Andy, Wall, Bob and Murphy, John P. (Eds.): *Proceedings of the Texas Conference on Performatives, Presuppositions, and Implicatures*. Arlington: Center of Applied Linguistics.

LAKOFF, ROBIN T. (1989): "The limits of politeness". *Multilingua* 8: 101-129.

LAVÉ, JEAN and WENGER, ETIENNE (1991): *Situated Learning: Legitimate Peripheral Participation*. Cambridge: Cambridge University Press.

LEE-WONG, SONG M. (1998): "Face support - Chinese particles as mitigators: A study of BA A/YA and NE". *Pragmatics* 8(3): 387-404.

LEECH, GEOFFREY N. (1983): *Principles of Pragmatics*. London: Longman.

LEECH, GEOFFREY N. (2007): "Politeness: Is there an East-West divide?" *Journal of Politeness Research* 3: 167-206.

LEVY, STEVEN (1984): *Hackers: Heroes of the Computer Revolution*. New York: Dell.

LEWIN, BEVERLY A. and DONNER, YONATAN (2002): "Communication in Internet message boards". *English Today* 18(3): 29-37.

LIMBERG, HOLGER (2008): "Threats in conflict talk: Impoliteness and manipulation". In: Bousfield, Derek and Locher, Miriam A. (Eds.): *Impoliteness in Language*. Berlin/New York: Mouton de Gruyter, 155-179.

LINKE, ANGELIKA, NUSSBAUMER, MARKUS and PORTMANN, PAUL R. (2001): *Studienbuch Linguistik*. 4th ed. Tübingen: Niemeyer.

LIU, RUNQUING (1986): *A Dream of Red Mansions*. Unpublished MPhil dissertation. Lancaster University.

LOCHER, MIRIAM A. (2004): *Power and Politeness in Action: Disagreements in Oral Communication*. Berlin/New York: Mouton de Gruyter.

LOCHER, MIRIAM A. (2006a): "The discursive approach to polite behaviour. A response to Glick". *Language in Society* 35(5): 733-735.

LOCHER, MIRIAM A. (2006b): "Polite behaviour within relational work: The discursive approach to politeness". *Multilingua* 25(3): 249-267.

LOCHER, MIRIAM A. and WATTS, RICHARD J. (2005): "Politeness theory and relational work". *Journal of Politeness Research* 1(1): 9-33.

LOCHER, MIRIAM A. and WATTS, RICHARD J. (2008): "Relational work and impoliteness: Negotiating norms of linguistic behaviour". In: Bousfield, Derek and Locher, Miriam A. (Eds.): *Impoliteness in Language*. Berlin/New York: Mouton de Gruyter, 77-99.

LONGACRE, ROBERT (1996): "Typology and salience". In: Longacre, Robert (Ed.): *The Grammar of Discourse*. New York: Plenum Press, 7-31.

LÜDELING, ANKE, EVERT, STEFAN and BARONI, MARCO (2007): "Using web data for linguistic purposes". In: Hundt, Marianne, Nesselhauf, Nadja and Brewer, Carolin (Eds.): *Corpus Linguistics and the Web*. Amsterdam/New York: Rodopi, 7-24.

MACAULEY, MARCIA (1996): "Asking to ask: The strategic function of indirect requests for information in interviews". *Pragmatics* 6(4): 491-509.

MAO, LUMING R. (1994): "Beyond politeness theory: 'Face' revisited and renewed". *Journal of Pragmatics* 21(5): 451-486.

MARKUS, HAZEL R. and KITAYAMA, SHINOBU (1991): "Culture and the self: Implications for cognition, emotion, and motivation". *Psychological Review* 98: 224-253.

MATSUMOTO, YOSHIKO (1988): "Reexamination of the universality of face: Politeness phenomena in Japanese". *Journal of Pragmatics* 12(4): 403-426.

MATSUMOTO, YOSHIKO (1989): "Politeness and conversational universals - observations from Japanese". *Multilingua* 8(2/3): 207-221.

MAYNOR, NATALIE (1994): "The language of electronic mail: Written speech?" In: Montgomery, Michael B. and Little, Greta D. (Eds.): *Centennial Usage Studies*. Publications of the American Dialect Society Series: University of Alabama Press, 48-54.

MCHOUL, ALEC (1994): "Discourse". In: Asher, Ronald E. and Simpson, J.M.Y. (Eds.): *The Encyclopaedia of Language and Linguistics*. Oxford: Pergamon Press, 940-949.

MEHAN, HUGH (1990): "Rules versus relationships in small claims disputes". In: Grimshaw, Allen D. (Ed.): *Conflict Talk: Sociolinguistic Investigations of Arguments and Conversations*. Cambridge: Cambridge University Press, 160-177.

MEIER, ARDITH J. (1995a): "Passages of politeness". *Journal of Pragmatics* 24(4): 381-392.

MEIER, ARDITH J. (1995b): "Defining politeness: Universality in appropriateness". *Language Sciences* 17(4): 345-356.

MEY, JAKOB L. (1993): *Pragmatics. An Introduction*. 2nd ed. Oxford/Malden: Blackwell Publishers.

MEY, JAKOB L. (1998): "Pragmatics". In: Mey, Jakob L. (Ed.): *Concise Encyclopaedia of Pragmatics*. Amsterdam: Elsevier, 716-737.

MEYERHOFF, MIRIAM (2002): "Communities of Practice". In: Chambers, John K., Trudgill, Peter and Schilling-Estes, Natalie (Eds.): *Handbook of Language Variation and Change*. Oxford/Malden: Blackwell Publishers, 526-548.

MILLER, LAURA (2000): "Negative assessments in Japanese-American workplace interaction". In: Spencer-Oatey, Helen (Ed.): *Culturally Speaking. Managing Rapport Through Talk Across Cultures*. London/New York: Continuum, 240-254.

MILLS, SARA (2003): *Gender and Politeness*. Cambridge: Cambridge University Press.

MILLS, SARA (2005): "Gender and impoliteness". *Journal of Politeness Research* 1(2): 263-280.

MILLS, SARA (2009): "Politeness and culture". *Journal of Pragmatics* 14: 1047-1060.

MÖHL, SILKE (1996): *Alltagssituationen im interkulturellen Vergleich: Realisierung von Kritik und Ablehnung im Deutschen und Englischen*. Master Thesis. Universität Hamburg.

MORISAKI, SEIICHI and GUDYKUNST, WILLIAM B. (1994): "Face in Japan and the United States". In: Ting-Toomey, Stella (Ed.): *The Challenge of Facework*. Albany: Suny Press, 47-94.

MORRIS, CHARLES W. (1938): *Foundations of the Theory of Signs*. Chicago: University Press.

MULLANY, LOUISE (2004): "Gender, politeness and institutional power roles: Humour as a tactic to gain compliance in workplace business meetings". *Multilingua* 23(1-2): 13-37.

MÜLLER, YVONNE, ZAUGG, ALEXANDRA DANIELA, DUBOIS, JULIEN, GALLSZ-LöWEI, ORSOLYA and HOFMANN, ANDREAS (2007): *Kulturelle Unterschiede im Beschwerdeverhalten - Ein Vergleich zwischen Deutschschweiz und Romandie*. Institut für Wirtschaftsinformatik, Abteilung Informationsmanagement, Universität Bern.

MURPHY, BETH and NEU, JOYCE (1996): "My grade's too low: The speech act set of complaining". In: Gass, Susan M. and Neu, Joyce (Eds.): *Speech Acts Across Cultures*. Berlin/New York: Mouton de Gruyter, 191-217.

MURRAY, DENISE E. (1985): "Composition as conversation: The computer terminal as medium of communication". In: Odell, Lee and Goswami, Dixie (Eds.): *Writing in Nonacademic Settings*. New York: Guilford, 203-227.

MURRAY, DENISE E. (1988): "The context of oral and written language: A Framework for mode and medium switching". *Language in Society* 17: 351-373.

MURRAY, DENISE E. (1990): "CmC". *English Today* 23: 42-46.

MYERS, DAVID (1987): "'Anonymity is part of the magic': Individual manipulation of computer-mediated communication environments". *Qualitative Sociology* 19(3): 251-266.

NAKABACHI, KEIICHI (1996): "Pragmatic transfer in complaints: Strategies of complaining in English and Japanese by Japanese EFL speakers". *JACET Bulletin* 27: 127-142.

NORRICK, NEAL R. (1978): "Expressive illocutionary acts". *Journal of Pragmatics* 2: 277-291.

O'BRIAN, JODI (1999): "Writing in the body: Gender (re)production in online interaction". In: Smith, Marc A. and Kollock, Peter (Eds.): *Communities in Cyberspace*. London: Routledge, 76-104.

OLSHTAIN, ELITE (1983): "Sociocultural competence and language transfer: The case of apology". In: Gass, Susan M. and Selinker, Larry (Eds.): *Language Transfer in Language Learning*. Rowley, MA: Newbury House Publishers, 232-249.

OLSHTAIN, ELITE (1989): "Apologies across languages". In: Blum-Kulka, Shoshana et al. (Eds.): *Cross-Cultural Pragmatics: Requests and Apologies*. Norwood, NJ: Ablex, 155-173.

OLSHTAIN, ELITE and COHEN, ANDREW (1983): "Apology: A speech act set". In: Wolfson, Nessa and Judd, Eliot (Eds.): *Sociolinguistics and Language Acquisition*. Rowley, MA: Newbury House Publishers, 18-36.

OLSHTAIN, ELITE and WEINBACH, LIORA (1987): "Complaints: A study of speech act behaviour among native and nonnative speakers of Hebrew". In: Bertuccelli-Papi, Marcella and Verschueren, Jef (Eds.): *The Pragmatic Perspective: Selected Papers from the 1985 International Pragmatics Conference*. Amsterdam/Philadelphia: Benjamins, 195-208.

OLSHTAIN, ELITE and WEINBACH, LIORA (1993): "Interlanguage features of the speech act of complaining". In: Kasper, Gabriele and Blum-Kulka, Shoshana (Eds.): *Interlanguage Pragmatics*. Oxford/New York: Oxford University Press, 108-122.

OWEN, MARION (1983): *Apologies and Remedial Interchanges*. Berlin/New York: Mouton de Gruyter.

PAOLILLO, JOHN C. (2011): "'Conversational' codeswitching on Usenet and Internet Relay Chat." *Language@Internet*. 8 (article 3), http://www.languageatinternet.org/articles/2011/Paolillo, retrieved March 20, 2012.

PENMAN, ROBYN (1990): "Facework and politeness: Multiple goals in courtroom discourse". *Journal of Language and Social Psychology* 9: 15-38.

PIKE, KENNETH L. (1967): *Language in Relation to a Unified Theory of the Structure of Human Behaviour*. Berlin/New York: Mouton de Gruyter.

PLASTIC (2001): "Plastic", *http://www.plastic.com*, retrieved November 19, 2005.

PÖCHHACKER, FRANZ (1995): "Simultaneous interpreting: A functionalist perspective". *Hermes Journal of Linguistics* 14: 31-53.

POTTER, JONATHAN and WETHERELL, MARGARET (1987): *Discourse and Social Psychology: Beyond Attitudes and Behaviour*. Thousand Oaks, CA: Sage.

RADER, M. (1977): *Complaint Letters: When is Conflict with Ought*. Unpublished Paper. University of California.

RAETTIG, TIM (1999): "Innovativer Sprachgebrauch bei computervermittelter Kommunikation", *http://www.linguistik.uni-bonn.de/downloads/ha01.html'5.%20Schlu%DF folgerung-gen*, retrieved October 18, 2005.

RAMPTON, BEN (1985): *Crossing: Language and Ethnicity among Adolescents*. London: Longman.

RAYMOND, ERIC (Ed.) (1993): *The New Hacker's Dictionary*. Cambridge, MA: MIT Press.

REID, ELIZABETH M. (1991): *Electropolis: Communication and Community on Internet Relay Chat*. Senior Honours Thesis, University of Melbourne.

REID, ELIZABETH M. (1994): *Cultural Formations in Text-Based Virtual Realities*. Master Thesis. University of Melbourne.

REYNOLDS, MIKE (1995): "Where the trouble lies: Cross-cultural pragmatics and miscommunication". *Papers and Studies in Contrastive Linguistics* 30: 5-15.

RHEINGOLD, HOWARD (1993): *The Virtual Community: Homesteading on the Electronic Frontier*. Reading, MA: Addison-Wesley.

RISAGER, KAREN (2005): "Cross-cultural and intercultural communication/Trans- und interkulturelle Kommunikation". In: Wiegand, Herbert E. (Ed.): *Handbücher zur Sprach- und Kommunikationswissenschaft*. Berlin/New York: Mouton de Gruyter, 1674-1683.

ROTH, RUTH-MARIA (2002): *Responding to Insults in British English*. Unpublished State Exam Thesis. English Seminar. Rheinische Friedrich-Wilhelms-Universität, Bonn.

RUBINO, ANTONIA and BETTONI, CAMILLA (2006): "Handling complaints cross-culturally: Italians vs Anglo Australians". *Studi Italiani di Linguistica Teorica ed Applicata* 35(2): 339-358.

SADOCK, JERROLD (2006): "Speech acts". In: Horn, Laurence R. and Ward, Gregory (Eds.): *The Handbook of Pragmatics*. Oxford/Malden: Blackwell Publishers, 53-73.

SANDERSON, DAVID (1997): "Lexicon der Emoticons". *Zeitschrift für Semiotik* 19(3): 307-315.

SAPIR, EDWARD (1962): *Culture, Language and Personality: Selected Essays*. Berkeley: University of California Press.

SCHIANO, DIANE J. (1997): "Convergent methodologies in cyber-psychology: A case study". *Behavior Research Methods, Instruments and Computers* 29(2): 270-273.

SCHNEIDER, KLAUS P. (1988): *Small Talk. Analysing Phatic Discourse*. Marburg: Hitzeroth.

SCHNURR, STEPHANIE, MARRA, MEREDITH and HOLMES, JANET (2008): "Impoliteness as a means of contesting power relations in the workplace". In: Bousfield, Derek and Locher, Miriam A. (Eds.): *Impoliteness in Language*. Berlin/New York: Mouton de Gruyter, 211-229.

DE SCHRYVER, GILLES-MAURICE (2002): "Web for/as corpus: A perspective for the African language". *Nordic Journal of African Studies* 11(2): 266-282.

SCHULZ VON THUN, FRIEDEMANN (1996): *Miteinander Reden 1. Störungen und Klärungen*. Reinbek bei Hamburg: Rowohlt Taschenbuchverlag.

SCHULZ VON THUN, FRIEDEMANN (1998): *Miteinander Reden 2. Stile, Werte und Persönlichkeitsentwicklung*. Reinbek bei Hamburg: Rowohlt Taschenbuchverlag.

SCOLLON, RON and SCOLLON, SUZANNE W. (1995): *Intercultural Communication: A Discourse Approach*. Oxford/Malden: Blackwell Publishers.

SEARLE, JOHN R. (1969): *Speech Acts: An Essay in the Philosophy of Language*. Cambridge: Cambridge University Press.

SEARLE, JOHN R. (1975): "A taxonomy of illocutionary acts". In: Grunderson, Keith (Ed.): *Language, Mind, and Knowledge*. Minnesota, MN: University of Minnesota Press, 344-370.

SEARLE, JOHN R. (1976): "A classification of illocutionary acts". *Language in Society* 5(1-23).

SEARLE, JOHN R., KIEFER, FERENC and BIERWISCH, MANFRED (1980): "Introduction". In: Searle, John R., Kiefer, Ferenc and Bierwisch, Manfred (Eds.): *Speech Act Theory and Pragmatics*. Dordrecht: Reidel, vii-xii.

SEARLE, JOHN R. and VANDERVEKEN, DANIEL (1985): *Foundations of Illocutionary Logic*. Cambridge: Cambridge University Press.

SEVERINSON-EKLUNDH, KERSTEN and MACDONALD, CLARE (1994): "The use of quoting to preserve context in electronic mail dialogues". *IEEE Transactions on Professional Communication* 37(4): 197-202.

SHAW, PHILIP (2000): "The intercultural validity of customer-complaint handling routines". *Document Design: Journal of Research and Problem Solving in Organizational Communication* 2(2): 180-193.

SHEA, VIRGINIA (1994): *Netiquette*. San Francisco: Albion.

SIEBENHAAR, BEAT (2006): "Code choice and code-switsching in Swiss-German Internet Relay Chat rooms". *Journal of Sociolinguistics* 10(4): 481-509.

SIEVER, THORSTEN (2006): "Emoticons: Gefühle und Zeichen", *http://www.mediensprache.net/de/websprache/chat/emoticons//*, retrieved June 2, 2006.

SIEVER, THORSTEN et al. (Eds.) (2005): *Websprache.net. Sprache und Kommunikation im Internet*. Berlin/New York: Mouton de Gruyter.

SIMON, BERND (2004): *Identity in Modern Society. A Social Psychological Perspective*. Oxford/Malden: Blackwell Publishers.

SIMPSON, JOHN ANDREW and WEINER, EDMUND S.C. (Eds.) (1989): *The Oxford English Dictionary*. Oxford/New York: Oxford University Press. *http://www.dictionary.oed.com/*, retrieved March 16, 2007.

SINCLAIR, JOHN M. and COULTHARD, RICHARD M. (1975): *Towards an Analysis of Discourse: The English Used by Teachers and Pupils*. Oxford/New York: Oxford University Press.

SLUGOSKI, BEN R. and TURNBULL, WILLIAM (1988): "Cruel to be kind and kind to be cruel: Sarcasm, banter and social relations". *Journal of Language and Social Psychology* 7(2): 101-121.

SMITH, ANNA DU VAL (1999): "Problems of conflict management in virtual communities". In: Smith, Marc and Kollock, Peter (Eds.): *Communities in Cyberspace*. London: Routledge, 134-166.

SMITH, CHRISTINE B., MC LAUGHLIN, MARGARET L. and OSBORNE, KERRY K. (1997): "Conduct control on Usenet". *Journal of Computer-Mediated Communication* 2(4), *http://jcmc.indiana.edu/vol2/issue4/smith.html*, retrieved February 17, 2006.

SPENCER-OATEY, HELEN (2000a): "Introduction: Language, culture and rapport management". In: Spencer-Oatey, Helen (Ed.): *Culturally Speaking. Managing Rapport Through Talk Across Cultures*. London/New York: Continuum, 1-8.

SPENCER-OATEY, HELEN (2000b): "Rapport management: A framework for analysis". In: Spencer-Oatey, Helen (Ed.): *Culturally Speaking: Managing Rapport Through Talk Across Cultures*. London/New York: Continuum, 11-46.

SPENCER-OATEY, HELEN (2002): "Managing rapport in talk: Using rapport sensitive incidents to explore the motivational concerns underlying the management of relations". *Journal of Pragmatics* 34(5): 529-545.

SPENCER-OATEY, HELEN (2005): "(Im)Politeness, face and perceptions of rapport: Unpackaging their bases and interrelationships". *Journal of Politeness Research* 1(1): 95-119.

SPENCER-OATEY, HELEN (2007): "Theories of identity and the analysis of face". *Journal of Pragmatics* 39(4): 639-656.

SPENCER-OATEY, HELEN and JIANG, WENYING (2003): "Explaining cross-cultural pragmatic findings: Moving from politeness maxims to sociopragmatic interaction principles (SIPs)". *Journal of Pragmatics* 35(11): 1633-1650.

SPENCER-OATEY, HELEN and XING, JIANYU (2000): "A problematic Chinese business visit in Britain: Issues of face". In: Spencer-Oatey, Helen (Ed.): *Culturally Speaking: Managing Rapport Through Talk Across Cultures*. London/New York: Continuum, 272-288.

STOKOE, ELIZABETH and HEPBURN, ALEXA (2005): "You can hear a lot through the walls: Noise formulations in neighbour complaints". *Discourse and Society: An International Journal for the Study of Discourse and Communication in their Social, Political and Cultural Contexts* 16(5): 647-673.

SUTTON, LAUREL (1994): *Using USENET: Gender, Power, and Silence in Electronic Discourse*. Proceedings of the Twentieth Annual Meeting of the Berkeley Linguistics Society, General Session. Dedicated to the Contributions of Charles J. Fillmore. Berkeley, CA, Berkeley Linguistics Society, 506-520.

SWALES, JOHN (1990): *Genre Analysis: English in Academic and Research Settings*. Cambridge: Cambridge University Press.

TAKAHASHI, SATOMI and BEEBE, LESLIE M. (1993): "Cross-linguistic influence in the speech act of correction". In: Kasper, Gabriele and Blum-Kulka, Shoshana (Eds.): *Interlanguage Pragmatics*. Oxford/New York: Oxford University Press, 138-158.

TAKAHASHI, TOMOKO and BEEBE, LESLIE M. (1987): "The development of pragmatic competence by Japanese learners in English". *JALT Journal* 8: 131-155.

TANAKA, NORIKO, SPENCER-OATEY, HELLEN and CRAY, ELLEN (2000): "'It's not my fault!': Japanese and English responses to unfounded accusations". In: Spencer-Oatey, Hellen (Ed.): *Culturally Speaking. Managing Rapport Through Talk Across Cultures*. London/New York: Continuum, 75-97.

TANNEN, DEBORAH (1990): "Silence as a conflict management in fiction and drama: Pinter's Betrayal and a short story 'Great Wits'". In: Grimshaw, Allen D. (Ed.): *Conflict Talk: Sociolinguistic Investigations of Arguments and Conversations*. Cambridge: Cambridge University Press, 260-279.

TANNEN, DEBORAH (1993): "What's in a frame?: Surface evidence for underlying expectations". In: Tannen, Deborah (Ed.): *Framing in Discourse*. Oxford/New York: Oxford University Press, 14-56.

TATSUKI, DONNA H. (2000): "If my complaints could passions move: An interlanguage study of aggression". *Journal of Pragmatics* 32: 1003-1017.

TAYLOR, TALBOT J. and CAMERON, DEBORAH (1987): *Analysing Conversation. Rules and Units in the Structure of Talk*. Oxford: Pergamon Press.

TERKOURAFI, MARINA (2005): "Beyond the micro-level in politeness research". *Journal of Politeness Research* 1(2): 237-262.

TERKOURAFI, MARINA (2008): "Toward a unified theory of politeness, impoliteness, and rudeness". In: Bousfield, Derek and Locher, Miriam A. (Eds.): *Impoliteness in Language*. Berlin/New York: Mouton de Gruyter, 45-74.

THOMAS, JENNY (1983): "Cross-cultural pragmatics failure". *Applied Linguistics* 4(2): 91-112.

THOMAS, JENNY (1995): *Meaning in Interaction: An Introduction to Pragmatics*. London: Longman.

TIISALA, SEIJA (2004): "Power and politeness: Languages and salutation formulas in correspondence between Sweden and the German Hanse". *Journal of Historical Pragmatics* 5(2): 193-206.

TING-TOOMEY, STELLA and KUROGI, ATSUKO (1998): "Facework competence in intercultural conflict: An updated face-negotiation theory". *International Journal of Intercultural Relations* 22(2): 187-225.

TRACY, KAREN (1990): "The many faces of facework". In: Giles, Howard and Robinson, William P. (Eds.): *Handbook of Language and Social Psychology*. Chichester: Wiley, 209-226.

TRACY, KAREN (2008): "'Reasonable hostility': Situation-appropriate face attack". *Journal of Politeness Research* 4: 169-191.

TRENCHS, MIREIA (1994): "Complaining in Catalan, complaining in English: A comparative study of native and EFL speakers". *Revista española de lingüística aplicada* 10: 271-288.

TROSBORG, ANNA (1987): "Apology strategies in natives/non-natives". *Journal of Pragmatics* 11(1): 147-167.

TROSBORG, ANNA (1995): *Interlanguage Pragmatics. Requests, Complaints and Apologies*. Berlin/New York: Mouton de Gruyter.

TRUONG, HOAI-AN (1993): "Gender issues in on-line communications". *Feminism and Women's Studies*, *http://feminism.eserver.org/gender/cyberspace/gender-issues-online.txt/document_view*, retrieved July 22, 2006.

TSELIGA, THEODORA (2007): "'It's all *Greeklish* to me!': Linguistic and sociocultural perspectives on Roman-alphabeted Greek in asynchronous computer-mediated communication". In: Danet, Brenda and Herring, Susan C. (Eds.): *The Multilingual Internet. Language, Culture and Communication Online*. Oxford/New York: Oxford University Press, 116-141.

TURNER, KEN (1996): "The principal principles of pragmatic interference: Politeness. State of the art article". *Language Teaching* 29(1): 1-13.

TYLER, ANDREA (1995): "The construction of cross-cultural miscommunication". *Studies in Second Language Acquisition* 17(2): 129-152.

VOLLMER, HELMUT J. and OLSHTAIN, ELITE (1989): "The language of apologies in German". In: Blum-Kulka, Shoshana, House, Juliane and Kasper, Gabriele (Eds.): *Cross-cultural pragmatics*. Norwood, NJ: Ablex, 197-218.

VUCHINICH, SAMUEL (1990): "The sequential organization of closing in verbal family conflict". In: Grimshaw, Allen D. (Ed.): *Conflict Talk. Sociolinguistic Investigations of Arguments in Conversations*. Cambridge: Cambridge University Press, 118-138.

WARTENBERG, THOMAS E. (1990): *The Forms of Power. From Domination to Transformation*. Philadelphia: Temple University Press.

WATTS, RICHARD J. (1989): "Relevance and relational work: Linguistic politeness as politic behaviour". *Multilingua* 8(2/3): 131-166.

WATTS, RICHARD J. (1991): *Power in Family Discourse*. Berlin/New York: Mouton de Gruyter.

WATTS, RICHARD J. (1992): "Linguistic politeness and politic verbal behaviour: Reconsidering claims for universality". In: Watts, Richard J., Ide, Sachiko and Ehlich, Konrad (Eds.): *Politeness in Language. Studies in its History, Theory and Practice*. Berlin/New York: Mouton de Gruyter, 43-69.

WATTS, RICHARD J. (2003): *Politeness*. Cambridge: Cambridge University Press.

WATTS, RICHARD J. (2005): "Linguistic politeness research". In: Watts, Richard J., Ide, Sachiko and Ehlich, Konrad (Eds.): *Politeness in Language: Studies in its History, Theory and Practice*. Berlin/New York: Mouton de Gruyter, xi-xlvii.

WATTS, RICHARD J., SACHIKO, IDE and EHLICH, KONRAD (Eds.) (1992): *Politeness in Language. Studies in its History, Theory and Practice*. Berlin/New York: Mouton de Gruyter.

WEINBACH, LIORA (1988): *The Realization Pattern of Complaints in Hebrew: Native Speakers and Learners*. Master Thesis. School of Education. Tel Aviv University.

WENGER, ETIENNE (1998): *Communities of Practice: Learning, Meaning, and Identity*. Cambridge: Cambridge University Press.

WENZ, KARIN (1998): "Formen der Mündlichkeit und Schriftlichkeit in digitalen Medien". *Linguistic Online* 1, *http://viadrina.euv-frankfurt-o.de/~wjournal/wenz.htm*, retrieved April 10, 2008.

WERRY, CHRISTOPHER C. (1996): "Linguistic and interactional features of Internet Relay Chat". In: Herring, Susan C. (Ed.): *Computer-Mediated Communication. Linguistic, Social and Cross-Cultural Perspectives*. Amsterdam/Philadelphia: Benjamins, 47-63.

WHORF, BENJAMIN LEE ([1940] 1956): "Language, thought, and reality: Selected writings of Benjamin Lee Whorf". In: Carroll, John B. (Ed.). Cambridge, MA: MIT Press.

WIERZBICKA, ANNA (1985): "Different cultures, different languages, different speech acts: Polish vs. English". *Journal of Pragmatics* 9(2-3): 145-178.

WIERZBICKA, ANNA (1987): *English Speech Act Verbs: A Semantic Dictionary*. Sydney: Academic Press.

WIERZBICKA, ANNA (1991): *Cross-cultural Pragmatics. The Semantics of Human Interaction*. Berlin/New York: Mouton de Gruyter.

WIEST, GEORG (1997): "Medienspezifische Kodes in computergestützten Kommunikationssystemen". *Zeitschrift für Semiotik* 19(3): 229-244.

WILSON, ANDREW (1992): "A pragmatic device in electronic communication". *California Linguistic Notes* 23: 42-43.

WOLFE, JOANNA and POWELL, ELIZABETH (2006): "Gender and expressions of dissatisfaction: A study of complaining in mixed-gendered student work groups". *Women and Language* 29(2): 13-20.

WOLFSON, NESSA (1988): "The bulge: A theory of speech behavior and social distance". In: Fine, Jonathan (Ed.): *Second Language Discourse: A Textbook of Current Research*. Norwood, NJ: Ablex, 21-38.

WOLFSON, NESSA (1989): "Speech behavior and social dynamics". In: Wolfson, Nessa and Judd, Eliot (Eds.): *Perspectives. Sociolinguistics and TESOL*. Rowley, MA: Newbury House Publishers, 125-139.

WRAY, ALISON and BLOMMER, AILEEN (2006): *Projects in Linguistics: A Practical Guide to Researching Language*. 2nd ed. London: Arnold.

YAHOO!, GEOCITIES (2001): "Geocities 2001 Ratings and Reviews", *http://www.us.geocities.yahoo.com*, retrieved June 16, 2007.

YATES, SIMEON J. (1996): "Oral and written linguistic aspects of computer conferencing". In: Herring, Susan C. (Ed.): *Computer-Mediated Communication: Linguistic, Social and Cross-Cultural Perspectives*. Amsterdam/Philadelphia: Benjamins, 29-46.

ŽEGARAC, VLADIMIR and PENNINGTON, MARTHA C. (2000): "Pragmatic transfer in intercultural communication". In: Spencer-Oatey, Helen (Ed.): *Culturally Speaking. Managing Rapport Through Talk Across Cultures*. London/New York: Continuum, 165-190.

ZIMBARDO, PHILIP G. and GERRIG, RICHARD J. (1999): *Psychologie*. Berlin: Springer Verlag.

Appendix

BrE complaints - data set: Item NR

No.	Complaint	Item	Date	Time
1	NO GOODS RECEIVED.... REPORTED TO EBAY.... AVOID!!!	7319348326	01-Jun-05	21:52
2	Item not received	7325458864	30-Jul-05	20:18
3	i still dont have my item	5174120421	22-Mar-05	16:11
4	i never did receive my item i paid for, my 1st bad ebay experience	5781065311	24-Jul-05	19:55
5	item paid for but never arrived. Promised april still waiting	7958919037	03-Jun-05	21:19
6	sent cheque and not recieved the goods	4378882611	29-May-05	14:54
7	Never received item , will not order again	8180938274	18-Apr-05	20:59
8	never got item paid for	Private	02-Mar-05	23:37
9	I still haven't recieved it!!!	4340650729	29-Dec-04	12:32
10	Its Now the 28th November And I'm Still awaiting Delivery sine paying On The 5th	7562432673	28-Nov-05	17:57
11	item never received from this seller	8249181140	24-Jan-06	19:35
12	STILL NO NAIL VANISH, 2 WEEKS LATER. WHAT A WASTE OF TIME	5641742939	22-Dec-05	14:33
13	never arived	7973711012	01-Jun-05	18:32
14	Purchased not received at all!	8186773276	12-May-05	12:13
15	i never receaved it	5398505474	15-Jul-05	16:51
16	This seller took my payment, and never sent the DVD. A THIEF and SCAMMER. Not the first time that they have done this either	6367859930	20-Apr-05	19:42
17	Item never arrived - seems to be a habit	5336591079	15-Dec-04	12:21
18	I paid over a week ago and didnt recieve goods!!	8185391468	07-Jun-05	12:56
19	never recieved goods,payed before xmas!!!!!!!!!!!!!!!!!!!!!! very poor	Private	23-Feb-06	16:08
20	did not get the pants, wre are they?????	6757416393	14-Jun-05	16:55
21	hi thankyou just one little things what have i won and when will it be here jay	5805859691	15-Sep-05	10:28
22	still waiting for my item this is not acceptable	4579752423	28-Oct-05	22:55
23	still have not recieved this item.	6504821806	09-Apr-05	15:57
24	NEVER RECIEVED ITEM YER..2 WEEKS???	8368374650	15-Jan-06	12:15
25	not recieved- unhelpful to 2 small boys who lost their birthday money - unkind	6133754340	11-Jan-05	11:14
26	BAD EBAYER SENT CHQ NEVER SENT ITEM, GET PAYPAL????	5985587906	09-Aug-05	15:27
27	i sent the money but the top never came???????????	5423227664	07-Nov-05	18:39
28	still waiting for this to arrive	6009845769	02-Feb-06	14:03

29	dont buy from seller! he lies and items dont turn up	4766825989	29-Oct-05	16:15
30	the item never arrived. i am very disapointed	8155924777	16-Jan-05	22:47
31	Utterly disappointed, 3 children waiting for an item which never arrived.	4343653607	14-Jan-05	19:18
32	NEVER DEAL WITH HIM - WORST EBAYER -	4372307501	11-Jul-05	16:27
33	explained paypal problems, then paid, have not received item	7944048594	24-Jan-05	22:01
34	did not have the itam after i won it	5768354554	01-May-05	22:32
35	07/12/04 not received record yet	4051061136	07-Dec-04	12:33
36	Appalling. Taken money without sending item. Reporting to Ebay. STAY CLEAR	2562651793	02-Dec-05	22:01
37	As at 10 Feb 06 (18 days after purchase) item not received	7581259618	10-Feb-06	17:55
38	I have still not recieved this item	5394015676	23-Jun-05	14:54
39	I sent the money but never recieved the DVD	6417094159	13-Aug-05	00:31
40	bored still aint come	8213544930	25-Aug-05	13:07
41	Never got the iteam or my postal order	5995698620	19-Sep-05	14:01
42	Never recived the waistcoat!!!!	6811201083	19-Nov-05	19:08
43	can you send me my vinyl pleaseeeeeeeeeee.	4069109042	22-Feb-05	16:15
44	very disapointed payed for item 26 feb still waiting for cd rom now five weeks	5166905810	02-Apr-05	13:01
45	after 2weeks of waiting and being told on the 25th it was posted still not here	3752439682	31-Oct-04	16:01
46	liar I has waited for more than 45 days my item!!!! Robber	6545384260	24-Aug-05	13:57
47	THE MONEY SEND LONGTIME AGO AND I DID NOT RECEIVE THE ITEMS	5554492198	29-Mar-05	23:55
48	still waiting for my item	6359007403	03-Mar-05	19:52
49	still waiting 4 to send my purchase to me	5039313477	29-Oct-05	19:59
50	never arrived so waste of time and money	7181482455	12-Dec-05	10:18
51	I DID NOT RECEIVE MY ITEM FROM THIS SELLER, BEFORE YOU BUY THINK TWICE!	8185399624	09-Jun-05	21:46
52	item never received payment sent and their feddback placed but no item beware	5346567462	26-Jan-05	08:34
53	did not get the item and i paid for it	5552932064	21-Mar-05	19:14
54	good never came still waiting for	7184991186	12-Oct-05	08:53
55	never recieved item.	7976027218	05-Jul-05	20:33
56	never received item, do not buy from this seller AVOID!!	7987342892	04-Sep-05	16:38
57	payment was made over 2 weeks ago and border has still not come	5925711655	03-Nov-04	21:13
58	NEVER RECIEVED ITEM	7326236210	29-Jun-05	22:27
59	i havent received items.	5365964060	24-Mar-05	11:22

60	still havent recieved the item i bought	4372634415	26-Apr-05	15:43
61	Never recieved the goods	5537938466	17-Dec-04	12:11
62	sent postal order for the item but didnt recieve it	Private	16-May-05	21:26
63	didnt receive	6460144364	12-Jan-06	09:41
64	never recieved	6602234794	18-Feb-06	12:01
65	Purchased and paid 4 August 2005, not received and now 11 August 2005	5795445720	11-Aug-05	07:29
66	Why does ebay allow such people to trade, no items sent like so many others !!!!	6726301398	02-Mar-05	23:36
67	never recieved my goods	5594072717	15-Jul-05	16:25
68	Charger not received, dissapointed	5807575186	19-Sep-05	13:46
69	Paid, but did'nt get item. Don't do business with Babe40_4	4965387987	11-Mar-05	20:07
70	i never recieved bands. i will NEVER buy from you again. DO NOT recommend!!!	7163955773	09-Sep-05	09:29
71	too useless for words	3864966790	20-Mar-05	19:13
72	Item not received	6473730155	19-Feb-06	20:00
73	Paid instantly, never received item. Avoid	6343527825	04-Dec-04	12:22
74	i've never received the item	5754637340	20-Apr-05	17:55
75	very upset with seller payment sent but never recieved.	7111226839	01-Jan-05	17:48
76	Item Never Arrived	5450227517	05-Jan-06	23:31
77	cheque sent and cashed but no goods received!!!!	4727138435	28-Jun-05	19:02
78	Payment sent,never received, looks like i got conned like I normally do on ebay	6004204135	03-Nov-05	08:48
79	I have never received this item	5439715703	31-Jan-06	12:21
80	Item never received	8732051458	09-Jan-06	07:30
81	dont buy here unless you like to be ripped off. my item never arrived at all!	5787543236	23-Aug-05	21:46
82	i paid but not item recived - nobody should buy any items from you its crap	6178594435	31-May-05	13:42
83	Item not received. Been waiting 3 weeks.	5822434887	15-Nov-05	10:35
84	Never received	6181469181	24-Jun-05	19:04
85	item never recieved a month after	4709104676	30-May-05	13:46
86	DID NOT RECEIVE GOODS	5525975874	16-Oct-04	19:15
87	this person is a big lair, i have waited for my item for a month but get nothing	5538325073	07-Jan-05	14:33
88	Total idiot & waste of space!!! cheque cancelled forthwith!!!	8157656511	12-Jan-05	12:14
89	I NEVER RECEIVED THE ITEM!!	5776471055	09-Jun-05	12:14
90	not reccommended to anyone took my money and have,nt received item. sad people	5008171945	18-Jul-05	11:56
91	Item not recieved	6229845778	16-Feb-06	19:27
92	item not sent	8005778107	14-Nov-05	23:28
93	didnt receive item	4746333291	03-Sep-05	01:37

94	goods never received!!!	5599589576	06-Sep-05	13:05
95	still not received	5373397521	01-Apr-05	09:04
96	never recieved item	5390980104	25-Jul-05	18:16
97	This guy ripped me off!! i sent payment and have never seen my item!	8200363926	04-Jul-05	09:38
98	avoid this seller at all costs. they take you money and dont send you the goods.	8003669499	27-Oct-05	16:04
99	DONT BUY ANY SO CALLED SKY PRODUCTS FROM THIS GUY NEVER GOT ANYTHING A CON!!!!	5727300831	02-Nov-04	20:32
100	item never recieved	5561500407	06-Apr-05	19:00

BrE complaints – data set: Item DIFF

No.	Complaint	Item	Date	Time
1	purchased this GR8 item used it once and the chuck fell off.Quality tools NOT!	4371635912	12-May-05	18:51
2	Very unhappy with my buy.COPY CD!!!! Not what i expected,false advert!DONOT BUY!	4758663245	06-Sep-05	20:48
3	item not as stated very dissapointed item had to be altered	5413182844	07-Aug-05	19:19
4	biggest piece of **** i've ever brought!!!	4968733295	06-Mar-05	22:54
5	stamp tiny, disappointed with it. please leave dimensions in details.	8221300882	05-Oct-05	22:30
6	CD case broken CD scratched	4709259111	01-Apr-05	09:16
7	Dissapointed with cd as it was live recording	4715745265	13-Apr-05	11:00
8	item listed as cream but no mention of the fact that they're patterned too.	6761181428	07-May-05	22:07
9	Didn't mention it was ten friggin years old did you? What flippin use is that?	8318864075	23-Jul-05	10:03
10	fast del but dissapointed very poor quality cheap film	6450702480	16-Nov-05	14:13
11	rubbish of the two items one did not work and the other fell apart	5762981037	21-Apr-05	18:45
12	item has been received but very dissapointed with it so negative feedback sorry	6036857636	06-Mar-05	20:44
13	Goods were not fit for sale ! Did not carry out there described functions.	5821182808	13-Jan-05	17:02
14	Very painful to use. I had to throw it away	5601164469	17-Oct-05	18:14
15	misleading description highly expensive for a set of copies total rip off	6480323369	03-Feb-05	09:38
16	Speakers described as stereo but does not say so on packet, poor sound quality	8720539588	17-Nov-05	18:02
17	the game gear had a really scratched screen volume does not work no adapter	8207708140	02-Aug-05	22:22

18	said i sent item in tiny food bag totally untrue was blue poly bag	6760872892	04-May-05	16:24
19	wrong size was sent	5322752039	05-Oct-05	05:40
20	Threw away, doesn't work out of range.	5808230458	02-Oct-05	12:57
21	false advertising . ebayers stay well clear	4811449453	02-Jan-06	12:54
22	Grubby plush + stinks of soap - fur feels vile.VERY disappointing.Buyers beware!	5919639723	28-Sep-04	21:34
23	charger doesnt stay in the phone, have to hold it in.	5792474866	26-Aug-05	14:46
24	I am reporting you to ebay the good's you sold me are scrap.	5782802576	30-Jun-05	17:46
25	The CR2032 batteries are crap.. lasted 3 days the original lasted 18 months.	5851336168	28-Jan-05	18:57
26	very poor quality would not buy from again.	6714291594	15-Oct-04	16:23
27	not impressed item ripped and dirty I'm disgusted.	5205884480	21-Jun-05	14:21
28	alot smaller than it looked,no size shown	7570504672	24-Dec-05	11:42
29	Was not impressed with jeans	5442011993	18-Nov-05	14:59
30	THE PLANTS WERE IN BITS WHEN I GOT THEM	7741728335	12-Feb-06	21:27
31	Waste of money. Items torn, dirty and most won't fit Barbie. very disappointed.	5619345430	11-Oct-05	12:17
32	these items were fit for the bin- beware of this seller	Private	12-May-05	21:20
33	O.k service, but record not picture disc as portrayed from picture!	2577713707	19-Dec-05	23:28
34	rubish	7554630183	16-Jan-06	22:43
35	this item was classed as the best wire saw you can get. yet it broke right away	7165143049	07-Jul-05	17:54
36	poor product	8178594975	05-Apr-05	13:48
37	not happy with game disk 2 wont load big crack in it bad EBAYER.	Private	16-Jun-05	16:15
38	Arrived promptly, although dirty and smelling of smoke and underarm stains	5364265047	02-Mar-05	13:14
39	unit sent waz u/s	6367144058	30-Apr-05	07:04
40	I was disgusted with this item, it arrived dirty,missing power lead waste of mon	4364219673	18-Mar-05	10:44
41	rare vintage shirts? More like cheap market copies! Not what I was expecting!	5223024439	22-Aug-05	20:27
42	quick delievery. Dress aged 18mths not 12mths as described. stains on back dress	4748431566	26-Jul-05	08:20
43	Really crappy item, donated to rubbish collections... terrible seller...	6733968086	16-Feb-05	21:43
44	GASH! GASH!! DO NOT BUY THIS CRAP.. I HAVE BEEN RIPPED OFF... BAD EBAYER AVOID	8032029819	28-Jan-06	21:37

45	Not Hush Puppies, but you thought they were, so that is good enough?	3968913241	28-Apr-05	19:02
46	does not cover ford 5000 series	7974435372	17-May-05	20:25
47	New to this person is secondhand to the rest of us.dont go near this seller.	6433398242	20-Oct-05	19:07
48	Not as advertised - lens cleaner doesn't work on xbox	5142495009	05-Feb-05	14:05
49	i didnt recieve the product shownin the picture - mine only has 1 candle holder	Private	22-Nov-05	13:43
50	I was disapointed that the item wasn't giant as described in add. had 2 buy agai	5968073028	30-Apr-05	21:13
51	disappointed in style and fabric	5392149635	27-May-05	23:04
52	not as described dissapointed with bangle as stones missing also wont lock toget	5069584076	11-Jan-06	16:21
53	Very disappointed, item had been stuck together with glue, this was not stated.	6183239165	14-Jun-05	11:31
54	Received promptly but item scratched, dirty, cracked and Facia silver worn off -	6323986849	29-Sep-04	13:41
55	Top was in bad condition with stitches loose and broken straps!	5385516696	05-May-05	22:14
56	poorly packed - all loose in envelope. should have been packed in jiffybag	8186629869	08-May-05	12:31
57	trainers came quick but ended up being size 9. BEWARE!!!	5465184629	04-Feb-06	15:55
58	Rec'd in a very sorry condition (worse than 2nd hand).Better DVD deals on Amazon	6415659543	28-Jul-05	20:04
59	SELLING ILLEGAL COPIED GAMES AS ORIGINALS DO NOT USE OR TRUST IF BUYING GAMES	6447262038	22-Nov-05	03:27
60	described as large but definately not , must be a second!!! VERY DISSAPOINTED	7211485137	24-Jan-06	20:42
61	not the size that i bid for	3983741607	09-Jul-05	16:07
62	Poor Condition. Not as described.	8735726668	14-Dec-05	13:50
63	Not as described: not made by de Havilland and unusable	3980980398	22-Sep-05	00:42
64	CD WASN'T AN ORIGINAL AND DOSEN'T PLAY AT ALL	4721536884	04-May-05	14:42
65	poor game did not contain any data on it	8149844609	08-Oct-05	22:20
66	Was not the real thing a copy	5857133747	11-Feb-06	20:39
67	post was fast, but shoes were awful, dirty, sequins missing, sole faulty, Sorry!	6787409808	27-Jul-05	11:36
68	Poor quality, advert suggest items is of a product other than cheep plastic :-(	5838853556	15-Dec-05	11:20
69	item torn only fit for the rubbish bin extremely disappointed	5368612000	16-Mar-05	21:04

70	Disappointed I paid over £5 for a burnt CD recording from Radio One!	4052400870	20-Dec-05	11:42
71	items were not working only fit for the skip thats putting it nicely lost money	3869860858	17-Feb-05	12:46
72	wrong item recieved!	6804700473	24-Sep-05	14:34
73	Buyer will not get what has been described and. Buyers Beware!	7522018680	08-Jul-05	13:47
74	did not work, computer expert tried, threw it in dust bin	6752019598	06-Apr-05	23:16
75	i didnt think i ordered a paper bra, it describes it as a sweet bra	5400080432	24-Jun-05	19:55
76	Product cover was ripped. Sleeve on inside was torn off. 2nd disc was scratched.	4740386000	08-Jul-05	10:04
77	LIAR! item not as described DON'T BUY FROM HIM! better sel porn then bike parts	7176440143	25-Aug-05	21:11
78	some pictures were of poor quality	7221031822	02-Mar-05	16:15
79	No cable supplied and in poor condition	3837685682	14-Oct-05	10:01
80	paints coming of the bowls. not very good	7509381789	19-May-05	22:15
81	WANT MONEY BACK, disgrace would not sell these boots even 2a blind person	5139713463	27-Nov-05	22:17
82	item wasnt what i exspected very disapointed should have been described better	6314854822	02-Sep-04	21:21
83	one of the neons was broke inside!!	8004510334	07-Nov-05	12:56
84	the perfume had gone off	5607704477	27-Aug-05	11:03
85	these are fake quiksilver t-shirts	3951556384	26-Jan-05	09:20
86	product is dirty and has cracks in it...	7581945926	27-Jan-06	11:28
87	BUYER BEWARE... Mixer tap purchased DOESN'T fit standard uk bath or sink!!!	5978419580	08-Jun-05	17:27
88	Item appears to have a fault with it, doesn't appear to match up to description!	6845547856	07-Feb-06	10:07
89	Junk. 100% Rubbish. Made in India. Cardboard Helmet.. Untruthful Seller. BEWARE!	6558950274	17-Sep-05	19:20
90	OLD SCRUFFY LIBRARY BOOK, WITH 16 PAGES MISSING - NOT STATED, A LOAD A RUBBISH!!	7184756885	27-Sep-05	11:18
91	Coat arrived - disappointingly though as I had to take it to Dry Cleaners	5445998451	06-Dec-05	20:12
92	the items are used not new and are both faulty unable to use bars are damaged.	7212847140	03-Feb-06	23:02
93	very disappointed. Item has 2 punched holes not mentioned in description	6183547927	14-Jun-05	19:41
94	I did not expect the chart to be over 15 A4 pages and of poor quality copy	8171672101	01-Mar-05	16:26
95	Item case scratched. can not give as a pressent. very disapointed.	5353067969	02-Feb-05	17:12

96	doesn't come in tiffany box or with bag and authenticy card	5041801346	30-Okt-05	20:39
97	not a good quality diamond and not hallmarked. very dissapointed	4975620799	16-Mar-05	23:55
98	Not satisfied with product, inferior, edges rough when seperated from card.	7562232137	11-Jan-06	19:29
99	WARNING: Goods were misrepresented and basically a breach of Copyright laws.	4792044994	27-Nov-05	22:20
100	I thought i was buying a rubiks Cube, but this one is a cheap immitation	5994046103	13-Sep-05	11:32

BrE complaints – data set: Item NR-D

No.	Complaint	Item	Date	Time
1	didn't recieve items bought. no responce to e-mails. Will not buy from again	6581139635	20-Dec-05	10:51
2	Item not received, no response from seller, very surprised as feedback is good	5053531190	30-Nov-05	21:43
3	Did not arrive , was no help ,would no buy from this person ,took the money ,	4724418758	17-May-05	22:09
4	no tape no response to emails rip off merchant nad conman avoid at all cost	4852777657	22-Apr-05	09:45
5	items never arrived, no response from seller, don't buy from him, con man, avoid	6767865365	02-Jun-05	15:51
6	Paid immediately vis paypal. After 2 weeks, no delivery or reply to email.	7390921713	03-Mar-05	13:27
7	beware !!!!!!!! item paid for but never received.no reply to e-mails	7101393856	27-Apr-04	19:28
8	Purchased on the 3rd Maech, still not received goods, sent 2 emails, No reply	5870508109	21-Mar-05	10:10
9	No item recived .no response to e mail..	6784157782	12-Aug-05	19:39
10	I have never received the goods I purchased and also have not had any reply	5857947211	26-Feb-06	16:09
11	DONT GO HERE ITEM NEVER TURNED UP ,TRYED TO SORT OUT BUT "WELL SAY NO MORE "	5967145813	07-May-05	00:40
12	SHOCKING SERVICE WORSE I HAVE RECEIVED - ITEM NOT RECEIVED NO REFUND/REPLACEME	7612327777	28-Apr-05	18:22
13	ink not recieved after 15 days!! no contact from seler even after i emailed um!	6738231185	16-Feb-05	02:14
14	I have never received item. payment was sent in cash. and have had no respose	6556273752	27-Sep-05	09:23
15	DIDN'T SEND ITEM,WAS RUDE,OFFENSIVE AND LIED.DO NOT BUY FROM HIM TERRIBLE EBAYER	8354573404	22-Jan-05	12:43

16	IGNORED DISPUTE & EMAILS. DONT DEAL WITH - HAD CHEQUE DIDNT DELIVER. DONT TRUST	6210287739	15-Oct-05	16:10
17	didn't receive goods and got no response to recent emails	6802495785	15-Dec-05	17:18
18	ignores messages & hasn't sent goods 11days after payment	7401424999	04-Apr-05	13:08
19	didnt receive item sent many emails no response.	8393578086	02-Apr-06	14:56
20	Item never received and no further communiction received despite emails sent!	6807112738	07-Nov-05	20:57
21	No charger recieved, no reply to e-mails, Do not buy from this e-bayer	5836387730	17-Jan-05	11:27
22	Payed, and not recvied. Paypal gave me refund. Doesn't reply to emails! AVOID!!!	4752350123	13-Sep-05	09:18
23	Never recieved 2 pair of jeans, and no reply when i asked for refund	6821404524	17-Mar-05	00:03
24	Item paid for on 13/10/2005. Haven't got goods or refund	7717350867	31-Oct-05	08:27
25	never recived item been waiting 4weeks and does not answer emails]	6480609407	02-Mar-05	13:20
26	Nothing received and no reply to numerous emails. Have they stopped trading ?	4729411164	25-Jul-05	14:37
27	Did not rcieve the product, took my money,did not answer any emails!	7380700541	18-Feb-05	07:56
28	item paid for not received emails ignored tried to contact seller many times	7743731242	06-Apr-06	16:44
29	paid up in full.item not recieved messaged seller many times no response..BAD!!!	7199931013	19-Dec-05	15:59
30	Paid for this beginning of Jan, still not received, ignoring my emails	4428769789	29-Jan-05	20:55
31	No item received and refused to answer many emails.	6586546961	10-Mar-05	08:55
32	Never arrived, no messages answered as to when it was sent :-(	8229973874	11-Dec-05	20:41
33	Item never turned up and seller didn't answer emails. Poor service overall	5656428985	17-Feb-06	18:27
34	I received no pens and no refund... Service not good ! !	8247444873	03-Feb-06	14:35
35	not received item or a e-mail sayin wen they will send it.very dissapointed.	5439436688	06-Nov-05	18:16
36	DO NOT USE! NO GOODS RECIEVED OVER 1 MONTH LATER. NO RESPONSE TO EMAILS. USELESS	5846601390	02-Feb-05	22:59
37	Goods never arrived - Seller ignored all correspondence...	6033994103	30-Apr-05	02:35

38	Goods never arrived and no response from messages.	5870867439	12-Apr-06	08:05
39	Sorry, been almost a month now, no replies to e-mails, would like money back pls	5410143062	25-Aug-05	20:01
40	Paid for item. Did not receive it. Did not reply to numerous contacts.	4383413155	08-Jul-05	17:35
41	Did not send item, nor respond to Paypal Investigation. BUYERS BEWARE !!!!!!!	3752880151	15-Dec-05	15:00
42	product did not turn up!!! messaged seller and no reply ..dodgy!	5560288462	15-Mar-05	21:23
43	TOP NEVER REC, DOES NOT REPLY TO EMAIL AVOID AT ALL COSTS	5396353953	21-Jun-05	13:14
44	TOOK MY MONEY AND NEVER SENT ITEM - DOES NOT REPLY TO EMAILS EITHER - AVIOD..!!!	7564577027	15-Dec-05	08:51
45	Taken money & have not recieved item now ignoring me trying to get hold of them	7197246598	07-Dec-05	18:25
46	Item not recieved after payment was sent, correspondence ignored, bad ebayer	6434367169	25-Oct-05	14:37
47	Still to recieve item a week after paying, and he is not answering my emails?	8272898766	14-Apr-06	14:29
48	Very unhappy, never received goods and never reply's to messages i sent!!!	8003796145	02-Nov-05	10:10
49	unfortunatly i have not recieved this item and no response to emails	5582905503	07-Jul-05	16:24
50	item never received and no refund given by seller very dissapointing	7563563459	22-Feb-06	20:01
51	TOOK MY MONEY AND I STILL HAVE NOT EVEN HEARD FROM THE SELLER . NOT HAPPY	4401351291	05-Sep-05	14:55
52	This items has never arrived and despite emails no response	5236420994	24-Oct-05	21:40
53	Really disappointing...no response to emails....item still not received.	5211612542	02-Jul-05	16:55
54	still havent received item, have left cple of emails still no replys	8363512492	04-Jan-05	18:12
55	would not use these as you never get the item and you don't get replys for them.	4441958962	28-Mar-06	14:15
56	PAID FOR CD BUT NEVER CAME OR REPLIED TO EMAILS. UNTRUSTWORTHY	4771185631	20-Oct-05	12:13
57	PAID STRAIGHT AWAY-NOTHING.SENT 3 EMAILS OVER 3 DAYS-NO RESPONSE.NOT RECOMMENDED	7739947772	09-Feb-05	17:56
58	nothing sent to me or answer. never again from this seller	6412111170	09-Aug-05	23:32

59	didnt even receive the item,egnored my emails 4 wks until paypal got my money .	6827310519	31-Dec-05	11:33
60	5 days still nothing no responce to e-mail	6426361487	31-Aug-05	20:49
61	Paid for the goods instantly, rec'd nothing, e-mails not answered - BUYER BEWARE	7568529263	29-Dec-05	18:17
62	worse e-bayer eva! Sent money neva received item! Neva replied 2 my emails	5579231636	27-Jun-05	11:55
63	Not recieved video,sent money, email's but no answer.bad ebayer	4186567710	20-Jun-04	13:42
64	Brought on 11/11/05,paid instantly with P/P.Still not received,no answer to emai	4588782641	19-Nov-05	11:39
65	No item sent, cheque cashed, no communication from seller, be careful here!	5594866648	17-Aug-05	11:57
66	its been 2 weeks i paid still no film . no message nothing this person rips you	9117392640	03-Apr-06	18:36
67	Refuses to reply to emails have not received any products AVOID!!!!!!!!	4549093537	26-May-05	09:41
68	not recieved item /emailed not replied to will not get anything elsel from them.	9118388174	30-Mar-06	02:42
69	not recieved,threatened on phone ,bad bad ebayer reported to ebay	4398001773	11-Aug-05	11:32
70	Item not received, no response to emails GET A PROPER JOB DEL BOY	7994141929	14-Sep-05	14:29
71	still not got my items, cheque came out, 3 weeks ago. emailed them, no reply.	5667765865	10-Mar-05	21:44
72	payment acknoledged,never recieved item promised refund,wich never arrived,crap	7009762814	06-Apr-06	16:29
73	Bloody useless conmen. No delivery, no communication	5461206928	24-Jan-05	17:31
74	readn ur feedbak, u aint answern me either, wheres my bloody dvd, bin waitn 14 d	6473529802	26-Jan-06	01:19
75	NOT SENT TROUSERS NOT GOT INTOUCH WITH ME WOULD LIKE MONEY BACK	5384446136	10-May-05	09:43
76	never recieved item never emailed me bak stay away from this seller	8371061978	07-Feb-06	14:16
77	2 WEEKS STIL AWAITIN ITEM, NO REPLIES, ##### bad ebayer #####	6445259587	11-Nov-05	17:04
78	i paid for this item on 3rd april & i still havn`t received it or had a response	9505068388	13-Apr-06	14:08
79	still not recieved the cd. very disappointed. No response from emails	4738419980	17-Jul-05	13:04
80	NEVER RECEIVED GOODS WORTH OVER £40 E BAY MEMBER NEVER REPLYS TO E MAILS	7569755623	22-Apr-05	20:29
81	never received item, and seller not in a hurry to respond taking me months now.	6763020532	18-Jul-05	12:12

82	4 items not sent no reply to 6 emails going to report to ebay!! Thief beware	8198204343	14-Sep-05	20:28
83	BEWARE - Goods paid for but not received also seller does not respond to email	6413882646	25-Jul-05	22:11
84	never got the item !sent loads email no ans STAY AWAY!	5453798812	25-Jan-06	19:15
85	terrible service, order not delivered, no contact from seller as to why!!!!!!!!!	8264356018	28-Mar-05	08:32
86	I have not recived my goods or had an email answered. ????????	5847714061	10-Jan-06	14:21
87	no comunication goods not delivered !!! Avoid !!!	8382066479	21-Feb-06	07:53
88	No record, no response to emails	4748450102	08-Sep-05	20:35
89	Never recieved payment, waited for 6 days, no contact or explination	9302704596	02-Apr-06	22:54
90	paid 5/12/05,STILL no item rec'd +no reply from her to 4 emails re RM claim	5640066477	09-Feb-06	13:14
91	bad ebayer- didn't recieve the item at all- BLANKED MY EMAILS	5844773575	16-Jan-06	23:58
92	STILL WAITING FOR ITEM AFTER 2 WEEKS AND IGNORES ALL EMAILS BE AWARE	5862592930	20-Feb-06	10:09
83	Telephone/ emails NO REPLY at all, NO item after 3 Weeks!! NEXT DAY DELIVERY???	7578808589	25-Mar-06	09:24
94	contacted seller several time, no reply no cd! DO NOT BUY NOTHING FROM HERE!!!	5606068259	28-Aug-05	13:48
95	never received the product and now haven't replied to my e-mails chasing it up	6846844615	10-Mar-06	14:10
96	I paid 4thnov. 4th dec. still waitin for item,AND reply!to email askin where n"y	5436230571	04-Dec-05	14:39
97	do not buy from this trader. have not received items paid for, or replys.	5581271911	25-Jun-05	22:38
98	i still didnt receive my item and they dont respond to my emails....	6415978640	22-Aug-05	18:45
99	NEVER RECEIVED ITEM.DID NOT REPLY TO E MAILS..ROBBERS	5873622202	12-Mar-05	19:48
100	Never arrived, didn't reply to emails,just took money...shit ebayers	8722180803	09-Feb-06	14:35

BrE complaints – data set: Item DIFF-D

No.	Complaint	Item	Date	Time
1	Poor quality item. No response to my email.	4572365013	22-Sep-05	12:19
2	item was water damaged tried to contact seller no replay to emails	5861383931	27-Feb-06	11:24
3	rip off!vouchers out of date and had to pay an extra £1.05 to recieve my package	6548543520	04-Aug-05	19:28

4	Poor product very ineffectual, Seller didn't want to know, AVOID	4391674486	18-Jul-05	22:07
5	Itemdidn't work, sent back to addres stated on site, no refund or item. Bad ebay	6003368938	19-Nov-05	16:48
6	Faulty item 6 emails asking for details to return no response. Shysters don't by	9303763187	27-Apr-06	16:06
7	Item described as leather, was vinyl,no response to repeated e-mails.	6796894450	14-Sep-05	19:50
8	TOTTALY IGNORANT PEOPLE, THEY SELL FAULTY GOODS THEN MESS YOU ABOUT FOR REFUND--	6828290314	13-Jan-06	20:57
9	Item not as described Spindles Pine not Mahogany Will not refund Buyer Beware	6001840294	11-Oct-05	09:57
10	plastic cover damaged when recieved, emailed but no reply.	7166042479	12-Sep-05	12:22
11	rubbish ebayer, advertised wrong sizes, numerous emails, no response!!!!!!!!!!!	5416801912	04-Oct-05	14:57
12	Sent me wrong ones DONT FIT GILERA DNA 50CC WILL NOT ANSWER EMAIL AVOID!!!!!!!!!	7975496569	01-Jun-05	17:42
13	Item was broken in the post, I returned it and was refused a refund	5968062966	27-Apr-05	10:53
14	Did not respond to my email asking why this did not work!!	5849704687	31-Mar-05	10:51
15	Item faulty, I returned item and received replacement, they wont pay my postage	5877426927	03-May-05	14:51
16	Not as described! Seller doesnt reply to emails! Avoid at all costs!	9120249866	09-Apr-06	13:33
17	Boots were FAKE unhappy with service - seller ignored e-mail of complaint	5469482588	22-Feb-06	13:13
18	NOT AS DESCRIBED, LEAVES PERSONAL INSULTS - DO NOT BUY FROM!!!	5228856878	22-Nov-05	14:42
19	crap quality & faulty returned but never received refund altho proof it returned	4436161437	04-Apr-05	08:07
20	disappointed with item condition not as described no response from seller	7361076666	15-Nov-05	07:51
21	Fast Delivery, product not as described. Very disappointed. Never replied	6441958058	29-Oct-05	09:15
22	item no good tried to contact seller but would not reply in bin now	4415869986	25-Jan-06	20:47
23	Not Region 2 would not play !!! Returned and never received refund CAUTION !!!	6439511650	15-Nov-05	18:36
24	bent product, not advertised as is. over charged postage,very disappionted	5076146558	18-Jan-05	19:30
25	when the razor came it was blunt, promised replacement but never came	6566334037	04-Nov-05	12:17

26	Sent wrong disc. Promised refund, but now ignores e-mails. Very poor service.	4732011681	05-Jun-05	16:04
27	Not happy at all with item, seller would not exchange for another item !Unhappy!	8401354971	11-Apr-06	14:00
28	Slippers stopped flashing after one day. Contacted seller but got no reply......	6784535028	11-Dec-05	08:34
29	Sells dirty clothes and ignores emails.	6846958537	25-Feb-06	17:48
30	POOR COND., 1 PR DIRTY GREY/BLUE, STUNK OF SMOKE, NO RPLY 2 EMAILS - NOT HAPPY	4857752127	17-Apr-05	21:14
31	Sent me fake not 'Faith' boots then offered me refund and didn't do it.	3964696017	13-Apr-05	14:57
32	Wrong Size, wouldnt refund money, dodgy eBayer!!!!	6862144272	03-Apr-06	22:24
33	The Item doesn't work, no reply to my messages, not happy	5232533745	27-Sep-05	20:21
34	delivery wasn't as stated, scratched surface, no email replys, wont buy from agn	4443218950	13-Mar-05	18:49
35	very poor quality camera-no refund agreed to by seller-dissapointed	7563818077	24-Nov-05	19:34
36	item misdescribed as light,not light holder. Did not reply to two questions- - -	5567175740	12-Apr-05	07:53
37	incorrect item sent /// 2 emails sent with no response	6837133337	12-Jan-06	12:37
38	Item delivery was quick but, CD was not sent as per ad; not response to e-mail	5868532758	08-Mar-05	00:24
39	useless ebayer does not reply emails useless item dont buy from this ebayer	7997917932	05-Oct-05	14:59
40	We got a T22 for a T23: crook! No reply to our request. Intend to sue	8754928370	04-Feb-05	09:34
41	hard drive was faulty wont answer emails	8762484321	03-Mar-05	09:27
42	Condition of item worse than stated. No reply to email from seller.	7714501310	12-Nov-05	16:05
43	non working item sent NO response to emails not in spirit of Ebay! AVOID!!!	5853981270	31-Jan-06	22:06
44	This is what there add should say ! WE SELL CHEAP CHINESE CRAP ! ignored emails	5855947203	14-Feb-06	04:15
45	Stereo didn't fit even though was told it would, refund was not an option !!	5791043617	17-Aug-05	22:22
46	items sent were different size refund was quick but only partial buyers beware	5465368260	22-Feb-05	11:08
47	Item not received as advertised, seller did not respond to my query - not good	6826559368	15-Dec-05	17:12
48	cable and drivers do not work. not happy. already tried contacting. no reponse.	5817545996	25-Oct-05	00:04
49	rod broken when deliverd, wil not replace	7174271584	16-Aug-05	20:25

50	Paper was very poor quality - not as listed. Seller ignoring my emails tosortout	6765453261	18-May-05	11:33
51	I've received wrong item. Have e-mailed you but, ignored.Please contact me asap	4733396885	24-Nov-05	19:06
52	Sent wrong battery, contacted seller no reply.	5796236755	15-Oct-05	08:41
53	took 3 weeks 2 arrive! stitching on the back is anything but quality..	6857096137	10-Apr-06	16:31
54	I've tried 2 contact more then twice but heard nothing!! item not working	5827502913	05-Dec-05	01:19
55	poor - imitation item - no responses to e mail. Never again	5411544527	06-Oct-05	13:08
56	Faulty monitor. Tried to contact seller many times no answer. BEWARE!!!!!!!!!!!!	5130340669	23-Nov-04	10:33
57	received item covered in pet hairs no answers to my emails disgusted!!!!!!!!!	6583397468	20-Dec-05	08:30
58	Product not as described,did not have the decency to reply to mails,steer clear!	5183612042	29-Apr-05	14:39
59	Wrong item sent, no replies to e-mails. Dumb-founded!!!!!!!!	5416094433	29-Aug-05	09:26
60	box crushed, item smelt smokey. long delivery time	8788359706	01-May-05	20:51
61	Wrong item sent. No response to EBAY message or email.	8268569368	28-Mar-05	08:57
62	crap. took ages and it isn't even the right one!!!	5877384097	30-Apr-05	11:13
63	'excellent/good condition without tags' means old/grubby.25% were new.no refund!	Private	27-Feb-06	10:28
64	received item and was not as described! contacted seller 3 times...no reply!!	9710547272	18-Apr-06	11:05
65	MAKE-UP ARRIVED USED AND DAMAGED, NOT NEW! - EMAILS IGNORED - DISPUTE OPENED!	5677147032	05-Apr-05	22:10
66	problem with bike no reply from seller thumbs down	7182213673	27-Sep-05	20:04
67	Not model shown in picture. No reply to email :(	7011576784	17-Mar-05	17:11
68	TSHIRT IS DEFINETLY NOT AUTHENTIC THATS A DEFINET DISSAPPOINTED EMAILED NO REPLY	8322106087	07-Sep-05	22:27
69	Item didn`t work and communication was rubbish! I mended it myself in the end!	7226301623	04-Apr-06	08:54
70	FAKE SUBWAY VOUCHERS NOT ACCEPTED IN THE UK - WILL NOT REFUND ME - NASTY PERSON	Private	14-Jul-05	12:21
71	Wrong size belt.No refund or exchange offered.Will be contacting Paypal soon.	5455871799	06-Feb-05	00:09
72	SPA FAULTY. SELLER WILL NOT RESPOND. No aftersales at all. BE WARNED!	4382605391	28-Jul-05	18:45

73	ITEM DAMAGED & WRONGLY DESCRIBED, RETURNED & NO REFUND RECEIVED	5074799634	01-Feb-05	11:08
74	Parts as described but missing a fitting bolt. No response from seller.	7169596691	05-Aug-05	09:10
75	Disappointing. Wrong item arrived and no reply to my emails.	8023445682	01-Jan-06	14:00
76	loose blade,split scabbard,non of which was in the DescriptionNo reply to email	6566755080	29-Oct-05	21:48
77	Item broken, cost refund offered £5.51, not postage, more than £11!!!	8198418894	30-Jun-05	17:00
78	badly damaged due to poor packaging, no reply to email sent 6 days ago	8216842766	25-Sep-05	15:22
79	buggie was dreadful emailed company and they never replied.KEEP WELL AWAY !!!!!	7749124817	04-Apr-06	19:12
80	Wrong item sent, they promised me spare ribbons as compensations but didn't send	6019729466	16-Feb-05	23:01
81	did say sml scratches looks like has been run over by a car did email seller n/r	5829012632	24-Nov-05	16:25
82	bracelet poor quality and ebayer refusing to recognise sale after complaint	5059721630	12-Dec-05	23:31
83	I sent the item bak cuz it was damaged & she still wudn't giv refund total CON!!	5586604134	18-Jul-05	10:40
84	advertising frame when only stickers that r overpriced.Didnt answer questions	7166424590	14-Jul-05	17:17
85	lingerie is a lot smaller than sizes state and you cannot return unlike shops	5393819431	01-Jun-05	20:17
86	Item had a large stain on it and did not reply to email about problem.	5390669039	13-Aug-05	12:45
87	DONT BOTHER!! Item not as described and faulty. V.Poor communication. !!BEWARE!!	7596754406	11-Apr-05	03:38
88	Do NOT recommend. Sent wrong brand. Offered part refund. NEVER got it.	7376828604	06-Mar-06	07:51
89	item faulty,refund refused,avoid,very unpleasant attitude.	5807282019	26-Sep-05	19:41
90	Not very happy. goods supplied did not work as described. No offer of refund !!!	6032263557	24-Mar-05	18:26
91	Torch smaller model than advertised. Refund offered but subsequent comms ignored	7520890278	18-Jul-05	19:26
92	Item NOT new! 3 emails to seller and 8 WEEKS ON!! Nothing done!!!!!! Unhappy!!!	4375496922	21-Jun-05	22:23
93	Received defect golf club..Sent 4 emails ..NO REPLY. You must NOT buy from him	7162380970	06-Jul-05	13:52
94	Phone arrived but didnt work.Seller wouldnt refund.reported to ebay/paypal.	5841388054	25-Jan-05	21:45

95	received item in poor used condition not brand new as stated no reply to emails.	8136691529	25-Oct-05	10:35
96	Attempted email contact as items smelt of cig smoke - no return contact	5468133663	23-Mar-05	09:37
97	supplied faulty charger, seller ignored my messages	5785945626	16-Jul-05	09:01
98	goods were missdiscribed,broken and bits missin!£5 for 2nd class delivery!	5960168477	16-Mar-05	19:33
99	does not fit BMW as said no response to e-mail	8017871082	14-Dec-05	11:19
100	item took 11 days, poor quality of goods	5062564029	06-Jan-05	10:03

German complaints – data set: Item NR

No.	Complaint	Item	Date	Time
1	wochenlanges warten, keine ware erhalten, wenigstens gab es das geld zurück.	8315204892	10-Aug-05	19:04
2	Geld überwisen ,Ware aber nicht erhalten : - (, so kann mann auch Geld machen	5803551946	21-Sep-05	15:42
3	meine ware kommt nicht!!!!!!!!!	7976711322	12-Jan-05	21:37
4	Ware nicht Bekommen !!!	5061480033	14-Jan-06	15:10
5	Ich habe die Ware noch immer nicht erhalten !!!	5815868739	09-Dez-05	17:28
6	Keine Ware erhalten	8709915668	17-Jan-06	16:54
7	Vorsicht!!-- Keine Ware bekommen!!-Behauptet Post ist schuld--Vorsicht!!!	6007750254	23-Nov-05	12:05
8	Bis heute keine Ware, diese Leute gehören eingesperrt !!!	6394863256	10-Jun-05	19:17
9	Rasentraktor nicht bekommen nicht zu empfehlender Verkäufer	4358460692	21-Mär-05	13:21
10	nie wieder!!!!!!!!!!!!!!!!!!!!!!!!!!!!!!!!!!!	8159827113	24-Feb-05	16:07
11	Voll die Zecke . Ware nicht angekommen !!Ein Großer Lügner	4753832466	06-Sep-05	17:21
12	ware bezahlt aber nicht bekommen	6161940885	13-Aug-05	23:57
13	VORSICHT! WARE BEZAHLT UND KEINE ERHALTEN - NIE WIEDER!!	5349339934	09-Jul-05	12:19
14	nicht erhalten	6804410992	08-Okt-05	11:57
15	Superschnell bezahlt, nach einer woche noch keine Ware. Das ist schlecht.Schade!	6393097936	14-Mai-05	16:29
16	Warte seit 6 Wochen auf meine Filme!!!!	6471733404	18-Feb-06	21:51
17	HABE DIE WARE BEZAHLT ABER NICHT ERHALTEN !!!	5077537138	23-Jan-06	18:07
18	Am 15.12. überwiesen, bis heute keine Lieferung !!!	5940493273	17-Jan-05	10:18
19	Wahre ist nicht angekommen !	3984327105	14-Aug-05	20:28
20	KEINE WARE ERHALTEN - Schade! Nicht zu empfehlen.	6417919908	03-Sep-05	15:01
21	30 Euro für nichts ! Anzeige ist unterwegs !	6438136265	17-Jan-06	21:27

22	Ware gab es überhaupt nicht. Lasst die Finger von dem Laden! 100 % NEGATIV!	7174436324	19-Aug-05	16:15
23	ware bezahlt nie erhalten!!	8356842135	08-Feb-06	10:43
24	Am 12.12.2005 die Ware zwar bezahlt aber bis heute 02.01.2006 nicht erhalten!	8361430838	02-Jan-06	14:06
25	bezahlt - keine ware erhalten!	4345007425	07-Jan-05	23:16
26	Überweisung nachgewiesen > trotzdem keine Ware erhalten	Privat	16-Aug-05	17:49
27	ganz klar: kassiert im voraus und liefert nicht.	4959231955	15-Mär-05	20:16
28	lieferte nie das gekaufte und bezahlte Artikel,kriegt bald ein Az beim Gericht	5782288609	25-Jul-05	15:08
29	habe leider mein spiel NICHT erhalten	8236276346	01-Feb-06	19:17
30	ware nicht erhalten!!	6405356683	05-Sep-05	17:06
31	Abzocke!!!!Hat Geld,aber ich keine Ware!!!Kauft nichts von diesem Banditen!	4073849907	03-Mär-05	16:47
32	gelt kassirt keine wahre erhalten ! betrüger!"!!!!!!!!!!!!!!!!!!	7995781991	22-Nov-05	20:04
33	Sorry ! Habe nie die Ware erhalten,17€ für nichts !!!!!!!!!!!!!!!!!!!!!!!!!!!!!!	5237440886	01-Oct-05	11:39
34	Ware nicht erhalten	8346018293	22-Nov-05	10:13
35	Achtung Betrüger-Ware bezahlt und nie erhalten-Strafanzeige wegen Betrug läuft	7983580489	08-Aug-05	19:02
36	Nach 3 Wochen immer noch nicht da!!! Echt peinliche Aktion!	5172719710	03-Apr-05	10:57
37	knapp 4 Wochen her, nichts erhalten, nie wieder! Ding ist noch nicht durch.....	6473159545	07-Feb-06	22:47
38	Ware ist bis heute nicht ankekommen Note sechs	4584407614	24-Nov-05	22:02
39	Habe bislang keine Ware erhalten! Ist doch absurd.Kannste inne Pfeife rauchen!!	5207297026	10-Jul-05	13:04
40	hab jetzt 2 Monate gewartet und keine Ware bekommen, schönen Dank	6401434506	15-Aug-05	12:20
41	Nimmt Geld, liefert aber nicht	5762986338	13-Apr-05	16:42
42	Ware per PayPal am 22.02.2005 bezahlt, Ware bis heute nicht erhalten!!!	6155436173	24-Apr-05	11:14
43	WARE HABE ICH BEZAHLT !!! LEIDER NACH 2 MON.IMMER NOCH NICHTS BEKOMMEN!!SCHLECHT	Privat	26-Jul-05	16:23
44	Ware nicht erhalten, Geldbetrag ist abgebucht!	6824231305	25-Dez-05	19:11
45	VORSICHT!!!Ware bezahlt jedoch nicht erhalten.Werde Rechtsanwalt einschalten	4428504174	14-Feb-06	12:17
46	Leider keine CD erhalten	4713682088	18-Mai-05	18:44
47	Artikel wurde bezahlt,nie geliefert,30,89€in den Sand gesetzt.Danke nie wieder	8102857945	31-Aug-04	22:11
48	ganz schlechter Partner,nach 5 Wo. immer noch keine Ware,trotz Zahlung nie mehr	7301405913	30-Mär-05	21:27

49	Geld überwiesen, KEINE WARE ERHALTEN!!! Finger weg! BETRÜGER!!!!	7521922443	08-Jul-05	18:18
50	habe ware lägst bezahlt, verkäufer war im urlaub ich habe keine ware erhalten!!!	7713838498	31-Okt-05	09:10
51	Nach 4 Wochen noch keine Lieferung der sofort bezahlten Ware.	7553132005	15-Nov-05	17:31
52	Gezahlt, Ware aber nicht erhalten. Warum auch immer........	3876163060	20-Mai-05	11:56
53	vorsicht !!!!!!!!! nimmt geld u. liefert nicht	7968341905	09-Mai-05	19:37
54	Ware nie gesendet. nicht empfehlenswert	7343053233	10-Sep-05	13:30
55	Nichts erhalten.	3879702204	22-Mai-05	06:55
56	Geld bereits vor 2 Wochen überwiesen - Buch immer noch nicht da! MIES!	8372559131	08-Feb-06	16:11
57	Ware bez.und Nicht Erhalten!	4950168161	09-Feb-05	22:52
58	Die Ware war trotz Bezahlung gar nicht vorhanden. Nie wieder!!!!!!!!!	8195264420	07-Jun-05	15:05
59	leider keine Ware angekommen	6796202313	15-Sep-05	18:40
60	!!!GELD ÜBERWIESEN, WARE NIE ERHALTEN!!!	8714529529	24-Jan-06	14:08
61	Ware bezahlt, aber nie erhalten. Nie wieder!	3984606509	08-Sep-05	13:39
62	Bezahlt, bis 11.06.05 nichts erhalten; Betrüger!! Anzeige wg. Betrug folgt!!	6750632814	12-Jun-05	06:11
63	artikel bezahlt..kommt nicht an..VORSICHT	Privat	10-Okt-05	13:42
64	Bezahlt. Keine Ware erhalten.H. Jack sagt: "Einfach Pech gehabt..." NIE WIEDER!	7376274323	01-Feb-06	20:17
65	die Bezahlung ist bereits am 7.03.2005 erfolgt; Artikel noch nicht erhalten!!!!	8166751875	10-Mär-05	14:25
66	Geld wurde gezahlt, aber keine Lieferung erhalten- Finger weg!!!	3842017586	20-Okt-04	14:13
67	Sofort bezahlt/Keine Ware trotz 2x Ankündigung/ebay informiert/Anwalt beauftragt	6412624587	29-Jul-05	18:51
68	Geld genommen und nicht geliefert. Wie bei vielen Anderen auch. Betrug	7309781415	05-Mai-05	19:46
69	Ware noch nicht erhalten Bin total sauer da das Geld gleich überwiesen wurde	5640863125	20-Dez-05	12:09
70	Ware nicht erhalten - schlamperei	6439909980	13-Nov-05	13:45
71	Tut mir leid ... aber ich habe die Ware nie bekommen !!	6394115967	26-Jul-05	21:20
72	Geld bezahlt,02,01,06 Ware noch nicht da,05,02,06,Geld zurüch???	7577387718	04-Feb-06	12:06
73	Artikel konnte nicht geliefert werden, da angeblich in den Müll geschmissen!!!	5725918017	26-Dez-04	13:48
74	schon lange bezahlt jedoch keine Ware erhalten	5770225759	29-Mai-05	13:46
75	ACHTUNG!!!!!scheiß laden keine ware bekommen! negativ schlechter ebayer achtung!	7932404082	24-Jan-05	18:34
76	Auch nach 8 Wochen keine Ware . Schade !!!	6765483945	07-Jul-05	17:36

77	VORSICHT BETRÜGER !!! BEZAHLTE WARE WIRD NICHT GELIEFERT!!!	7715791482	03-Dez-05	17:49
78	Trotz Zahlung (Barzahlung i.H. von € 5,50) wurde der Artikel nicht geliefert !!	7509883292	15-Mai-05	13:44
79	ware wurde bezahlt und bis heute nicht geschickt	5016577686	17-Sep-05	22:57
80	das buch wurde bezahlt ist aber nie angekommen	4516788367	11-Jul-05	14:16
81	Nach 3 Monaten noch keinen Ware erhalten werde die Sache meinm Anwalt übergeben	5426572784	14-Dez-05	14:41
82	ACHTUNG!!! Ware bezahlt bis heute nicht erhalten !!!!	4335657057	20-Dez-05	23:36
83	Alles Lüge, geld kassiert und Ware nicht schicken, Mein Anwalt freut sich!!!!!!!	7110773153	17-Nov-05	10:46
84	habe das geld am 4.3.2005 an ihn überwiesen und die ware kam bis heute nicht.	6372112942	03-Apr-05	19:31
85	Betrüger, keine Lieferung nach Zahlung am 14.03., Anzeige erstattet	7955301638	13-Mai-05	19:50
86	ware nie angekommen. hände weg von diesem verkäufer!	6940072771	25-Mär-05	13:03
87	Am 26.9 ersteigert am 29.9 überwiesen..bis heute noch keine ware bekommen.	8002159703	07-Okt-05	12:25
88	Ware leider nie angekommen!	7946758698	10-Mär-05	14:40
89	Artikel nicht erhalten, wurde angeblich nicht von der Post abgeholt,Finger weg!!	7356606333	20-Dez-05	20:12
90	Habe meine Ware bis heute nicht bekommen	7135785261	15-Mär-05	07:52
91	ACHTUNG!!!!!! AUFPASSEN MEINE WARE DIE ICH GEKAUFT HABE IST NICHT ANGEKOMMEN!!!!	6473754345	06-Feb-06	19:14
92	artikel bezahlt aber kein ware bekommen!!	7191553980	24-Nov-05	13:38
93	ware bezahlt ,bis heute noch keine ware erhalten	6383202952	24-Apr-05	19:11
94	ware nie bekommen,total mieser betrüger	6419858508	02-Okt-05	22:46
95	Die bezahlte Ware ist bei mir nie angekommen.	3819463507	21-Okt-04	20:41
96	Bis heute noch nichts bei mir angekommen	5228715317	21-Sep-05	18:02
97	HABE SEIT 30. MAI GELD BEZAHLT UND BEKOMM KEINE WARE. BEWEIS: KOPIE GEMACHT	7516782626	12-Jul-05	17:43
98	Vorsicht Falle !!!! Ware angeblich abgeschickt - nie erhalten !!!	3746287236	08-Okt-05	09:57
99	ware bis jetzt noch nicht eingetroffen	8010788469	18-Nov-05	00:01
100	ich warte seit 10 Tagen auf mein Rad	8701091153	18-Okt-05	14:10

German complaints – data set: Item DIFF

No.	Complaint	Item	Date	Time
1	nicht wie in beschreibung, gekürzten Dämfer gelifert	7973601357	23-Mai-05	12:01

2	Gegenstand und Hülle waren sehr beschädigt. Kein guter Service!	8704381648	31-Okt-05	21:11
3	ware funktioniert nicht !!!	4752328458	21-Aug-05	15:01
4	Richtige hülle aber ein falsche kasette nie wieder	4752463986	06-Aug-05	11:19
5	Das angebliche "Sahnestück" hat 2 Tintenflecken und 2 Risse.	6783111385	22-Jul-05	18:16
6	leider nicht die bestellte Ware geliefert	8723503260	08-Jan-06	21:29
7	Das Zippo was ich erworben habe war teilweise ein imitat und in schlechtem zusta	6219509811	16-Nov-05	06:51
8	Für Induktion ungeeignet. Einfach nur dünnes Blech.	4422871889	27-Dez-05	21:21
9	voll der witz chip passt zwar aber auto springt nicht mal an damit.	7949208630	09.02.2005	16:04
10	Die Sachen sind BEIDE total verwaschen und m. E. nur noch was für die Tonne!	6752976026	18-Mai-05	22:41
11	schuhe i.d. falschen größe bekommen,	6785614777	28-Jul-05	12:45
12	Sritzlappen auf dem Bild sind ein Paar und solten so auch abgegeben werden	4540570733	27-Apr-05	11:17
13	kleid hut gürtel verdreckt überall flecken und riecht übel schade	8171201844	08-Mär-05	11:23
14	Das Telfon Ist nicht ISDN fähig. Man sollte es auch nicht als dieses Verkaufen!!	6463549589	29-Dez-05	12:47
15	platte entsprach vom zustand nicht den angaben(vg++!); max g!	4797409943	01-Dez-05	16:58
16	Schuhe färben ab	8179708668	30-Mai-05	16:55
17	riechen nach schimmel	8335873518	16-Okt-05	17:44
18	Evo-X-Pro defekt	7189597127	06-Nov-05	21:24
19	Die Software lief nicht, wie behauptet, unter XP!	7194273879	23-Jan-06	12:32
20	Vorsicht Betrug, auf Bild war mehr abgebildet als ich erhalten habe. wurde betro	6031887003	11-Feb-06	14:09
21	Schickt nicht bestellte Ware, grau ist nun nicht mal oliv !!!!!!	6776271402	12-Jul-05	19:40
22	ACHTUNG! KLEINE PRÖBCHEN!!! KEINE ORIGINALGRÖSSEN WIE AUF BILDERN	7175255152	15-Sep-05	12:15
23	Bezahlung und Belieferung OK, allerdings Ware defekt!	5753511729	24-Mär-05	09:12
24	1700mAh .gekauft aber nur1500mAh bekommen. Achtung nicht emphehlenswert !!!	6475524736	22-Feb-06	00:10
25	Ware 2. Klasse-Beschädigungen, i.d. Artikelbeschreibung aber kein Wort erwähnt	7524548570	05-Jul-05	08:48
26	Hallo, ich bin sehr enttäuscht über das Paket nur Ramsch	5406734447	20-Jul-05	15:03
27	Dass sind einfach nur Betrüger die verkaufen falsche Ware Vorsicht nichts Kaufen	5211899706	17-Jul-05	18:40
28	ich war nicht zufriden da die cd hüllen teilweiß beschätig waren	8753147135	21-Feb-06	16:19

29	ware stinkt, so wie lange in sehr feutchte keller gelagert war...	6824609425	04-Dez-05	20:20
30	einfach nicht wundern, bei halbem Preis=halbe Beutelgröße	7508384600	11-Jul-05	23:20
31	verkauft billig Version (Best of, PAL,..) als Deluxe!! BETRÜGER	8764717862	04-Mär-05	14:48
32	Buchzustand schlechter als in Beschreibung, Buchrücken fast abgelöst, fleckig	8372281476	31-Jan-06	16:49
33	Foto und Beschreibung/Inhaltsangabe stimmen nicht mit der Ware überein	6327212914	27-Okt-04	15:39
34	Betrug durch falsche Angabe des Produktes, nie wieder mit so einem Ebayer	7967307338	05-Jun-05	17:21
35	Verkauft eine Gratisbroschüre des Verkehrsverbands als "Toller Reiseführer"	7003539487	14-Feb-06	12:34
36	Artikel in schlechtem Zustand, Artikelbeschreibung "fabrikneu" war gelogen.	6518404922	30-Apr-05	11:10
37	Als neuwertig angegeben, Sohlen gebrochen und Hacken abgelaufen! Nicht gut!	8147982576	21-Dez-04	14:47
38	ware sehr schnell angekommen, leider gefälscht, vorsicht!!!!!!!!!!	7701528990	22-Jul-05	15:27
39	Ware nicht richtig kabel fur SE V600 bestellt, fur k750 gekommen VORSICHT !!!!!!	6478539214	07-Feb-05	21:43
40	100% kein Original, Ärmel viel zu kurz, Kindergröße???	3961808771	13-Mär-05	12:19
41	Wurden als sehr gut beschrieben, doch teilseise sehr schlechter Zustand. Schade!	4047067860	07-Dez-04	12:34
42	Schnelle Lieferung , aber sehr enttäuschende Wahre	4327547439	17-Okt-04	19:36
43	"Zustandsbeschreibung "gut" = nicht zutreffend - enttäuschend - schade !	4586491734	29-Nov-05	20:07
44	Material nicht gut	Privat	23-Feb-05	14:27
45	kein echtes gold ist nur müll nicht empfelenswert	Privat	20-Feb-06	23:12
46	Minderwertige Ware!	7132922482	24-Mär-05	20:06
47	sah nicht so aus wie auf der Abbildung	9108047277	02-Mär-06	16:08
48	schmutziger, unvollstÃ¤ndiger, stark gebrauchter MIST... danke nie wieder	6020861524	01-Jan-06	11:04
49	Kleidung von QS(by S.Oliver)als Original Markenprodukt von Quicksilver verkauft	6829727627	27-Dez-05	21:59
50	lieferung pünktlich - schuhe miese qualität, 2 h getragen, erste Schäden!!!	3970425437	13-Jun-05	22:02
51	Lieferung unvollständig - nicht zu empfehlen!	7706062211	23-Okt-05	23:16
52	Die Vorstellungen waren andere.	7717552629	07-Jan-06	09:48
53	Produkt war Fälschung billigster Bauart, Betrug, eine Frechheit, solche Leute!!	Privat	30-Aug-05	19:09
54	ganz schlechte ware, bin entäuscht, nicht mal angehabt schon kaputt,schade!!!!!!	8343045525	12-Nov-05	19:40

55	Muffig, bröselig und total verbrannt. Schmeckt absolut gruslig. Kein Kaffee!	7209240014	28-Jan-06	15:01
56	"Gebraucht "war noch geschönt. Buch ist total verranzt,,Seiten fallen raus,Müll!	5229146187	01-Sep-05	12:14
57	Abwicklung OK, Ware mangelhaft.	5796112668	28-Aug-05	17:00
58	verkratztes, passungenaues nokia cover, sieht nach b-ware aus!!! :-(	6346590288	16-Dez-04	13:19
59	Artikel entspricht nicht der Abbildung!	5840164235	28-Feb-06	14:02
60	Diese CD ist Betrug, nur Industrieaufnahmen	6535456973	28-Jun-05	09:43
61	schnelle lieferung aber schlechte verarbeitung,schon nach 1 woche kaputt	5131603966	15-Nov-04	18:13
62	ware hat flecken	4334583818	14-Nov-04	15:14
63	läßt sich nicht fixieren, fabrikneuer Schrot - leider	4398687428	28-Aug-05	22:21
64	schade, ware ist vollkommen kaputt, nur noch zum wegschmeissen...bin sehr entäu	4389147622	23-Jun-05	23:21
65	Ware wurde mit Feuchitgkeit und Schimmelflecken geliefert	7359808035	13-Nov-05	19:52
66	Schuhe waren nicht so gut, vorne direkt eingerissen	6757288839	23-Mai-05	22:39
67	entäuschent	4986279444	25-Apr-05	17:50
68	Ware als XXL(xl ausgewiesen) verkauft, ist aber reell nur Größe M! Ärgerlich	7738524840	10-Feb-06	23:53
69	Verkauft Kopien als Originale Billiger Fotoscan!!! Sehr schlechter Zustand	6207511142	17-Sep-05	11:31
70	Gehäuseklappe defekt (pin war abgerissen) und das bei dem Preis lächerlich!!!!	6790446994	18-Aug-05	15:44
71	das feuerzeug ist kein zippo es stand in der falschen rubrik	6123934098	26-Okt-04	10:12
72	Vorsicht!Unwahre Angaben.Mußte Rechtsanwalt einschalten.	Privat	16-Mai-05	15:05
73	Ware in einem Schlechten Zustand. Rueckabwicklung.	4427250679	31-Jan-06	08:25
74	Ventilator lässt sich nicht an der Decke befestigen,da die Bohrungen falsch sind	7538402576	18-Okt-05	15:16
75	gelogen...das md ist nicht voll funktionstüchtig......ärgerlich bin reingefallen	3840096208	15-Okt-04	10:29
76	Glatter BETRUG! Statt LED-Lichterkette wurde eine mit Glücklampen geschickt.	4430977253	18-Feb-06	08:30
77	material läst sehr zu wünschen übrig farbe nicht so wie angegeben alles schund	Privat	09-Mär-05	21:50
78	Luxus Taschenuhr ! ? Mehr als Schrott ! Einmal und nie wieder !!!!!!!!!!!!!!!!!!	Privat	05-Okt-05	19:55
79	Von 50 Chlortabs waren mehr als die Hälfte zerbrochen. Wollte kein Granulat	4373687685	02-Mai-05	10:17
80	Es wurde nicht die Originalware die bei Ebay angeboten wurde geliefert !!	8005035084	13-Nov-05	08:44

81	viel Geld für nichts - der reinste Müll - nie wieder !!!!	5956113055	24-Feb-05	08:31
82	SCHNELLE LIEFERUNG ABER PASST NICHT	8006073259	20-Oct-05	16:14
83	VORSICHT ! Verkauft defekten Schrott mit Beschreibung " Topzustand " ! Forget it	4527297609	21-Apr-05	14:37
84	Schuhe viel zu klein!!!	8180878706	25-Mai-05	22:29
85	Markenblock mit rücksetigen Beschädigungen, Wasserflecken und Zackenfehlern	5607345774	08-Sep-05	22:59
86	Nur Abfall und Schrott - Frechheit - fehlten nur noch Reste vom Boden	5628224093	09-Nov-05	15:36
87	Vorsicht: Verkauft Software ohne darauf hinzuweisen, dass es Testversion ist!	4503919108	28-Nov-04	20:32
88	foto besser als die realität, beide letzten seiten große einrisse, schade!	6536147595	19-Jun-05	20:59
89	schulranzen nicht brauchbar, ungeeignet für kinder	7533735962	10-Aug-05	09:04
90	Sehr schlechte Qualität der Pflanzen, erwäge Anzeige wegen Betruges.	Privat	21-Apr-05	19:07
91	Hatte bessere Qualität erwartet. Artikel ist nicht Schadstoffgeprüft !!!!	Privat	02-Nov-05	09:37
92	Was soll diese Schönfärberei ?Artikel in"gutem Zustand"war mehrfach beschädigt.	7955102495	20-Mär-05	00:26
93	ein body war mit vekalien beschmutzt-kann ich leider wegwerfen!!!!!	7305531879	18-Mär-05	10:04
94	die uhr ist uhralt und kaputt!	Privat	19-Apr-05	21:11
95	USB-Kabel zwar günstig,jedoch nicht passend zu angegebenem Handy.	6386710725	04-Jul-05	17:35
96	anstatt abgebildete Original-DVD nur Promo-DVD mit 3 Titeln!!	7315784469	09-Mai-05	21:44
97	Kein Funkscanner, ein moderneres Radio mehr nicht, leider falsche angaben!!!!!!!	5768369386	28-Apr-05	13:48
98	Laut Bezeichnung soll die Ware neu sein, war sie aber nicht.	4567462830	30-Aug-05	20:47
99	Nicht wie auf Foto angegeben geliefert; m.E. keine gute Verpackung für "Neuware"	4347325614	12-Jan-05	21:06
100	ES WAR KEIN ZIPPO!!! NUR EIN NORMALES BENZINFEUERZEUG	6191305742	26-Jul-05	01:18

German complaints – data set: Item NR-D

No.	Complaint	Item	Date	Time
1	Keine Ware kein Geld zurück ANZEIGE WEGEN UNTERSCHLAGUNG FOLGT	7596382235	28-Apr-05	22:21
2	Geld kassiert, keine Ware erhalten; Verkäufer reagiert nicht auf E-mails	6605165180	29-Mär-06	21:19
3	NIcht geliefert, reagiert nicht mehr auf e-mails.	7605378068	12-Mai-05	15:18

4	Achtung!!!! Geld gern genommen, Ware nie angekommen. Keine Antwort auf Mails.	6459220395	09-Jan-05	16:13
5	habe bezahlt den Artikel nie erhalten und auf Mails wurde nicht reagiert!!!	7730506258	02-Jan-06	12:13
6	Ware bezahlt und nie erhalten!!!Nach 4 Wochen noch kein Geld zurück!Finger weg!!	6748284172	07-Apr-05	20:59
7	Geld sofort überw.keine Ware erhalten,Keine Rücküberweisung,Anwalt eingeschaltet	5214632709	09-Jan-05	10:07
8	artikel nie erhalten und geld erst nach mehreren wochen zurück gekriegt	5229215087	28-Okt-05	12:00
9	2 Monate!! Immer noch keine Ware erhalten VORSICHT! Keine Antwort auf Mails.	6478271939	15-Mär-06	07:17
10	Artikel NIE angekommen, ausserdem unfreundlicher Verkäufer :-(	8016480627	15-Mai-06	21:11
11	Schickt ware nicht und antwortet auf keine mail. nicht empfehlenswert	6756547306	10-Mai-05	11:03
12	Ware nie erhalten, hat sich nie gemeldet	6396982018	06-Aug-05	11:48
13	keine Lieferung / kein kontakt möglich, antwortet nicht	6022996149	21-Jan-06	13:05
14	Geld bezahlt, Dvd nie erhalten, antwortet nicht auf emails	9105058508	21-Mär-06	15:08
15	Ware kam nie an! Ich habe 4 mal gemahnt. Keine Reaktion.	6969494819	02-Nov-05	11:44
16	Ware bezalt und nicht erhalten, Geld wurde trotz Reklamation nicht erstattet!!!!	6964482501	18-Jul-05	11:08
17	Achtung !!!!!!!!! Bezahlt aber keine Ware! Kein E-mail Kontakt. Keine Reaktion !	Privat	20-Mai-06	11:24
18	Warnung Verkäufer liefert die wahre nicht! und auch kein Geld zurück.Nach 5 Woch	7513366930	20-Jun-05	22:08
19	Artikel nicht erhalten-eingezahltes Geld auch nicht. Anzeige wegen Betrug 6.2.06	5832156512	07-Feb-06	22:05
20	Keine Ware, Keine Antwort auf Mails. Betrug !!!	9128679286	14-Mai-06	19:33
21	Am 10.04. bezahlt - keine Ware - keine Erstattung des Kaufpreises !!!	6862229637	10-Mai-06	13:59
22	Keine Ware erhalten...Schade. per Telefon nicht erreichbar.	6786166872	08-Aug-05	14:45
23	Ware bezahlt und nix bekommen, Kontaktaufnahme unmöglich! Das letzte!!	8166172031	25-Feb-05	15:53
24	Nie die Ware erhalten, auch nach mehrfacher Aufforderungen keine Stellungnahme	7514353291	25-Jan-06	14:18
25	ACHTUNG HATT AUCH MICH BETROGEN KEINE WARE KEINE ANTWORTEN AUF MAILS	6439529783	20-Dez-05	10:50
26	Vorsicht!!Verdacht auf Betrug!! 2Wo. nach Onlineüberw.: Keine Lieferung o. Antwo	4559413886	25-Jul-05	08:41
27	Ware nicht bekommen, nicht mal Geld retour	7546134617	29-Dez-05	18:32

28	habe bis heute keine ware erhalten vorsicht schlechte komunikation	6850483656	22-Mai-06	21:47
29	Geld weg, keine Ware. Nach mehrfacher Auffoderung keine Reaktion Achtung Betrug!	8010012880	25-Jan-06	17:36
30	gezahlt, keine Ware erhalten, auf Emails keine Antwort. Betrug vermutet	6034373370	04-Mär-05	22:48
31	Habe den Deckel bis heute noch nicht erhalten und auch nichts vomVk gehöhrt	4562943654	01-Okt-05	15:24
32	Warte jetzt einen Monat vergeblich auf Lieferung. Keine Reaktion auf E-Mails!!	6575018532	18-Dez-05	07:57
33	ACHTUNG BTRÜGER! GELD ÜBERWIESEN WARE TROTZ VERSICHERUNG NICHT ERHALTEN! KEINE R	7593806444	20-Mai-06	16:38
34	Artikel bezahlt aber nicht erhalten, antwortet nicht auf mail	6412642306	26-Jul-05	22:30
35	Verschlist Die Wahre nicht, und reagirt nicht oder kaum auf eMails!!!	7605542585	23-Mai-06	18:51
36	bezahlt, jedoch die hose nie bekommen und auch keine antwort auf emails	6797120933	24-Okt-05	09:46
37	Ware nie bekommen, obwohl sofort bezaht, Rückbuchung erst 8 Wochen später.	4426118331	15-Feb-06	17:02
38	keine ware bekommen, läßt nicht mit sich reden!!!	6407378458	07-Aug-05	19:01
39	warte seid knapp einem monat auf meine ware und antwortet nicht	9111450949	02-Apr-06	14:00
40	Ware leider nie erhalten! Geld nicht zurück bekommen!Nie Wieder!!!!!!!!!!!!!!!!	8731171124	03-Mär-06	06:41
41	Geld am 31.05. überwiesen; keine Ware erhalten; Kontakt abgebrochen;VORSICHT!!!	7159054777	24-Jul-05	21:34
42	Nicht empfehlenswert!!! Warte seit 20.04. auf meine Ware bzw. Rückerstattung!!!	Privat	13-Mai-06	07:50
43	keine Lieferung von DHL erhalten, kein Support trotz versichertem Versand.Beware	Privat	11-Feb-05	14:10
44	seit 6 wochen keine lieferung trotz sofort bez., keine antwort auf mails achtung	4385593773	06-Jul-05	07:13
45	keine Ware erhalten, reagiert nicht auf eMails,schade	9102829820	28-Apr-06	20:09
46	ware nicht geliefert,reagiert teilweise nicht auf email,käufer soll sich kümmern	6219754457	08-Dez-05	13:02
47	Ware in 3 T. bezahlt, Ware noch nicht erhalten, Verkäufer weiß von nix mehr	7153206485	26-Mai-05	11:36
48	Ware sofort bezahlt, jedoch nicht erhalten, auf Nachfrage keine Antwort!	6392270217	03-Jul-05	19:44
49	VORSICHT!! Verkäufer antwortet nicht. Geld bezahlt. Keine Ware. -> Staatsanwalt!	8051330739	27-Apr-06	13:14
50	sorry,habe bezahlt u.nichts erhalten,bat um Nachforschung,keine Rückmeldung mehr	6997429163	18-Mär-06	21:26

51	Bezahlte Wahre nie angekommen, Nachfrage nicht erhört, blooooß nicht!!!!!	8741662180	26-Jan-06	22:12
52	Keine Ware erhalten! Und es wird nicht auf meine EMails reagiert! Finger weg!!!!	8747673647	05-Feb-06	21:25
53	Nicht geliefert, Antwortet auf Fragen nicht, Sehr negativer Eindruck	6795208687	08-Okt-05	15:15
54	Keine Ware erhalten, kein Kontakt möglich, bin super sauer!	8396631273	08-Mai-06	12:28
55	Ware nie erhalten,antwortet auf E-mails nicht,wo ist die entschuldigung?ABZOCKE!	9131105334	01-Jun-06	20:57
56	Geld Überwiesen nur keine Ware erhalten Trotz Mail Keine Antwort >Anzeige <	4387962577	19-Jul-05	16:08
57	Keine Ware erhalten, auf Anfragen keine Antwort !!!	8922679950	11-Mai-06	09:17
58	Ich habe meineWare nie erhalten. Der Ebayer topwertig nannte mir keine versandnr	7537105025	29-Sep-05	19:21
59	!!!!!!!!!!!!!!!!!!!!!!!!!KEINE WARE UND KEIN GELD ZURÜCK !!!!!!!!!!!!!!!!!!!!!!	7350494405	23-Nov-05	12:46
60	Leider nicht versendet und nach mehrere Aufrufe keine Reaktion	9111887908	25-Mai-06	17:30
61	Keine Ware erhalten, nicht auf Mails reagiert! Geld weg.	3970313907	31-Mai-05	07:45
62	VOR EINEM MONAT BEZAHLT, KEINE WARE UND KEIN GELD ZURÜCK. FINGER WEG....	9127451459	13-Mai-06	20:46
63	nix gekommen,keine reaktion von verkäufer!!!!	9129002740	14-Mai-06	12:39
64	!!!Versteigert Ware und liefert dann nicht!!!Antwortet nicht auf Mails!!!	5813813242	24-Okt-05	17:06
65	keine ware keine antwort auf mails.werde Rechtsanwalt einschalten	6875734728	19-Mai-06	11:10
66	Ware nicht geliefert! Reagierte erst auf dringende Aufforderung.	7501014301	18-Apr-05	21:36
67	Achtung! Keine Ware und kein Geld zurück, Vorsicht ist geboten !!!!!!	5626534703	02-Dez-05	17:47
68	Liefert nicht.Kein Kontakt. Unverschämt!Nicht zu empfehlen!!!!	6870894983	16-Mai-06	21:10
69	Ware nicht erhalten. Keine Rückerstattung des Kaufpreises.	9117393459	24-Apr-06	14:32
70	NIE WIEDER---GELD FUTSCH-KEINE WARE ANGEKOMMEN-IGNORIERT EINFACH---NIE WIEDER	5653346652	01-Mär-06	10:09
71	Ware 14 Tage überfällig,Verkäufer reagiert nicht auf Mitteilng.Vorsicht	5721410613	26-Okt-05	12:12
72	Hände weg, keine Ware, kein Kontakt möglich!!	4385622978	10-Jul-05	12:00
73	Ware nie erhalten & keine Reaktion auf meine Nachfrage	8209865079	03-Sep-05	20:53

74	reagiert nicht auf mail , keine ware , schlechter gehts wohl nicht , abzocke !!!	7237985992	29-Mai-06	19:11
75	KEINE WARE UND KEIN GELD ZURÜCK SEHR SCHADE BEI DIESEM BETRAG !!!!!!!	5410478713	19-Sep-05	10:14
76	Habe lange bezahlt, Ware kommt nicht, bekomme keine Information	7165635053	15-Jul-05	09:35
77	Keine Ware da - keine Reaktion ! Bei dem Betrag - mehr Zuverlässigkeit bitte !	7378352481	25-Jan-06	11:21
78	Artikel kam nie an, keine reaktion auf nochmalige Nachfrage, echt fies sowas!!	5216238336	30-Aug-05	13:00
79	BETRÜGER!!!!!!!!!! WEDER WARE NOCH GELD!!!!!!!!!!!! HABE ANZEIGE ERSTATTET!!!!!!	4612506976	09-Mär-06	11:03
80	Artkel nicht erhalten und ungehobelte Antwort auf den Verbleib !!!!	6991293540	24-Jan-06	20:09
81	Ware nie erhalten, hinterher keine Kooperation, nie wieder!!! SAUEREI !!!	5207311702	10-Sep-05	18:11
82	Gekauft 06.11.+bezahlt 07.11.-trotz Anfrage keine Ware +auch keine Antwort mehr	5826432035	08-Dez-05	19:11
83	Vorsicht. Geld kassiert und keine Ware geschickt. Antwortet nicht auf E-Mail.	7752335671	11-Apr-06	20:25
84	Wahre bezahlt, bis heute keine Nachricht oder Lieferung!! Sehr serh schlecht, fi	8378696012	01-Mär-06	20:25
85	Habe 5 mal geschrieben und nie Antwort erhalten, Ware NIE angekommen	7761956274	11-Mai-06	13:18
86	bezahlt, aber keine ware, wochenlang keine reaktion! Nie wieder!	7714151169	10-Nov-05	15:26
87	Ware nie erhalten! Trotz email keine Antwort!!!!! Vorsicht!!!!!!!!!!!!!!!!!!!!!	8732688459	13-Feb-06	11:33
88	Hab die Ware nach 1 Monat immer noch nicht. Antw. nicht auf E-mail! Nie wieder!	8712836791	01-Dez-05	17:11
89	Habe mehrfach versucht an zu rufen, ohne Erfolg. keine Ware bekommen.	Privat	20-Mär-06	09:20
90	ACHTUNG Gezahlt und kein Artikel, jeder Kontakt unbeantwortet !!! ACHTUNG	8239761380	27-Dez-05	15:19
91	Ware nie erhalten, Verkäufer meldet sich nicht mehr!!!	5651866167	04-Apr-06	20:03
92	WARNUNG! Habe nie Ware erhalten-Geld ist weg.Keine Antwort auf emails. WARNUNG!	4556790302	01-Nov-05	12:04
93	keine Reaktion, von der Ware fehlt jede Spur und der Händler reagiert nicht	6466838030	14-Jan-06	13:07
94	Artikel wurde nicht geliefert, versprochene Gutschrift nicht erhalten.	8323883391	17-Nov-05	08:18
95	Bezahlte Ware nicht erhalten trotz mehrfacher Anfrage keine Antwort	6962359176	24-Jun-05	14:27

96	!!! NACH 1 MONAT NOCH KEINE WARE & ANTWORT ERHALTEN, ANZEIGE FOLGT HEUTE NOCH!!!	7960520608	22-Aug-05	19:49
97	Liefert nicht u. antwortet nicht mehr. Zahlung bereits vor 3 1/2 Wochen erfolgt!	7510704306	01-Jun-05	22:29
98	Am 18.05. ersteigert-bis jetzt keine Ware und kein Geld zurück!Nie wieder!!!	5168272716	04-Aug-05	12:24
99	KOHLE KASSIEREN!NICHT MELDEN!KEINE WARE!MIESER LADEN!	4601150004	12-Jan-06	11:16
100	habe ware nicht erhalten und kein vermerk,warum nicht?schade!!!!!!!!!!!!!	5083796233	28-Feb-06	14:22

German complaints – data set: Item DIFF-D

No.	Complaint	Item	Date	Time
1	Ware wurde Defekt versendet & VersandKo. selber zahlen um Heile Ware zu bekomm!	6228972367	22-Dez-05	15:36
2	Falscher Artikel, Verkäufer meldet sich nicht, will keinen ersatzt leisten Note6	7379779000	26-Jan-06	15:16
3	Nicht beschriebenes HC sondern billiger Paperback. Keine Rückvergütung.	8380569887	23-Feb-06	12:39
4	Achtung Ebey'er! Defekte Ware erhalten. Reklamation schwierig bis zwecklos.	7760011075	11-Mai-06	10:23
5	Ware beschädigt bekommen, keine Antwort auf Reklamation. Nicht zu empfehlen	Privat	19-Okt-05	20:34
6	auf e-mail nicht reagiert, schuhe sind verschmutzt und haben löcher!	9315231307	21-Mai-06	23:00
7	Beschreibung "Top"?ha ha keine Reaktion auf Beschwerde!	6801536448	07-Dez-05	12:59
8	Ware entspricht nicht der Ankündigung - keine Antwort auf Anfrage	7609016966	21-Apr-05	17:51
9	Artikelbeschr. stimmte nicht; keine Rücknahme möglich	8358674182	10-Dez-05	09:11
10	ware falsch verpackt, beschädigt, ersatz versprochen, nicht geliefert	7385486654	19-Mär-06	23:00
11	4 Wochen Lieferzeit und dann noch falsches Kabel!!! Finger weg!!!	7569362008	02-Mai-05	16:05
12	Hat überhaubt nicht funkuniert wie beschrieben. Und Kahm keine Antwort	7231929853	12-Apr-05	19:04
13	Druckerpatrone nach 20 Seiten leer. Keine Antwort auf Emails	6833497467	10-Jan-06	21:45
14	falsche Ware geliefert- Keine Rückerstattung trotz Zusage- nie wieder!!!	6003072810	29-Nov-05	21:36
15	Ware war defekt, hat auf Reklamation nicht reagiert	Privat	11-Dez-05	20:57

16	Falsche Ware!!! Nachlieferung nach 2Wochen noch nicht angekommen	8056915242	01-Jun-06	20:11
17	keine antwort auf mail wahre minderwertig	7161437575	06-Jul-05	17:33
18	Ware war mies, hab zurückgeschickt und kein Porto ersetzt bekommen.	7584658281	23-Apr-05	14:13
19	Ware war unbrauchbarer Schrott, Geld trotz Zusage bis heute nicht zurück	8787823754	02-Mai-06	17:31
20	Völlig anderes Buch geliefert, auf E-Mails keine Reaktion	8304913046	07-Aug-05	09:27
21	ACHTUNG!!! Verschickt defekte Ware! Umtausch wegen Inkompetenz nicht möglich!	8706536289	26-Nov-05	14:19
22	!!! Plasma TV 22.5 ersteigert 23.5 bezahlt Ware DEFEKT bis jetzt kein Ersatz !!!	9729161633	06-Jun-05	20:52
23	falsche Ware, umtausch mit schwierigkeiten, VORSICHT nix gut	6802768900	23-Okt-05	17:21
24	Stuhl ist total zerbrochen angekommen und dazu hat er noch wochen gebraucht.	4384192694	30-Jul-05	10:00
25	Schrottware erhalten, Verkäufer reagiert nicht auf Versuche zur Klärung, mies!!!	7622984612	10-Jun-05	11:41
26	Achtung,Achtung verschickt CD die nicht gehen und antwortet nicht	7198590724	05-Dez-05	07:59
27	Betrug:Abartiger verbrannter Kaffee,Kerosingestank.VK reagiert nicht	Privat	08-Jan-05	16:25
28	Vorsicht! Teils supermiese Ausschuss-Ware. Verweigert Rücknahme und Rückzahlung.	7757362937	01-Mai-05	18:39
29	Karte ließ sich nicht freischalten, keine Antwort auf Reklamation	9123296824	24-Apr-06	21:33
30	ACHTUNG!!!Zubehör fehlt,keine Antwort,werde andere Schritte einleiten müssen!!!!	3748778918	04-Okt-04	13:11
31	Buch ist Mängelexemplar gebraucht,falsches Bild,Versandk.1,15 zu hoch,nie wieder	8749795278	26-Jan-05	18:20
32	falsche Ware geliefert, Rückzahlung dauerte 3 Wochen nach Rücksendung	6865850285	05-Mai-06	20:43
33	die sim karte geht nicht verküfer antwortet nicht schade	9108540710	20-Apr-05	22:53
34	Ware defekt. Keine Reaktion auf mehrere Reklamationen. Nie wieder.	Privat	16-Mär-06	07:17
35	Liefert falsche Ware, antwortet auf mails nicht! unseriös!	5245812925	16-Okt-05	20:28
36	betrug ! kein messing nur farbe ! verweigert geldrückgabe - ebay ist informiert	4365150298	29-Apr-05	09:35
37	DVD-Recorder defekt. Rücknahme strikt verweigert. Garantie nur für Erstbesitzer	5776069540	17-Jun-05	19:20
38	artikel war defekt, Kopfhörer fehlten, keine Anwort auf mein mail ! Vorsicht !!!	7592986361	24-Mär-05	10:24

39	sehr unfreundlicher kontakt über defektes buch-- nie wieder t-stalk	6565168845	22-Nov-05	20:30
40	Sehr schlechte Ware,nach Anfrage wegen Umtausch unverschämtes Angebot.Nie wieder	6771190682	21-Jun-05	17:59
41	Echt dreiste Abzocke*Bilder ausgeschnitten*Seiten fehlen-Unfreundlicher Kontakt	7000334282	26-Jan-06	09:34
42	Katastrophenpartner!! Schickt nicht wie ersteigert USB, keinerlei Reaktion !!!	5845894750	29-Jan-05	20:09
43	Extrem lange Lieferzeit - Patrone nach 10x Drucken verklebt! Finger weg!!!	6811732166	03-Dez-05	17:59
44	Vorsicht! Liefern falsche Ware und reagieren nicht auf Telefon und Email!	7367879797	07-Dez-05	18:41
45	ware im schlechtem zustand nicht wahrheitsgemäße angaben, kontakt mangelhaft	7540338109	05-Sep-05	18:41
46	Karte hat weniger MB Speicherplatz als angegeben, dreifache an Porto verlangt	7604938431	20-Mai-06	02:03
47	DVD leider fehlerhaft. Trotz 14 tägiger Rückgabemögl. keine Antwort. Schade!	6400562656	24-Jun-05	08:52
48	Ware teilweise defekt! Bei Nachfragen zum Umtausch keine Antwort!	7620746240	03-Jun-05	14:32
49	Artikel funktioniert nicht. Auf meine Fragen wird nicht eingegangen.	9126413572	16-Mai-05	14:45
50	ernie funkioniert nicht richtig,schade!!Auf mehre mails keine Antwort	6002319250	13-Okt-05	14:53
51	nie wieder: 2 ungekühlte Gammel-Enten erhalten. Pfui! Keine Reaktion auf Mail.	7215071276	18-Feb-05	10:06
52	Lange Lieferzeit,Falsche Ware,Nie wieder bei Euch	7388308682	15-Mär-05	16:03
53	Durchgebrochener Stein, defekte Schliffkanten, Kratzer! 0 Reaktion auf Rückfrage	6563970955	27-Dez-05	14:26
54	BETRÜGER Firma keine anwort auf email , WARE defekt und falsche farbe	6463446072	07-Feb-06	15:22
55	Ware war defekt ,warte seit 2 Monaten auf Rückerstattung, meldet sich nicht	9121356886	14-Jun-06	13:39
56	Ware in mühl Qualität aus China. Hier wird Porto als ware verkauft! Aufpassen	7614227075	26-Mai-06	14:01
57	MIESE QUALITÄT,SELBSTGEMACHTE BILLIG-FOLIEN,KEINE ANTWORT AUF UNZÄHLIGE MAILS!!!	7974182076	10-Aug-05	22:32
58	Lieferung erst nach Anmahnung! Einfachste Qualität absolut ohne Geschmack	7175612861	05-Sep-05	19:39
59	Anderer Monitor geliefert(FP71E+), keine Antwort auf E-Mails und Fax!	8728895337	17-Dez-05	22:48
60	Vorsicht! Meine richtige Ware nie erhalten! Auch nur schwer erreichbar! nie mehr	8383499420	15-Mär-05	10:43

61	habe ein defektes Mainboard zurückgeschickt und kein Geld zurückgekriegt	6772115968	18-Jul-05	12:19
62	Ware entsprach nicht Artikelbeschreibung; keine Antwort auf mehrere Nachfragen	7583487691	06-Mär-06	20:16
63	schrauben fehlten reagiert nicht auf nachfrage	7703545072	11-Sep-05	04:48
64	DVD NICHT wie beschrieben, Asien Import, Rückabwicklung erfolglos, NIE WIEDER	6395773546	05-Okt-05	21:13
65	Habe nur die Hülle erhalten. Er war nicht bereit, Ersatz zu leisten. nie wieder!	6393071125	20-Jun-05	15:57
66	Ware defekt! Abgesprochene Rücksendung verweigert! Kann nur abraten!!!!	4411954416	16-Nov-05	16:06
67	falsche Patronen bis heute kein Geld zurück Rechtsanwalt ist eingeschaltet frech	6811502283	03-Apr-06	18:32
68	VORSICHT!Bewußt falsche Angaben!Sehr schlecht verpackt!Dann kein Kontakt mehr!	Privat	01-Aug-05	11:11
69	Niemals kaufen!!Mangelhafte Ware, Ware zurückgeschickt, kein Geld zurückbekommen	7389786718	20-Mai-06	00:37
70	Spiel nicht funktionstüchtig! Ware zurückgesendet! Verkäufer reagiert nicht!!!!!	5981490748	17-Okt-05	22:03
71	KriechstromFische tot,lampe eingeschickt,weder Lampe noch Geld zurÃ1⁄4ck erhalten	7730877001	25-Jan-06	17:55
72	devekte ware erhalten! reklamiert und warte noch immer auf ersatz echt super!!!	5246255089	10-Nov-05	18:12
73	1 GB Stick hat nicht im Sony Ericsson P910i funktioniert; kein Umtausch möglich!	7591229050	28-Feb-06	21:24
74	keine übereinstimmende Artikelbeschreibung-Kontakt???ungeklärt-sehr enttäusht	6804420321	12-Okt-05	16:35
75	Nette emails aber leider ware nicht ok und geld hab ich nicht zurück bekommen	6561019347	17-Dez-05	14:11
76	Artikel keine "Rarität", sondern billiges Imitat. Verkäufer lehnt Rückgabe ab.	8014720835	29-Nov-05	12:23
77	Ware bei Lieferung kaputt. Auf Mail keine Reaktion. Keine Bestellung mehr.	7545388074	07-Nov-05	15:25
78	Neuteil bestellt, verkratztes u. gebrauchtes Teil bekommen! Verk. reagiert nich!	7228744865	26-Apr-05	00:14
79	Bettlaken zu klein, paßt nich / auf meine Mail hat keiner reagiert	4422308335	20-Dez-05	12:15
80	Hose Fäden gezogen nicht im Angebot angegeben trotz Mail kaum Reaktion Schade!	6801619508	10-Okt-05	10:37
81	andere Ware, als auf Foto bekommen; hohe Versandkosten	6803589075	15-Nov-05	19:38
82	UNSERIÖS! Verkauft Gebrauchtware als Neuware! Reagiert nicht! Ganz mies!!!	6835673466	01-Feb-06	11:50
83	Päckchen 4,50 EUR bezahlt, Brief 2,20 EUR erhalten, Ware nun z.T. verschmutzt !	6788233802	11-Aug-05	20:43

84	Falsche Größenangabe in der Auktion, weigert sich, mir den Schaden zu ersetzen	6801671331	06-Dez-05	14:56
85	DAS HANDY IST DEFEKT, KUNDE MELDET SICH NICHT! HIER NICHTS KAUFEN	6447856874	18-Nov-05	13:52
86	Nein danke! Erst paßt nix und dann ewig auf Antwort/ Rückzahlung warten;o(((	7933320329	17-Okt-05	16:52
87	Ware war gebraucht und unvollständig keine Reaktion auf E-Mail nie wieder	8756813441	01-Mai-06	10:48
88	Dünner Stoff reißt an den Nähten! Keine Antwort auf Reklamationsmail!	Privat	12-Aug-05	11:55
89	liefert falsche Ware und meldet sich nicht	8379497319	26-Feb-06	12:24
90	Ware funktioniert nicht! Verkäufer reagiert nicht auf E-mails !!!	7589004848	03-Apr-06	11:05
91	15 tage wartezeit, superlautes netzteil, selber zusammenbauen->NIE WIEDER!!!	8725324268	15-Dez-05	14:28
92	Die Ware ist in tausend Scherben hier eingetroffen, leider keine Geldrückgabe!	4435366253	03-Mai-06	11:34
93	Ware im schlechten Zustand . lange (6 Wo)gewartet.nichts funktioniert.schade!!	6194719029	16-Sep-05	00:01
94	Lieferung entsprach nicht der Erwartung, war nicht bereit nachzubessern	5576083945	06-Jul-05	17:35
95	Uhr kaputt, Verkäufer unkooperativ und frech, Finger weg!!!! Mies!!!	5018590122	05-Okt-05	10:41
96	Lange warte zeit und die ware ist auch nicht so besonders	7757700246	15-Mai-06	11:53
97	bietet eindeutig gebrauchte CD als neu an ; keine Reaktion auf Reklamation/EMail	4830546490	05-Apr-05	19:21
98	Das Nokia Cover ist billigware! Farbe geht ab! Reklamation bleibt unbeachtet!	6443585951	20-Dez-05	22:19
99	Kette Kaputt und sollte eine neue kriegen und warte schon 4 wochen	8723100866	21-Dez-05	17:37
100	unvollständige lieferung und sehr lange wartezeit nach rücksendung...........	8227294399	10-Dez-05	00:08

KULTUREN – KOMMUNIKATION – KONTAKTE

Bd. 1 Tobias Spelz: Kommunikation in den neuen Medien – Französische und brasilianische Webchats. 332 Seiten. ISBN 978-3-86596-261-4

Bd. 2 Michael Scholz-Hänsel: Inquisition und Kunst. *Convivencia* in Zeiten der Intoleranz. 340 Seiten. ISBN 978-3-86596-248-5

Bd. 3 Hartwig Kalverkämper: Lexikographie der Körperkommunikation. ca. 200 Seiten. ISBN 978-3-86596-265-2

Bd. 4 Claudia Bliesener: Wenn Worte zu gefährlich werden ... Zensur in der DDR – Zensur in Spanien unter Franco. Ein interkultureller Vergleich. 132 Seiten. ISBN 978-3-86596-320-8

Bd. 5 Stephan Theilig (Hg.): Historische Konzeptionen von Körperlichkeit. Interdisziplinäre Zugänge zu Transformationsprozessen in der Geschichte. 252 Seiten. ISBN 978-3-86596-333-8

Bd. 6 Susanne Beck: Körpersprache in italienischen Printmedien. 190 Seiten. ISBN 978-3-86596-258-4

Bd. 7 Jennifer Sandner: Medium und Gender. Geschlechtsspezifische Höflichkeit in französischen SMS. 114 Seiten. ISBN 978-3-86596-374-1

Bd. 8 Mareike Kühn: Opera dei pupi. Sizilianisches Marionettentheater im Wandel. 118 Seiten. ISBN 978-3-86596-382-6

Bd. 9 Ursula Wiedemann: Biometrie – Stand und Chancen der Vermessung des Menschen. 200 Seiten. ISBN 978-3-86596-389-5

Bd. 10 Kristin Voigt: Informelle Wissenschaftskommunikation und *Social Media*. 166 Seiten. ISBN 978-3-86596-408-3

Bd. 11 Christoph Schubert/Teresa Pham (Hg.): RaumTexte – TextRäume. Sprachwissenschaftliche Studien zur Verortung im Diskurs. 244 Seiten. ISBN 978-3-86596-364-2

Bd. 12 Sabine Rohmig: Literarischer Kulturtransfer. Afrikanismen in frankophonen Romanen Schwarzafrikas. 492 Seiten. ISBN 978-3-86596-459-5

Bd. 13 Christoph Strosetzki: Konversation als Sprachkultur. Elemente einer historischen Kommunikationspragmatik. 2., durchgesehene und ergänzte Auflage. 464 Seiten. ISBN 978-3-86596-482-3

Bd. 14 Belén Santana López: Lachen – Humor – Komik. Eine systematische Interkulturalitätsanalyse. Deutsch und Spanisch. 172 Seiten. ISBN 978-3-86596-484-7

F Frank & Timme

KULTUREN – KOMMUNIKATION – KONTAKTE

Bd. 15 Christina Hofmann-Randall: Das spanische Hofzeremoniell 1500–1700. 310 Seiten. ISBN 978-3-86596-431-1

Bd. 16 Stephan Theilig: Türken, Mohren und Tataren. Muslimische (Lebens-)Welten in Brandenburg-Preußen im 18. Jahrhundert. 408 Seiten. ISBN 978-3-86596-525-7

Bd. 17 Jenny Metzig: Die Wahrnehmung kultureller Eigenheiten im Zusammenleben bikultureller Paare. 322 Seiten. ISBN 978-3-7329-0003-9

Bd. 18 Marja E. Meinl: Electronic Complaints. An Empirical Study on British English and German Complaints on eBay. 330 Seiten. ISBN 978-3-7329-0030-5

Bd. 19 Michael Scholz-Hänsel/David Sánchez Cano (Hg./eds.): Spanische Kunst von El Greco bis Dalí. Ambiguitäten statt Stereotype/Arte Español del Greco hasta Dalí. Ambigüedades en lugar de estereotipos. 336 Seiten. ISBN 978-3-7329-0063-3

Bd. 20 Ramona Jakobs: Der kultivierte Dialog in der italienischen Renaissance. Eine sprechakttheoretische Analyse des *Libro del Cortegiano* (1528). 350 Seiten. ISBN 978-3-7329-0111-1

Bd. 21 Bianka Schönbrunn: Emotionalität in der Berichterstattung deutscher und französischer Tageszeitungen. Ein interkultureller Vergleich. 192 Seiten. ISBN 978-3-7329-0157-9

Bd. 22 Daniela Marcantonio: Gesten im interkulturellen Vergleich. Deutsche in Italien und Italiener in Deutschland. 246 Seiten. ISBN 978-3-86596-247-8

Bd. 23 Yvette Bürki/Henriette Partzsch (eds.): Redes de comunicación. Estudios sobre la prensa en el mundo hispanohablante. 390 Seiten. ISBN 978-3-7329-0129-6

Bd. 24 Sarah Wille: Hablando The Chilean Way. Anglizismen im gesprochenen chilenischen Spanisch. Die Informationssendung „El Informante". 100 Seiten. ISBN 978-3-7329-0287-3

Bd. 25 Sylvia Jaki/Annette Sabban (Hg.): Wissensformate in den Medien. Analysen aus Medienlinguistik und Medienwissenschaft. 348 Seiten. ISBN 978-3-7329-0201-9

Bd. 26 Gianluca Pedrotti: Diktatur der Rhetorik oder Rhetorik der Diktatur. Gezeigt an ausgewählten Redesituationen von Mussolini und Hitler. 594 Seiten. ISBN 978-3-7329-0215-6

Bd. 27 Stefanie Unger: Soziolektale Herausforderungen: Weibliche Emanzipation in der spanischen Pressesprache des 20. Jahrhunderts. 400 Seiten. ISBN 978-3-7329-0519-5

Bd. 28 Richard Brütting: Interkulturelles Mosaik Europa. Essays zu Deutschland, Frankreich und Italien. 354 Seiten. ISBN 978-3-7329-0507-2

KULTUREN – KOMMUNIKATION – KONTAKTE

Bd. 29 Henriette Schneider: Ausdruck von Emotionen in der Zweitsprache. Möglichkeiten und Grenzen. 156 Seiten. ISBN 978-3-7329-0590-4

Bd. 30 Elisabeth Buhl/Katharina-Elisa Wolf: Wunden Lateinamerikas. *Rassismus in Peru* und *Frauenmorde in Nordmexiko*. Zwei Beiträge. 210 Seiten. ISBN 978-3-7329-0246-0

Bd. 31 Diana Haußmann: Zelebrieren, Vergessen, Erneuern. Das Spannungsfeld der Afrikanität bei Fatou Diome, Léonora Miano und Alain Mabanckou. 444 Seiten. ISBN 978-3-7329-0581-2

Bd. 32 Sandra Hinckers: Lateinische Übersetzungsreflexion in der Römischen Antike. Von Terenz bis zur *Historia Augusta*. 210 Seiten. ISBN 978-3-7329-0614-7

Bd. 33 Anne-Britt Ueckermann: Kommunikationskultur. Orientierung für eine erfolgreiche Kommunikation. 746 Seiten. ISBN 978-3-7329-0595-9

Bd. 34 Elisabeth Buhl: Das Bild der Fremde in deutschsprachigen Reiseführern. Beschreibungen und Vorstellungen von Peru. 122 Seiten. ISBN 978-3-7329-0687-1

Bd. 35 Stéphane Hardy: *Der largonji du louchébem* – die Geheimsprache der Pariser Metzger. 382 Seiten. ISBN 978-3-7329-0912-4

Frank & Timme